NEW ESSAYS ON CANADIAN THEATRE
VOLUME SEVEN

CANADIAN PERFORMANCE HISTORIES AND HISTORIOGRAPHIES

ALSO IN THIS SERIES

ASIAN CANADIAN THEATRE
EDITED BY NINA LEE AQUINO AND RIC KNOWLES

NEW CANADIAN REALISMS
EDITED BY ROBERTA BARKER AND KIM SOLGA

LATINA/O CANADIAN THEATRE AND PERFORMANCE
EDITED BY NATALIE ALVAREZ

THEATRES OF AFFECT
EDITED BY ERIN HURLEY

DANIEL MacIVOR
EDITED BY RICHIE WILCOX

PERFORMING INDIGENEITY
EDITED BY YVETTE NOLAN AND RIC KNOWLES

ALSO BY HEATHER DAVIS-FISCH
LOSS AND CULTURAL REMAINS IN PERFORMANCE: THE GHOSTS OF THE FRANKLIN EXPEDITION
PAST LIVES: PERFORMING CANADA'S HISTORIES

NEW ESSAYS IN CANADIAN THEATRE
VOLUME SEVEN

CANADIAN PERFORMANCE HISTORIES AND HISTORIOGRAPHIES

EDITED BY HEATHER DAVIS-FISCH

PLAYWRIGHTS CANADA PRESS
TORONTO

First edition: May 2017
Printed and bound in Canada by Marquis Book Printing, Montreal

PLAYWRIGHTS CANADA PRESS

Playwrights Canada Press
202-269 Richmond Street West, Toronto, ON M5V 1X1
416.703.0013 :: info@playwrightscanada.com :: playwrightscanada.com

Cover photo of E. Pauline Johnson provided courtesy of Library and Archives Canada
Cover design by Leon Aureus

LIBRARY AND ARCHIVES CANADA CATALOGUING IN PUBLICATION
Canadian performance histories and historiographies / Heather Davis-Fisch, editor. -- First edition.

(New essays on Canadian theatre ; v. 7)
ISBN 978-1-77091-775-0 (softcover)

1. Theater--Canada--History. 2. Canadian drama-- History and criticism. I. Davis-Fisch, Heather, 1979-, editor II. Series: New essays on Canadian theatre ; v. 7

PN2301.C346 2017 792.0971 C2017-901361-0

We acknowledge the financial support of the Canada Council for the Arts, the Ontario Arts Council (OAC), the Ontario Media Development Corporation, and the Government of Canada through the Canada Book Fund for our publishing activities.

Canada Council for the Arts Conseil des arts du Canada
ONTARIO ARTS COUNCIL
CONSEIL DES ARTS DE L'ONTARIO
an Ontario government agency
un organisme du gouvernement de l'Ontario
Canada
Ontario
Ontario Media Development Corporation

For Scott, for all the things, and for Briscoe, who will always be my favourite writing companion.

CONTENTS

GENERAL EDITOR'S PREFACE

ROBERTA BARKER

It is a privilege—though a somewhat daunting one—to pen my first preface as general editor of New Essays in Canadian Theatre (NECT). To have the chance to collaborate with some of the best, most innovative scholars and artists in the field of Canadian theatre and performance is a thrilling honour. To follow in the footsteps of the series's first general editor, is, however, a tall order. Ric Knowles and his work at Playwrights Canada Press have for many years been a source of tremendous inspiration and insight for everyone engaged in Canadian theatre studies. As I take up the editorship of this series with deep gratitude for my own good fortune and deep consciousness of how much I have yet to learn, I can only hope to labour along with this wonderful community to build on the strong foundations he has laid.

When Ric Knowles founded NECT in 2011, he set out to complement his previous book series for Playwrights Canada Press, Critical Perspectives on Canadian Theatre in English (CPCTE). Each volume of the CPCTE series offered a critical history of a key topic in Canadian theatre studies; most of the essays featured in these volumes were reprints of important articles in the field, though they were supplemented by newly commissioned works that brought novel perspectives to the questions at hand. With NECT Knowles chose to foreground new work, under-explored subjects, and fresh viewpoints. As he wrote in his General Editor's Preface to *Performing Indigeneity* (2016), these volumes

> are designed to fill what I perceive to be gaps in the critical record, often . . . taking new approaches, often . . . from minoritized and

> under-represented perspectives, and in almost every case introducing topics that have not received book-length coverage . . . [T]hey are designed at once to follow, lead, and instantiate new and emerging developments in the field. (v)

Paired with play anthologies, many of them specially created as companions for the NECT volumes, these books strive to open exciting new avenues of exploration for artists, students, and scholars of Canadian theatre.

The six volumes published under Knowles's editorship richly fulfill this mandate, covering in the process a wide range of topics and approaches. Some, like *Asian Canadian Theatre* (edited by Nina Lee Aquino and Knowles) and *Latina/o Canadian Theatre and Performance* (edited by Natalie Alvarez), illuminate the vibrant and important work of key communities within the Canadian theatrical ecosystem. Others, like *New Canadian Realisms* (which I co-edited with Kim Solga) and *Theatres of Affect* (edited by Erin Hurley), strive to reconsider established genres and forms of theatre through new theoretical lenses. The 2015 volume, *Daniel MacIvor* (edited by Richie Wilcox), brings long overdue scholarly attention to the work of one of Canada's most beloved and innovative theatre artists. Finally, 2016's volume makes a particularly mighty contribution: *Performing Indigeneity*, edited by Yvette Nolan (Algonquin) and Knowles, is the first Canadian collection of essays on the topic to offer an all-Indigenous list of contributors. Many of these volumes, or the articles they feature, have been garlanded with scholarly prizes and awards: a fitting tribute to their impact on the field.

With such groundbreaking work firmly in mind, it may seem odd that—after accepting Knowles's generous invitation to take over from him as general editor—my first thought was to commission a new volume on Canadian performance histories. Histories, after all, are generally perceived to be concerned with the vagaries of the past rather than with the possibilities of the future—with the old, rather than with the new. Moreover, some of the best-known works of theatre and performance scholarship to emerge from the land mass we currently call Canada explore theatre histories and historiographies. In the first paragraph of her introduction to this collection, editor

Heather Davis-Fisch cites Eugene Benson and L.W. Conolly's short guide to *English-Canadian Theatre* (1987), Don Rubin's anthology *Canadian Theatre History: A Sourcebook* (1996), and Alan Filewod's monograph *Performing Canada: The Nation Enacted in the Imagined Theatre* (2002); one might also mention the work of such pivotal theatre historians as André-G. Bourassa and Jean-Marc Larrue, Kym Bird and Paula Sperdakos, Stephen Johnson and Patrick O'Neill, to name but a few. How, in the context of such great and influential contributions, might we conceive Canadian theatre history and historiography as in any sense an emerging field or a site of new—and perhaps under-represented—discoveries?

The answer, for me, lies in the transformative impact of recent developments in Canadian theatre and performance studies—including many of the developments explored in earlier volumes of NECT—on the very idea of what might constitute a Canadian theatre history. The influence of performance studies methodologies; the renewed focus on diverse and under-explored forms of theatre and performance; and, above all, the insights offered by scholars and artists who speak from under-represented and minoritized perspectives: all of these have fundamentally challenged familiar ways of approaching the Canadian past. As the discussion between Indigenous scholar-artists Jill Carter, Karyn Recollet, and Dylan Robinson, featured in this volume, underlines, long-dominant settler understandings of past and present, of nation and community, and of knowing and unknowing—the understandings that phrases like "Canadian theatre histories and historiographies" seem to take for granted—are facing radical and very necessary revision. The time, then, feels right to revisit Canadian performance histories, asking afresh—as Heather Davis-Fisch and her collaborators set out to do—what such histories might reflect upon, and how. In a year of "Canada 150" celebrations, this latest entry in the NECT series showcases the path-breaking work of scholars who shun easy assumptions about Canada, history, and time, and who remind us—once again—that the past is ever-present, ever-changing, and ever-new.

ACKNOWLEDGEMENTS

As a historian, I would be remiss if I did not begin by acknowledging the role my own disciplinary genealogy played in the development of this book. Alan Filewod looms large in this volume and in all my work on Canadian performance histories; I was fortunate enough to work with Alan throughout my graduate studies at the University of Guelph, and the insight he brought to our conversations and the critical rigour of his work continue to challenge me. I am also deeply grateful for the mentorship of Stephen Johnson, Ric Knowles, Danny O'Quinn, and Jerry Wasserman, all of whom contributed to my understanding of the intersection of ethics, methodology, and rhetoric essential to historical research and writing.

The Canadian Association for Theatre Research has provided me with a disciplinary home, generating many of the conversations that led to the essays in this volume. In particular, I must thank Roberta Barker, Kirsty Johnson, Laura Levin, Marlis Schweitzer, and Kim Solga, my co-panellists in a 2013 seminar on Performance Genealogies, and the many participants in the ongoing Performance History working group and seminars: the questions raised in these sessions have challenged me, introduced me to new ways of thinking about the performative past, and engendered many of the questions that drive my own work.

I would also like to thank my colleagues and friends in English and Theatre at the University of the Fraser Valley for their interest in and support of my work, the research office at UFV for providing me with teaching releases for completing this book, and the dean's office in the College of Arts for encouraging my research activities. My students in Canadian drama and theatre courses have been a motivation and inspiration. Phay Gagnon, my research assistant, has provided invaluable editorial assistance in the preparation of this manuscript.

Roberta Barker, the general editor of this series, has been unfailing in her enthusiasm and care for this project. I deeply appreciate her invitation to edit this volume and her astute, supportive guidance throughout the process. I also can't say enough good things about the folks at Playwrights Canada Press—Annie Gibson, Blake Sproule, Stephanie Nuñez, Mandy Bayrami, Jessica Lewis—who have made the process of editing this volume and its companion anthology of plays an absolute pleasure.

Finally, I would like to thank my extended families and friends, who generously did not ask if I was finished this collection yet. My two canine companions—Briscoe and Pickles—kept my feet warm and ensured I took sufficient breaks from staring at a computer screen. My husband Scott has been indefatigable in his support for this project. I am eternally grateful for his ability to handle—even embracing and managing—the domestic and hormonal chaos caused by my signing on to edit two books then proceeding to have not one but two children before they—the books, not the children—went to print. Jasper: thank you for making sure I was playing as much as working. And Baby Quinn: thank you for staying inside until I finished editing this book.

DOUBLE LIVES AND DISAPPEARING ACTS: CANADIAN PERFORMANCE HISTORIES

HEATHER DAVIS-FISCH

Where—or when—does one begin in introducing a collection of new essays on Canadian performance histories in the nation's sesquicentennial year? A quick and dirty, but by no means complete, survey of key Canadian theatre histories presents a few candidates. Eugene Benson and L.W. Conolly's concise survey of *English-Canadian Theatre* (1987) begins with "The Native Peoples," briefly outlining the "indigenous drama of great richness and complexity" that "flourished" pre-European contact (1),[1] before reverting to the position that "the drama of the native peoples, however, had little influence on subsequent theatrical developments in Canada, which originated in Europe" (2). *Canadian Theatre History: Selected Readings* (1996), edited by Don Rubin, begins with a section titled "The Annexation of our Stage, 1750–1916," implicitly locating the origins of Canadian theatre practice in proto-nationalist anxiety concerning cultural colonization by British and American forces. Alan Filewod's 2002 monograph *Performing Canada: The Nation Enacted in the Imagined Theatre* identifies Marc Lescarbot's 1606 masque, *The Theatre of Neptune in New France*, as the first European theatrical performance in what is now Canada (xi). Filewod situates this performance, which likely featured French actors portraying Aboriginal peoples welcoming the French to

1 Benson and Conolly do not capitalize indigenous when referring to Aboriginal, First Nations, Inuit, or Métis performance. Throughout this introduction, I use capitalized versions of Indigenous, Indigeneity, etc. to refer to such performances, performers, and cultures. I use the lower-case "i" to reference critical or historical examples of the term being used in non-Aboriginal contexts, for example, to refer to an indigenous, homegrown Canadian (rather than English or American) theatre.

Mi'kmaq territory, as the de facto starting point for his "radical rethinking of the conceptual foundations of Canadian theatre" (x). All three works, albeit in very different ways, place and re-enact Canadian theatre history against the backdrop of colonialism.

The reader's experience with this volume begins with its cover image: an 1895 photograph of Tekahionwake, or E. Pauline Johnson, in "Indian dress." Johnson (1861–1913) was the daughter of a hereditary Haudenosaunee (Mohawk) chief, himself of both Indigenous and European ancestry, and an English-American immigrant mother. Johnson was a renowned interdisciplinary performer; however, she is today best known for widely anthologized poems that celebrate her Indigenous heritage and the Canadian wilderness, such as "The Song My Paddle Sings." Although Johnson has received some critical attention for her contributions to Indigenous performance,[2] she is not widely acknowledged as an important figure in Canadian theatre history. For instance, she is present in the *Oxford Companion to Canadian Literature*, but absent from the *Oxford Companion to Canadian Theatre*. This is a disappointing oversight for several reasons. Johnson's performances exemplify many of the obsessions of late nineteenth-century Canadian theatre and, through their episodic structure, demonstrate how distinct genres and styles were integrated in practice. An evening with Johnson might have included recitations of literary drama, romantic enactments of Canada's Indigenous past, and comic scenes imported from England. The "Indian dress" in which she frequently appeared mirrored the overt performativity of her act: Johnson changed from European to "Indian" dress during the course of her performance and, while the costume included "authentic" items collected from a range of Indigenous nations, it was not an "accurate" representation of traditional Haudenosaunee clothing. Johnson's theatrical work not only tells us a great deal about the complexity of popular performance practices during her lifetime, but also exemplifies the ongoing, messy relationship between colonialism and performance, a relationship that this volume positions as central to understanding

2 See, for example, Norman Shrive and Julie Rak for early and more recent critical perspectives on Johnson's work.

Canada's theatrical past. Furthermore, historians' attention, or lack of attention, to Johnson and to specific aspects of her professional practice reveals a great deal about the nature of performance historiography and raises ethical questions about historiographical practice.

Johnson's performance practices, as captured in the cover photograph, may be positioned within the chronologies that flow from the originary moments I outlined above. However, I introduce her image not to mark a "bead . . . of a rosary," a moment in a historicist sequence of teleologically progressive events (Benjamin 255), but as what Terry Eagleton, drawing on Jacques Derrida's work in deconstructive criticism, terms a symptomatic point: an "apparently peripheral fragment in the work—a footnote, a recurrent minor term or image, a casual allusion" (133). In her preface to *Of Grammatology*, Gayatri Chakravorty Spivak explains Derrida's process of deconstructive reading as follows:

> If in the process of deciphering a text in the traditional way we come across a word that seems to harbor an unresolvable contradiction, and by virtue of being *one* word is made sometimes to work in one way and sometimes in another and thus is made to point away from the absence of a unified meaning, we shall catch at that word. If a metaphor seems to suppress its implications, we shall catch at that metaphor. We shall follow its adventures through the text and see the text coming undone as a structure of concealment, revealing its self-transgression, its undecidability. (lxxv)

While Spivak is focused on reading literary works, the method she describes might be applied to the image of Pauline Johnson. Following Johnson's imaginary adventures through, against, and across the "texts" of Canadian theatre history opens up critical space in which one might destabilize or dismantle the oppositions that underpin such texts and their historiographical assumptions. The image of Johnson in "Indian dress" symptomatizes the central tensions and contradictions in Canadian performance historiography that the essays in this volume seek to investigate: between settler and Indigenous world views and identities, between nationalist and post- or decolonial agendas, between embodied performance practices and dramatic texts, between the archive and the repertoire as modes of cultural memory, and between macro- and micro-historical methods. Working out from Johnson's image—not as an originary moment but as a symptomatic point in a rhizomatic structure of past performance practice—allows us to challenge essentialist conceptions of national identity and performance by introducing Indigenous and hemispheric perspectives, to critique the agendas that determine what and who is included—or omitted or erased—from the stories we tell ourselves about past performance and the stories that survive in cultural memory, and to contemplate the processes by which we remember and engage with past performances today.

IMAGINING THE NATIVE/NATION

The name Tekahionwake is generally translated as "double wampum" or "double wampum belts," not only reflecting multiple facets of Johnson's family ancestry but also positioning her between cultures and nations. The Haudenosaunee, along with other Indigenous peoples from what is now known as eastern North America, traditionally exchanged wampum shells as gifts and, in the early contact period, used the shells as a form of intercultural currency. The shells' political and historical significance, however, extends beyond this economic function: strung together, they served as a memory aid, a storytelling device, and as a form of treaty. Perhaps most importantly, the Haudenosaunee Great Law of Peace, the oral constitution of the Six Nations, was written on wampum belts. Johnson took her name from her great-grandfather, Jacob Johnson Tekahionwake, who, like many Haudenosaunee following the American Revolutionary War, migrated to what is now known as the Six Nations Reserve: lands that the British granted the Haudenosaunee as compensation for their losses of territory in the war (E. Johnson 104–05). From my historical vantage point, the doubleness cited in the first Tekahionwake's name seems retroactively to reflect both his ability to navigate between two cultures in the early colonial period, and his contribution to peaceful relations between the Haudenosaunee and the British.

Pauline Johnson adopted the name Tekahionwake in 1894. Her mother, Emily Howells, was born in Britain and immigrated to the US as a child; in her early twenties, she moved to Six Nations to join her sister, who was married to an Anglican missionary. Johnson herself was thus not only of mixed-race ancestry but also inherited, inhabited, and performed her great-grandfather's position between cultures. Her decision to call herself Tekahionwake goes beyond citation of her genealogy, however. Alexandra Kovacs argues that Johnson's "adoption of 'Tekahionwake' had benefits that were cultural, theatrical and commercial," demonstrating not only her "deep reverence for her family history" but also "her connection [to] and reclamation of Kanien'kéha (Mohawk) language"; the name served "as a refutation (even inversion) of colonial-settler practices that attempted to erase and assimilate Indigenous histories and identities. The Mohawk stage name consolidated her 'right' to the presentation of her particular history" (138). I would add that Johnson's use of Tekahionwake might also be understood as a gesture forward, to a future in which reclamation of Indigenous languages and names is assumed as a step toward decolonization.

Johnson's double name, its relationship to her lineage, and her performance practice illustrate the complex and various relations between Indigenous peoples, Americans, and British settlers in the colonial history of the land that became Canada. Furthermore, identifying Pauline Johnson as a "Canadian" writer or performer points to the temporal, spatial, and cultural tenuousness of that term. Not only was she born six years before Confederation, but she was born on the Six Nations Reserve, territories that Haudenosaunee and Euro-Canadians have disputed since at least the 1780s.[3] Raised there, in what was first Canada West, then Ontario, the child of an Anglo-American mother and a Haudenosaunee chief, himself of mixed-race

3 Chiefswood, where Johnson was born, is less than twenty kilometres from the present-day town of Caledonia, where disputes over unresolved land claims led to a heated dispute between Six Nations, developers, and the Ontario Provincial Police in 2006. See DeVries.

ancestry, Johnson quite literally occupied and embodied the intersection of at least four nationalities. This positionality, I contend, makes Pauline Johnson not exceptional but symptomatic of "Canadian" identity. Efforts to categorize her identity—as Indigenous, as Canadian, as English; as writer, as actor, as performer—or to critique her lack of "authenticity" (a critique that Kovacs's essay in this volume dismantles) point to a central preoccupation—one might even say an underlying anxiety—with national origin that runs through Canadian theatre history. What is exceptional about Johnson, I believe, is the extent to which she enacted such intersections, the extent to which her performance practices—arguably epitomized by the image of her in "Indian dress"—demonstrate the contingency and theatricality of national identities.

Returning to an originary moment that I initially set aside—the 1606 performance of *The Theatre of Neptune*—allows us to trace this anxious relationship between nation, authenticity, and performance. In Lescarbot's spectacular nautical masque, Neptune and his Tritons welcome the French to the territory, followed by four "savages," likely played by French performers, who offer their submission and allegiance to the king of France. The play was apparently performed for an audience that included both French and Mi'kmaq spectators. Alan Filewod argues that "all of Canadian theatre, and the nation it stages, can be seen as a replaying of *The Theatre of Neptune*, a constant historical citation and recitation of the post-colonial crisis of authenticity and displacement" (*Performing* xvii). He refers specifically to the enactment of aboriginality by French performers: "Postcolonial nationhood," he continues, "is founded on fantasies of absent authenticity," and in post-colonial settler colonies such as Canada, that "imagined cultural authenticity" is "enacted" in theatre culture (1). Following Filewod, I would add that in Canada absent and imagined notions of authenticity are intimately linked to absent and imagined notions of aboriginality: performance practice and historiography are each dependent on both the desire for constructed indigeneity and the evacuation of actual Indigeneity, on the disappearance—whether accidental or deliberate, literal or rhetorical—of Indigenous bodies.[4]

The concurrent and systematic exclusion of Aboriginal subjects and the creation of imagined aboriginalities is, Daniel Coleman argues, central to the production and reproduction of settler Canadian identity, particularly in English Canada. The figure of the "Noble Savage," integral to the European Enlightenment tradition, provided a way to imaginatively generate civility, allowing for the concurrent production, marginalization, and exclusion of Aboriginal peoples from the civil sphere (Coleman 14). In settler colonies (or settler-invader colonies) such as Canada, with actual rather than imaginatively and discursively produced Indigenous populations (as in Europe),[5] this process was complicated: the settler had to construct, "by a double process of speedy indigenization and accelerated self-civilization, his priority and superiority to latecomers; that is, by representing himself as already indigenous, the settler claims priority over newer immigrants and, by representing himself as already civilized, he claims superiority to Aboriginals and other non-whites" (Coleman 16). Coleman's study focuses on literary, rather than theatrical, representations of Canadian identity; however, one can easily trace a genealogy of such representations, both of the already indigenous settler and of the process Coleman describes, through Canadian drama. The descendants of Lescarbot's masque, in such a genealogy, might include Charles Mair's *Tecumseh* (1886),[6] Gwen Pharis Ringwood's *Maya, or Lament For Harmonica* (1959), George Ryga's *The Ecstasy of Rita Joe* (1967), and Colleen Murphy's

---

4 Filewod makes this point in relation to Charles Mair's poetic drama *Tecumseh*, arguing that the proposal of aboriginality as an authenticator of nationhood effectively negates the aboriginal presence itself. In effect, the battle that forges the nation also incinerates aboriginality, so that (to continue the smithing metaphor that Mair's generation used so well), the sword of the new nation is tempered with the spirit of the old. ("National Battles" 82)

5 Of course, there are many Indigenous peoples of Europe, such as the Basque of Spain and France or the Samoyedic-speaking peoples of Russia; however, these populations did not significantly figure into the creation of the "Noble Savage" in early modern European thought.

6 See Davis-Fisch, "Complicated."

Pig Girl (2013), which represents a fictional serial killer eerily reminiscent of Robert Pickton. While these plays all express sympathy for Indigenous peoples, each also erases Indigeneity, whether through tragic dramaturgical structures that promote affective engagement and closure, or through production histories that privilege casting non-Indigenous performers to play Indigenous characters.

A similar phenomenon occurs across Canadian theatre and performance historiography. In the quest to produce first a canon of "Canadian" dramatic literature, then a national theatre, then a body of theatre criticism, critics and historians sought to create and promote the idea of a post-colonial, "indigenous" Canadian identity. Post-colonial, in this case, is a paradoxical concept, referring to a post-British, post-French, or post-American identity in which settler Canadians emerge as "indigenous" and in which the ongoing colonization of Indigenous peoples is ignored. A few key passages from L.W. Conolly's 1982 collection, *Theatrical Touring and Founding in North America*, illustrate Coleman's argument, demonstrating how widespread the perception of an absence of "indigenous" Canadian identity was and how the discursive construction of such an "indigenous" identity depended on the erasure of Indigeneity.[7] Robertson Davies, for instance, writes:

> Canada did not cease to be a colony, psychologically, until long after I was born, and in matters relating to the arts its colonialism was absolute. A national culture arises from the depths of a people, and Canadians knew where those depths were, and certainly it was not here. There were too many Canadians who were physically loyal to the new land, but who remained exiles in matters of spirit. You might as well have asked for an indigenous form of government, or an indigenous religion, as ask for Canadian art. Theatre, music, and literature did not originate here. They came from home, wherever home might be. ("Mixed Grill" 41)

7 One might, of course, argue that the perceptions present in Conolly's anthology are still widespread today.

The idea that Indigenous governance, religion, or artistic practice predated the arrival of Europeans was apparently inconceivable to Davies. Andrew Parkin's contribution, unironically titled "The New Frontier: Toward an Indigenous Theatre in British Columbia," attempts to identify "indigenous" theatre traditions in the province, contrasting dramatic and performative histories:

> [T]he emergence of regional drama has been slow and, until recently, disappointing. Not so the theatre history of the region. This has been rich and interesting. To investigate the founding of indigenous professional theatre in British Columbia is to discover a wealth of amateur and professional activity and the building of many theatres. This activity can be charted alongside the economic and social factors that stimulated and depressed it: the Cariboo gold rush, the transcontinental railroad, the Yukon boom, the post-1918 Little Theatre boom, the Depression, and then post-war growth, with the effort to build a Canadian culture having its own identity. (101)

One wonders what someone like Margo Kane might make of Parkin's belief that "indigenous" theatre

> arose from the amateur activities of settlers, forming a tradition from the naval and military performances to the activities of the British Columbia Drama Association, the Vancouver Little Theatre Association, the regional stimulation of the Dominion Drama Festival, and the growth of university and school drama as well as the little community theatres. It also arose from the stimulation of American and British touring companies, the stock companies of gold rush days and later, together with a local determination to provide an alternative (legitimate) theatre to the fare offered by the vaudeville circuits. (103)

These are but two among many examples of the widespread and long-standing conflation of "indigenous" and "native" with "Canadian" in Canadian theatre criticism and historiography. A diverse range of theatre critics—including Merrill Denison, Tyrone Guthrie, Herbert Whittaker ("The Theatre"), and Rick Salutin[8]—and historians—including Don Rubin ("Creeping" 322), Murray Edwards (168), and Diane Bessai (7)—use the language of indigeneity, variously to express a desire for a nationalist drama or theatre, to call for the representation of regional or local experiences on stage, and to advocate for acting and production roles for Canadians. This cursory survey demonstrates that the idea of "Canadian theatre" or "Canadian drama" has historically relied upon a simultaneous imagination and evacuation of Indigeneity.

The essays in this volume reflect a significant shift, from a desire for an (absent, imagined, unmarked) "indigenous" Canadian theatre (history) to a recognition that the study of performance history in a settler colony—whether obviously *about* Indigenous performance or not—must always consider the historical relationships between settlers and Indigenous peoples and the related historical patterns of movement and circulation. Performance in Canada—that is, in the territories now called Canada—always takes place against a backdrop of colonial histories; it always takes place on Indigenous lands. As the summary of the final report of the Truth and Reconciliation Commission of Canada states: "we are all Treaty people" (Truth and Reconciliation 8).

Furthermore, the essays in this volume recognize that performance practices and performers of the past—like those today—were not bound by the geographic or political borders of what is now Canada or by those of its provinces, a fact that Pauline Johnson's genealogy and touring practices underscore. Conceptual and methodological frameworks emerging from Indigenous and hemispheric studies challenge the geographic anachronism

8 A quick glance through Rubin's collection *Canadian Theatre History* revealed all four examples: see Denison's 1929 comment "there is this to say about a native theatre" (93); Guthrie's rhetorical question as to whether "Shakespeare should not seem as indigenous to Western Ontario as he does to Northumberland?" (212); Whittaker's 1957 comment that "the theatre instinct, however, showed up elsewhere, and in a humbler, more indigenous form" ("The Theatre" 221); and Salutin's assertion, in 1981, that "in Toronto in the post-war period there was an indigenous theatre movement, with people like Mavor Moore at the centre" (381).

underscoring "Canadian" theatre historiography. For example, transmotion, a concept coined by Anishinaabe scholar Gerald Vizenor, allows for a complex consideration of the interrelation between patterns of human movement, territory, survivance (a term Vizenor coined to suggest both survival and resistance), and—ultimately—national sovereignty (*Fugitive*). Transmotion, Michi Saagig Nishnaabeg scholar Leanne Simpson explains, refers to pre-colonial movement patterns, wherein "movement, change and fluidity were a reality" for Nishnaabeg people, who were not "wandering" but moving outward from a territorial centre to a place of encounter, "where one needs to practice good relations with neighboring nations" (*Dancing* 89). It is important to note that the concept of transmotion addresses not only physical movement across the land but also the cultural, political, and spiritual implications of these patterns, encompassing the ways in which Anishinaabe understandings of territory were defined not by physical borders but by language, philosophy, way of life, and political structure. Anishinaabe understandings of the land are inextricably tied to all of their relationships with their surroundings. Vizenor explicitly links Indigenous patterns of movement to enactments of sovereignty:

> The connotations of transmotion are creation stories, totemic visions, reincarnation, and sovenance; transmotion, that sense of native motion and an active presence, is *sui generis* sovereignty. Native transmotion is survivance, a reciprocal use of nature, not a monotheistic, territorial sovereignty. Native stories of survivance are the creases of transmotion and sovereignty. (*Fugitive* 15)

Challenging the very notion of national borders, the concept of transmotion is an example of an Indigenous theory that makes an uncritical discussion of "Canadian" theatre history untenable.

Like Vizenor's conceptualization of space, time, and nation, hemispheric studies also offers theoretical and methodological challenges to nationalist approaches to performance history. Most obviously, hemispheric studies foregrounds the spatial to suggest the transgression of national and geographic boundaries. A hemispheric approach to performance privileges patterns of movement, relationship, and circulation and allows for connections between performance practices across national boundaries to emerge. Jill Lane suggests that not only does a hemispheric approach cause us to rethink space, it also allows us to understand time in new ways. By considering "deep time" ("time that exceeds the lineaments of European monochromic temporality" ["Hemispheric" 116]), a hemispheric approach "allows us to see sociality against the relief of other temporal scales" ("Hemispheric" 117) such as seasonal time, oceanic time, carnival time, and—I would add, drawing on Tracy C. Davis's work—performative and theatrical time.[9]

Appropriately, considering this volume's explicit framing of Canada as a settler colony, hemispheric approaches to performance emphasize the role that colonialism and other forms of political violence play in shaping national and cultural formations. In their introduction to *Hemispheric American Studies*, Caroline Levander and Robert Levine point out that the idea of post-colonial national independence in the Americas is inherently contradictory, given that national independence "facilitated internal colonialism through institutionalized slavery of certain portions of the population and through the repression of indigenous histories, knowledge, and cultural forms" (5). Their recognition of nation not as "the realization of an original essence" but as "a historical configuration designed to include certain groups and exclude others" allows one to view Canada "as a relational identity that emerges through constant collaboration, dialogue, and dissension" (5). Lane specifically addresses the contribution hemispheric studies makes to performance studies, noting that work by performance historians like Paul Gilroy and Joseph Roach has challenged us "to reimagine how performance has participated in the histories that produced colonial, neocolonial and neoliberal geographies in the first place" ("Hemispheric" 114). A hemispheric focus, Lane continues, "delineates the shared historical experiences

9 Theatrical time, according to Davis, is the time of the theatrical event—the represented time, whether it is "unified" in an Aristotelian sense or not—in contrast to the "real" time within which a spectator experiences life (147). Performative time "allows for nonlinearity, or nonseriality, as a factor in perception as well as the teleology of time's asynchronicity, as a factor in perception . . . overturning a straightforward concept of temporal succession . . . [P]erformative time participates promiscuously in the past yet is ongoing" (149).

of North, South and Central America—conquest, native genocide, colonialism, slavery, independence wars, nation formation and histories of migration and deterritorialization—and illuminates the formative role of performance in these historical contexts" ("Hemispheric" 114). While the essays in this volume are certainly not the first to situate Canadian performance history hemispherically, as Marlis Schweitzer's essay notes, the hemispheric approach employed by Schweitzer, Kovacs, Stephen Johnson, and others in this volume specifically "recognizes the violent histories of hemispheric thinking that have shaped the grounds on which we now stand" (J. Lane, "Hemispheric" 115).

Pauline Johnson's performances, particularly her acts of renaming herself Tekahionwake and of openly changing her costuming from "European" to "Indigenous," cited and enacted her position as *both* Euro-Canadian and Indigenous. These practices, as Kovacs discusses in her essay, opened Johnson up to charges of inauthenticity during her lifetime; today, however, one can argue that they demonstrate the contingency and performativity, to use Judith Butler's terminology, of national identity. To paraphrase and reframe Butler's well-cited discussion of gender performativity:

> That disciplinary production of [nation] effects a false stabilization of [nation] in the interests of the [settler] construction and regulation of [nationality] within the [cultural] domain . . . According to the understanding of identification as an enacted fantasy or incorporation, however, it is clear that coherence is desired, wished for, idealized, and that this idealization is an effect of a corporeal signification. In other words, acts, gestures, and desire produce the effect of an internal core or substance, but produce this *on the surface* of the body, through the play of signifying absences that suggest, but never reveal, the organizing principle of identity as a cause. Such acts, gestures, enactments, generally construed, are *performative* in the sense that the essence or identity that they otherwise purport to express are *fabrications* manufactured and sustained through corporeal signs and other discursive means. That the [national] body is performative suggests that it has no ontological status apart from

> the various acts which constitute its reality . . . In other words, acts and gestures, articulated and enacted desires create the illusion of an interior and organizing [national] core, an illusion discursively maintained for the purposes of the regulation of [nationality] within the obligatory frame of [settler culture]. (73)

Johnson's performances, staging as they did the instability of national identity particularly when projected onto a (female, Indigenous) body, demonstrate the extent to which the nation is relational, embodied, individuated, and performative.

PERFORMANCE/PERFORMING ARCHIVES

If Johnson's position within racial and national formations is contentious, symptomatizing the instability of categories like Indigenous, white, American, British, and Canadian, her position in the academy today is no less so. Like many women working in cultural industries in the nineteenth and early twentieth centuries, she was a public figure at a time when women were often expected to be private. Furthermore, as a poet, actress, and performer, her work spans fields that are now often imagined as discrete areas of cultural production. Perhaps because her literary work has "survived" intact, perhaps because literature was imagined as a more socially acceptable vocation for a woman than acting, Johnson is typically remembered as a Canadian literary figure and was, until relatively recently, more or less forgotten for her contributions to Canadian theatre and performance history.

Exclusions like that of Johnson from the narratives of Canadian theatre history are closely related to dominant methodologies in the field. Theatre history practice in Canada from the 1970s until the 1990s tended to focus on a few tangible, painstaking tasks: the creation of performance calendars, the preservation and archiving of material records (playbills, programs, promotional material), and the collection of play scripts and other textual documents. In short, the focus was on the creation of archives that accounted for what had happened in the past and on ensuring that such materials were publicly accessible, whether through university libraries or documentation practices like microfilming and digitization. Without diminishing the exemplary and ambitious work of those historians, it is important to note that these types of archives produced particular types of histories: histories that tended to emphasize surveying and analyzing dramatic texts, summarizing key developments, and macro-narrative approaches. Alan Filewod points out the shortcomings of such strong emphasis on the textual and easily archived remains of the past: "Most theatrical performances, even if they can be called plays, are never published. Most human performances are unrecorded. They pass by unremarked, traced through the survival of the exceptional" (*Committing* 2). Because of historiographical practices that emerged "in the interstices of archaeology and literary history," performance historians "developed investigative techniques that sought evidence in both material and written sources;" as a result, " 'Theatre' thus becomes that which is findable by theatre historians" (*Committing* 3).

What do these histories of what's "findable" in the archive miss? Diana Taylor's well-known description of the archive and the repertoire is instructive: Taylor uses the "archive" to refer to textual and material remains, the supposedly permanent and tangible traces of practices, and the "repertoire" to refer to "the corpus of embodied and socially transmitted memory, to the supposedly ephemeral, and to performance as practice" (*The Archive* 19–20). As Taylor's work in *The Archive and the Repertoire* demonstrates, historiographical practices that privilege the archive over the repertoire also privilege certain performance practices over others, habituating us to and reproducing what Rebecca Schneider terms the "patrilineal, West-identified (arguably white-cultural) logic of the archive" (*Performing* 97). Performance practices that are not easily archived—non-textual practices, extra-theatrical events, or nonprofessional productions, for example—tend to be overlooked; the combination of a devotion to the archive and a disproportionate investment in archival preservation of some performance practices over others means that performance histories skew toward and reproduce dominant practices and world views.

The essays in this volume reflect the fact that in the last twenty years theatre history has been substantially informed by performance studies, influenced not only by performance theory but also by developments in dance studies, anthropology, and a number of other fields. Performance historians have developed methodologies for researching and analyzing embodied practices remembered and preserved in the "repertoire." For instance, in 1996 Joseph Roach's work in *Cities of the Dead* set out a groundbreaking framework for describing the cultural impacts of performances of the past; although no authors in this volume cite Roach's theorization directly, his influence on Canadian performance historiography has been enormous. Perhaps most notably, he describes and models a method for "juxtapos[ing] living memory as restored behavior against a historical archive of scripted records" (11), drawing together the archive and repertoire as forms of cultural memory. Rebecca Schneider's *Performing Remains* (2011) further problematizes the relationship between the archive and repertoire, arguing that theatre, by its very nature, complicates "the issue of remains as material document and the issue of performance as documentable" (98). Challenging Peggy Phelan's contention that performance is that which "cannot be saved, documented, or otherwise participate in the circulation of representations" (146), Schneider argues not only that "it is precisely in live art and live theatre that scores of late twentieth-century and early twenty-first century artists explore history—the recomposition of remains *in and as the live*" (98), but also that there are ways in which "the archive depends upon performance . . . ways in which the archive *performs* the service of 'saving' " (99).

In 2014, Ric Knowles pointed out that the field of Canadian performance history is at a "moment of consolidation and revitalization, where early historical, archival, and literary methods are being regenerated and are meeting and merging with more recent methods in an expanded field in ways that have recently proven to be extraordinarily productive" ("Theatre/Research" 228). The essays in this volume address not only theatrical performances, like Pauline Johnson's, that were previously ignored by theatre historians, but also non- and extra-theatrical performances, demonstrating an awareness that the line between theatre and "non-theatre" is culturally and historically determined, and that the bounds of what Rosemarie K. Bank terms "theatre culture" extend beyond the temporal and spatial boundaries of a theatre space (4). Many essays build on the disciplinary foundations laid by archive-focused historians, rethinking how performances of the past were interpreted, drawing attention to the mechanics of archival work, and alerting readers to blind spots or omissions from previous surveys of theatre history.

OF ROSARIES, TREES, AND RHIZOMES

Theatre historiography, as distinct from theatre history, has emerged relatively recently, arguably because theatre history was long "defined strictly as the accumulation of factual knowledge about the dramatic literature and staging practices associated with the canon of Western civilization," its methodology characterized by a valorization of the archival document, its debates focused on interpretations of archival records (Bial and Magelssen 1). In Canada, this approach produced a historical narrative of late-nineteenth- and twentieth-century Canadian theatre practice, basically, as emerging as a site of resistance to American cultural imperialism, but stymied by the lack of a Canadian dramatic canon, theatre buildings, or theatre "culture." This narrative

> argues that the cause of Canadian playwriting was artificially inhibited by the absence of a professional theatre system until the post-war years, at which point the introduction of public funding established a "mainstream" that generated a radical "alternative" theatre movement in which Canadian playwriting came into its own. (Filewod, *Committing* 9)

Not only does this narrative reinscribe the primacy of dramatic text over embodied performance, it is also "historically dubious;" however:

> [I]t provided a critical genealogical sequence that allowed for the maturation of a professional theatre in which the drama and the

> theatrical system function as reciprocal engines of growth: new dramatic "voices" encourage new forms of theatre production; new theatres enable new drama, and so on through the generations. In this positivist account, the theatre "evolves" in stages that superseded colonialism; every accomplishment is a step closer to deferred autonomy. (Filewod, *Committing* 9)[10]

This narrative is problematic for a number of reasons, not the least of which is its ability to gloss over "anomalous" examples that don't fit into the disciplinary bounds it sets for theatre at each stage of its progression toward a professional expression of post-colonial Canadian identity.

Above all, this narrative and the methodology that produced it exemplifies a Hegelian, historicist approach to the past. Critiquing the legacy of Hegelian historiography in relation to intercultural performance in Oceania and the South Pacific, Margaret Werry explains that Hegel offers

> a precise articulation of the peculiar spatiotemporal logic that undergirds modernity's mythos. His absolute distinction between time and space rests on his definition of time as linear, progressive, and singular and space as a surface, static and objective, logically divisible into distinct units, knowable and ownable; time can have but one closed narrative, space but a single trajectory. (99–100)

This understanding of history, Werry argues, is hardly politically neutral but rather "the cornerstone to the familiar discourse of modernity that consigns non-Western peoples without such political forms to the 'waiting

10 Eugene Benson and L.W. Conolly's 1987 *English-Canadian Theatre* reiterated and popularized this thesis (Filewod, *Committing* 9). This narrative, however, was not unreservedly accepted. In the years immediately following the publication of *English-Canadian Theatre*, for example, both Alan Filewod ("Erasing") and Barbara Drennan challenged it, with Filewod terming this an "evolutionary fallacy" (206) and Drennan noting that within this narrative, "[w]hen theatrical experiences elude our points of reference . . . they are often dismissed with a perplexed shrug."

room' of history, occupying an earlier spot in the historical queue" (99). Walter Benjamin uses the term "historicism" to describe this linear, causal, teleological approach to history; in its attempt to arrange "the sequence of events like the beads of a rosary," Benjamin argues, "historicism contents itself with establishing a causal connection between various moments in history." Benjamin suggests an alternative: historical materialism, which, by taking into account the historian's present affective and ethnical engagements with the past, can break with such linear causality, take "hold of a memory as it flashes up at a moment of danger," and allow the historian to grasp "the constellation which his own era has formed with a definite earlier one" (*Illuminations* 255, 263).

The advantages of historical materialism, recognized by many of the contributors to this volume in implicit or explicit ways, lie in its ability to help historians to better articulate how the past was experienced and to position themselves in relation to the histories they recount. Greg Dening, taking up Benjamin's call for complexity and positionality over linear causality and assumptions of progress, argues in favour of "attempt[ing] to represent the past as it was actually experienced in such a way that we understand both its ordered and disordered natures" (*Mr. Bligh's* 5). Writing nearly sixty years after Benjamin, he also articulates the relationship between the past as it was experienced, the "relics of the past" (i.e. the archive), and the past as it can be known in the present:

> The relics of the past, the only ways in which the past survives, *are* cargo to all the present moments that follow. We all stand on the beaches of our present and make of our past, even of our past person, an object. The past is me; the past is it . . . All relics of the past, even if they disappear . . . have a double quality. They are marked with the meanings of the occasion of their origins and they are always translated into something else for the moments they survive. (*Performances* 46–47)

How, then, might historians buck against narrativizing the events of the past as if they were beads on a rosary? How might they address the messiness and unknowability of the past and their own complicity in creating it through the histories they create? Two interrelated material-semiotic approaches that run through this volume—genealogical and rhizomatic—constitute methodological and theoretical alternatives to historicism.

Joseph Roach describes his work on circum-Atlantic performance as fundamentally genealogical, arguing that performance genealogies "document—and suspect the historical transmission and dissemination of cultural practices through collective representations," and attend both to "bodies—to the reciprocal reflections they make on one another's surfaces as they foreground their capacities for interaction," and to " 'counter-memories,' or the disparities between history as it is discursively transmitted and memory as it is publicly enacted" (25–26). Roach draws heavily on the work of Michel Foucault, who in "Nietzsche, Genealogy, History" describes genealogy as "gray, meticulous, and patiently documentary" (76); the genealogist demonstrates an "indispensable restraint . . . record[ing] the singularity of events outside of any monotonous finality" (76). Genealogists operate on the micro rather than macro level, making their work akin to microhistory, which Giovanni Levi explains as a practice "based on the reduction of the scale of observation, on a microscopic analysis and an intensive study of the documentary material" (95), rather than metahistory (Foucault, "Nietzsche" 77). Genealogy "opposes itself to the search for 'origins,' " focusing instead on descent: "Genealogy does not pretend to go back in time to restore an unbroken continuity that operates beyond the dispersion of forgotten things . . . it is to identify the accidents, the minute deviations—or conversely, the complete reversals—the errors, the false appraisals, and the faulty calculations that gave birth to those things that continue to exist and have value for us" (Foucault, "Nietzsche" 77, 81). Genealogy remains a linear, temporal approach, examining patterns moving—one assumes—chronologically forward, but unlike historicism, it does not presuppose progression or improvement over time.

A second approach—which is more radical than the "tree logic" of genealogy (12) but continues to use a biological metaphor for relationships over time and space—is the rhizomatic one, as outlined by Gilles Deleuze and Félix Guattari. As they write, "[m]ost modern methods for making series proliferate or a multiplicity grow are perfectly valid in one direction, for example, a linear direction" (6); these methods can be spatially imagined as trees or roots and assume a central order. Multiple, multi-dimensional, and multidirectional systems, however, are better described as rhizomes:

> [U]nlike trees or roots, the rhizome connects any point to any other point and its traits are not necessarily linked to traits of the same nature . . . The rhizome is reducible neither to the one nor the multiple . . . It is composed not of units but of dimensions, or rather directions in motion. It has neither beginning nor end, but always a middle (milieu) from which it grows and which it overspills . . . Unlike a structure, which is defined by a set of points and positions, with binary relations between the points and biunivocal relationships between the positions, the rhizome is made only of lines . . . Unlike the tree, the rhizome is not the object of reproduction: neither external reproduction as an image-tree nor internal reproduction as tree-structure. The rhizome is an antigenealogy. (21)

While "tree logic" focuses on "tracing and reproduction," rhizomatic logic "is altogether different, a *map* and not a *tracing*" (12). Importantly for our purposes, Deleuze and Guattari note that "[t]he map has to do with performance, whereas the tracing always involves an alleged 'competence' " (12–13). Thinking of past performances rhizomatically allows us to see connections between performances over time and across spaces, better addressing the relationships between human and non-human actors, the possibility of time moving multidirectionally, and the inter(in)animation of past and present.[11]

Returning to our initial example of Pauline Johnson's performance practice, and using both genealogical and rhizomatic approaches, we can track

11 Deleuze and Guattari's rhizomatic approach has clear links to actor-network theory. See Latour; Schweitzer, "Networking."

how her performance practices connect to others. Approaching Johnson genealogically, not as a point of origin or ending, but as occupying a position from which other performance practices descend, we might first consider her most literal legacies: as Kovacs points out in her essay, Johnson has been represented on Canadian stamps, in the 2015 opera *Pauline*, and was, at the time of writing, a candidate for depiction on a new Canadian banknote. Moving beyond such overt legacies, however, we can find deeper traces of Johnson's embodied practice in a range of performance examples, particularly those created by Indigenous women. One might argue, for instance, that elements of Johnson's performance practice, particularly its embodiment and explicit display of racial slippage and hybridity, can be traced forward in lines of descent running through display practices that occurred at World's Fairs and in museums throughout the late-nineteenth and early-twentieth centuries, through dramatic representations such as Monique Mojica's *Princess Pocahontas and the Blue Spots* (most notably its representations of La Malinche and of Métis women) and Daniel David Moses's *Almighty Voice and His Wife* (particularly its second act, which takes the form of a minstrel show to point out the performed, regulated nature of Indigenous identity), and through contemporary performance artworks such as Rebecca Belmore's *Wild* or Lori Blondeau's *A Moment in the Life of Belle Sauvage*.[12] Locating Pauline Johnson's performance as a point on a rhizome allows us to map the interconnections between her performance as a cultural practice and the challenges it poses to essentialized concepts of race and nation, and to use her performance practice to explore other historiographical and theoretical concerns. Looking only at examples that appear in this volume, the rhizomatic model allows us to connect Johnson's performances to the minstrel performances that Stephen Johnson discusses—through their foregrounding of racial difference as a performance convention rather than an essential identity category—as well as to the performances of hybridized culture and language that Nicole Nolette discusses in her essay on Acadian theatre and drama. We might connect her exclusion from mainstream Canadian theatre histories to the patterns of

12 I thank Carla Taunton for pointing out this relationship to me.

erasure and omission that Allana Lindgren notes in relation to ethnic dance in the Massey Commission Report, that Jessica Riley notes in reference to suggestions of violence against women in David Freeman's *Creeps*, or that Robin Whittaker notes as plaguing nonprofessionalizing theatre. We might make connections, via Pauline Johnson's performance practice, to the value of hemispheric approaches that Marlis Schweitzer suggests in her essay on child performers in the nineteenth century, or to the value of Indigenous creation methods that Margo Kane's work models and that Jill Carter, Dylan Robinson, and Karyn Recollet discuss. In short, rather than seeing Johnson as an isolated "deviation" from the maturation narrative that has often governed Canadian performance historiography in the past, we might see her performances as part of multiple lines of genealogical descent or as components of a complex, rhizomatic network of performance practices.

ESSAYS

Rather than trace the history of Canadian performance, the essays in this volume provide a map of the field of performance history in Canada in 2017. They fall, roughly, into three groups: explorations of performances that have been under-represented in or excluded from mainstream theatre histories; re-evaluations of case studies that typically appeared in narratives of Canadian theatre history, often with authors introducing new archival findings or applying methods from performance studies and other fields; and critical considerations of performance history methodologies and historiographical practices. Many of the essays flag the actual and affective labour of the authors, locating the historian as both "I" and "eye" in the production of historical narratives. They reflect Ric Knowles's observation of changes in the field—while in the 1970s and '80s, research was "distinctly nationalistic" with a goal of "establishing roots . . . and insisting that Canadian theatre . . . had a distinctive past upon which to build" ("Theatre/Research" 227), in the 2010s, " 'Canada' as subject is taken-for-granted rather than belaboured" ("Theatre/Research" 228). Questions here focus not on what happened but on how performances past were remembered, why some pasts have been remembered and others forgotten, how to address omissions, and what narratives to tell.

The first section of this volume—(Re)Integrations—includes four essays exploring performance practices that have been excluded from many theatre histories to date. Alexandra Kovacs's chapter, "Beyond Shame and Blame in Pauline Johnson's Performance Histories," takes up the questions of this introduction, arguing that critical shame and historical blame are not only responsible for Johnson's long-standing exclusion from theatre history narratives but also have validated such exclusions in ways that reinforce prejudices. Beginning by asking whether there is a history of Acadian theatre and noting that histories produced to date generally situate Acadian theatre within nationalist models, Nicole Nolette's essay "Chiac and the Linguistic Detour of Acadian Theatre History" contends that by taking a linguistic rather than nationalist approach, one can better understand the apparently anomalous detour of Chiac performance in Acadian theatre history. In "Untold Histories of Canadian Theatre in Higher Education," Glen Nichols notes a significant disconnect between the conflicting outcomes of liberal education and (pre)professional training in university and college programs, traces this disconnect to how the histories of post-secondary theatre training in Canada have been discussed—or more often virtually ignored—by theatre historians, and argues that in order to challenge the neo-liberal, utilitarian agendas rampant in today's post-secondary sector, we must develop historiographical tools and appropriately complex and comprehensive historical narratives to address how post-secondary theatre training has developed in Canada. In the final contribution to this section, Michelle La Flamme notes several significant oversights in existing histories of Aboriginal theatre in Canada and, through her interview with Margo Kane, suggests that both a broader perspective and methodological reconsiderations are necessary to redress these omissions.

The essays in the second section of this volume, Returns and Re-examinations, shed new light on performance practices that have received critical attention in the past. At first glance, Alan Filewod's chapter appears to address two relatively well-described aspects of Canadian dramatic literature: "closet" drama and literature representing World War I. After establishing the historiographic and theoretical challenges that unpublished and unproduced plays pose to theatre historians, Filewod explores William Stabler Atkinson's play *Glory Hole*, suggesting that considering such a work as an example of life writing allows for a critical rethinking of not only the surviving script but also the object and practice of theatre history. Examining the 1951 Massey Commission Report's treatment of dance, Allana Lindgren's essay, like Filewod's, also covers territory that is arguably well-addressed in Canadian theatre histories to date. By returning to the commission's source texts—testimony provided to commissioners—and explicitly addressing how dance testimony opens the door for examinations of mid-century attitudes toward diversity, Lindgren argues that revisiting historical sources can not only complicate well-established understandings of nation and culture but also allow us to resist "the ossifying effect of primary sources." The final two essays in this section provide timely rethinkings of the "alternative" theatre movement of the 1970s, the movement so crucial to the narrative of Canadian theatre's professional maturation. In his case study of Alumnae Theatre's production of Anne Hébert's play *Le Temps Sauvage*, Robin Whittaker argues against the dismissal of nonprofessionalizing theatre companies' practices and, employing the methodology described by Michel Foucault in *The Archaeology of Knowledge*, contends that this example "challenges the flawed anthropomorphic narrative that has come to define Canadian theatre history as a history of professionalizing practices maturing from amateur theatricals." In "Invisibility and Early New Play Dramaturgy: Bill Glassco's Development of David Freeman's *Creeps*," Jessica Riley considers the impact of two "unseen" aspects of Freeman's play, drawing links between the invisibility of Glassco's dramaturgical practices and the play's unseen female character Thelma, shedding new light on both playwriting practices and the representation of women and disability at a crucial moment in Canadian theatre history.

The final section of this volume, Rethinkings, explicitly addresses historiography and methodology. The first of the contributions to this section, an edited transcript of a round table convened at the 2016 Canadian Association for Theatre Research conference, brings Jill Carter, Karyn Recollet, and Dylan Robinson together to discuss how explicitly applying Indigenous epistemologies to examinations of the performative past enriches practices for performance historiography. Yves Jubinville's essay then asserts the need for comparative approaches to Québécois theatre history, arguing that by considering theoretical understandings and practices of theatrical modernism in Québec alongside similar developments in English Canada and the United States, we can better understand the cultural specificities of all three traditions. Stephen Johnson's essay, " 'Shield Us From This Base Ridicule': The Petitions to Censor Blackface Circus Clowns, Toronto, 1840–43," employs a microhistorical methodology to examine a case study that could also well appear in the first section of this volume: petitions submitted to Toronto City Council protesting blackface performance. Johnson's essay demonstrates the rich questions microhistory can generate and how such questions—rather than firm conclusions—shed light on the cultural power of performance, both in the past and today. Employing a similar microhistorical and self-aware approach to Johnson, Marlis Schweitzer's essay deconstructs three sentences that appear in the memoirs of the nineteenth-century star Mrs. John Drew, tracing both Drew's travels and Schweitzer's own journey through archival remains of Drew's performance history. Schweitzer's essay demonstrates that combining microhistorical and deconstructive methodologies with a hemispheric perspective creates space for productive rethinkings of received narratives concerning nineteenth-century popular performance. Finally, Nikki Cesare Schotzko takes up the timely critical, historiographical, and theoretical challenges performance documentation practices pose today, in a performance culture shaped by social media and digital-virtual archives. Applying a phenomenological frame to her analysis of contemporary performance art, she asks us to consider urgent questions, "as performance, both in the mainstream and on the more experimental edges, seems to ask, what does the mode of perception do to the time of performance? And what happens to the future of performance when the simultaneity of the event of performance with its socially mediated documentation turns the present now into a concurrent historical event?"

Carter, Recollet, and Robinson and Cesare Schotzko's contributions, which bookend this volume's final section, lead readers from considering

Canada's performing pasts to imagining the futures of performance historiography. It is my hope that by (re)locating Canadian performance histories and historiographical practices today and (re)situating Canadian performance practices within decolonizing, interdisciplinary, digital, and global contexts, the essays in this volume not only map the ground of Canadian theatre and performance history today but also chart future courses for students and scholars (re)turning to Canada's performative past.

PART 1: (RE)INTEGRATIONS

BEYOND SHAME AND BLAME IN PAULINE JOHNSON'S PERFORMANCE HISTORIES

ALEXANDRA KOVACS

In December 1892, E. Pauline Johnson took the stage at Association Hall in Hamilton, Ontario, to perform a play about shame. Alongside Owen Smily's Charlie McDonald, Johnson played Christine McDonald in a "dual rendition" of a "Romance" that she wrote herself ("Recital"). In the program for the playlet, the audience is offered some context for the presentation:

> CHRISTINE McDONALD is the child of red and white parentage, her father, a Hudson Bay Factor, having married a Northwest Indian girl. Christine also marries an Englishman who, in the employ of the Government, has spent some years at the Hudson Bay Post. The scene begins when Charlie McDonald and his wife reach home after attending the Lieut.-Governor's ball at the provincial capital. ("Recital")

Though there is no script that documents the actual performance given in December 1892 by Smily and Johnson, a short story by the same title was published in February 1893 in *The Dominion Illustrated*. This document offers some insight into the action Johnson and Smily probably performed. The inciting incident in the story is Christine's open discussion, at a society party, of the details of her parents' marriage. She admits to a curious crowd that there were "no missionaries" in the "part of the country" where her parents had wed ("A Red Girl's Reasoning" 22). The confession that her parents were married according to "Indian rites" causes a frenzy amongst the high society guests, with many calling the situation "horrify[ing]" (23). In the story,

Christine's husband is embarrassed by his wife's confession and a domestic argument ensues upon their arrival home from the ball.

> "Christie," he said harshly, "do you know what you have done?"
>
> "Yes,"—taking a step nearer to him—her whole soul springing up into her eyes, "I have angered you, Charlie, and—"
>
> "Angered me? You have disgraced me, and, moreover, you have disgraced yourself and both your parents."
>
> "*Disgraced?*" (23)

To this accusation, Christine responds:

> "Shame? Why should I be ashamed of the rites of my people any more than you should be ashamed of the customs of yours—of a marriage more sacred and holy than half your white man's mockeries?" (23–24)

In a resounding climax to the work, Christine confronts Charlie, and then walks out on him, standing up for an acknowledgement of her complex identity while confronting the assumptions that turn Indigenous expressions of identity to "disgrace." In short, Christine rejects the framework that disciplines her behaviour and history through applications of "shame."

Johnson's performance of this strong woman marked the end of a year that represented a turning point in her artistic development. Prior to 1892, Johnson was known as a talented writer with a unique personal history. Born 10 March 1861 in Chiefswood, her family home on the Six Nations community near Ohsweken, Ontario, the Kanien'kehá:ka (Mohawk)–English Johnson was the daughter of hereditary Pine Tree Chief Onwanonsyshon (George Henry Martin Johnson) and English settler Emily Susanna Howells ("Emily Pauline Johnson"). She began publishing her poetry near the end of her father's life in 1884. Soon, her writing regularly appeared in periodicals such as *Saturday Night*, *The Week*, and *The Globe*. On 16 January 1892 all that changed: Johnson became a figure of great public interest when she recited her poem "A Cry from an Indian Wife" at the Canadian Authors Evening arranged by the Young Men's Liberal Club in Toronto, Ontario. After that event, she was catapulted into fame, and embarked upon a year of heavily scheduled performance engagements. By September 1892, she had assembled various costumes to enhance the theatricality of her presentations. In December of the same year she added more dramatic flavour by working with a stage partner on what would have been one of her first attempts at a "dual rendition."

From 1892 until her breast cancer diagnosis in 1909, Johnson toured across Canada nineteen times (Rogers), performed twice in London, England, and was engaged in various performance circuits throughout the United States. She performed alongside various stage partners in costumed entertainments that were scripted by her own pen or by other dramatists. Though Johnson died in 1913, her legacy endures: her portrait's appearance on a Canadian postage stamp in 1961 speaks to her incorporation into projects of Canadian nationalism; Margaret Atwood and City Opera Vancouver's 2015 production of *Pauline*, based on Johnson's life, evidences the artistic community's continued fascination with her life; and, more recently, the Bank of Canada's nomination of Johnson as a contender to be featured on the next bank note represents the influence Johnson still holds over the Canadian public's cultural imagination (Shypula).

However, despite the impact of Johnson's performance practice on audiences during her lifetime and the enduring impression she continues to make on both Indigenous and settler publics today, Johnson's theatrical activities rarely enter substantively into discussions of her larger biography or into scholarly discussions of Canadian theatre history. Rather, critical focus has remained on Johnson's poetic output: her poems like "The Song my Paddle Sings" and "Cry from an Indian Wife" are recited in classrooms and valued as cultural heritage for both Indigenous and settler communities (qtd. in Anderson x). Her history as a prolific theatre artist who recited her poetry during costumed entertainments and adapted her literary short stories for dramatic presentation is, far from being commemorated, often ignored.

This contribution to a collection on Canadian theatre historiographies responds to that omission by focusing on two histories of shame related to Johnson's performances—first, the critical shaming of Johnson's costume and, second, the historical blame assigned to Johnson's sister for the inaccessibility of Johnson's performance archive. This contribution argues that these two histories function as interpretive distractions, constructed to validate a lack of scholarly focus on Pauline Johnson's theatrical activity. Beginning with an assessment of the historicization of Johnson's costume through the prism of affect theory, the essay identifies the dominant prejudice associated with Johnson's costume. How do contemporary scholars assess Johnson's costume? Why is it a site of such difficulty and disgrace? Offering an alternative to the prevailing interpretations that discredit the costume's sophistication, this essay recontextualizes the constituent parts of Johnson's dresses by viewing them alongside the theatrical conditions within which they operated. This recontextualizing practice analyzes reviews to identify Johnson's repertoire, and then addresses how these performed selections demanded a multi-functional set of costumes that could represent a plethora of both settler and Indigenous identities. This essay also puts Johnson's choice of describing her costumes as "correct" into context, carefully articulating how this billing is produced within a particular performance culture of costumed entertainment. Next, I address how the paradigms of authenticity that buttress the shaming of Johnson's costumes are replicated in the historical record's negative characterization of her sister Evelyn Johnson. Here, I consider depictions that suggest Evelyn Johnson obstructed access to Pauline Johnson's performance archive, or even destroyed materials related to Pauline's performance history. This more personal and confessional section of the essay reflects on the way in which I, as an early career researcher, accepted an entrenched narrative that vilified Evelyn Johnson, and how that "distracted"—in Graham Hingangaroa Smith's sense of the term—from my own responsibility to locate primary source materials that could illuminate the nuance at work in Johnson's performance repertoire. Inspired by the resistance to constructions of shame that Johnson herself performed via Christine McDonald in 1892, this essay reveals how assessments of Johnson's performative talent or aptitude typically depend on the damaging assumption that Johnson only ever performed her own identity. I argue that the interpretive focus on authenticity and biography at the site of the Indigenous performer is pernicious and tenacious—Johnson is certainly not the only target of this critical apparatus. So while the work presented in what follows seeks to offer a new set of materials and approaches with which the theatre and performance research community may begin to recuperate a sense of agency and pride at the site of Johnson's performance, it also seeks to instigate a retooling of the approaches by which both early and present-day Indigenous performers are viewed and reviewed.

SHAME ON YOUR COSTUME

It is worthwhile to begin a discussion of the interpretations of Johnson's performance history by citing the perspective on Johnson held by the "personification of Canadian literature" (Kapuscinski 98). Novelist Margaret Atwood admits that E. Pauline Johnson was an artist of considerable sophistication "despite her habit of dressing up in costumes" (qtd. in Martin). Atwood's anti-theatrical view of Johnson's artistry is characteristic and evocative. The author shames Johnson's theatrical strategies, chiefly by targeting her use of costumes. It is Johnson's bad "habit"—her "dressing up"—that needs to be ignored in order for Johnson to receive validation as an artistic forebear of national importance.

Atwood's uneasiness with Johnson's costume is typical of scholarly engagement with Johnson's theatre history. Cultural historians Anne Collett, Martha Viehmann, and Rick Monture similarly echo or identify the worry and hesitation over Johnson's performances, locating the "disappointment" at the site of her costume (Viehmann 261). As Anne Collett notes, "Johnson-Tekahionwake's portrayal (both in word and costume) of the 'red Indian' lacked the authenticity she demanded of Canadian novelists" ("Fair" 167). Rick Monture is particularly concerned about the semiotics of Johnson's costume change into a Victorian ball gown. For Monture, this strategy "symbolizes the process of Native assimilation into Canadian mainstream society" (123), "imply[ing] that all Native people would simply be better off if they would adapt to Euro-Canadian ways" (129).

It is Johnson's costume, then, that is one of the central "problems" of her performance history. Interestingly, the difficulty of her "habit" is not limited to only modern criticism—even Pauline Johnson herself, when she first wrote to her friend William Lighthall in September 1892 with her idea for a costume, notes that the process of creating it was "the most difficult thing in the world":

> This season I am going to make a feature of costuming for recitals—always an interesting topic with ladies, but I am beset with difficulties on all hands. For my Indian poems I am trying to get an Indian dress to recite in, and it is the most difficult thing in the world. Now I know *you know* what is feminine, so you can tell me if the "Indian Stores" in Montreal are *real* Indian stores, or is their stuff manufactured? I want a pair of moccasins, worked either in colored moose hair, porcupine quills, or very heavily with *fine colored beads*, have you ever seen any such there? [. . .] [I]f you see anything in Montreal that would assist me in getting up a costume, be it, beads, quills, sashes, shoes, brooches or indeed anything at all, I will be more than obliged to know of it. (qtd. in Strong-Boag and Gerson 110; emphasis in original)

Almost all biographies of Johnson's highlight the moment when she confesses to Lighthall the "difficulty" she was having in constructing her "Indian costume." In these interpretations, her desire to "[get] up a costume" that was "real," by inquiring about the "store" from which she could obtain it, speaks to her alienation from authentic sources and calls into question Johnson's theatrical motivations.

Johnson's undiscerning sourcing of materials (she asks for "anything at all") is, according to the typical interpretation of Johnson's request to Lighthall, made more troubling because in May of 1892, months before she sent her letter, she released a non-fiction essay that advocated for authors to approach the representation of Indigenous characters with a careful eye to distinctiveness. In "A Strong Race Opinion: On the Indian Girl in Modern Fiction" Johnson expresses concern about the impoverished nature of generic portrayals, pointing out that "tribal distinction [. . .] among North American aborigines" is seldom negotiated by authors in their creation of fictional characters:

> The Indian girl we meet in cold type [. . .] is rarely distressed by having to belong to any tribe, or to reflect any tribal characteristics. She is merely a wholesome sort of mixture of any band existing between the Mic Macs of Gaspé and the Kwaw-Kewlths of British Columbia, yet strange to say, that notwithstanding the numerous tribes, with their aggregate numbers reaching more than 122,000 souls in Canada alone, our Canadian authors can cull from this huge revenue of character, but one Indian girl, and stranger still that this lonely little heroine never had a prototype in breathing flesh-and-blood existence! (178)

Johnson sarcastically criticizes writers that create Indigenous "national" characters "without having ever come in contact with [them]" (qtd. in Gerson and Strong-Boag 183). With this in mind, Johnson's confession that she had difficulty finding a costume for her performance poses a critical problem for many modern interpreters of Johnson's performance. Why would Johnson, who so fervently and passionately noted the necessity of "tribal distinction" in the creation of "flesh-and-blood" characters, "ma[ke] no effort to replicate the actual clothing of any specific Native group" (Strong-Boag and Gerson 110) and instead create, according to modern interpretations, a "bricolage of personal and public iconography of 'the Red Indian' " (Collett 161): a costume, as seen below, made up of a buckskin skirt and fringed leather bodice with wampum belts, a firebag, pelts, ermine tails, bear claws, and various medallions attached as embellishments?

The "semiotic confusion" (Lyon) of Johnson's approach to costuming has been defined as contradicting her stance on fictional portrayal—an implicit evasion of the prescriptions of the "real live Indian girl" that she extols in

Fig. 1. Johnson's costume as it appeared in a program circa 1894. Provided courtesy of the William Ready Division of Archives and Research Collections, McMaster University Library, Pauline Johnson Fonds, box six, file six.

her prose writing. The dichotomy between Johnson's written advocacy and performance choices has meant her costume has been viewed "either as an act of dishonesty, or even one of prostitution" (Collett, "Fair" 162). The fact that Johnson's costume was "syncretistic to the point of being fanciful" has been viewed as an indicator that Johnson's performance was "ideologically undeveloped" (Goldie 61, qtd. in Lyon). Rick Monture calls it an indication of Johnson's "hollow activism" (138).

Many interpretations have evaluated Johnson's performance history according to one costume's adherence—or lack thereof—to Johnson's own demands for "distinctiveness." Embedded within these approaches is a discernible bias that culminates in a negative judgment: Johnson's performance is a failure on account of her costume's inauthenticity. This critical response to Johnson's performances corresponds to what theology professor and philosopher Stephen Pattison calls the "means of social control" enforced by "shame-based cultures" (132). Such cultures produce shame by monitoring an individual's "conformity to unwritten rules, the maintenance of honour and appearance, and the avoidance of pollution" (132). Johnson neither conforms to her own written rules, nor maintains the appearance of a seemingly desired authenticity. Worst of all, the cultural pastiche of her costume only serves to validate a kind of pan-Indian "pollution." Pattison cites the work of sociologist Richard Sennett, who addresses how these practices of shaming have " 'taken the place of violence as a *routine* form of punishment in Western societies,' becoming 'an everyday tool of discipline' " that is connected to paternalistic authority (Pattison 140; emphasis in original). If anything, the ongoing critical anxiety about Johnson's performance of Indigeneity—the consistent negotiation of whether or not Johnson was performing "right" (read authentically) and the defensive justification of her performance (even when it is well-meaning)[1]—culminates in the discursive violence to which Sennett and Pattison allude. The costume's fancy and overt theatricality has provoked

1 For an example of an interpretive approach that attempts to justify and celebrate Johnson's aesthetic choices as performance art, see Emily Landau's reading of Johnson's theatrical strategies in her article "Double Vision."

the "impossible question" that "haunts Johnson's career (and that even got to her on occasion) [. . .]: 'Pauline Johnson: was she really Mohawk?' " (Fee 119). Especially because the critical shaming of Johnson's theatricality (as represented by the spectacle of her costumes) threatens her claim to her own Indigenous nationality (a nation of which she was very proud),[2] it is imperative to return to the artifact of Johnson's performance history that is most troubling—her "Indian" costume—and ask if its shaming has distracted historians from assessing its function within a particular theatrical context that served to embody a repertoire of several characters and personalities.

To proceed with this examination I will now address what costumes Johnson initially used in her early performances, and how her "Indian" costume transformed over time in tandem with changes in her repertoire. By November 1892, only a month after her plea to Lighthall, Johnson was preparing for a performance in Ottawa at St. John's Hall under the patronage of the governor general and Lady Stanley. For that performance, reporters noted that Johnson appeared "in three costumes, the every day dress of a lady, a sailor costume and an Indian costume" ("Mohawk Poetess"). The reporter from *The Evening Journal* outlines the particular intrigue offered by Johnson's "Indian" costume:

> [It is] made of doeskin patterned after the dress supposed to have been worn by Minnehaha in the long ago. The front of it bears a number of silver brooches of many shapes which were given her by an old Indian pagan woman, aged 90, who lived on the reserve and had worn them on her costume and who in turn received them

2 It is worth noting that Johnson's expression of Haudenosaunee pride is as complex as her performance history. For instance, Johnson's commitment to emphasizing the "undeniable fact" that the "Iroquois stand far in advance of any Indian tribe in America" (Johnson, "The Iroquois") resists the more present-day conception of Indigenous nationhood as expressed by the discourses of Indigenous literary nationalism. In that orientation, nationhood reflects "a common social interdependence within the community, a tribal web of kinship rights and responsibilities that link the People, the land, and the cosmos together in an ongoing and dynamic system of mutually affecting relationships" (Fagan et al. 20).

> from her mother. Thus these ornaments have been worn for over one hundred years. The back of the skirt is adorned by a "fire bag" manufactured by the Blackfeet Indians. She [Johnson] has various samples of Wampum, some of which are very rare and of great value, the art of making the beads of which they are composed of being lost. One is an Iroquois Wampum and the Indians of that particular branch of Indians can trace by the Wampum the history of every treaty entered into between the Six Nations and the British Government. The red blanket which she will wear around her shoulders to-night is the identical one on which Prince Arthur stood when he was made a chief of the Six Nations when he visited Canada in 1870. ("Mohawk Poetess")

Throughout her performance career, Johnson bought and sold various accoutrements, adding and subtracting materials from the two-piece costume described above, while also assembling a wardrobe of other dresses (boating costumes and silk Victorian gowns) that she would use in her presentations. By her 1893 season, Johnson's use of multiple costumes and her presentation of many personalities made the national news. She even began to bill her performance, which now featured a collaboration between her and new stage partner Owen Smily, as a "dual costume recital" ("Amusements").

The diversity of the repertoire Johnson performed indicates the reason she may have required so many different outfits, and also why her "Indian" number, in particular, featured such a variety of materials. It is useful to return here to the program for Johnson's December 1892 performance at Association Hall, discussed at the start of this essay, as it gives some insight into the dramaturgical structure of Johnson's performance with Smily, as well as the repertoire they both performed. Smily and Johnson gave solo performances at the start of their act, with Johnson scheduled to perform "Cry from an Indian Wife," "As Red Men Die," and "The Song My Paddle Sings" (some of her most famous poems) in between Smily's renditions of "Abner Brown," "Sunny," "Demon Ship," and "A Fish Yarn" (an adaptation of "Three Men in a Boat"). At the *end* of the program, Johnson and Smily came together to perform the fifteen-minute "dual rendition" of "A Red Girl's Reasoning" (see "Recital"). The evening's program required a set of costumes that could functionally serve the expression of a variety of characters: "Cry from an Indian Wife" is a soliloquy given from the perspective of a Plains Cree wife on the eve of the battle at Cut Knife Creek, "As Red Men Die" requires a contrapuntal performance in the voice of a Huron captor and "Mohawk brave," "The Song My Paddle Sings" certainly would have been made more striking by its performance in a boating costume, and "A Red Girl's Reasoning" would have required Johnson to wear a gown (as the program notes make clear, the character Christine is returning from a ball at the provincial capital).

Further attention to the development of Johnson's costume over time suggests that changes she made by 1896—for instance, the addition of a knife to her costume—were motivated by the changing requirements of her repertoire. By this time, Johnson was performing in the United States. For her performances in Grand Rapids, Michigan, a reviewer noted that the repertoire consisted of:

> "Ojisdah [*sic*], the White Star of the Mohawks" in which was related a thrilling incident of the wars between the Mohawk and Huron tribes, "The Cattle Thief" a tragic poem including a Cree maiden's appeal; "The White Wampum" in which was told a legend of the prairies and the northern lights, and "His Sister's Son," showing the tragic results of the system of civilizing the Indians of the British Northwest [. . .]. ("Mohawk Princess")

According to this reviewer, Johnson "embodied" these selections with the help of many props. The first of these new performance props was "her father's steel dagger," which she carried "in her belt, using it to portray passages in her readings."

Presumably, a dramatic recitation of "Ojistoh" (what the reviewer names "Ojisdah") benefitted from the use of the knife. This poem recounts the capture of a Mohawk woman named Ojistoh. She is "flung [. . .] on [the Huron's] pony's back" (qtd. in Gerson and Strong-Boag 115) and "bound with buckskin to his hated waist." Pretending to be disloyal and unfaithful to her husband, Ojistoh convinces her Huron captor to "cut the cords" and "cease [. . . the] maddening haste." Then, she uses her knife to obtain her freedom:

> I wound my arms about his tawny waist;
> My hand crept up the buckskin of his belt;
> His knife hilt in my burning palm I felt;
> One hand caressed his cheek, the other drew
> The weapon softly—"I love you, love you,"
> I whispered, "I love you as my life."
> And—buried in his back his scalping knife. (116)

The poem concludes with a gripping description of Ojistoh's return "[b]ack to [her] Mohawk and [her] home." What is noteworthy here is how the props Johnson attached to her costume support the performance of the poem. When the costume is reanimated by the various primary sources cited here, its function as a tool to express several distinct characters is highlighted and Johnson's costume, though not faithful to an "authentic" self, is faithful to her advocated desire for the unique representation of multiple characters.

These costuming choices, now contextualized by the repertoire they animated, offer some rationale for why, by 1900, Johnson was advertising that she performed her "dramatic recitals" in "correct costume" (Johnson, "To Sir"). Cynthia Cooper, in her study of Canadian fashion in the late nineteenth century, examines how the cultural "passion for costumed entertainments" heightened correctness as a metric for success in performance (41). Cooper importantly notes that correctness had little to do with authenticity, but was measured by an individual or performer's adherence to certain codes for particular characters that were laid down by "fancy dress" experts like Ardern Holt. Authorities like Holt even published manuals to clarify the protocols involved in the development of costumes. These compendiums, treasured by high society, "careful[ly] circumscrib[ed] [. . .] the fantasy experience" of dress culture in Victorian society (Cooper 42). Included in Holt's 1887 compilation is a listing for the suitable portrayal of "American Indian Queen North" that might have been negotiated by Johnson:

> INDIAN DRESSES should come veritably from the country, and are of great variety. North American Indian Queen for fancy dress wears a brown satin cuirass bodice and skirt, or black cloth embroidered with red, yellow and white, bordered with cut leather fringe; sandals; a diadem of coloured eagles' and vultures' feathers; bird's wings in front, and a great many beads for jewellery. (Holt 199)

Of course Holt's description is indeed the kind of generic representation that Johnson admonishes in her non-fiction writing, and it does not describe Johnson's garb precisely. But Holt's insistence that "Indian dresses should come veritably from the country" reflects Johnson's emphasis, in her letter to Lighthall, on the need for "real" materials, and her subsequent sourcing of materials from different regions for the presentation of very different characters. It also contextualizes her request for "moccasins" that are "worked [. . .] very heavily with fine colored beads" and her choice of a two-piece outfit (a brown "cuirass bodice and skirt"), ornamented with fringed hems (qtd. in Strong-Boag and Gerson 110). Johnson works with these codes, but also beyond them, to develop a costume piece that had the functional capacity to represent more than just Holt's one generic character. Consequently, the very nature of the costume's composition—the collage to which many critics refer—afforded Johnson the space to allow for the distinctiveness of various characters to emerge. As a performer especially interested in the portrayal of female characters, her use of targeted accessories may have enhanced (at least in her own mind) her portrayals of "Indian girls" from nations and regions other than her own. As such, Johnson did not "simply lack the talent needed to see beyond the inscriptions of her time" (Lyon). On the contrary, reading her costume's development within the context of the characters it served to embody supposes that Johnson was "see[ing] beyond" more conventional inscriptions, and complicating them through a nuanced performance that evidenced a great deal of "talent" and effort.

BLAMING EVELYN JOHNSON

Interestingly, the critical assumption that metonymically links Johnson's performance to her own identity is damaging to more than just Johnson's legacy: it also, as I will argue now, is intrinsically tied to the other history of shame entangled in Johnson's performance history and related to Johnson's sister Evelyn. Added to the critical "difficulty" of her costumes, many biographers of Pauline Johnson note that their hesitancy toward a discussion of her performance is on account of limited access to scripted performance materials. Interestingly, the blame for this dearth of resources is assigned to Johnson's sister, Evelyn (commonly known as Eva), who allegedly "culled" Pauline's "effects"—burning her private papers (Strong-Boag and Gerson 10). As such, there is general agreement across biographies that, on account of Evelyn, "Johnson's skits and dramatic presentations [. . .] experienced a particularly high mortality rate surviving only in accounts by newspaper reviews" and that "[t]he likelihood that much more may be found is rather slim" (Strong-Boag and Gerson 6–7).

Fig. 2. Pauline Johnson's sister, Evelyn (Eva) Johnson. Provided courtesy of the William Ready Division of Archives and Research Collections, McMaster University Library, Pauline Johnson Fonds, box two, file four, envelope two.

In my own early work on Johnson, I believed the narrative blaming Evelyn for the destruction of Pauline's materials. That acceptance was reinforced by representations of Johnson's sister in both biographies and live performances (*Pauline*). Many of these sources described how jealousy motivated Evelyn to destroy her sister's materials.[3] I had faith in the veracity of this sibling rivalry. This was a convenient narrative that allowed me to excuse the inferences I often made (I thought I *had to make)* about Johnson's performance career.

I now realize that my confidence in this history was a distraction that impeded my responsibility to both Johnson's and her sister's legacies. I use the term distraction strategically, evoking Maori scholar Graham Hingangaroa Smith, who in his study of Sami culture notes how "issues of lesser importance," which tend to focus on identity, are constructed by the mainstream academy and colonial societies to "distract from the larger picture of long-term objectives and more urgent and real concerns" of an Indigenous community or subject that might be under study (qtd. in Kuokkanen 278). Smith outlines how "dominant white non-Indigenous interests" have developed the "politics of distraction," usually by embracing discussions of a subject's identity politics (211). Indeed, the dramatic story of the Johnson sisters distracted me from accessing sources that revealed Johnson's multi-faceted dramatic ability.

I only broke out of this distracted fog when I came across a description of one of Johnson's performances that seemed very uncharacteristic. An undated *Ottawa Citizen* review of Johnson's performance in Orme Hall ends with a surprising report of Johnson's stage work with her other stage partner Walter McRaye: "in company with Mr. McRaye, [Johnson performed] *At the Ball*

3 Most biographies take some time to discuss the Eva/Pauline rivalry. Marcus Van Steen writes, "[a]mong those who disapproved strongly of Pauline's chosen way of life was her sister Evelyn, and the gulf between them grew to the point that they ceased communicating with each other" (20). Likewise, Charlotte Gray confirms that Evelyn had an issue with Johnson performing at the end of her book when she cites Lionel Makovski as saying that " 'Eva seemed to feel that Pauline's life as a "trouper" was something not to be mentioned' " (395–96). Betty Keller rounds out this oppositional narrative when she argues that "Pauline's sister strongly disapprove[d] of the proposed recital tour" and was "firmly opposed to Pauline making a career of [performance] in case it reflect[ed] badly on the family" (11).

[. . .] an amusing incident supposed to occur at a ball in an insane asylum, where two visitors mistake each other for patients" ("Miss E. Pauline Johnson: Canada's"). *The Daily Examiner* gives a more detailed outline of the performance's content as it was presented in Peterborough in 1903:

> The latter half of the programme was opened with a playlet entitled "At the Ball," in which Miss Johnson acted the part of Clara Manners while Mr. McRaye took the part of Captain Fielding. The scene of this selection was a ball given in Kensington lunatic asylum for patients who were not very violent. Miss Manners and Captain Fielding were the guests of Dr. Adams. The two guests seek refuge from the throng of dancing maniacs, and meet in a small room. Here each takes the other for a lunatic and acts as such. They, however, discover their mistake prior to the conclusion of the very clever little piece of acting. ("Delightful")

This performance certainly seemed to have little to do with Johnson's ancestry, her Indigenous identity, or her political advocacy (as expressed in her non-fiction writing). With this in mind, I did something I had never done before (and certainly would never advocate a student of theatre history to ever do): I opened my computer, loaded up an Internet browser, and typed the name of the character Johnson played—Clara Manners—into Google. Her performance, in that once-empty field, now took centre stage.

Suddenly, Google led me to a script, hitherto deemed "untrace[able]" (Strong-Boag and Gerson 235): W.R. Walkes's dramatic sketch *A Pair of Lunatics*. Published by Samuel French and performed at Drury Lane and the Avenue Theatre in 1889, this sketch features two characters: "He (otherwise Captain George Fielding) played originally by Mr. George Alexander" and "She (otherwise Clara Manners) played originally by Miss Maude Millet" (Walkes). Pauline Johnson had a previous association with George Alexander (an actor and producer): he had introduced both Johnson and McRaye to the agent of the American Slayton Lyceum Society, and so it is likely that Johnson came by this script through that professional association (Keller 103). This script corresponded entirely to the descriptions of Johnson's sketch *At the Ball* that were offered in reviews. I had suddenly come upon the Johnson historian's "holy grail": the script that hitherto was deemed untraceable now laid before my eyes.

Much can be said about this script (and hopefully will be said subsequent to this essay), but what is most important to note here is that Evelyn did not destroy it. Furthermore, she is not to blame for my oversight of these materials. What made this script inaccessible was, rather, my supposition that Johnson was always performing her own identity. Never before had I thought to make the character Johnson played the subject of my search. This is more than just a singular error of historical methodology located at the site of Johnson's performance—it is a habitual interpretive strategy that has historically been applied to Indigenous performers. Theatre scholar Rob Appleford notes:

> When there was talk in 1970 of adding the name of Chief Dan George to the list of Oscar nominees for his performance in the film *Little Big Man*, the idea was quashed by a Los Angeles movie critic who, with what seemed like breathtaking logic at the time, pointed out that "it would be ridiculous to give an Academy Award to an Indian for playing an Indian." ("The Desire" 21)

The critical apparatus that failed to recognize Chief Dan George's talent has kept the historical negotiation of *Johnson's* performance at an impasse too: the assumption that Johnson was not an actor, but was always playing herself, distracts from the existence of scripts that illustrate Johnson's dramatic dynamism, shows that she had an interest in developing commercially successful work, and proves that such success did not always focus on the performance of her own Indigenous ancestry or self.

The very knowledge of these scripts offers an entirely new understanding of the tone and approaches Johnson took to her performance. Plays like these suggest that Johnson's performance was more than an "act in which she externalized the duality of a 'mixed-blood' inheritance through the device of costume" (Collett, "Red" 362). It certainly indicates that she performed more than the "sides" of herself. To be sure, Johnson did often perform her own poetry in a sequence of costuming where she changed from an "Indian costume" into a gown or other outfit (and often vice versa), but her use of these costumes in tandem with modifications in vocal delivery, as well as her choice of repertoire, suggests that she was doing more than merely "externali[zing] the duality of [her] 'mixed-blood' inheritance through the device of costume" (Collett, "Red" 362). The very existence of these scripts alters understandings of Johnson's performances, and frees Johnson's sister Evelyn from blame for erasing her entire performance archive.[4] The over one hundred year oversight of these materials also asks our field, more broadly, to reconsider the approaches taken, thus far, to the study of early Indigenous performing subjects.

LOCATING AND APPRECIATING JOHNSON'S TALENT

Johnson herself is no longer able to return and offer a defense of her performance choices, nor is she able to confront the critical interpretations that have

4 Evelyn Johnson was dedicated to the preservation of Six Nations culture and history as a local historian and a member of the Brant County and Ontario Historical Societies. According to Strong-Boag and Gerson, "she took considerable pride in her accuracy" (54). It is Evelyn who eventually willed the materials she did possess (and that related to her sister) to the Brant I.O.D.E (Imperial Order Daughters of the Empire). This same collection would eventually come to represent the first accrual of the Pauline Johnson fonds at the McMaster University William Ready Division of Archives and Research Collections. In addition, as Michelle Hamilton notes in her article "Borders Within: Anthropology and the Six Nations of the Grand River," Evelyn "turned to Museums to preserve Native material culture" and "after Pauline's death in 1913, [. . .] donated numerous items owned by her sister to the Brant Historical Society and later [. . .] willed seven False Face masks to their museum" (195). It is then to Evelyn Johnson, the very woman that many have characterized as a pariah of archival ethics, that researchers owe most of their findings regarding not only Pauline Johnson's life, but also a great deal of material culture related to the Six Nations of the Grand River.

labelled her performance, too often, as an example of her artistic compromise. Despite the absence of her voice and body, however, there are materials available that alert one to the complexity and mutability of Johnson's performance career—her fluency in various theatrical codes and languages is revealed across sources that frame Johnson's performances as at times powerful, often political, certainly dependent on economies, sometimes just plain fun, and always a great deal of work. Johnson's performances were always changing, and they certainly offered more than just a vision of her self or her own identity. Johnson's individual experiences, yes, are deeply present in the characters she plays, but that only goes to further evidence her artistic talent. This early artist's adaptation and performance of short stories like "A Red Girl's Reasoning" alongside her poetry and comedic sketches indicate a versatility that should no longer be a target of shame, but should be treated with respect and attention.

How that attention is generated is key to the project of reconsidersing Johnson's performance history. Of course, if Johnson's image in her "Indian dress" had been chosen to appear on the next hundred-dollar bill, it would be complimentary for her legacy. But as Thomas King warns, flattery is "especially dangerous when we do not even see that the premise from which we start a discussion is not the hard fact that we thought it was, but one of the fancies we churn out of our imaginations to help us get from the beginning of an idea to the end" (10). The assessments of Johnson's performance history that have excused it, or else dismissed it, have been guided by "fancies" that shame Pauline Johnson, but also blame important figures in the Six Nations community like Evelyn Johnson. Hopefully, the sources revealed here and the methodological considerations they inspire begin to do more than congratulate.

Indeed, as research work continues to be conducted about Pauline Johnson and her theatre history, revelations of her sacrifices and mistakes will also come to the fore—and things will not always be complimentary. But if the engagement with her history instigates at a point that can validate Johnson as a *talented* performer, then her theatrical legacy will no longer be flattened into a two-dimensional expression of only her duality or ancestry.

It is my hope that the analysis offered begins a process whereby the complex ability, expressed through Johnson's performances, can be assessed through equally multi-faceted methodologies and resources that give it animation, space, and life.

CHIAC AND THE LINGUISTIC DETOUR OF ACADIAN THEATRE HISTORY[1]

NICOLE NOLETTE

A HISTORY OF ACADIAN THEATRE?

Is there a history of Acadian theatre? If Acadian theatre history is to include all performance practices in Acadia, then the story starts with Marc Lescarbot's 1606 *Le théâtre de Neptune* in Port Royal. What follows, in this history, is a long period of oral traditions and *séances* featuring comedies or melodramas imported from France or Québec alongside other forms of performing arts. But if this history is to include only dramatic literature written by Acadian authors, according to Zénon Chiasson, who attempted such a history, it would begin in 1969, and is concurrent with the emergence of theatrical infrastructure outside of the parishes, convents, and colleges that hosted earlier performances. Two amateur theatre troupes were founded that year in Moncton: Les Feux Chalins and the Théâtre amateur de Moncton. Les Feux Chalins featured the writing of Antonine Maillet, most notably in its 1971 production of *La Sagouine*, directed by Eugène Gallant and showcasing Viola Léger in the title role. The Théâtre amateur de Moncton also promoted new works by Acadian authors, setting the stage for professional theatre in Acadie. Meanwhile, the recently founded Université de Moncton opened a department of dramatic arts and a few graduates created professional companies that remain today: the Théâtre populaire d'Acadie (TPA), established in 1974

1 This chapter is a translation and adaptation of material previously published in French in my book *Jouer la traduction. Théâtre et hétérolinguisme au Canada francophone*. I would like to acknowledge and thank the University of Ottawa Press and the Social Sciences and Humanities Research Council of Canada for their support.

in Caraquet, and l'Escaouette, created in 1978 in Moncton. Though l'Escaouette defined itself early on by its process of collective creation, one of its participants emerged as its main playwright: Herménégilde Chiasson. While Maillet dominated the perception of Acadian theatre from outside the borders of Acadie (mostly in Québec), Chiasson was her counterpart *within* Acadie.

Several scholars have compiled compelling histories of Acadian dramatic literature and theatre practices, but few have located Acadian theatre outside of a model of the concurrent emergence of a national consciousness and of a national literature.[2] In order to move beyond—or at least trouble—this model,

2 Zénon Chiasson wrote, for example, of Acadian theatre as "engaged and militant," as a "specific cultural space that compensated for other [more state-oriented] forms of national existence" ["D'un théâtre de divertissement et de subsistance, le théâtre acadien est donc devenu, au fil des ans, un théâtre engagé et militant. Coupé de ses racines, privé de pouvoir politique réel et maintenu à l'état de minoritaire, il était normal que le peuple acadien cherchât à se façonner un espace culturel spécifique mais compensatoire et à se donner ainsi une forme d'existence nationale."] (78). After testifying to the continuing maturity of Acadian theatre in a series of articles published throughout the 1980s, Chiasson started the laborious work of finding and describing existing literary works, ending with the compilation of an exhaustive bibliography. Glen Nichols further developed Chiasson's work in his 2005 article "Building Bridges," applying post-colonial models developed by Bill Ashcroft, Gareth Griffiths, and Helen Tiffin to classify Acadian theatre from the 1960s onwards. Their prominent formulation of post-colonial studies provided four models by which literature could be read and conceptualized: the national model with its insistence on the national (or pseudo-national) differentiation of literatures; the race-based model that cuts across literatures to grasp commonalities inherited from race; the comparative model that explores specificities shared by two or more post-colonial literatures; and, finally, the model that establishes hybridity or synchreticity as the basis of post-colonial literatures (Ashcroft et al. 16). For Nichols, Antonine Maillet's work fits into a nationalistic, myth-building dramaturgical model. Herménégilde Chiasson's drama, on the other hand, ascribes to a comparative model that deplores the neo-colonial role of Québec in regards to Acadie. Meanwhile, the more international theatre repertoire of and co-productions by Théâtre populaire d'Acadie and l'Escaouette reflect an increased openness to the world, corresponding to a model of hybridity and syncreticity. In 2007, Nichols added Collectif Moncton-Sable to his post-colonial history, as an example of a company characterized by its postmodernity and post-nationalism. For Nichols the company, which started working outside the established theatre infrastructure in the late 1990s, signalled an important

I focus in this essay on a particular aspect of dramatic literature and theatrical practice: its language.[3] Alain Masson, an early observer of Acadian literary modernity, noted in 1974 that "speaking of bilingualism in New Brunswick is a euphemism," because "francophones actually carry within them a genuine swarm of languages" ("*Étranglement*" 59).[4] At the heart of this bustling activity are the quaint, archaic language of the Sagouine; the dialects of Northern New Brunswick, of Québec, and of Canada; a variety of French considered to be international; Parisian slang; and, finally, Chiac, the dialect of the Moncton area that mixes French and English. The language of contemporary Acadian

---

milestone in the short history of Acadian theatre, because it "look[ed] beyond boundaries in so many ways—structurally, artistically, culturally, and politically—and in so doing contribute[d] to the construction of new visions for Acadian theatre and new dimensions of Acadian identity in a postmodern world" ("Collectif" 11). Like Zénon Chiasson before him, Nichols's Acadian theatre historiography relies heavily on the emergence of a national identity, although he does point to companies that rework and challenge the relationship between nation and theatre. While acknowledging the significant work done by Chiasson and Nichols to untangle the mimetic, myth-making, and post-national connections between Acadian theatre and representations of Acadian identity over the past fifty years, in this essay I take another point of departure, which I hope will bring dramatic and theatrical form to the forefront while shifting national concerns to the background.

3 Québécois scholar Lucie Robert first promoted language as a point of departure for writing theatre history in 1988. Pointing to what she perceived, at the time, as the absence of a history of drama in Québec, she noted that the first issue for any such endeavour to tackle should be language. Québécois drama, she argues, obsessively asks questions about language. It "never stops asking how to speak? In what circumstances? To say what? To what effect? In what language? What does this obsession teach us about ourselves as a collective?" ["La dramaturgie québécoise pose de manière obsessionnelle, et sous toutes les formes possibles, la question de la langue. Elle n'en finit plus de demander comment parler? dans quelles circonstances? pour dire quoi? avec quels effets? dans quelle langue? Qu'est-ce que cette obsession nous apprend sur nous-mêmes en tant que collectivité?"] ("Pour" 167–68). While applying Robert's questions about Québécois drama to Acadie may seem to reproduce a neo-colonial relationship between the two, these questions are also pertinent to playwriting and theatre-making in Acadie.

4 "Parler du bilinguisme au Nouveau-Brunswick est [. . . un . . .] euphémisme [puisqu'en réalité] les francophones portent en eux-mêmes un véritable grouillement linguistique."

theatre is not any more established than Masson observed in 1974, and again in 1994,[5] though the languages of Maillet, Laval Goupil, and Chiasson form inescapable historical models for playwrights. In this essay, I survey these foundational models before exploring the bustling playground on which Acadian theatre practitioners play, specifically considering Chiac artists like Collectif Moncton-Sable and Paul Bossé. These artists, I argue, have bypassed or detoured around the linguistic and institutional models that earlier Acadian practitioners established. Focusing on these discontinuous examples within Acadian theatre history as aesthetic and cultural turning points, I suggest, exposes how by prioritizing dramaturgical questions over national ones, we can better understand practices that criss-cross boundaries between historical periods previously categorized as nationalist or post-nationalist.[6] Ultimately,

---

5 Masson expanded on this linguistic analysis during the World Acadian Congress of 1994 by insisting on its literary value:

> As, in fact, there are multiple ways of speaking in Acadie—two languages, dozens of speech registers—the attachment to ambient speech patterns necessarily take a very singular turn. The Acadian writer finds himself in a very interesting position: instead of building a style, he determines a language. The language of this literature is not an established language.
>
> Comme le fait de l'Acadie est une parole multiple : deux langues, des niveaux de langue par dizaine, ces attachements à la parole ambiante prennent nécessairement une tournure très singulière. L'écrivain acadien se trouve donc dans une position très intéressante : au lieu de construire un style, il détermine une langue. La langue de cette littérature n'est pas une langue établie. ("Une idée" 128)

6 National or regional identity has been a contentious issue in Franco-Canadian literary studies. From a Franco-Ontarian perspective, for example, Lucie Hotte has argued that most readings of this minority literature have been marked by a singular search for identity that blocked other, more aesthetically oriented readings (66). From an Acadian perspective, however, Raoul Boudreau has countered that not all Franco-Canadian literatures are the same, and that models that hold true for Ontario do not necessarily apply in Acadie, not only because of cultural factors but also because of material ones:

> Acadie is bound to resurface periodically in Acadian poetry, because Acadian literature will never get out of its minority situation. Whether he likes it or not, the Acadian writer is always confronted with this question, if not in the theme

we see that the grandiose and grandiloquent treatment of Chiac by Bossé and Moncton-Sable is profoundly ambivalent, to the extent that the legacy of Chiac in the theatre itself comes into question.

LANGUAGE MODELS INSIDE AND OUTSIDE THE THEATRE INSTITUTION

In contemporary Acadian theatre institutions, vernacular language has had two major functions: turning the world upside down with language and exorcising linguistic alienation. These functions characterize the work of its two main playwrights, Antonine Maillet and Herménégilde Chiasson, and, to a lesser extent, the unclassifiable Laval Goupil. By its public reading in Montreal in 1968, Maillet's play *Les Crasseux* (*The Scum/The Grimy*) already marked an important turning point in giving Acadian theatre (and literature) a language of its own. The eponymous characters in this play spoke an Acadian parlance similar to the better-known Sagouine, an archaic form of language that Maillet dug out from the origins of Acadie, a dialect closer to that of Rabelais than anything Acadians speak today. Maillet invented a literary language that was "more French than France French because [it was] older, and preserved"

> of his work, then because of the conditions under which the work circulates and is received—which, as we know, end up influencing the content and even the form of the works. The Acadian writer will never pretend that the question of Acadian identity is settled or obsolete, because it shows up in the dependency in which he practices the activity of writing itself. ("La poésie" 89)

If the question of identity is unresolvable not only because of nationalist concerns but also because of the institutional structures determining how Acadian literature circulates, then moving into a period of "post-nationalist" theatre neither settles the question nor makes it obsolete. In this sense, writing the history of Acadian theatre should not mean pointing to periods during which Acadian concerns resurface or disperse, but rather examining the different forms these answers can take, and how they circulate.

(Boudreau, "L'hyperbole" 79).[7] According to Annette Boudreau and Raoul Boudreau, the linguistic liberation that started with *Les Crasseux* and continued with Maillet's next play, *La Sagouine*, proceeded first and foremost from the playful "transposition of a rich oral literature into a written literature" (170).[8] For them, this literary transposition had major effects: settling an oral language into its written form, it also "enhanced its value by making it into a literary language with which Acadians could proudly identify rather than be ashamed" (171).[9] The language of popular tradition, by imposing itself on theatre, became available for written literature. Maillet would go on to write a series of plays inspired by rural and traditional Acadie following these linguistic conventions, aggrandizing the dimensions of the action "to planetary dimensions" (Boudreau, "L'hyperbole" 76) through self-fulfilling, hyperbolic comments by her characters. Beyond Maillet's prolific playwriting, usually staged in Montreal, her invented language lingers in the Bouctouche, New Brunswick, theme park Le Pays de la Sagouine. Yet few subsequent Acadian authors have made Maillet's language their own.

When Acadian theatre was first moving toward professionalization, Laval Goupil also experimented with the languages at his disposal. With the play *Tête d'eau*, produced by Les Feux Chalins in 1974, Goupil distinguished himself from Maillet through his modernity, but maintained some of her playfulness. The character of Onil ironically comments about his "gradual death by asphyxia. Made in Acadialand!" (27),[10] plays football in English, and swims in a love-induced delirium in a "beetle language" (61).[11] Fantasy drifts into the explosion of language and its reinvention. A similar linguistic innovation, but with a more realistic basis, is afoot in Goupil's next play, *Le*

---

7 "[U]ne langue plus française que le français de France parce que plus ancienne, préservée."

8 "[L]a transposition d'une riche littérature orale en littérature écrite."

9 "[F]ixer une langue orale [mais aussi celui] de la valoriser en en faisant une langue littéraire à laquelle on peut désormais fièrement s'identifier au lieu d'en avoir honte."

10 "La mort par axphysie [*sic*] graduée. Made in Acadialand!"

11 "[L]angage coléoptérien."

Djibou (*Dark Owl*, TPA, 1975). Like Maillet before him, the author dwells on the literary transposition of Acadian language registers to allow them to proliferate on stage. According to Laurent Mailhot:

> The play that Laval Goupil rightly calls *le Djibou* marks the (bloody) exchange between the past and the present, between the concrete and the abstract, between orality (reported, recalled, imagined) and the (proposed, imposed) written word. This exchange, this passage is the very plot of the play. There is no other. Which explains, to a certain point, the excessive importance Laval Goupil gives to language and languages. (54)[12]

Though Goupil's subsequent plays would continue to use languages in similar ways to *Le Djibou*, few of them would be staged in Acadie or elsewhere.

Herménégilde Chiasson's counterproposal to Maillet's orientation toward the past, a focus on contemporary language use, had more critical success. In a 1979 interview with Anne-Marie Robichaud, Chiasson put his finger on the challenge of representing contemporary Acadie in the absence of essential language models: "We can't connect to a single language, and that's hard. To account for Acadie, we need to write in French, in Chiac, in English; in short, we need to write all about alienation" (72).[13] With these words, Chiasson echoes the preoccupations Masson voiced five years earlier, but connects them with dispossession from the French language, whose elite Parisian ideal

---

12 "La pièce que Laval Goupil intitule justement *le Djibou* marque l'échange—de sang—entre le passé et l'avenir, entre le concret et l'abstrait, entre l'oral (rapporté, rappelé, imaginé) et l'écrit (proposé, imposé). Cet échange, ce passage est l'action même de la pièce. Il n'y en a pas d'autre. Ce qui explique, jusqu'à un certain point, l'importance excessive que Laval Goupil accorde au langage et à la langue. Il abuse des barbarismes précieux, des savoureux archaïsmes, des anglicismes ingénieux. On ne fait que *vironner, tchaquer, (s')bouscailler* dans cette pièce aux allures de conte mi-naturaliste mi-fantastique."

13 "On n'arrive pas à se brancher sur un langage, sur une particularité, et ça c'est dur. Pour rendre compte de l'Acadie, il faudrait écrire en français, en chiac, en anglais, bref, il faudrait écrire sur toute une aliénation."

Acadians could not hope to master. While Chiasson's poetry, essayistic prose, visual art, and films are attempts to communicate in a French language that could circulate beyond Acadie, his theatre ambivalently explores the linguistic variation of his surroundings. As Glen Nichols indicates, Chiasson's transposition of Acadian dialects goes hand in hand with the relationships his characters establish with Acadie and with their political and social engagements ("Bard" 34–35), all of which are amply expressed by the characters themselves. Conversely, the use of standard French on stage works as a shorthand for negative character traits similarly to how dialect signifies such characteristics in other genres. Speaking a standard French, for example, a bureaucratic tax collector in Chiasson's *Pour une fois* (l'Escaouette, 1999) elicits a strong antipathy from spectators.

In this play, however, Chiasson also allows Chiac a rare incursion, giving voice to two taxi drivers in a passage surprisingly devoid of the metalinguistic consciousness that characterizes dialects in the playwright's work. Rather, it seems as if those who speak Chiac do not worry about the language diversity at their disposal, as if their lower socio-economic background frees them from the linguistic *surconscience* typical of francophone writers (Gauvin 6). *Pour une fois* showcased Chiac with an intensity unheard of on l'Escaouette's institutional stage in 1999, but the dialect had become a literary and performative tool earlier, during an underground event held in Moncton in November 1993. As Marc Arsenault recalls, the "Tableaux de backyard" event

> was a night of poetry and music in homage to Guy Arsenault. Around 500 people young and less young participated. We had the impression that many generations were ready to meet. In presenting the writers, Marc Poirier and I intentionally ended every introduction with "lives in Moncton": for example, Gérald Leblanc lives in Moncton, Jean-Marc Dugas lives in Moncton, etc. The project became clear: affirming the creative dynamism of the city and of its imaginary,

> recognizing the Chiac language. Being a minority became a worthy attribute, as postmodernism obliged.[14]

With this, Chiac joined the swarm of literary languages used in poetry, prose, and—more subtly and later—theatre.

Up until the late 1990s, access to theatre institutions was essentially limited to Chiasson, Maillet, and a few others. Chiasson exercised a "quasi monopoly" (Lonergan 337) over the creation of new works at l'Escaouette. In these conditions of institutional drought, Collectif Moncton-Sable, like the "Tableaux de backyard" event, took a detour around Acadian theatre institutions, their languages, and their typical processes. Following Édouard Glissant, François Paré uses the phrase "culture of the detour" to describe the "greater creolization" of Acadian culture in southwest New Brunswick and the "promotion of Moncton's Chiac"[15] by its artists (*La Distance* 195). Collectif Moncton-Sable modelled the theatrical detour Paré explains by creatively bypassing institutional hurdles and by valuing playful stagings of Chiac. Founded in 1997 by Louise Lemieux, Philip André Collette, Lynne Surette, Amélie Gosselin, and Jean Surette, Collectif Moncton-Sable aimed to create theatre outside the established traditions of dominant institutions. They returned to collective creation models, which defined the early work of l'Escaouette; their performances were based on improvisation and on physical materials. After early collaborative performances with author France Daigle, which involved working with sand (which gave the collective its name), chalk,

---

14 "En novembre 1993, a lieu un événement marquant, Tableaux de backyard, nuit de poésie et musique en hommage à Guy Arsenault auxquel [*sic*] participent environ 500 personnes, jeunes et moins jeunes. Nous avions l'impression que plusieurs générations s'étaient donné rendez-vous. En présentant les écrivains, [Marc] Poirier et moi faisions exprès de terminer chaque présentation par 'vit à Moncton': par exemple, Gérald Leblanc vit à Moncton, Jean-Marc Dugas vit à Moncton, etc. Le projet devient alors évident : l'affirmation du dynamisme créatif de la ville, de son imaginaire et la reconnaissance de la langue chiac. La minorisation devient digne, le post-modernisme l'oblige."

15 "[C]ulture du détournement"; "la créolisation accrue"; "promotion du chiac monctonien."

and hay, Moncton-Sable began adapting Daigle's poetic prose for the stage. Vernacular language (Chiac in particular) had—until then—been absent from Daigle's literary practice, but she drew directly from the collective's improvisations, which sometimes occurred in Chiac, to write using the actors' names for characters and their words for dialogue (Mallet 19).

Daigle's and Moncton-Sable's early work opened a door for Chiac on stage, which Paul Bossé, an emerging poet and filmmaker at the time, stepped through when he began working with the collective. Their collaboration yielded four major projects: *Empreintes* (2002), *Linoléum* (2005), the text "Vénus et la Fourrure" in the collective performance *Papier* (2006), and *Pellicule* (2009).[16] Of these projects, *Empreintes* would make the greatest use of Chiac, not only in its dialogue but also in its plot: Chiac is used by Moncton's residents in the play's present timeline, recorded in the machine memory of the future, and unlocked by a clever translator who rewrites history to free humanity. Beyond *Empreintes*'s hyperbolic world-making, worthy of Antonine Maillet, Bossé's play also proves as linguistically ambivalent as Herménégilde Chiasson's scripting of Chiac. Bossé's Chiac detour is best understood not only in relation to Maillet and Chiasson's work but also in connection with Laval Goupil's linguistic delirium: its historical exchange between the past, present, and future, as well as its indeterminate legacy.

CHIAC IN THE MISTS OF TIME

Translating from English to the partial French of Chiac, Paul Bossé grounds *Empreintes*'s expansive reach in time and space in an adaptation of the classic film *2001: A Space Odyssey*. Time and space oscillate between a prehistoric African savannah, a university auditorium in Acadie in 2001, and an Antarctic media library located in a future in which cyborgs control humans. The

16 A few texts and performances by Moncton-Sable are available in English, notably *Craie* (1999) and *Papier*, as published in the pages of *Canadian Theatre Review*.

omnipresent Aline-9000, a "cyber-sapien with mother-hen tendencies" (16)[17] who resembles HAL 9000 in *2001*, ensures that David Beaumont, the play's counterpart to *2001*'s David Bowman, submits to "watching videotapes of the glorious seasons" (30)[18] of human beings. While watching a home video of a sports event filmed in 2001, David witnesses what he thinks is the murder of a gorilla by archaeologist Lucie Malenfant. He then enlists the help of Ève (based on *2001*'s EVA pod and Acadian cultural icon *Evangeline*), a revolutionary cyborg from a previous generation, to assist him in decoding Chiac to solve the mystery of the gorilla's murder. Ultimately, she also frees David from the hands of other cyborgs. Freedom and imprisonment are at the heart of *Empreintes*, from the captivity of melancholic gorilla Mojo, to that of David, the human whose only beacon of hope comes from the glimpses he receives of Acadia in 2001. These themes are also at play on a symbolic level, in the tension between Chiac's freedom to circulate within Acadian theatre and its imprisonment by material conditions that mean the dialect can only reach relatively small audiences. While these are larger concerns of theatre written

17 "Ordino [ordinateur] avec des tendances mère-poule." Translations of Bossé's *Empreintes* in this text are from Glen Nichols's translation *Traces*. Attentive readers will notice many creative translations of Chiac by Nichols. These translations are discussed in my book, *Jouer la traduction. Théâtre et hétérolinguisme au Canada francophone*. They are also discussed by theatre critic Russ Hunt, who commented on Nichols's public reading of the English translation in the following terms:

> Whether the shifts from standard French to the "Sheac," [*sic*] the creole which has arisen in the French-English Acadian community around Moncton, actually work in an English play isn't so clear. One kept wondering whether something like a shift from standard English to an offshoot like the creoles of Jamaica or the Australian bush might work better. Of course, then the whole location of the play would have to be shifted, and it would become something entirely new, not a translation. What we need, and what to some extent we get, though probably a good deal less than in Bossé's original, is the sense that somehow it's the vibrancy of the language itself which gives Evangeline the imagination and initiative to help the human escape his captivity—escaping, in an interesting theatrical device, directly on the footsteps of the australopithecines we began with.

18 "*[W]atcher* les *videotapes* [des] saisons glorieuses."

in dialects or languages of lesser circulation, Bossé's magnification and symbolic treatment of this theme are unique within Acadian theatre.

Subverting the negative sociolinguistic portrayal that appeared in Herménégilde Chiasson's theatre, Bossé amplifies the presence of Chiac in the 2001 timeline of *Empreintes*. As in Chiasson's *Pour une fois*, a lower-class taxi driver is the first to use Chiac in the play, when Pierre "Lerat"/"Lil Rat" Léger replies gleefully to Lucie Malenfant's request for a speedy ride to her lecture at the university: "Pas de problem. Me an' my gas pedal 'ere, we make de beautiful music togedder [. . .] Do ya min if I open de radio?" (18–19).[19] His Chiac contrasts with the standard French of the scholar in the back seat, and yet it indicates neither illiteracy nor iconoclasticism against the university system.

LUCIE: You're interested in anthropology?	**LUCIE:** L'anthropologie vous intéresse?
LIL RAT: Da study a ants?	**LERAT:** L'étude des entrepôts?
LUCIE: Yeah . . . right . . .	**LUCIE:** Ouais, c'est ça . . .
LIL RAT: Jus' jokin' ya. J'sais fer shure what it is, d'antropologie. Jus cause I drive de cab don mean I'm missin de screws. (20–21)	**LERAT:** J'*jokais* juste . . . ben sûr que j'sais qu'osse qu'é d'l'anthropologie . . . juste parce que je vis dans une cave sa veut pas dire que j'suis cave . . . (38)

Avoiding the conflation of linguistic register with level of education, Lerat shows off by playing with social expectations as well as homophony. Such punning participates in making Chiac legitimate as an intellectual language—that is, not solely the slang of the lower classes.

19 "Pas d'troubles . . . moi, pis l'*accelerator*, on s'adounne ben ensemble [. . .] *Mind*-tu si j'mets la radio . . ."

Lerat's Chiac is so remarkable that the cyborg Aline-9000 can only be offended for the human she subjects to it in the futuristic timeline: "That's disgusting! David, we cannot permit you to listen to these archives" (18).[20] Even though the carefree human proclaims that he doesn't "even understand anything [the radio personality] said" (19),[21] Aline persists: "The language is not appropriate for you" (19).[22] With these words, she seems to echo two negative perceptions of Chiac: "either that it symbolizes linguistic alienation by reflecting contact with the oppressor, or that it constitutes a linguistic ghetto that risks alienating Acadians from other Francophones" (Boudreau and Gadet 58).[23] In fact, however, the danger Aline perceives does not derive from these sociolinguistic attitudes, but rather from the creative potential of the dialect. Aline elucidates her antagonistic position in the following terms: "Chiac is a corrupt hybrid of bad French and bad English spoken mostly by teenagers and young people in Moncton and south-east New Brunswick. David, if you listen to it too much, you might start writing poetry . . . " (19).[24] Indeed, in *Empreintes*, Chiac is dangerous because it alludes to a current of legitimation through Moncton-based poetry spearheaded by Gérald Leblanc and followed by Paul Bossé himself (Leblanc 520). There is self-deprecation in the dangers attributed to the dialect in the play. The playwright reflects on his poetic practice and on its contagious social reach, which extends beyond Moncton through *time* to be heard by a human subjected to the cyborg regime where it becomes a symbol of the imagination necessary to dream of freedom.

As *Empreintes* legitimizes Chiac in the present timeline, it also aggrandizes its reach to the past and the future, through the character of an interpreter

---

20 "Oh! Comme c'est grossier! David couvre-toi les oreilles!"

21 "[C]omprend même pas ce qu'il dit."

22 "Ce n'est pas un langage convenable pour toi."

23 "[S]oit parce qu'il symbolise l'aliénation linguistique en reflétant le contact avec l'oppresseur, soit parce qu'il constitue un ghetto linguistique qui risque d'isoler les Acadiens des autres francophones."

24 "Du chiac urbain, un dialecte acadien issu du français. Si tu en écoutes trop, tu vas te mettre à écrire de la poésie . . ."

who is key to writing the past and establishing a better future. This interpreter, found at the Centre d'Études Acadiennes (Centre for Acadian Studies) in the futuristic timeline, has the polysemic name Évangéline-zéro-un-un. The name evokes the tragically passive Acadian heroine of Henry Wadsworth Longfellow's epic poem *Evangeline*, from 1847, as well as her multiple reincarnations under Acadian pens, from Pascal Poirier's nineteenth-century *Accordailles de Gabriel et d'Évangéline* (*The Betrothal of Gabriel and Evangeline*) to Antonine Maillet's *Évangéline Deusse* (*Evangeline the Second*).[25] By the sum of her suffix (zero + one + one = two), Évangéline-zéro-un-un intensifies her affiliation with Maillet's rewriting of Évangéline. Like Maillet's Evangeline, she legitimizes an Acadian language that has become archaic. Yet unlike the older figurehead, she is a young, Chiac-speaking cyborg. Her affirmation of the language in the futuristic timeline confirms not the traditional Acadian parlance, but Chiac as a language for Acadian theatre in the 2000s.

Évangéline-zéro-un-un's supposed role is to translate Chiac for David. Her nickname Ève—a palimpsest of EVA, the Extravehicular Activity Pod from *2001: A Space Odyssey*, that is, a vehicle that moves beyond the spaceship—hints to a conception of translation as transfer or as physical displacement toward the outside. But as a translator, Ève refuses binaries of inside and outside, and barriers between French and English. Rather than eliminating regionalisms or anglicisms from her speech, a tendency observed in real-life translators working in Canadian contact zones (Collombat 26), Ève flaunts the diatopic variation of Chiac as her translation language. Consequently, Ève foils ideologies that define Chiac as a kind of French contaminated by English, or as a sign of forthcoming assimilation. When the cyborg Aline insists that "[e]veryone knows how fast bad language can corrupt their mother tongue" (22),[26] Ève responds inversely, "Same thing for me, eh . . . I got to watch I

25 See Usmiani, "Antonine"; Bourque; Thériault.

26 "[O]n connait la vitesse avec laquelle des mots infectés corrompent leur langue maternelle."

don't get infected with dictionary French" (22).[27] Ève uses her hybrid language to mock the "dictionary" French of the pure, inflexible cyborgs of the next generation represented by Aline. She also quickly reveals her secret mission: she was sent by Deep-Blue-Two, a chess-conquering computer from the first generation of machines that enslaved humans, to save the latter from the new generation of cyborgs. Reminding David of the game of chess that determined the secret history of human captivity in Chiac, she ends up infecting him, but with ideas of hope and freedom rather than bad language use.

2001: A SPACE ACADIE, OR AN AMBIVALENT THEATRE UNIVERSE

The use of Chiac and of translation both seem fully embraced as tools in the resistance to a standard French in the hyperbolic and self-deprecating drama of Bossé, yet they are also paradoxically subject to the themes of freedom and imprisonment explored in the play. In this sense, the theatre universe the performance builds plays on a dual positioning of Chiac "in resistance to English (dominant language) and to standard French (dominant variation)" (Perrot 150).[28] The resistance to English in Bossé's play connects with Herménégilde Chiasson's profound ambivalence toward the linguistic alienation contained by Chiac, giving credence to Catherine Leclerc's affirmation that in Acadian literature written in the dialect, "the need to trace zones of contact [with English] coexists with the need to delimit space, creative crossovers cohabit with airtight resistance" ("Ville" 154).[29] Free to roam the science-fiction universe of *2001: A Space Odyssey*, which it translates, Chiac

---

27 "Moi c'est la même chose . . . y faut pas que je me fasse *contaminaté* par des francicismes."

28 "[D]ouble positionnement"; "en résistance à l'anglais (langue dominante) et au français standardisé (variation dominante)."

29 "[L]e besoin de tracer des voies de contact cohabite avec celui de délimiter l'espace, la transversalité créatrice avec la résistance étanche."

gradually imprisons English as the source language in a palimpsest that is only revealed in glimpses. Similarly, the ambient English of 2001 Moncton is expelled from the stage and confined to the grammar of code switching.

This amplification in the use of Chiac operates first in the city of Moncton, where the visiting academic, Lucie Malenfant, meets only residents who speak Chiac as she explores the urban surroundings. An employee of the Mont Magnétique cable car, for example, communicates spontaneously in the dialect that has gone from a vernacular to the vehicular language of the city.[30] Moncton's English is evacuated in favour of Chiac, constructing an Acadian city out of a linguistically divided one. Paradoxically, resistance to English coexists with a certain amount of accommodation. While the utopia of a Moncton life in Chiac establishes a partial francization of the urban space, a reciprocal language exchange takes place between the city represented and the Anglophone world. Pushing the hyperbole of a Chiac Moncton to its logical geographic limit, Bossé makes Chiac not only the language of the city (what François Paré calls "Acadie City" [19]), but of the whole universe (a space Acadie). The influence of Moncton spreads to Hollywood, where Vanna White takes the Acadian surname LeBlanc (Bossé 51). In contrast to this international reference, local references to "Université de Monk [. . .] Pavillon Bud Powell" (18) circumvent the important Acadian institution that is the Université de Moncton, pulling the linguistic play in two complementary but opposite directions. Like author Jean Babineau, who adds a "k" to Moncton in his novel *Bloupe*, Bossé associates the city with the origin of its name, Lieutenant Colonel Robert Monckton, one of the architects of the Deportation of the Acadians (Leclerc, "De Bloop" 290). On the one hand, then, as Leclerc explains, this word choice "closely links the city to the English domination that is exercised there" ("De Bloop" 290).[31] On the other hand,

30 Bossé's portrayal of a Chiac Moncton finds echoes in France Daigle's novel *Petites difficultés d'existence* (*Life's Little Difficulties*), published the same year as Moncton-Sable's performance of *Empreintes*, and after Daigle's own detour into Chiac theatre with the collective. In the novel's "utopic" Chiac representation of the city (Doyon-Gosselin and Morency), Daigle "evacuat[es] the English component almost completely" (Leclerc, "Ville" 156).

31 "[L]ie étroitement la ville à la domination anglaise qui s'y exerce."

"monk" is also a wink to the stereotype of the monkish university scholar. The Acadian university, reinvented by the performative playfulness of Chiac, can then consecrate Harlem jazz pianist Earl Rudolph "Bud" Powell, in a "transversal consciousness that fuses all of urban America from Moncton to New York" (Paré, "Acadie City" 28).[32] As the microcosm of Moncton extends to other urban centres, the Magnetic Hill at the centre of the city merges with the strange magnetic resonances in *2001: A Space Odyssey* to "open our consciousness" (77).[33] As an adaptation, Bossé's *Empreintes* plays upon habitual linguistic attributions and insists on cultural exchanges based on reciprocity, which can only come about through the hyperbole that makes Chiac available as a language for Acadian theatre.

Following on an interview with Bossé, Leclerc confirms how, though not as explicitly as Herménégilde Chiasson, the author is ambivalent regarding his use of Chiac:

> Between the freedom afforded by Chiac and its codification, it is sometimes difficult to take a stance. Writer Paul Bossé, for example, insists simultaneously on these two aspects and cannot help but take note of their contradictory orientation. On the one hand, Bossé describes himself as a defender of Chiac, the ultimate language of Acadian urbanity. He appreciates its "anarchic" character since everyone can use whatever amount of French and English they choose. On the other hand, Bossé creates a hierarchy of different degrees of hybridity. He opposes Chiac to "Frenglish," a massive Anglicization of French that he perceives as a trap. He immediately resists this stance, however, adding: "But I don't want to sound like a teacher at

32 "[C]onscience transversale [qui] fusionne toute l'Amérique urbaine de Moncton à New York."

33 "[I]l nous ouvre la conscience."

> [local high school] Mathieu-Martin." In sum, Bossé prefers to remain ambivalent. ("Ville" 171)[34]

In the same manner, the space delimited for English in the Chiac universe of *Empreintes* is mocked and transgressed. The dialect is imposed like a cage from which English cannot escape without being parodied. Imitating the imperious queen of the chess game between Deep-Blue-Two and Katastrov, Ève proclaims, "*Out-of-my-way people, out of my way people this is crown property!* . . . like a queen" (61).[35] As a wink to the Deportation of the Acadians, a subtle denunciation of the continued presence of the British crown, and a quip on the necessity of making the "bad guys" speak English, these words embody the difficulty of opening up to the Other in a context of linguistic asymmetry. At the same time, her words exhibit pleasure at proceeding to do so . . . until the opponent is checkmated. By metonymy, the performance plays on issues encountered in creating art in Chiac: accommodation and resistance to English, ambivalent detours, and inside jokes. It also showcases how playing on these issues does not empty them of their relevance, but rather amplifies them for those who identify with them. In other words, the magnification of these issues anchors the performance in a specific space and time, in a certain mode of theatrical-language recognition.

---

34 "Entre la liberté octroyée par le chiac et sa codification, il est parfois difficile de prendre position. L'écrivain Paul Bossé, par exemple, insiste simultanément sur ces deux aspects, et ne peut que noter leur orientation contradictoire. D'un côté, Bossé se décrit comme un défenseur du chiac, langue par excellence de l'urbanité acadienne. Il en apprécie le caractère 'anarchique' sans règles, où chacun peut, en toute liberté, avoir son propre dosage de français ou d'anglais. De l'autre, [. . .] Bossé hiérarchise lui aussi diverses catégories d'hybridation. Il oppose le chiac au 'franglais,' une anglicisation massive du français qu'il perçoit comme un piège. À ce balisage, il met cependant aussitôt un frein en ajoutant : 'Mais je veux pas sonner comme un prof de Mathieu-Martin.' En somme, Bossé préfère rester dans l'ambivalence."

35 "[C]omme une reine."

CHIAC'S HISTORY AS VANISHING POINT

The specificity of the time and space represented in the play may suggest that the meaning of *Empreintes* was circumscribed to the hundred or so spectators who saw it produced in Moncton in 2002. Referring to Bossé's book of poetry *Saint-George/Robinson* from Québec City in 2008, for example, Benoit Doyon-Gosselin declared that he "got three readers likely to appreciate his poetic approach to read it. From their comments, it became clear that *Saint-George/Robinson* could only truly be appreciated within 30 kilometres of the streets in question."[36] Yet Bossé also inscribes a historical metaphor for Chiac into *Empreintes*, one that could extend beyond any foreseeable past or future. The metaphor lies in the imaginary language shared by australopithecines in times primeval and Mojo the gorilla in 2001. Confined to the Magnetic Hill Zoo since his birth, Mojo is highly melancholic because of his captivity and the need to perform every day to get visiting children to laugh. Scholar Lucie and zookeeper Frank debate over two possible solutions for his depression: releasing him into the "outside world [where] he would starve to death in no time" or sending him back to Tanzania where "[h]e would meet another gorilla and start talking to him in his frigged up zoo-accent . . . and they would reject him" (78).[37] The gorilla, like Bossé's and Moncton-Sable's Chiac theatre, faces an aporia: it dreams of a life that offers something other than a cage in a zoo or the region of Moncton, but the outside world offers him nothing other than reception based on a language difference and ultimate rejection. Between these two options, Lucie Malenfant chooses to euthanize the gorilla. This suggests that Bossé might prefer the absolute dissolution of the Chiac of *Empreintes* to its depressing performance for spectators eager for its exotic

36 "[J]'ai fait lire le recueil de Bossé à trois lecteurs susceptibles d'apprécier son approche poétique. À entendre leurs commentaires, j'ai fini par croire que *Saint-George/Robinson* ne peut véritablement être apprécié que dans un rayon de 30 kilomètres autour des rues en question."

37 "[D]ans l'*outside world*, y crèverait dans moins qu'un mois"; "y rencontrerait un autre gorille pis y s'mettrait à lui parler avec son accent *fucké* de zoo pis y s'ferait rejeter."

qualities and easy laughs, the end of the detour of Chiac in Acadian theatre history to a period of prolonged ambivalence.

While the perspective the text expresses may seem depressing, Chiac's assisted suicide is less definitive. In this optic, the strange resemblance between the language of the gorilla and the language of previous primates, the australopithecines, needs to be taken into account. Fin and Fang, two australopithecines from prehistoric Africa, share this language, "Mamagaya" ("Mama Gaya"), that combines Greek, Latin, incongruous rhymes, and phonetic puns. Lucie the archaeologist can only speculate about its meaning and hypothesizes that it must have disappeared by 2001. Mojo, however, still mysteriously speaks it. Further, Ève legitimates the language by acknowledging that it is too complex for her to translate: "The language Mama Gaya speaks is still too complex even for us. The only cyber-sapien who came close to understanding her was Deep Blue Two" (81).[38] From the vantage point of the future, Ève makes a rhetorical turn, transforming the disintegration of the creole of the australopithecines into the traces of a linguistic complexity that remains elusive, of a game that even the greatest of the cyborgs has not yet mastered. The same qualities might apply to the way Acadian theatre history remembers the Chiac encapsulated in *Empreintes*, as a recognition fleeting toward the future.

Mary Louise Pratt tells a similar story about another text from another linguistic contact zone, a 1,200-page manuscript sent by Felipe Guaman Poma de Ayala to King Philip III of Spain, written in 1613 "in a mixture of Quechua and rough, ungrammatical Spanish" (2). Peruvianist Richard Pietschmann found the manuscript in 1908 in the Danish Royal Archive in Copenhagen, where "[n]o one knew (or knows) how" it got there, "or how long it had been there. No one, it appeared, had even bothered to read it, or even figured out how to read it. Quechua was not known as a written language in 1908, or Andean culture as a literate culture" (2). It was only in 1970, with the post-colonial turn, that the text became *legible*: unreadable by the imperial power at the time of its writing, the manuscript gradually gained legibility as readers

38 "[L]e langage que Mamagaya parle est encore trop complexe pour nous. La seule Ordino qu'est venu proche à la comprendre, c'te langue là . . . cé Deep-Blue-Two."

caught up to its linguistic and cultural complexity. The story of this manuscript, like the renewed interpretation of the language of primates, suggests an alternate way of reading the history of the Chiac detour taken by Bossé and Moncton-Sable. Like the language of Mojo the gorilla in *Empreintes*, the performance might be only simulating linguistic euthanasia, and awaiting future spectators who can grasp its complexity.

Two years after the production by Moncton-Sable, Glen Nichols translated the play as *Traces* and staged a reading of it at the NotaBle Acts Theatre Festival in Fredericton. Bossé's play served as the "anchor production" for the festival and provided a window into francophone drama in New Brunswick ("NotaBle"). Theatre critic and scholar Russ Hunt, in his review of the public reading, grasped the linguistic issues at stake in the play. The themes of authority, power, creativity, and freedom, he notes, are "maybe [. . .] a matter of language. [. . .] It's the vibrancy of the language itself which gives Evangeline the imagination and initiative to help the human escape his captivity." His review of *Traces* ends with the desire to see the project go further than a public reading. Notwithstanding Hunt's wish, *Traces* honours its name and its archaeological resonances: the public reading was, at least at the time of writing, the last layer in the story of *Empreintes*.

THE END(S) OF CHIAC?

The play's use of Chiac, like Laval Goupil's wild linguistic explorations, has not had a widespread or long-lasting influence on Acadian drama. Among Bossé's contemporaries and successors, Jean Babineau wrote the play *Tangentes*, performed at Théâtre l'Escaouette in 2006, and Sonya Malaborza translated Don Hannah's *Running Far Back* into Chiac as *La Batture*, which had a public reading in 2005, and wrote the short play "La Septante," staged as part of Moncton-Sable's *Papier* in 2006. By 2010, Moncton-Sable, like Bossé and other Chiac writers, had ceased creating new performances, making the Chiac detour seem a lot like a dead end. The new generation of creators and writers interested in circumventing the main Acadian theatre institutions has not invested in Chiac as a language of performance, preferring mime, puppetry, and dialects closer to a neutral stage French with the hope of improving possibilities of touring beyond Acadie.

Perhaps the legacy of the Chiac detour can best be explained by recognizing that its ambivalence connects it with that of other playwrights and theatre practitioners working in Acadian languages and with concerns that criss-cross historical periods previously categorized as national or post-national. A similar ambivalence characterizes the response of contemporary spectators of Chiac theatre, some of whom question its raison-d'être. Malaborza summed up the 2005 reception of her Chiac translation of *Running Far Back* in the following terms:

> Many spectators felt the need to tell me, almost in secret, that, "that's exactly how we speak here." Others, however, wondered why I had missed the opportunity to "write a nice story in proper French." In other words, we can't please everyone, and mostly, it is all the more urgent to produce more translations that reflect a use of language that clearly causes some unease in Acadie. (10)[39]

In short, the unease around dialectal theatre might have signalled a need for a more widespread use of dialects in Acadian theatre, a need to go beyond the Chiac detour and invest in creating performances in the swarm of languages identified by Masson. This appears to begin with *Les trois exils de Christian E.*, a highly successful piece of autofiction created by Christian Essiambre and Philippe Soldevila and performed at l'Escaouette and at Québec City's Théâtre Sortie de secours in 2010. The performance renewed both the parlance Maillet created for the Sagouine and the perspective on Chiac (and English) explained by Herménégilde Chiasson as linguistic alienation.

39 "[P]lusieurs spectateurs ont senti le besoin de me confier, presque en secret, que 'c'est exactement comme ça qu'on parle chez nous.' D'autres, par contre, se sont demandés pourquoi je suis passée à côté d'une occasion d'écrire 'une belle histoire en français comme il faut.' C'est dire qu'on ne peut pas plaire à tout le monde, et surtout, qu'il est d'autant plus pressant, selon moi, de produire d'autres traductions qui sachent refléter un usage de la langue qui cause manifestement un malaise en Acadie."

Paradoxically, Essiambre and Soldevila's performance, by employing other Acadian dialects, also signalled the end of the Chiac detour taken by Moncton-Sable and Bossé at the end of the twentieth century. Interspersed with the story of his three cousins, the character Christian E. gives a virtuosic demonstration of the swarm of languages in Acadie, strategically omitting Chiac. Spectators have to wait until the end of the performance, when the character from Northern New Brunswick visits Moncton, for Chiac to appear as part of the linguistic landscape; when it does, it is in the mouth of a junkie to whom Christian E.'s cousin Marc owes drugs: "Quoi? *Why the fuck* qu'les *cops* sont v'nus 'checker' *out* pour Marc icitte? Marc est *gone* man!" (73)[40] Contrary to the theatre of Bossé and Moncton-Sable, where Chiac gains legitimacy in a hyperbolic and erudite universe, *Les trois exils de Christian E.* returns to a slightly bleak reflection on life in Moncton,.where Chiac only reveals the low socio-economic status of its speaker. Speaking in 2010, from and about the present, on stage at l'Escaouette, Moncton's major Acadian theatre institution, Christian E. thus certifies the end of the Chiac detour in Acadian theatre history.

So is there a history of Acadian theatre? *Empreintes* certainly attempts to make history, to extend the reach of the twenty-year Chiac detour even beyond the four hundred years of Acadian theatre practices to times primeval and times far ahead. Yet, without critical attention to Chiac works, Acadian theatre history might remember very little of the Chiac detour, of Paul Bossé and Moncton-Sable's counter-institutional linguistic performances, aside from their post-nationalist tendencies. *Empreintes*'s representation of the future, however, as continuous with the language-based history of Acadian theatre, suggests the Chiac detour might not be complete, that there may be more still to come, following in Ève's footprints, or in the primate code's mysterious ways, playing more tricks with time, geography, and history . . .

40 "The cops came here looking for Marc. He's gone, man. He left me to deal with the dealer." The translation provided here is from the surtitles for the Théâtre français de Toronto performance by Gunta Dreifelds and Guy Mignault.

UNTOLD HISTORIES OF CANADIAN THEATRE IN HIGHER EDUCATION

GLEN NICHOLS

> If university theatre could cultivate knowledgeable and articulate audiences, that was goal enough.
> —Ross & Ann Stuart, "University Theatre"

A few years ago, I began to observe a contradiction between what we tended to say about our drama studies program at Mount Allison University (MtA) and what our students think they are doing, between what students think they are learning and how they actually use their learning after graduation. Attempts to sort out what seemed a simple observation led to the research and thinking that suggested the thesis of this essay: that a new examination of the historiographical treatment of theatre in higher education in Canada might lead to important benefits both for our students and for the security of our programs in the face of neo-liberal threats.

This essay investigates the historical sources of an apparent contradiction between Canadian scholarship on university theatre programs and actual learning outcomes and student success stories. The histories of university and college drama and theatre programs are shaped around four characteristics that in turn dominate the ways we talk about our programs today: 1) the lack of a comprehensive history of university theatre education; 2) the view that university theatre is all about professional training; 3) the discounted value of extracurricular theatre on campuses; and 4) the lack of conceptual frames for pedagogical and curricular discussion. This essay contends that a fuller understanding of the history of post-secondary drama and theatre education and richer historiographical approaches to this field could have positive implications for some of the challenges our programs are facing in the current neo-liberal climate.

THE PROBLEM

The Mount Allison University calendar explicitly states that the drama studies program is "designed to provide an education in drama rather than professional training for the theatre" ("Drama Studies"), and we pride ourselves on our contribution to the broad liberal education goals of our institution and the long-term success of our students. Nevertheless, our marketing materials, website, and personal contacts with prospective students focus on stories of grads who are working in theatre as actors, artistic directors, technicians, etc., regionally and across the country. While many students touched by our program do go on to further education and work in theatre, the majority of our former students find success in many fields beyond theatre (a positive result of our mandate and emphasis on liberal education). This contrasts both what our marketing promotes and what many of our students think the program is about: job training for the industry. This apparent disconnect began to niggle at my conscience. Then the second penny dropped.

That most of us esteem the broader liberal education outcomes associated with theatre and drama studies became clear to me when I had opportunities to assist as external reviewer of several theatre and drama programs across the country. This allowed me to observe first-hand that drama and theatre programs as vastly different as, for example, the University of Victoria's studio-based BFA and UPEI's small English-department-centred minor in drama (not to mention many more in between, including that at MtA), all employ the language of "liberal education" or "liberal arts" to describe what they do.

Every year, thousands of Canadian university students[1] take theatre and drama courses, create hundreds of productions, and participate in countless

1 Statistics Canada collects data on enrolments and graduates through the CANSIM database (Postsecondary Student Information System or PSIS). Total number of enrollments

theatre-performance activities. All this creative and exacting work delivers an extensive range of learning outcomes for students. Ours is a discipline that, while never forgetting a grounding in language and words, is by its nature engaged in the examination of human experience in action and in embodied forms. The integration of literature, theory, and practice at the heart of university drama and theatre activity "encourage[s] reflective and integrative thinking, promote[s] effective communication skills and encourage[s] social responsibility" as core learning outcomes for our students (Kindelan 1–2). These high-level connections between theatre studies and the real world are reinforced by students' abilities to "learn quickly, solve problems in new ways, [develop] self-esteem, imagination, promptness, integrity, [and] team work," among so many more (Gressler 120). The evidence of this complex learning can be seen in the success of theatre and drama graduates in so many walks of life.

And yet, again reflecting my observations at MtA, campus recruitment campaigns and department websites from across the country reveal how we entice new students to our programs by focusing almost exclusively on stories of graduates who are now directors, designers, technicians, and, especially, actors working in Canadian theatre.[2]

---

in drama, theatre, and stagecraft programs grew from 4,200 students in 2004 to 7,230 students in 2013. The number of graduates grew from 1,113 to 1,974 in the same period. These numbers count only students registered in such programs. In most cases our programs touch far more students through our courses and extracurricular theatre activities. So these numbers are very conservative.

2 Similar observations have also been made about America institutions:

> [S]uccess in the professional world of theatre, film and television is the only meaning of success. While departments may pay lip service to the value of theatre training in other careers, they do not display their successful teachers, drama therapists and children's theatre specialists in their glossy ads . . . The desire to study theatre as a literary art and to master its philosophies, traditions and literature . . . has been relegated to second class status. (Loughlin B4, qtd. in Gressler 123)

While at first relieved to realize the MtA situation is not unusual, my relief was soon tempered by the glaring fact (and somewhat dubious ethics) that despite implicit promises of recruitment marketing, and buoyed by their own hopes, the vast majority of the two thousand drama and theatre university graduates every year in Canada are clearly not getting jobs as actors. So, ironically, while we salute, in some contexts, the ways that liberal education benefits our students, who clearly find success in many fields, these benefits often get lost or misrepresented in disconnected and mixed messages about what our programs do. This is where the final penny dropped.

At first I was puzzled by how the same liberal-education and liberal-arts vocabulary could be used to describe programs so different from one another. It didn't take long, however, to connect this observation to a very troubling implication: the terms "liberal education" and "liberal arts" have "so many and so varied uses" that, despite their "rich historical meanings, the question now arises of whether and how liberal education is any longer a useful construct" at all (Mulcahy 2). This in turn begged the question as to what the relationship might in fact be between the way we muddy the messages about liberal education and theatre practice in our university drama programs and the threat our programs are experiencing from the neo-liberal agenda, which similarly sidelines the importance of liberal education in favour of job training.

A desire to sort out the conundrum led me to investigate the literature on drama and theatre education at Canadian universities (HEDTPS),[3] but I

And these comments still don't even begin to address the success of the majority of our students who work in fields completely outside of theatre altogether.

3 The essay will use the acronym "HEDTPS" (Higher Education Drama, Theatre, and Performance Studies) to encompass the diversity of post-secondary theatre/drama programs for which the issues discussed here may be relevant. The first attention of this essay is on B.A. programs at universities, which tend to have ambiguously framed outcomes: to varying degrees marketing themselves as having or operating with some level of assumed pre-professional ambitions for their students, while acknowledging, even highlighting, liberal-arts or liberal-education contexts. Other programs (BFAs and M.F.A.s at universities, community-college, and CEGEP (Collège d'enseignement général et professionnel) programs, as well as independent theatre schools and conservatories) are generally more

found relatively little pertinent scholarship, either historical or contemporary. And what there is focuses almost entirely on professional training, in particular actor training. This focus in our scholarship validates the marketing face of our programs, but in these times of threat it offers dangerously little perspective on larger issues such as our important relationship to liberal education; meaningful analysis of pedagogical or curricular approaches; an unpacking of the premises behind the focus on training; why we haven't engaged more fully with the reality of our complex programs; and, especially, the diverse outcomes our students achieve. If our own scholarly research does not illuminate the importance of our programs to the broader education and success of our students, if we're instead focusing so much on the job-training outcomes of our programs, then how complicit does that potentially make us in the neo-liberal contentions for job-specific programs and diminution of liberal education?

A key piece in drawing my attention to this connection was the 2015 collection of articles in *Canadian Theatre Review* (volume 161) derived from a panel entitled "The Academy According to Dickeson: How Can Theatre and Performance Studies Thrive in the Corporatized University?" that was convened at the 2014 Canadian Association for Theatre Research conference.[4] These papers provide a diversity of perspectives on how to "defend" university theatre programs in light of economic and institutional threats. However the dominant "defensive" posture of the collection is its weakness, and a telling one at that, given the diffident hope that the exercise should be to "maintain

explicitly mandated for professional training. However, in contrast to Ric Knowles's 1995 contention that there are "fundamental distinctions" between the two ("This Discipline"), today at least there is considerable crossover among these distinctions, for example the manifestation of BFA programs alongside B.A. programs in the same departments (often with at least some shared courses) and the ambiguity and variety of B.A. programs.

4 Robert Dickeson's work, *Prioritizing Academic Programs and Services: Reallocating Resources to Achieve Strategic Balance* (1999, revised 2009), is one oft-cited source used by university administrations to justify reducing or eliminating certain programs, like drama and theatre, which are not seen to fit the neo-liberal definition of job-training-based education.

a strategic foothold in the margins" (Alvarez 74). Each of the papers provides an interesting piece of a puzzle: for example, the interdisciplinarity of theatre studies and social justice (Gallagher, "A Foothold"), the development of more sophisticated local audiences (Guay), or the need to prepare language that can counter the inevitable big-data steamroller (Finn). However, each writer's effort to defend their particular corner of the discipline results in a picture that is ultimately unclear, leaving the reader with little sense of what the pieces, together, actually advocate for. Despite the suggestion of the "usefulness of theatrical methods in other disciplines and professional contexts" (Freeman 81), the broader educational values of HEDTPS programs get lost, and this seems to show how vulnerable we are.

The nearest thing here to an exception is Barry Freeman's contribution. He attempts to engage the importance of liberal education outcomes and advocate the need to examine the core student experiences in our programs. He suggests that "whether students will go on to be theatre artists or otherwise, the most successful among them will have learned what it takes to be resourceful, flexible, and information savvy," and he asks, "How can we make more of a virtue—and a pedagogy—of the usefulness of theatrical methods in other disciplines and professional contexts?" (81). But even here, Freeman is still restrained by the unexamined premise that "it is difficult to translate a theatre degree into a viable, innovative practice and sustaining career, and difficult, too, to maintain autonomy and integrity in *theatre training programs* given the material constraints" (80; emphasis added).

Serious examinations of acting and other technical-training aspects of our programs are obviously needed and important. But by not looking beyond the professional-training preoccupations, by not questioning the assumptions that have led to this emphasis, by not clarifying the more complex intersections of education and theatre training, we leave ourselves at best "defensive" against serious structural and cultural threats. Instead, a re-examination of the sources of these approaches may in turn develop a new scholarship that puts drama and theatre not at the margins of the university, but at its centre.[5]

HISTORICAL SOURCES

The source of today's inadequate discourse on the role of university theatre education can indeed be traced to the way Canadian university theatre has been discussed in the past, in the way our historical narrative has framed our contemporary views. A review of some recent histories quickly delineates four particular ideas that frame the discourse today: 1) the lack of a comprehensive history of university theatre education in Canada which fosters, 2) the dominant view that university theatre is about professional training. As a result, 3) the diversity of extracurricular theatre on campuses is overlooked or denigrated in imitation of the way amateur theatre is treated vis-à-vis professional theatre. And all of these are sustained by 4) the lack of conceptual frames for the investigation of pedagogical and curricular thinking.

The 1985 collection of essays edited by Anton Wagner, *Contemporary Canadian Theatre: New World Visions*, contains two pieces that explicitly address training and education and which introduce two of these key ideas. The first, Don Rubin's article "Training the Theatre Professional," decries the Canadian approach to professional preparation (in contrast to what he describes as the more selective "European approach"). According to Rubin, the haphazard Canadian model of many forms and avenues of open-door training results in an oversupply of under- and unemployed actors and professionals (284). Citing Malcolm Black's 1977 *Report of the Committee of Inquiry*

5 For example, and not unusual in the much richer American discourse on these issues, is Nancy Kindelan's rousing call to arms in her 2012 book, *Artistic Literacy: Theatre Studies and a Contemporary Liberal Education*. She argues that the powerful learning that theatre studies and activities frames for students gives HEDTPS faculty a significant tool to bring to institutional-level curricular discussions. Her argument is that such moves counter the prevailing ideology that theatre studies are merely "frill and fill" programs, easily cut in times of economic difficulties.

into Theatre Training in Canada, Rubin acknowledges the approximately fifty undergraduate university, college, and CEGEP theatre programs existing at the time, but declares that the only ones worth mentioning are those at the University of British Columbia (UBC), University of Victoria, University of Alberta, University of Calgary, York, Ryerson, Concordia, Université du Québec à Montréal (UQAM), and Dalhousie because these represent "commitment to serious theatre training within an academic context" (289–90). Rubin then introduces the term "pre-professional" to emphasize that indeed the university is merely "context" (or perhaps *pre*text) for the real work of these schools: professional "training." Rubin thus clearly marks that university theatre programs exist for training professionals. Furthermore, the majority of such programs, in his opinion, are simply not very good at it. Any other educational values these programs might deliver are not even on his radar.[6]

Despite its title, "Drama in Education," by Wayne Fairhead, also in the 1985 collection, does not address higher education at all but only reviews approaches to drama curricula at the primary and secondary levels. The only mention of HEDTPS relates to teacher training and the influence of international theatre-in-education (TIE) specialists in faculties of education. This is the second foundational premise that turns any discussion of drama pedagogy or curriculum towards the pre-university levels, as if discussions of pedagogy or curriculum have no relevance to higher education drama programs. Sporadic mentions of university theatre appear elsewhere in the Wagner volume, again generally reiterating the premise that university theatre is about building the

---

6 Rubin is merely formalizing an attitude that goes back to much earlier thoughts on the role of university drama. Although published two years after this collection appeared, Eugene Benson and L.W. Conolly's brief overview of *English-Canadian Theatre* includes a section entitled "Drama and the Universities." Here they cite the "first Chair of Drama at a Canadian university" at the University of Saskatchewan in 1945, Emrys Maldwyn Jones, as "envision[ing] a major role for university drama departments in supporting a National Theatre for Canada," thus setting the stage, as it were, for the professional-training focus of HEDTPS scholarship to come. The section then cites Jones's complaint that universities were "slow to respond to the challenge of participating in the 'expression and development of a truly Canadian culture through the medium of Drama' " (63).

industry, such as in the chapter on how seminal companies such as Tamahnous and Touchstone were formed by UBC drama graduates (169). And there is, of course, no mention of pedagogy or curriculum anywhere.

However, a third new thread is introduced in the chapter on drama and theatre in Nova Scotia, when it is noted that "[c]olleges and universities have been frequent leaders in the field of community drama" (Perkyns 107), and in Mira Friedlander's article on "Community and Grass Roots," which addresses how early twentieth-century little theatre groups such as the University College Alumnae Association and Hart House Theatre contributed to the origins of professional theatre (229). Each of these articles regrets university theatre as merely amateur until such time as a "proper" program arrives that links the academy to professional training.[7] These articles also prompt the recognition that the industry model of the professional versus amateur binary is recreated in the hierarchy of curricular versus extracurricular theatre in the university. Given that many university students' exposure to theatre is through extracurricular work on campuses, and given that this work is often mentored or guided by faculty, it seems short-sighted to ignore the important impact of this component on student learning.

Perhaps most importantly from a historiographic perspective, it is worth noting that, as in much of today's Canadian literature on the subject, there is no unpacking of any of these assumptions in Wagner's collection: the essays offer no critical vocabulary to examine how the hierarchical relationships among amateur, professional, or educational theatres are constructed, or of the effects they produce; what ideologies are reproduced in these unexamined binaries; and certainly no consideration of any value, implicit or otherwise, in HEDTPS beyond job training for the theatre.[8]

---

7 This thread is also picked up in the 1987 Benson and Conolly chapter "Drama and the Universities" noted above (see note six), which ends with the very revealing statement that "the next crucial phase [for English Canadian theatre] consisted of moving from that amateur achievement to a fully professional status," dismissing the HEDTPS programs as no more than, pejoratively intoned, "amateur" (*English-Canadian* 66).

8 An important exception to this is Robin Whittaker's work on "nonprofessionalizing" theatre in Canada. See p. 89, later in this essay.

Benson and Conolly's *Oxford Companion to Canadian Theatre* (1989) reproduces the same thinking as the Wagner collection. Gordon Peacock's article, tellingly entitled "Education and Training,"[9] repeats the familiar story about the founding of drama programs at the Universities of Saskatchewan and Alberta, as well as mentioning Regina's, UBC's, and Ryerson's programs, but with no dates or curricular specifics beyond noting that these programs meet certain professional standards for technical qualifications in areas such as stage management. There are some broad statistics about the growth of programs (eight full-time instructors for 120 students at four universities in 1955 to "forty-eight programs, 280 faculty, and over ten thousand enrolments" in 1987 [193]). As in the Wagner volume, other articles in the *Companion* include occasional notes about universities and theatre programs, but these are all singing from the same hymnal: they include passing apologies for the amateur contribution of university theatres as, at best, precursors to the real professional work that came later (Stuart 11; Todd 62), or, more often, address university theatre as a second-rate activity that is best overlooked as quickly as possible (O'Neill, "Nova Scotia" 392). An intriguing and slightly less derogatory attitude towards theatre, both outside of and associated with universities, appears in the "Theatre in Quebec (French)" article, where amateur work is seen in productive discourse with the "theatrical revival led by numerous alternate professional companies" (David 448).

In this survey of historical sources, a final example—Ross and Ann Stuart's chapter on "University Theatre" in Ann Saddlemyer and Richard Plant's *Later Stages: Essays in Ontario Theatre* (1997)—stands out because it comes closest to addressing some of the common issues problematic in earlier sources. First, it attempts a more comprehensive history of HEDTPS, albeit limited to only one region and mostly focusing on programs in southern Ontario at that. The paper traces longer trends in theatre curriculum, outlining the development of drama in Ontario universities from its beginnings as a barely

9 This article was republished with some updates as "Theatre Education" by Joyce Wilkinson, Anthony Adah, Gordon Peacock, and Laurin Mann in the online *Canadian Encyclopedia.*

tolerated parascholarly activity enhancing the teaching of classical languages and rhetoric in the nineteenth century, to a valued extracurricular activity enriching undergraduate life in the early twentieth century, to the curricular confusion over drama studies as liberal education versus professional theatre training at the end of the century. Although it does not offer detailed analysis of the curriculum, the paper at least admits there is an educational relationship between extracurricular and curricular theatre in higher education and that it plays some role in larger liberal educational values.

What is also interesting here is the authors' suggestion that the root of these contesting ambitions may be seen in British versus American models of HEDTPS. The authors link the hiring of American faculty in the many newly created Canadian drama programs in the 1960s to the shift toward the more professional-training orientation of the "American" model and away from the "British" model, which emphasized the extracurricular side of theatre in higher education. Despite the twenty years since the publication of this volume, however, very little scholarship has yet followed up on any of these ideas.[10]

The slim and inadequately theorized historical literature on drama and theatre education at universities in Canada has laid the foundations for contemporary thinking on the subject. There is no macrohistory of how university theatre has developed: only spotty references touching some regions (Ontario, Saskatchewan, and Alberta in particular), with only fragmented information referring to a few institutions at seemingly random moments. More importantly, there is no analysis or history of pedagogical or curricular trends other than repetitions of unexamined connections between university training and

10 This also in spite of Ric Knowles's 1991 work "Otherwise Engaged: Towards a Materialist Pedagogy" arguing for a shift in the pedagogy of drama courses toward "examining the interests served by the various theatrical, social and cultural discourses with and through which the texts speak" (194). Despite that Knowles opened the door for larger discussions and followed it up with two additional articles, published in 1995 ("Discipline") and 1998 ("Alternative"), on the roles of practical theatre in "academic" settings and "alternative pedagogies" at the graduate level, his comments seem to have had little effect on the general discourse concerning university theatre.

professional training outcomes. Without either a broad or deep history of the subject, we see instead an overarching, but virtually unexamined, premise that university theatre is about professional training: a maxim that is repeated starting from the earliest establishment of university drama departments. A consequence of the fixation on the professionalization of university programs is the denigration of extracurricular activities on campus, paralleling the depreciation of amateur theatre off campus.

WAYS FORWARD

Our actual classroom and studio contributions to student learning have been far more dense and sophisticated than the minimal Canadian scholarly literature on theatre education suggests. Current scholarship on HEDTPS reiterates the narrow past premises and fails to explain the value of what our programs are doing and thus may not be providing us with the necessary tools to operate in changing administrative climates. I contend that a new examination of the four key premises outlined in the historical literature is needed in order to enrich contemporary views. This re-examination needs to begin with a more comprehensive study of the history of HEDTPS in Canada than that available in the present literature.

Getting a clear handle on the history of our work is daunting: what we do, and have done, in the one-hundred-plus drama and theatre programs[11] across this country is very diverse, with every program operating in unique ways as a result of different institutional histories and structures. Although we need a stronger sense of the whole, the challenge of trying to study something as complex as the history of university theatre is likely insurmountable. Much can be gained, however, from the development of detailed microhistories: careful examinations of the development of HEDTPS programs in particular

11 The University Study search engine published by Universities Canada lists 101 undergraduate theatre and drama programs in English and eight in French delivered by forty-three different universities. This includes eighty-five B.A. (and iBA) programs, and twenty-four BFAs ("Search Programs").

institutions or perhaps in closely related regions. Such a project is underway to examine the curricular and practical history of the nearly half-century of drama studies at Mount Allison. Without studies of other programs to provide context, however, the results of such microhistories are hard to interpret. I suggest, therefore, that a combination of microhistorical and comparative approaches will best allow us to connect individual programs with the history of theatre in HEDTPS more generally, allowing us to address questions like: What aspects are merely idiosyncratic and which represent important commonalities? Have the roles of our grads in the world of theatre and elsewhere been typical or atypical? How does the relationship of our program to the much longer tradition of extracurricular activity on campus relate to similar connections elsewhere? How does the history of theatre on the MtA campus compare to that of other institutions? While our educational work across Canada has much in common, each HEDTPS program has such unique histories and conditions of operation that only once there are sufficient examinations to test the range of issues can we really begin to ask the necessary contextual questions.

Further to this, the more inclusive coverage of regions and institutions must be informed by sufficiently theorized conceptual frames brought to bear on the material, both historical and pedagogical. Knowles's call for a materialist-informed pedagogy that informs "study based on concepts and methods rather than content" and so counters the increasingly "perceived need to disseminate information" ("Otherwise Engaged" 196) could be one such approach. Likewise, Laura Levin argues that performance studies is the key to making "theatre more relevant to our students and stave off administrative types always looking for budgets to slash" ("It's Time" 167). Other avenues for investigation might be an interrogation of suggestions noted in earlier histories, for example those concerning how "British" versus "American" models of HEDTPS programming may have influenced the developments in Canada and the intriguing idea that English and French Canada have different understandings of the relationship among educational, amateur, and professional theatre.

Another way to revisit the historical material would be to underpin new scholarship using similar critical sophistication as that seen in the TIE work at lower grades, inspired by the likes of Kathleen Gallagher's groundbreaking 2014 book, *Why Theatre Matters*. Theatre in Education is of course an international and mature discipline, with distinct and diverse definitions and approaches, supported by nearly a hundred years of scholarly and practical work. No one can deny the importance of research on the role of theatre in Canada's primary and secondary levels, such as Gallagher's international ethnographical TIE project. Surely, HEDTPS stimulates comparable personal and social transformations for post-secondary students as those Gallagher has identified as occurring for grade-school students. This leaves one to wonder why similar critical and scholarly attention has not been paid to theatre education at higher levels.

The specific application of concepts to adult learners and the questions raised by the intersection of liberal education and theatre training will differ in detail from those in typical TIE work, but the inspiration is the same in that

> [t]heatre, when it meets education, often articulates deeply felt social aspirations as well as giving shape and form to the circumstances and difficulties faced by young people in the here-and-now. (H. Nicholson 43)

Our discipline has focused on studying the history, literature, performance, and politics of professional theatre in Canada. Now it's time to turn our attention to the many intersections of university and theatre by "asking profound questions about the purpose of education, the social role of theatre and its ability to affect the lives of young people" (H. Nicholson 43). It seems a question raised in 1996 may be useful here. Although he was examining the financial fundamentals underpinning post-secondary funding, Frank Strain drew attention to a peculiar facet of universities who "are not investing enough in R&D into their own operations and [. . .] have failed to employ relevant knowledge to change the education process" (162–63). Are we in HEDTPS investing enough of our scholarly resources in actually investigating the role of theatre in higher education and the real impact of what our programs have been doing for Canadian theatre?

The other major premise that needs re-examination is that HEDTPS work is merely "amateur" and therefore not valuable until the transition to professional/pre-professional training occurs. The key, though, to revisiting the historiographical premises that prioritized "professional" over "amateur" is a shift in fundamental thinking to recognize that important learning through theatre has never ended at the boundary of credit courses and performances, but extends into the co-curricular and even extracurricular activities associated with our programs (whether we admit it or not).

We need scholarship that gets under the skin of exactly what the relationships among HEDTPS, the professional world, and "amateur theatre" really are. Robin Whittaker's examinations of "nonprofessionalizing practice" at Walterdale Theatre and the Alumnae Theatre are steps in this direction. Whittaker not only frames a significant critical vocabulary but also initiates discourse around how the amateur, professional, and educational theatre worlds can be seen as "fundamentally complex and intertwined, in turns competitive and mutually beneficial" ("Entirely" 53). Other institutions like Hart House Theatre or the UBC Players Club also blurred the lines between educational, amateur, and professional in various ways. I suspect that all our programs and their seasons negotiate this same territory to varying degrees: a territory that needs to be much better mapped in order for us to better articulate the important things our programs do.

By studying the co-curricular and extracurricular activities related to our programs, as well as the strictly curricular training they provide; by assessing the evolution of learning outcomes in our programs from B.A. options to BFA requirements; by investigating the history of university theatre activities from the purely extracurricular to the most exacting professional-standard, for-credit performances; by tracing influences from before the advent of pre-professional programs through the modern diversification of theatre, drama, and performance programs; and by developing the critical vocabulary that underpins all of these, we can stretch the way we conceive the power of our programs to shape theatre beyond their walls. Building scholarship that fully appreciates all of the student learning associated with our programs, not just the training of elite professionals, means expanding the understanding and validation of the power we have in the realization of an informed public, whether directly involved with theatre or not, and the significance of that on Canadian theatre.

CONCLUSION

Since the establishment of drama and theatre programs at Canadian universities starting in the 1940s, the impact on the training of theatre professionals has been considerable.[12] But I wonder, given the diverse outcomes of our programs, if the narrow focus on professional-training ambitions has not actually sold our programs short. Might not the development and success of modern Canadian theatre actually have had at least as much to do with the broader and deeper influences of our programs and activities on the formation of audiences, supporters, volunteers, board members, and so on, who also play significant roles in the development and sustainability of theatre in Canada, yet who don't usually get bylines in theatre programs?

Most students touched by our programs do not work in theatre, but in many other walks of life where their actions and decisions can and do have important implications for the success of theatre. The learning derived through university theatre work affects the decisions of those business owners, voters, taxpayers, journalists, parents, politicians, scientists . . . which in turn shape the conditions for the minority of our students who actually become professional theatre makers.

However, by stressing vocational training as is the case in so much of our scholarship now, how have we, in effect, contributed to the utilitarian, neo-liberal arguments dominating some institutions? By highlighting our programs

12 Or has it? There is in fact very little scholarship available to back up this widely held assumption, or to analyze what in fact such a relationship between HEDTPS and the professional world actually means.

as, effectively, job training, whether explicitly or simply by default through not applying our research tools to articulate the fuller picture productively, are we not simply complicit with claims that higher education should be about preparing youth for specific jobs? To what degree is our mixed messaging, despite the best of intentions, weakening our position: in one moment emphasizing the histories of our successful stage graduates for competitive recruitment and playing up the pre-professional ambitions of our courses, while in the next appealing to institutional vocabularies that pay lip service to "liberal education." But without having the detailed scholarship to explain what either of these mean or how they relate, how effectively are we really able to do justice to either?[13]

Since HEDTPS programs started to be established in the 1940s, thousands of Canadian students have participated as theatre makers and audiences through our institutions: one could argue more theatre has taken place in universities than anywhere else in Canada, so clearly our programs have had a significant impact on learners across the country, well beyond the training of theatre workers. But how much do we actually know about this? And how much does our lack of knowledge leave us vulnerable? The complexities of studying these questions are difficult, but the stakes are high . . . in some cases perhaps the survival of our HEDTPS programs. But just as importantly one could also say the future of theatre in Canada itself is in play due to the far reach of our students in public decision-making, as well as in theatre-making.

In contrast to the picture painted by historical and current scholarship, our programs do an awful lot more for our communities than what happens in the acting studio or lighting lab. And we forget at our peril the armies of graduates who have ended up not working directly in or for theatre, but whose experience through our programs and activities has been instrumental in shaping their educational outcomes, informing their world views and life choices. However, it is not only the impact of broad learning on the individual students that needs research, but also the collective social impact of

13 See Schechner who, among others, articulates fairly graphic concern that HEDTPS, by not clearly understanding our roles, are not reaching any of our goals very well.

our programs that is lost in the unexamined focus on professional training. We have important influence on a strong component of a broader public that goes to the polls; decides where to spend their disposable income; chooses where to devote their spare, leisure, or creative time; and makes all manner of business, political, and social decisions . . . all of which impact Canadian theatre. Maybe even more important than how we are training our actors and stage managers, or even our future audiences, the future of Canadian theatre may depend on better understanding and communicating how we are training our wider public.

BC ABORIGINAL THEATRE HISTORY IN THE MAKING: TALKING WITH MARGO KANE ABOUT THE HISTORY OF FULL CIRCLE AND THE TALKING STICK

MICHELLE LA FLAMME[1]

Canadian theatre history, particularly since the 1980s, has been impacted by a phenomenal explosion of Aboriginal talent. Across Canada new plays have been performed in communities, in mainstream theatres, and unique and inspirational Aboriginal plays are being seen throughout the nation and internationally. Contemporary Aboriginal theatre practices in Canada must be considered in global contexts, within an international Indigenous performance movement that has enabled Aboriginal artists to tour shows and create new alliances that lead to exciting, syncretic performances. In addition to this proliferation and circulation of talent, companies like Full Circle First Nations Performance and Native Earth Performing Arts have mentored and trained a generation of Aboriginal actors, writers, directors, designers, choreographers, singers, and dancers whose visions and powerful presences have changed Canadian theatre forever. In order to make sense of this emerging area of Canadian theatre, some start by asking the routine and overdetermined question: When did all of this begin?

Answering this question, however, reveals that the history and historiography of Aboriginal theatre in Canada is contentious and fraught with complexities reflecting our colonial history. For many, Aboriginal theatre

1 The author wishes to acknowledge the work of Taylor Breckles, who provided valuable assistance with transcription and background research.

is created within the context of a ten-thousand-year legacy of performance practices that include orature, ceremony, song, and culturally embedded performances. Others argue that Aboriginal theatre in Canada began when mainstream theatres began to produce plays with Aboriginal content. Yet for others, it began when Aboriginal writers and storytellers began to use the forms and conventions of Western theatre to share their stories. A more radical view is that theatrical spaces in a settler colony are always-already colonized spaces and therefore a truly sovereign Aboriginal theatre movement has yet to emerge. Others add that since contemporary Aboriginal theatre is primarily written in English, it always involves a necessary act of translation. This argument suggests that the standard use of English (or French) in Canadian theatre can only lead to plays that present watered-down versions of traditional cosmologies, protocols, and worldviews that were embedded in the Indigenous languages that once thrived in North America. From this perspective, one might argue that contemporary Aboriginal theatre has not yet begun, that we simply are creating simulacra: stories that are weakened and lost in translation. Social-justice advocates and traditionalists insist that the performances we see today are entirely severed from the rich performance cultures that were the reality in the past. Following this line of thought, one might argue that Aboriginal theatre in Canada will not truly begin until plays are written in Indigenous languages, traditional land bases are restored, modern treaties are respected, and a cultural revitalization of traditional modes of performativity is evident.

Given the complexity of the topic and the incompatibility of the different paradigms I have briefly traced, I suggest setting aside the question of a foundational moment. Perhaps more useful questions we might ask are: What is the impact of this rich infusion of stories and cosmologies on writers, directors, actors, and scholars? How might an enquiry into these performance practices contribute to the overall objective of reframing the major narratives of Canadian theatre history? What are some markers or key moments in contemporary Aboriginal theatre history that allow us to further interrogate the broader questions above?

One set of developmental milestones emerges when one considers how Aboriginal content has made its way onto mainstream Canadian stages.

Scholars often point to plays such as George Ryga's *The Ecstasy of Rita Joe* (1967) or Sharon Pollock's *Walsh* (1973), as indigenized moments in Canadian theatre history. In both plays, non-Indigenous playwrights offer humane representations of Indigenous characters. Ryga's play should be lauded for bringing a sympathetic portrayal of a complex Aboriginal character to the mainstream (read: non-Native) stage. In Pollock's play, the central Aboriginal character—Chief Sitting Bull—exists primarily to allow for a meditation on justice and a contemplation of the actions of the Canadian government. It was not until 1986, the usual historical narrative goes, that an Aboriginal playwright would have a noticeable effect on the development of Canadian theatre. I am, of course, referring to the premiere of *The Rez Sisters*, by Tomson Highway, which was the first Canadian Aboriginal play to reach mainstream audiences and tour Canada.

The development of Aboriginal theatre in Canada was supported and complemented by the development of Aboriginal theatre companies. Toronto's Native Earth Performing Arts and Manitoulin Island's Debajehmujig Theatre, both founded in the early 1980s, played important roles in ushering in new plays and developing new talent through mentorship and training. Without diminishing the work of these two companies, however, it is important to note that histories of Aboriginal theatre tend to emphasize their importance at the cost of ignoring developments in other parts of Canada. For example, Montreal's Ondinnok Theatre and the National Arts Centre have both played important roles in developing and circulating Aboriginal theatre. Mainstream accounts of the history of Aboriginal theatre tend to focus on eastern Canada and on the contributions of male artists. However, companies like Vancouver's Urban Ink, Gordon Tootoosis Nīkānīwin Theatre (formerly the Saskatchewan Native Theatre Company), Turtle Gals Performance Ensemble, and Winnipeg's Red Roots Theatre have all been actively engaging performers and creating new and inspired work. Yet their impact is sometimes overshadowed by the focus on eastern Canadian theatre history, prominent male playwrights, and the work produced by Native Earth and Debajehmujig.

In addition to the importance of a new narrative about Aboriginal theatre history that includes Western Canada and female creators, we must also remember the important impact of theatre developed in community contexts. Any consideration of Aboriginal theatre history in Canada should consider the practical uses of theatre for healing and social justice that are occurring in many communities. Vancouver-based Theatre for Living (formerly Headlines Theatre), for example, has been invited for many years now into Aboriginal communities to create plays by, for, and about the communities. Through Forum theatre, Theatre for Living's performances often address issues such as language loss, community revitalization, and the long-term impacts of colonialism. Their 2017 mainstage show, *šxʷʔam̓ət (Home)*, engages its Aboriginal cast and others in addressing the question: "What does reconciliation mean to you?"

In addition to this professional company going into communities, Aboriginal actors also travel frequently to communities, and the impact of their mentorship on emerging Aboriginal artists cannot be overstated. The Gemini Award–winning actor Michelle Thrush, for example, regularly performs in small communities and recently travelling to Attawapiskat to share her characters with the community. Veteran actors Adam Beach and Tantoo Cardinal have also made efforts to travel to Aboriginal communities in Canada and inspire youth with performances and discussions about theatre. Young actor Cliff Cardinal has taken his show *Huff*, a visceral take on suicide and substance abuse, into communities and spoken to at-risk youth about the play. Such community-engaged performances facilitate dialogue with at-risk youth, women, Elders, and children. Although these performance practices are frequently excluded from mainstream narratives about Aboriginal theatre history, they are important because they save lives, revitalize communities, and inspire new storytellers.

Aboriginal theatre practices in Canada also transcend the boundaries of the Western theatre genre and creative arts disciplines. To appreciate this aspect of Aboriginal theatre, one can consider Aboriginal performers who cross-appropriate hip hop to tell their stories in a new format. Oz12, JB the First Lady, Christie Lee Charles, and Rapture Rising are all urban youth grounded in their cultures and they use new vocal, visual, and performative forms to share narratives that evoke contemporary realities. A history locating Aboriginal performance in an interdisciplinary context might consider the highly successful band A Tribe Called

Red and the collective of artists known as Beat Nation. The work of these new artists offers critical moments in the development of Aboriginal performance.

In addition to these talented musical performers, the work created by performance artists like Archer Pechawis, Lori Blondeau, Dana Claxton, and Rebecca Belmore is also integral to a contemporary Canadian Aboriginal performance history. Though the work they create is technically performance art and thus the analysis of it tends to be located in performance studies, a new complex history emerges when we take into account the phenomenal work that this handful of performance artists have created. In my essay "(re)animating the (un)dead," I offer an analysis of the kinaesthetic and synaesthetic aspects of the international touring exhibition *Walking With Our Sisters* and *The REDress Project* by Jaime Black as performative events that represent a cosmology in line with Marie Clements's play *The Unnatural and Accidental Women*. Clearly we are not following the disciplinary rigidity that characterizes much scholarship. Scholars have tended to focus on playwright-driven work, work that translates well to the printed page, and plays that fit into generic and stylistic conventions familiar to non-Indigenous readers. We must be vigilant to incorporate the diversity of Aboriginal performance practice and stretch the boundaries of European aesthetics and academic disciplinary boundaries in order to capture this rich performative history—and present.

A final way to trace the development of contemporary Aboriginal theatre is through its entry into the discipline and the academy. One key moment in Aboriginal theatre history, then, is the publication of Monique Mojica and Ric Knowles's two-volume anthology *Staging Coyote's Dream: An Anthology of First Nations Drama in English* (2003, 2009), which made major plays more readily available for scholars and students. Scholarship in the field has been advanced through recent Canadian and international conferences dedicated to the analysis of Aboriginal theatre and through the efforts of the Canadian publishing industry. For example, Rob Appleford's anthology *Aboriginal Drama and Theatre* (2005) and *Theatre Research in Canada's* special issue on Marie Clements, edited by Reid Gilbert in 2010, undoubtedly mark an increase in the scholarly gaze on Aboriginal theatre. Of particular note is *Performing Indigeneity* (2016), edited by Yvette Nolan and Ric Knowles, which examines

Indigenous performativity in its broadest sense and is the first such collection to feature only the work of Indigenous authors.

With this wide historical scope and these critical questions as background, I want to shift our gaze to Western Canada and call Margo Kane, the founder and artistic director of Full Circle Performance, to centre stage. In the interview that follows, I have tried to tease out Margo Kane's contribution to Aboriginal theatre in Canada while allowing her voice and process to remain the focus. The methodological choice of interview, rather than scholarly overview, allows Kane and her company's history to emerge in an anecdotal, storytelling format. What follows is a sharing that resists the easy, playwright-driven, masculine, Ontario-based narrative of the development of Aboriginal theatre history in Canada.

Margo Kane is of Cree and Saulteaux descent and is committed to encouraging Aboriginal voices in the arts: regionally, nationally, and internationally. She is an accomplished interdisciplinary artist and has been a powerhouse in the development of Aboriginal theatre in Canada. After more than forty years in the performing arts, Kane is still driven to perform, create more work, and run Full Circle First Nations Performance, which she established in 1992. Throughout her career, she has been a storyteller, writer, dancer, director, producer, teacher, and singer. She has worked across artistic disciplines, in live theatre, visual art, video art, and performance art. She is well known for her collaborative work and for her two powerful monodramas: *Moonlodge* (first performed in 1990), considered a classic of Aboriginal theatre, and *Confessions of an Indian Cowboy* (first performed in 2001). In addition, Kane was Artistic Director of Vancouver's first Aboriginal theatre company, Spirit Song Native Theatre School, and it is this point in time that I use as the opening for the interview. In Western Canada, Margo Kane has been a central force in the rebirth of Aboriginal theatre for four decades: influencing a new generation of performers, invoking traditional approaches to performance through her ensemble training program at Full Circle, and introducing new and accomplished Aboriginal artists through the platform of the Talking Stick Festival. Kane has been running her company for twenty-four years and the festival for fifteen. What started as a one-day cabaret has blossomed into a ten-day festival held in multiple locations throughout Vancouver. The examples of Full Circle Performance and the Talking Stick Festival offer a foil to mainstream narratives that—intentionally or not—focus on individual playwrights, professional practices, largely non-Native theatre spaces, and Western-derived creation methods.

Two of Kane's works deserve special mention here, particularly for readers unfamiliar with her body of work. *Moonlodge* sets the story of Agnes, a young Aboriginal woman, against the historical backdrop of Native children's experiences in the child welfare system. The play uses powerful drama, song, dance, and humour to explore the impact of the Sixties Scoop, which was a blatant effort on the part of the Canadian government to disconnect children from their Indigenous heritage by separating them from their families and preventing them from experiencing their cultures, enacted through repeated relocations within the foster-care system and adoption into non-Aboriginal families. In 2017 *Moonlodge* was presented at the Talking Stick Festival for the first time with a new actress. This is one obvious marker of change. It would be an entirely innovative project to collate a Canadian Aboriginal theatre history based on these markers within each Aboriginal theatre company in Canada to truly offer a counter-narrative.

Kane's performances have roots in the stories and legends of various Aboriginal communities as well as in stories from the lives of her students. A second significant work that shaped Kane's future artistic practice was 1992's ensemble dance performance *The River-Home*. This piece combines traditional Aboriginal performance techniques such as oration and ritual with contemporary technologies such as video projection and recorded soundscape to capture the intimate relationships between Aboriginal peoples and waterways. Each iteration of the performance was different as it was informed and developed by various students from the ensemble training program. Such communal approaches to development and theatricality are common in many Indigenous performance contexts.

While Kane was working on *The River-Home*, she was also establishing Full Circle First Nations Performance, a group dedicated to fostering opportunities for Aboriginal artists. According to the company's mandate on its website:

> "Full Circle" evokes many images: inclusiveness, wholeness, a full gathering. It is both a traditional symbol of completion and of

> continuous movement—action with no beginning or end. Full Circle First Nations Performance supports these principles in our practice. We honour the contributions of all our members within a diverse circle of cultures, communities and perspectives; we initiate projects and bring them to completion; we renew traditional practices to allow for our continuation through time. ("About Us: Mission")

Although it has been difficult for Aboriginal artists to be heard, Kane says that:

> We are entering a new era, I believe, and historically many changes have already begun which will lift the spirits of our people and share more stories and experiences of the First Peoples of this land. ("Re: Full Circle)

In June 2015, Kane received an Honorary Doctor of Letters degree from the University of the Fraser Valley (UFV). She returned to the university in May 2016 to deliver an informal talk, punctuated by performances of select excerpts from her own plays. Watching this, I was reminded of the extent to which her work, her vision, and her art have impacted students, audiences, and communities all over the country. When I first met Margo decades ago I was struck by her energy, fierce determination, and creative vision. I was inspired to witness a woman who pressed on despite the odds, offered her own expertise with candid clarity, and fought tirelessly to manifest a specific creative vision while mentoring others along the way. Recently I began talking with her more formally about the impact of her life's work and the legacy she has created. In this edited interview, Kane and I discuss the events that led to her creating *Moonlodge* and establishing her company Full Circle and developing the Talking Stick Festival. Then we address some of the challenges Kane faced as an Aboriginal artist at a time when there were few venues for Indigenous experiences and world views to be expressed artistically. While we explore her own story as a woman and an artist, a larger picture of Aboriginal theatre history in (Western) Canada emerges.

MLF: So, [on your journey toward creating Full Circle and *Moonlodge*], you've left Spirit Song, you've come back, and what happens in that period where you start thinking about, y'know, what would it be like to have a company or could I do it or . . . where were you at?

MK: [W]hen I first landed in the early eighties in Vancouver there were no [Indigenous] actors, per se . . . And I'm just kind of getting to know who everybody was, so by the time I had been away and starting to create my own work, coming back into town and meeting Jeannette [Armstrong],[2] and meeting Lee Maracle,[3] and meeting various Aboriginal writers, and I was starting to read and listen and find out what are the issues in their world, their artistic world. And I found that I was just soaking it all up. Every discipline I could, I would see what the visual artists were doing; I was really keen to know what was happening for Aboriginal artists at that time across disciplines. It all interested me very much . . . that's got to be around the end of the eighties, so what's happened is I decided to write a grant. I was asked to sit in a jury, I think that's what happened, and I started to see what was going on. I went up to Haida Gwaii for a [Canada Council] Explorations jury, when they still had Explorations, and I met Chris Creighton-Kelly[4] . . . so that became another period where I started to not only be around people who were very experienced in critiquing art and art practice and were discussing all those kinds of issues. I was also then working across disciplines and I then decided that I would write a grant to bring us all together, so I brought a bunch of artists together in a couple of grants at the end of 1989 and 1990. Around that time [we began] telling our own story and [addressing] the issues of cultural appropriation . . . The Artist-run Centres movement was happening, and so

2 Jeannette Armstrong (Okanagan) is a prominent Canadian author, artist, educator, and activist. Her 1985 novel *Slash* is considered the first novel written by an Aboriginal woman.

3 A granddaughter of Chief Dan George, Maracle is a Stó:lō writer and specialist in First Nations culture and history.

4 A South Asian/British artist, critic, and writer who was very involved in organizing gatherings for artists of colour.

Western Front [Art Gallery, in Vancouver] and the [Helen] Pitt Gallery [in Vancouver] were doing stuff . . .

I started to do exploratory work like I had done in the Artist-run movement because I could do whatever I wanted and I didn't have to be a playwright. I didn't have to conform with known forms that I really wasn't interested [in]. I was interested in my own process and my own orality, if you will, and my ritual, my sense of movement and bringing all these elements in to create a work. And there were a lot of us that started to come and work together in that period that had been actors or had gone through Spirit Song or were doing various things. And as well that was around the time [I was invited] to sit on the two big committees—the First Peoples Committee and the Culturally Diverse Committee—that helped to develop the Aboriginal Secretariat and the Equity Program for the Canada Council for the Arts. So all of a sudden I was also with all these, like, high-powered thinking artists—senior artists, and some not so senior, but like serious thinkers in the arts, and so I was part of that for several years. That was when Women in View, when Jane [Heyman] commissioned a show and I did *Moonlodge*. [W]e went to the Weesageechak Festival at Native Earth . . . It was just all of these things were coming together all at the same time. [I felt as though] I [was] starting to get to know who [. . .] all the Aboriginal artists in the country [are], so that was really keen. The other thing that happened [was] all of a sudden I was moving, going to Montreal, and I was getting to know the work of the Québec artists, the really movement-based works, some really incredible work that I loved, Carbone [14], all of these incredible artists.

And so I started to refine *Moonlodge*, I still was writing; we videotaped it and wrote it all down and then I went back and forth between the videotape on my [feed] to refine it because I wasn't, I didn't feel I was a writer and I didn't like to just sit and write. So it was from that . . . we mounted [*Moonlodge*] in the Vancouver East Cultural Centre and from there I carried that piece for over ten years, I toured a lot of places in the world, just me and a technician . . . I still did some TV work and the occasional film . . . but I never really took to that business, I didn't really want to be a famous film star, it was something about the business . . . that continually interfered with my creative process and

I found I just stopped. I was surprised to find I just totally didn't really care, because I was very much interested in creating my own work or the process of things. I had a very interesting artistic life already.

I was surprised by how well received [*Moonlodge*] was. I remember doing it and I was being on the edge wondering if they were going to get it, if they were going to enjoy it; it was very interesting so I kept working on it . . . It gave me an opportunity to work on my craft, on my touring. I didn't have to wait for a play with an Aboriginal person or a person of colour in it and I didn't really care about the canon of Canadian work or British-American work. "The role of an actor in the world": I wasn't interested in that, I was really into what *I* was doing, so *Moonlodge* was a way for me to keep working on my craft . . . I would tweak it every time I work[ed] on the script, every time I remount[ed] it. I really enjoyed having the conversations with the audience, the artist's talks, or going to [the] community [to] talk about the work.

I was able to do the work in a variety of situations. One situation we were sort of north of Kamloops on a rez somewhere outside of Barriere or someplace, and I remember they had brought in some lighting for me but it really was pretty bare bones and the show was really bare bones. It was a suitcase show, so you can make do with lots of things, and I remember at the very end, [when] I'm sitting in the Moon Lodge and all of a sudden this little child, sitting in her mother's lap in front of me, like six feet away, comes out and crawls towards me into my lap: things like that happened. It was just precious. That's what I want, that's the kind of theatre that I want to do, where the audience is immersed and they're so close that they can become part of it.

I have never yet successfully done the work that I still want to do, to that end, but [that immersive kind of performance] is something that stayed with me for [a] long [time], since I think I was a child playing steeple chase through the woods; just an immersive environment where the audience can become part of your show at any moment. So that show really gave me a lot of experience and kept me working.

MLF: Did you get to a point where you said, "Now I know this is good"? Because you've had such success with [*Moonlodge*].

MK: It took me a long time . . . The other thing is there were a couple of companies, main regional theatres that picked it up. But, y'know, people aren't really *big* on solo shows and you'd be in the second space, the small space . . . but I met people, then I was invited to do various things . . .

I worked with the students for Spirit Song Theatre Company in Vancouver. I trained and worked with them, and I love to do that, I love to teach and create characters with my students . . . that was fun . . . Somehow I managed to keep working and, because I could do a lot of things and I liked to do a lot of things. I like to direct a bit, choreograph, I like to teach, I like to try things, and . . . *Moonlodge* was still being called on occasionally. [F]or instance . . . we opened the Youth and Arts Centre, that was early 90s, so right after Native Earth and being in The Cultch, Women in View,[5] y'know it started, it had a life of its own. It maybe . . . didn't get into the regional theatres in the way that I would hope to one day but it started to. The Grand Theatre did it when . . . one of the people . . . who had worked on *The Tempest* up in the North [with me] . . . became [the] artistic associate up at the Grand Theatre in [London, Ontario] so he got me, my show, into the studio. . . . [T]hat was the other thing it's like you're trying to sell your own show, like I don't know that world . . .

And then I got invited to the Dreaming Festival in Sydney. I got to play in the Sydney Opera House. It was incredible, it was in the playhouse there in a series called "Women's Business" and it was all women's solo shows [by] Aborigine women, and I was invited over to do my work there. And so then I got to see what they did for three weeks. The first of the four festivals that led up to the Sydney Olympics. So it was the first one and it was *huge*, I was so impressed! It had art from all the galleries, all the Artist-run Centres, the big art gallery on the Circular Quay was all Aboriginal art, the Shakespeare Theatre had an Aborigine adaption of Shakespeare: the dance, the storytelling, the real traditional people coming, they put a big sand pit, sand, a dirt pit, in front of the gallery and they did their work outside, all their traditional

5 Women in View (WIV) is dedicated to the documentation of females in screen-based media in Canada. The documented women range from writers to cinematographers to directors. The purpose of this organization is to bring to light the challenges women face in media-related employment to encourage more female participation in the future.

dance and song. Oh my god! Like everything for three weeks was just full . . . I was so impressed by that and I thought, "Oh, could we have that one day?" It really, really inspired me, to be in Australia. I went several times with my show there. I think probably when I formed my company [Full Circle], it would have been 1992, because I was by this time drawing on napkins and place mats in restaurants trying to figure out what we had to do to get our own thing going here and so in 1993 . . . I just wanted to gather people and work together, train together, do something together, and so that's when we started our little training workshop . . . and I met a few people [at the Dreaming Festival, there were also] a few non-Native artists who I had a good rapport with . . . It was very hard though to find people who wanted to work at this all the time, who could. It took a long time.

MLF: So you started the company in 1993? You sort of have a vision around 1992 . . .

MK: 1992, incorporated as a society and 1993, we were doing workshops, were starting to work together and I'm working primarily with people who don't have the same level of training or experience that I do, but we're working with people and I'm working in my collaborative manner and I'm trying to develop a way of working . . .

MLF: What did you create for your first show? After you developed your company, what did you have in mind?

MK: I wanted to create something that honoured the place that we were living in, so it was called *The River-Home*, and there were at least three versions of it, maybe four. That was the thing about it, it varied, it was different each time because they had a different cast, different voices, and I was always honouring the voices that were in the room so I was pulling from them but it was still based on where we are, the river, the river of life, all of those metaphors you want to use but all those different voices were around the river, were in the river with me.

Every time it would be different because it was their voices, and the collaborative way, and video image. I was really wanting to work with video images . . . from working in the Artist-run Centres in the early 90s and creating performances, exploring my voice, what form that would take, I became interested in video, installations, and all kinds of various ways you could use things to tell your story . . . We were all creating work [at Video Inn, in Vancouver] because that was a place that we were really welcome. We didn't have to write a well-written play, or whatever, the theatre demands a different kind of set of circumstances . . . And we did it [at] the Roundhouse [Community Arts & Recreation Centre] in Vancouver as if the audience was sitting on either side of the river, so it was a corridor staging, which means both ends were open so there was still the rear-projected screen. I was fortunate to get a very well-known set and lighting designer who teaches up at UBC, Robert [Gardiner] . . . And he did the two projectors from the ceiling, lighting the stage with the river running, and it was so beautiful, oh my god, and then we had the big banks of the audience on either side. It was a beautiful work . . . I still look at the video and I go "Oh man, that was . . . " I know it wasn't yesterday, obviously, I'm much older but it still has the essence of what I wanted.

I want us to find our own voice, our own way, our own forms. I don't want to write a well-written play. I'm not interested in that. I'm interested in, as Indigenous people, what is inspiration for the work and what does that form look like. It's not a proscenium stage where we all sit in the dark and the actors are on the stage. It's much more where we're involved, we're immersed in what's going on and creating staging whereby the audience feels that they're part of the scenario. They're not in that Euro-centred, colonial gazing at [the actors]. But it's a challenge to create that and I found it so hard because I was doing everything and I had no help, I had no management. I was writing the [grants and] working long hours. I had help with the video editing, a really great gal that I met at Video Inn, and we went to the Banff Centre to develop some ideas. Around that time too the Banff Centre started Aboriginal programming. I was part of the advisory [committee] to talk about the relationship of the Aboriginal artistic community and the media. It was the media people that started it . . .

[We developed] the Winter Camp and we took *The River-Home* in and we got a grant to bring a dozen of us in to Banff and work for several weeks and stage one of our performances there and work on some new video. Oh, it was a fantastic, explorative time! The challenge was where, who's going to see this? Nobody's seeing this work, only a small group of us is seeing this work, and so we're always plagued by the fact that nobody's coming to see our work. So then you don't have a chance to produce it again or it takes so much energy just to raise the money to bring everybody together and then have the time. By the time the production was done I was burnt out. I was still young and I was burnt out! [I]t took so much effort in those days and it was discouraging, the amount of production administration that I had to do myself. So I guess I learned how to do it but man it was hard! And then no one would come or the mainstream people or the artists wouldn't come and see the work, and then your own community [would] come but there's not that many of you anyway, you know what I mean? Who's going to be influenced by it? Who's going to see it and talk about it and understand it?

MLF: So would you say those conditions plus your experience in Australia led to the creation of the Talking Stick Festival?

MK: I would say definitely, because along the way we'd get invited to maybe go over and be part of a reading at Weesageechak Festival in Native Earth . . . We always had fun playing with ideas, I mean that was the one thing that came out of Vancouver was we weren't writing plays the way that other people were doing them. All that creative exploration of form was really what we were about over here, whereas they [companies in eastern Canada] were more about writing plays. And they did a lot of plays over there . . . there's like pages of lists of all the productions that maybe only had one production or two productions at most, but we were much different over here, we were creating different kinds of work.

MLF: So, I just want to recap that point. So the Artist-run spaces here on the West Coast, plus working this way you've got artists at various spaces with those skill sets and you've got the spaces themselves to do the shows, and you have a much more liberated idea about what a performance consists of, so you have a totally different . . . aesthetic and development [of Indigenous performance practice] here. Because if you're a young person watching and getting a sense of what's possible, your mind is going to be so much more broad from seeing and experiencing these other kinds of storytelling or theatrical events, really, rather than being confined to this idea of a "play" and sitting there, disengaged, watching some people do some stuff [in central Canada].

MK: Yeah, and that may or may not be speaking to you because you may not be reflected on that stage. And it's not your story; the story of your people . . . because we didn't have any theatres, only Artist-run Centres. It was a different, eclectic kind of audience too, that's really interesting, and I really enjoyed seeing some of those non-Native performance artists. There was such a diversity of voice. Anyway, it didn't matter if they were Native or non-Native, [there] was just a diversity of formative styles. It's fantastic. And you were encouraged! Nobody was critiquing you because it wasn't a well-written play for god's sake, or you didn't have to live up to some standard; it was a much freer environment for exploration.

MLF: So you landed in the right city. You could've been somewhere else and been really constrained. So did you decide, "I'm going to start a festival" or did the ensemble training come before the Talking Stick?

MK: Well the training aspect, that's how we started. We started workshopping together, so that was always kind of a part of it from the beginning, training together. And I wanted to create an ensemble, that's why *The River-Home* was very much about the ensemble, but I discovered that I kind of stuck out like a sore thumb because I had an incredible amount of training and nobody else did. It's very hard to create a chorus if you stick out like a sore thumb. And I felt disappointed by that. And the other thing is that because they [her students] don't have all that level of training and because they're not necessarily performers or they're [not] going to be able to have a performing career or life like I had, then therefore they were always going away, and so I was always left alone. Again. It was very tough, it was very tough that way. And then of course some people would start to work on their own ideas, their own careers, so of course they'd go away, so nobody was really into working together with me . . . So I was always the pioneer, I was always the one ahead of the pack, I was always the one out exploring the world by myself, coming back, trying to get something going, then discovering that I could for a short time, but nobody stuck around because they were pulled in other directions or [to] any number of things and I was left alone again.

It was very disturbing. It was very depressing actually, I was depressed for many, many years but I would keep working, I would gird my loins and go again . . . I've been pretty lonely most of my life . . . Even my own father said to me before he passed away, we were having a few heart-to-hearts and he said, "You're always a pioneer, it's just who you are, so just accept that. You're always going out, exploring places, so we saw that, we knew that, we could tell that." And I thought, "Oh, well, okay then, suck it up. You're not going to have everything you want necessarily." And it's taken a long time and there's still areas where maybe I don't trust myself enough, but I'm learning that maybe I have a lot of respect for what I've been able to do, finally. I'm really hard on myself, I've learned that, whatever I was taught, it took me a long time to not be so hard on myself, to respect myself, to trust; [I] have a lot more trust in my ability now. I've gone through a lot of heavy things and come through them so that I know that I can. There were many times where I thought I wouldn't make it, emotionally.

My depression was very long, was full of lots of sorrow, and I just struggled along and I would just work. Work and work and work. I became a real workaholic for a long while because I couldn't face the loneliness. I'd stop and I would feel like I hadn't done anything because the world around me wasn't changing, and all this effort I put in wasn't making any difference. There were no Aboriginal works on stage still, I was still having to fight with some of the officers for granting. I was still having to struggle with getting audiences of any kind, you know what I mean? So, for a long time it felt like all the effort made no difference in the world and so I would keep working. I'd say, "Oh

I'll just do that some more and I'll just work on it," and so it took me a long time to really recover from my own sense that I wasn't doing a good enough job, or that I couldn't do the job, or that there were no people around to help me do the job.

It took me a long time to get to a place where I could see some results of my efforts and to be satisfied with them, that maybe I was going to see it all in my life. So maybe I'm trying to build an ensemble with the company and they keep swimming away like salmon and I'll have to keep bringing them back. I just kept holding that circle and it was very hard but I started to realize, "Oh my god, I do respect the work and the effort that I've done. I am starting to trust myself. I am giving time to myself and giving things to myself and I am doing for other people too, I'm giving to other people, I'm doing this for them as well as for myself."

So it's starting to feel like I've started to embody that teaching that was my life's work with the company. [After] twenty-three years I'm starting to feel like, "Oh, it's cool, it's working, time has passed." It was long and slow for a long time but in around 2000, almost ten years after I formed the company, we did the Talking Stick Cabaret and I had met Lisa Ravensbergen[6] by the phone; we didn't meet face-to-face for like a year and a half or two years before we actually saw each other . . . Somehow I'd reached out and I'd found her, we'd found each other and we started to create the cabaret and we wanted to bring disciplines together . . . [W]e had a woman who had poetry but she wanted to do some movement, she liked dance so we brought poetry and movement together, so we helped direct that and we brought along someone from the Artist-run Centre movement, we brought along Daina Warren[7] who was in visual arts and performance art. [W]e brought her in to be an assistant director intern to work with Lisa. We did this with a number of people, we started to try and work with a couple of disciplines together because we were interested in that, and so that's how the Talking Stick started. It was

6 An established theatre artist of Ojibway/Swampy Cree and English/Irish descent.

7 Co-Curator of the Talking Stick Cabaret, she is currently (as of 2016) the co-director at Urban Shaman Contemporary Aboriginal Art Gallery. She is of Montana Cree descent.

built around [a concept that] we'd seen at the Firehall Theatre; we saw that as part of their dancing . . . they did an eight-minute-max [timeframe] so [every performance] was eight or nine minutes [long]. [For Talking Stick, performances also] had to be an eight or nine-minute piece and we have eight or nine performances that night, and we opened that year with Chief Ian Campbell[8] and some youth that he was working with, singing and doing their stories and dancing, and so we started with that, so we used the local cultural community. So that's been my whole thing—bringing these people together. That's how the festival started. We slowly added things each year.

MLF: So from one night of cabaret performances to week-long, two weeks even . . .

MK: [Because of the enthusiastic response we have received, the event has been consistently growing in size and popularity.] We're trying to condense it right now because it's getting a little out of hand. There's just a lot to program and a lot of work so we're at about twelve days right now, I think . . .

You see, I wish I had known about some of that [the positive responses of viewers] earlier because it was very hard to do the festival because, again, you have limited resources . . . I always feel like I don't know what the hell I'm doing . . . [But now] I have a bit more help which is great, and people that have consistently returned to help build the company so it's not a different team every year; there's a core of people and so that's very fulfilling. But the first number of years I was so exhausted at the end of every festival that I just want[ed] to stop and go, "It's too hard, I can't do this," because it's so nerve-racking, you know what I mean? And I'm really sensitive and I'm on my case all the time so I kind of get wound up and it's exhausting. Now, I know it's been a few years where I've started to relax and go, "Oh man, it's been great all along you just didn't realize it! You just have to relax . . . " I always have that kind of inferiority complex, this kind of thing that I'm trying to live up

8 Campbell is a chief of the Squamish Nation who acts as their representative and elected political spokesperson.

to, that maybe I'm not quite good enough. It's still there, it's like a little underground stream, it's still there . . . [but] I managed to get over my depression, my suicidal thoughts. I had help for a while and I went into counselling . . .

For a long time I had a lot of traditional practice that kind of grounded me, so that helped too. [I found encouragement from] a certain number of artists who I respect, who have been in the field, in their own artistic field, and have struggled with their own communities and built things in their communities that nobody else could have done. [A] lot of women, mostly women, [were the ones to build in their communities]. *Moonlodge* was all about the women in my life. I've had a lot of women in my life who have made me crazy but they also are fun and funny and were supportive of each other and of me . . . I was adopted [and had a complex childhood, with] blended families, four mothers, all this stuff, but the thing is, I realize—I did a talk, and then I realized as I was talking about them [my teachers and family] . . . "You know what, even though I had a very complex early childhood and lots of families and mothers and whatever, the thing is that I was wanted. Like everybody wanted me. Like I was loved." I mean, maybe I didn't feel, you know you're a kid, you're a teenager, you don't feel like people loved you, but really everybody loved me . . . Those people loved me and wanted me and when you have that kind of background, no matter the troubles you go through, eventually I started to realize, oh my god, that's how I'm able to go out into the world and challenge myself and face all these things, it's because people gave me a sense of strength and security early on, along with my own, of course . . .

[F]or me the festival is that too, it's a place where I don't care how developed or how perfect your work is, I want you to feel like you can come back year after year if you can afford it, [if] we can afford it. I want to find a way to give voice to any voices at any level of development. Yes, we want some very excellent work, we want some highly professional work, but we need to give our people a chance to try things, we need to give them a stage at different stages of their own development. So that's why the festival is very eclectic, cross-discipline . . . [and] not very formalized yet, the development part of it. Some work comes to us that's still very raw, some work comes to us farther along, some work is already on tour, but it changes because it depends on what's out in the world. Right now, there's not much theatre this year touring 'cause it's taken a long time for our people to not just create the show but then have the capacity in their company to make the touring path, to figure out how that all works, to find other companies that want to tour their work to two or three places. It's taken us a while to get there but we're getting there . . . We come back to the fact that we're building on people, we're building on their strengths and we're building on relationships we've built with, like, Café Deux Soleils, who welcomes what we're doing every year. We're building on the Roundhouse and the relationship we have there and that's really fabulous. Last year the Powwow outgrew the space, it was huge . . . so this year the Powwow's going to go in the big gym now because it's so big. I mean [the festival's] just, it's built on who's available to do what. I used to say I keep holding the circle even if nobody's in it because that's all I can do, I want everybody to contribute, I want them to feel valued, I want them to know they have a voice that can be heard, I want to facilitate different performance styles that come out. It's for anybody that has a desire to perform and create something for the stage or stages, I want to give voice to that. I want our people to come, just be inspired by the art, I want the artists to take their place in that circle of tribal leadership which includes the healers and the teachers and the storytellers and the dancers and the singers and the theatre-makers and the spoken word artists. I want those artists to be recognized, and they're still not. We're still dealing with issues where our politicians are so colonized and having to grapple with their own issues that they don't fully understand how important the artistic voice is. So we have some work to do, but I think we've come a long way. Maybe I don't have fully what I want but what I do have is, there are people gathering every year for this and finding ways to work across the country, inviting people . . . Different people are doing different work. I'm invited to [the United States], I'm invited to Australia, so I'm starting to feel like, "Oh wow, there's more of us to do this and to help make all of this happen now."

Margo Kane was the first Aboriginal woman in BC to run her own theatre company. West Coast Indigenous cultural practices informed her creativity.

In addition, Vancouver's artist-run gallery spaces encouraged experimentation with multiple narrative perspectives, which inevitably affected Kane's development as an artist and contributed to a unique vision that has enabled Talking Stick to become "Western Canada's premier Indigenous Performing Arts Festival" ("TSF 2017"). As her story indicates, Margo Kane has nearly exhausted herself in pursuing her goals for Full Circle and the Talking Stick. This arduous path has evolved into a big annual festival that includes scholarly conversations about the field of Indigenous performance. As this discourse continues to grow we will inevitably recognize the impact of Margo Kane's work on Canadian theatre history.

PART 2: RETURNS AND RE-EXAMINATIONS

AFFECT AND THE UNPRODUCED: 420016 SGT. ATKINSON W.S. AND *GLORY HOLE: A PLAY OF THE GREAT WAR OF 1914–18*

ALAN FILEWOD

There is a way in which theatre history can be understood as the reconstruction of the ordinary as traced through the survival of the exceptional. Most theatre work disappears without record; most plays go unpublished; most performances are remembered by only a few. To say that the narratives we construct out of the work that does survive are always metonymic is a critique not just of positivist historiography, in which extrapolation from evidence fills its interstices to create an image of wholeness.[1] It is also true of post-structuralist historiography, which, in challenging the wholeness of the positivist narrative, is no less dependent on incomplete evidence, the trace from which something can be surmised and modelled.

Of the materials that comprise evidence, the most slippery for theatre historians may be the playtext because although it is material, it is at the same time indeterminate. On the surface the text is a graspable thing. It may or may not be a record of production, it may or may not be important,

---

1 The shift from positivist to post-structuralist historiography does not mean that one supersedes the other. Both modalities have their purposes and values; they pose different questions and produce different results. In Canadian theatre historiography, that shift was profoundly influenced by feminist theory that challenged researchers to situate themselves in the field of inquiry, and to question its social and political premises. The Canadian experience of that shift is the throughline of the collected essays in my book *Theatre Histories*.

it may or may not typify a genre, period, or movement. A text that may be of immense importance to a literary scholar may be of little interest to a theatre historian, and vice versa. But the indeterminate playtext is an unstable and exceptional object. We can posit that most plays in human history were never preserved as texts (because not all cultures wrote them out, or because, as today, market economics dictate that only a tiny fraction of performed plays appear in print), and for this reason extrapolating conclusions about the theatre culture of a place and time on the basis of its surviving texts inevitably leads to error.

If the published text is an uncertain trace, what do we make of the unpublished text, the play that exists only in manuscript? When the manuscript is stabilized by an awareness of a theatrical provenance, we assign value and significance according to the importance of the author, or because it reveals something previously unknown (such as a theatrical technique or an overlooked or marginalized community). But if there is no recorded theatrical provenance, no record of performance, the unproduced and unpublished play's historical value is contingent on the significance of the playwright; an unproduced manuscript of an unknown play by a famous writer may command critical attention (although historically detheatricalized as "closet drama") but the provisionality of an unproduced play by an unknown or obscure writer is a problem for theatre historians. If noticed at all it offers evidence of little more than the aspirations of its author, who may or may not have been typical of an unknowable number of others. Consequently the unpublished and unproduced play is an erratic idiosyncracy that disturbs theatre-historical structures of evidence-based critical value.

This essay is an exploration of one such play, *Glory Hole: A Play of the Great War of 1914–18*, written by William Stabler Atkinson in 1929. It arises out of a larger project that examines a body of plays, some published and performed, some performed and never published, and some that remain unpublished and unperformed, written by returned soldiers after the First World War. These plays are a small part of a substantial literature produced by soldiers. In *The Canadian Experience of the Great War: A Guide to Memoirs*, Brian Tennyson includes two plays among the 1,885 texts—memoirs, autobiographies, letters, diaries, poems, short stories, and novels—in his exhaustive list of life writing from the war. Tennyson makes the point that he included novels and poems (he does not explicitly mention plays) "on the grounds that they also constitute a creative form of memoir of their author's war-time experiences" (xxv).

These plays, whether written as commemoration or personal exorcism, constitute a form of life writing, defined by Marlene Kadar as a critical practice that "comprises texts that are written by an author who does not continuously write about someone else, and who also does not pretend to be absent from the [black, brown, or white] text himself/herself" (10).[2] Approaching these plays as life writing, as what Kadar and Jeanne Perreault call "unlikely documents" of "auto/biography," solves one theatre-historical question by contextualizing them as *theatrical* but not *theatre*, but it raises another: if they are to be understood as life writing, what do they have to offer to theatre historiography (Kadar et al. 2)? Why include a discussion of such a play in this disciplinary conversation? The answer, I suggest, is that they offer insights into both the object and the practice of theatre history. The unproduced and unpublished play has no stage history to reconstruct and no apparent evidential value. But it has inferential value because it can be a window into theatre culture that reveals how people in a time and place perceived theatre and its affects. In that case, the atypical may provide insight into the horizons of theatrical possibility that are occluded by practice at a given moment, as was the case of Georg Büchner's *Woyzeck*, written in 1836, published in bastardized form some forty years later and unproduced until 1913, and now recognized as a major precursor of German Expressionism.

For the historian the unproduced/unpublished play can foreground the sensuality of research, a delight in the play of primary evidence, detective work, and storytelling that may itself be the deep subject of the process. A historiography that is process-centred rather than argumentative is one that seeks

2 Life writing is in this way a broader, more inclusive term than "autobiography" or "memoir" (both of which carry the weight of long histories of literariness, critical discourse, and convention). It can include texts as diverse as diaries, websites, Twitter feeds, photo albums, medical records, and graphic comix. See Rifkind and Warley, and Smith and Watson, *Interfaces*.

comprehension rather than proof. Approaching William Stabler Atkinson and his play in this way enables me to use a life writing methodology to frame an answer to the deeper puzzle his play presents.

Life writing, according to Kadar, "is a way of looking at more or less autobiographical literature as long as we understand that 'autobiographical' is a loaded word" (10). She adds that

> this way of seeing literature is really a way of knowing that does not necessarily judge the text according to how "realistic" the autobiographical truth may be, and therefore how good or bad the life disclosed. If anything, it acknowledges that the involved reader takes great pleasure in inventing a persona for himself or herself as he or she reads. (11)

The pleasure we take in inventing the persona of the author is the sensual pleasure the historian finds in amassing evidence into narrative. Sensual pleasure is always about affect, and when I examine *Glory Hole* in terms of its affective power, I can begin to understand why a veteran in a small town in the interior of British Columbia might choose theatre as his medium when he sat down to write his war experience, knowing it had almost no chance of production or publication. Taking Tennyson's figure of 1,885 war memoirs as a benchmark, we can surmise that one of every three hundred of the six hundred thousand Canadian soldiers in the war produced some kind of memoir, and that fewer than a dozen of them wrote plays. This inquiry begins with the observation that a soldier who recorded his experience in dramatic form was an exceptional figure. Therefore there had to be a reason that compelled dramatic form. And that is a theatre-historical lure. The answer, I will suggest, has to do with the affective power of theatre and its ability to recreate and re-embody memory.

The text of *Glory Hole* is one of 781 play typescripts collected by the late theatre historian Patrick O'Neill, who in the 1980s identified them as Canadian submissions to the United States Copyright Office in the first half of the century.[3] As part of his never-ending quest to catalogue every play ever written in Canada, he arranged to have them microfilmed, and they are available today in the forty-six reels of the *Canadian Drama Collection* held by Mount Saint Vincent University (MSVU). Although it contains some plays that have entered the canon (by authors such as Merrill Denison and Herman Voaden), the O'Neill codex is a valuable scholarly resource primarily because it is an archive of the unproduced and unpublished. The published catalogue itemizes the plays by thematic topics, in which historical and religious themes predominate. These plays are more often than not melodramas and comedies. Their dramatic models tend to be derived from the popular stage or classical drama, but a few startling examples of visionary modernism stand out. We might consider these authors for the most part to have been hobbyists, or amateurs (although that word has such shifting meaning it is not really useful). But they were also aspiring "professionals" who made the effort to copyright their work internationally.

Between 1928 and 1941 Atkinson registered fifteen plays for copyright. Most of them he listed explicitly as comedy (such as *Ogopogo, or The Sea Serpent: a farce comedy of the Okanagan, Kelowna, B.C.* in 1926 and *The Chicago Lady Duxington: a comedy in three acts and one set* in 1931). O'Neill mentions Atkinson in passing in his article on Carroll Aiken and his Home Theatre in the Okanagan, and alludes to a performance of Atkinson's comedy *Meet the Wife* in Vernon in February of 1925 (71). Atkinson was more than an amateur; he was a practising playwright for a theatre that barely existed. He had some significant successes: his comedy *So This is Canada* (about three returned soldiers trying to make a go of fruit farming in the Okanagan) ran for six weeks in Vancouver and was picked up by the impresario John Shuburg, who promoted it as "World's Funniest Show" and gave it a Western Canadian tour in October 1926 ("'So This is Canada'").[4] Atkinson had a

3 O'Neill actually located 933 plays, but 152 of them were too fragile to be microfilmed (Mount Saint Vincent iii).

4 *So This is Canada* had some modest success after its tour: in 1934 it was in the repertoire of the Holden Players's first season in Muskoka.

follow-up success in 1931 with his *Man from Saskatchewan* at the Dominion Theatre in Winnipeg.

All but one of Atkinson's plays are comedies. The anomaly is *Glory Hole: A Play of the Great War of 1914–1918.* It is one of twenty-eight plays in the MSVU catalogue under the heading of "World War 1914–1918" (28–29), and one of three that can be reliably ascribed to a returned soldier by matching the playwrights with army attestation papers in Library and Archives Canada's *Soldiers of the Great War* database. The other two, *The P.B.I. or the Mademoiselle from Bully-Grenay*, written by four returned soldiers in 1920 at the University of Toronto, and *Dawn in Heaven*, by Simon Jauvoish, a veteran of Vimy Ridge, both received theatrical productions. Jonathan Vance alludes to all three of these plays in his study of Canadian memorialization of the war, *Death So Noble*, but only comments on them cursorily. To Vance, as a military historian, the plays are not important in and of themselves; they are of interest only to the extent they demonstrate social responses to the war. He dismisses *The P.B.I.* because of its "stock characters and improbable situations" (84), mentions *Dawn in Heaven* only to give a brief but very inaccurate plot summary (111), and cites *Glory Hole* only for the fact that one of the main characters is francophone (252).

Because Vance is focused on the themes, motifs, and politics of commemoration, he does not examine the plays as serious war literature. But seeing them only as minor representational dramas precludes seeing them for what they really are: theatrical re-enactment memoirs that embody lived experience. They are re-enactments insofar as they restage the procedures and experiences of the past, and memoirs in that they re-enact the personal experience of the authors. It is understandable that historians might not perceive the actual operation of re-enactment in these plays because they are cloaked in genre conventions, which reframe testimony in terms of narrative plot and showbiz tropes. Sidonie Smith and Julia Watson offer an insight into this in the introduction of their influential *Getting a Life: Everyday Uses of Autobiography*, when they write that "*In telling their stories, narrators take up models of identity that are culturally available.* And by adopting ready-made narrative templates to structure experiential history, they take up culturally designated subjectivities" (9; emphasis in original). *The P.B.I.* offers a clear example of this. It is a collective act of life writing and witnessing, with four principal authors and a cast of forty veterans, for whom the play was participatory documentary re-enactment and testimony built on the material culture of their war experiences. But that documentary impulse is contained in the frame of a light melodrama that in itself re-enacts the skits of the front-line entertainment troupes like the Dumbells that Jason Wilson documents in his book *Soldiers of Song*. For the soldiers who took part in the show (and in the veterans' productions of R.C. Sherriff's classic British war drama, *Journey's End*, noted by Vance), the plays were an opportunity to form up in uniform and relive the collective experience of the daily routines of the trench and *estaminet* (the makeshift cafés, often in farmyards, that were central to the social experience of the soldiers behind the lines). Both *Glory Hole* and *Dawn in Heaven* contain a scene in which a soldier is picking lice from the seams of his tunic.[5]

5 *Dawn in Heaven* is another clear instance of life writing. In its key episode the idealist protagonist, who joined the army to fight in what he believes will be the final war of human history, is subjected to the notorious Field Punishment No. 1, in which soldiers were tied with their arms outspread to a wagon wheel for two or three hours a day, despite rain, mud, and lice. Jauvoish's service record indicates that he, like his protagonist, was sentenced to "3 days F.P.No.1 on 26-2-17" for "refusing to give his name and number to an N.C.O." (Service Records for Simon Jauvoish). Jauvoish served with the 46th Battalion, nicknamed "the Suicide Battalion" because of its high casualty rate. The 46th took part in the assault on Vimy Ridge, and Jauvoish was shot in the shoulder and sent home two weeks later.

THE EYE THAT SPEAKS

Far, far from Ypres I long to be,
Where the Allemand cannot get me;
Think of me crouching where the worms creep
Waiting for Sergeant to sing me to sleep.
Sleep? Sergeant—sleep?
Does anyone sleep?
They certainly sleep; everyone sleeps.
But not—surely not, Sergeant!
Not in the Yeep-res Salient.
—Marching song of the 16th Battalion CEF (Urquhart 154)

In his preface to *Glory Hole*, Atkinson is explicit about the need for theatricalized documentation. He had begun writing the play in 1928 but seems to have run into problems with the generic requirement to shape his memories into a dramatic plot with its conventions of reversals, intrigue, and denoument.

In his "Author's Note" (dated 8 February 1930) he writes:

> "GLORY HOLE" had been laying aside for over a year—then I had the pleasure of reading "Journey's End" as published in the Royal Magazine in three issues. I have followed the doings of various companies through the medium of theatrical papers ever since it was produced professionally [*sic*], and enjoyed the wonderful reception it receive [*sic*] everywhere. It seemed to me to fill a long felt want in the hearts of those who having been through the war, still had a desire to see it again in the part of the looker on. "GLORY HOLE" had a trench as well as a dugout scene originally—I now decided one set adequate, and that it could safely be split into various scenes without taking away from the interest of the play. I summarized it again, taking my characters from actual persons for the most part, the experience being my own, except for the climax, my own battalion being withdrawn two days before it blew up, but the trench wasn't

> empty when it did, I was told, there being much loss of life—whether this is so or not I have no actual proof—only hearsay to go by . . .

The single set—an officers' dugout—of Sherriff's *Journey's End* appears to have given Atkinson the theatrical solution of a single confining set that enables narrative compression. That compression is the element that makes the play work as drama and memoir, because it reconciles the conflicting demands of dramatic narrative and documentary re-enactment. Setting the play in the compressed atmosphere of a claustrophobic and filthy trench dugout, Atkinson found a way to minimize plot and keep most of the narrative action offstage.

The returned soldiers of the Great War who recreated their memories in plays like *Glory Hole* shared a need to remember theatrically, to stage the affect and sensory experience of war, but had no dramatic models other than popular genres. They were naive modernists, who adapted conventional dramatic forms to replay their memories. In doing so they invented new, provisional dramatic forms—provisional because some of these plays were performed only once, and most not at all. *The P.B.I.* is a parade of embodied memory that documents routines, activities, character types, and language (in effect the cultural experience of the war as shared by forty veterans) staged in a comic sequence of songs, vaudeville skits, sentimental monologues, and melodramatic plot twists. In contrast, *Glory Hole* is an explicit restaging of what one man saw and heard in the trenches. It positions the spectator inside the author's witnessing body but at the same time distances us from identification. There is no point of empathic connection to any of the characters, although the play invites us to pity the doomed teenaged soldier whose fate gives the play its minimalist plot. One of the characters, who rarely speaks but coughs incessantly, may be construed as Atkinson's staged self, but the play does not foreground him. As we see what Atkinson saw, we also see what he remembered; we see him seeing himself in memory.

Behind the thin scrim of the "ready-made narrative template" of a war drama, *Glory Hole* is a staging of memoir and re-enactment. It can be authenticated by contextualizing it against Atkinson's experiences as documented by another genre of life writing: the official dossier. In Atkinson's case there are two: his homestead file in the Saskatchewan Archives and his military service file in Library and Archives Canada (Service Records for William Stabler Atkinson). Both provide information about his war service. Together they produce a simulacrum of his life—a hollow biography that connects the facts but tells us nothing about the person who lived them. But they do confirm the events of the play as memoir and its affective structure as re-enactment. The dossiers provide the outward narrative frame of his service; the play reenacts the affective experience of it. This goes some way toward explaining Atkinson's "desire to see it again in the part of the looker on" because to see it again as a spectator recreates the feelings of sharing cramped, dangerous space with men he knew and the experience of watching their interactions, entrances, and exits. The autobiographical I that speaks is, in memoir reenactment, the eye that watches.

THE SERVICE RECORD AS LIFE WRITING

As an "unlikely" form of life writing, the dossier presents the subject as constituted by institutions. The dossiers in this case tell us little about William Stabler Atkinson, but they tell us a great detail about 420016 Sgt. Atkinson W.S., 16th Battalion CEF. Atkinson's service record is a 138-page file that records in detail not what he did, but what was done to him as a soldier between 1915 and 1919. The army was a regime of ongoing surveillance that routinely monitored him to ensure that he conformed to orders and was healthy enough to be sent to die. The file records his physical data; his unit assignments and transfers; his military character and promotions; his pay; and, most tellingly, his medical boards, examinations, lab reports, weight charts, and hospitalizations. We know, for instance that when he enlisted in 1915 at the age of twenty-four, he stood 5'11" and had no tattoos; when he was discharged he had a tattoo of a snake on his right leg and his chest expansion had shrunk an inch and a half. He had a "Very Good" military character, but once had his pay suspended for five days for gambling. The outward details of his military life are plentiful but they tell us nothing about who he was. Reading him a century later, we can only know him as the army knew him.

When Atkinson joined the army in Winnipeg on 8 January 1915, he gave his profession as "accountant," and indeed for the rest of his life he worked in clerical and administrative jobs. But he was also a failed homesteader for whom the army offered a relief from precarious work. Four years earlier, at the age of twenty, he had taken over a homestead grant near Prince Albert, Saskatchewan, which had been abandoned a year prior by the original grantee. Atkinson appears to have been a recent immigrant.[6] The land grant carried minimum conditions of ground breakage and cultivation, and on the evidence of the homestead file, Atkinson failed to meet them. In a 1913 statement "[i]n the matter of his homestead," he explains his failure to meet his cultivation requirements: "Lungs weak through pleurisy of 3 years ago, & and at last have been compelled to come to town to be under care of a doctor who says it is necessary for me to rest and be attended until I'm fit."[7] This is the first reference to the pleurisy that would plague him in France and would eventually compound as tuberculosis.

Atkinson travelled eight hundred kilometres to Winnipeg to enlist in the Canadian Expeditionary Force (CEF), and was in a hurry to get there. The

---

6 Atkinson's army attestation form lists his birthplace as Darlington, Durham, England, in 1891, and in the Canadian census of 1911 there are only two William Atkinsons listed. One lived with his family in Smiths Falls, Ontario, and the other lived in a worker's hotel in Regina and gave his occupation as bricklayer. We know that William Stabler Atkinson was a resident of Regina in 1911 because that was his city of residence for the purpose of the homestead grant. Positing that the man listed in the census was in fact William Stabler Atkinson, we know that he arrived in Canada in 1908. He would have been seventeen at that time, which makes him just old enough to have completed the six months of military service with the Northumberland Hussars (a Territorial Army unit in England) that he claimed in his attestation papers.

7 In 1918, Atkinson again appealed to retain the homestead, explaining that his absence was due to war service: "Special Circumstance: Breakdown thro. active service & gas shell. Was examined by Private Medical Man in Prince Albert (Dr. Chisolm) before going to Winnipeg to enlist. He said old illness had utterly disappeared, & I was sound. Paid own fare to Winnipeg to get access as soon as possible."

sixteen battalions that comprised the First Contingent, numbering 30,170 men (two thirds of whom were born in the United Kingdom), had reached their recruitment goal quickly, and—largely untrained, underequipped, and barely organized—had landed in England in October 1915. When Atkinson signed up, the Canadian army had not yet entered battle; the original contingent was in the process of being organized as the First Division in preparation for embarkation to France. Atkinson was one of 9,363 men who signed up in January 1915 (Morton and Granatstein 30). But why travel to Winnipeg and not Prince Albert or Regina to sign up? In mid-December 1914, the Cameron Highlanders of Canada, based in Winnipeg, had announced the formation of the 43rd Battalion CEF in the second wave of recruitment. For whatever reason, Atkinson wanted to enlist in that unit, rather than one of the units announced at the same in time in Saskatchewan. Perhaps he felt the romantic draw of a Highland regiment. Although the numbered battalions of the CEF were intended to supplant the regimental affinities and rivalries that were common in the Canadian militia, battalions raised for Highland regiments kept the kilt (which features prominently in *Glory Hole*).

The 43rd Battalion trained in Winnipeg through the winter and spring of 1915, and on 1 June 420016 Pvt. Atkinson W.S. embarked on the troopship SS *Grampian* in Montreal. After a month of training at the Canadian depot at Shorncliffe, he was sent to France on 13 July in a reinforcement draft for the 16th Battalion (the famed Canadian Scottish) of the First Division to replace the casualties sustained in the Second Battle of Ypres. He joined the battalion at the front near Ypres on 22 July and would spend the next nine months there.[8]

He was "tall, erect, not rugged but fairly well built," his complexion was fresh, his eyes were blue and his hair was fair, but Private Atkinson would not stay healthy for long. He was recurrently sick during his nine months in the trenches of Ploegsteert and the Ypres Salient, suffering from lice-induced

8 The official war diary of the battalion records the arrival of Atkinson's draft: "386 reinforcements from 43rd Battalion arrived. They were accompanied by five officers who made examination of the trenches and return to England this afternoon (Friday 23rd). Reinforcements met by Pipe band. All Camerons: fine healthy lot of men" (*War Diary*).

trench fever, influenza, bronchitis, appendicitis, and inevitably pleurisy. The gist of his war service is captured tersely in the "Medical Report of an Invalid" written in July 1917, at which point he was posted as a sergeant to the Canadian Casualty Assembly Centre (CCAC) at Shorncliffe, near Dover:

> 9 mos in France—full duty. To England May 1915; Trained at Shorncliffe. During training was always fit—always able for route marches ie.
>
> To France, July 1916, as a draft of 16th Battalion. No delay at base—right up the line, carried out full duty, in and out of the trenches until 31 Aug, 1915, when he had an attack of trench fever & was off duty for 8 days at Bailleul. Returned to unit and again carried on until end of November, had pain in left neck, bad cough and was sent to CCS [Casualty Clearing Station] Romarin with Bronchitis and Pleurisy, then to 3rd FA [Field Ambulance] at Bailleul for 9 days. Returned to duty and remained with battalion until receiving leave on March 31st, 1916. When crossing to England caught cold, was an outpatient at Woodside V.A.D. [Voluntary Aid Detachment] Hosp, Darlington for short time, then for 5 days was in Queen Alexandria Hosp. Millbank Road—Discharged to CCAC, Folkestone. Boarded there on April 17 & given 8 weeks B.B. duty. On Aug. 14 again boarded for dyspnoea—no TB found in sputum. In April had been appointed to staff of medical department of CCAC and moved with that unit to Shoreham in October. Suffered from a chill when arriving at Shoreham & cough again became tuberculosis. On leaving Folkestone was 172 in weight, one month after being in Shoreham was 160 1/2 lbs. Cough full sputum, was examined & found Positive TB. Was sent home for one month, gained 4 lbs which increased to 8 lbs later on. Named

> to Hastings with CCAC, cough became worse. Present weight is 160 lbs & frequent exams of sputum give Positive T.B.[9]

He seems to have been an effective and reliable staff NCO (non-commissioned officer), promoted to corporal on assignment to the CCAC, and to sergeant four months later. The result of his final medical board in England was a recommendation that he be invalided to Canada for further medical treatment, and in his final months in England he had the rare privilege of a domestic life. The reference to "home" is unusual, because unlike British soldiers who could return to their homes on leave, the Canadians were in Europe for the duration. But at some point in that year of administrative service and recuperation, Atkinson met a woman and fell in love. He married Edith Marion in March 1917, and for a period of time was one of the few Canadian soldiers, and certainly one of the very few enlisted men, who could return to home and spouse at the end of the day. His commanding officer, Captain A.W. Hough, went out of his way to accommodate him:

> C.C.A.C. Hastings June 19th. 1917
>
> Dear Sutherland
>
> The bearer is No. 420016 Sgt. W.S. Atkinson, who has been with me over a year and is now being invalided to Canada as a T.B. Patient. He is coming through the Canadian Military Hospital, and proceeding to the Sanitarium where he is going to help in the orderly room until the boat sails. Can you arrange for him to sleep out as his wife is here and has been for at least three weeks. I have spoken to Capt. Wellwood about him, and if you can allow him this privilege while he is at the Can.Mil.Hosp. I will be greatly obliged.

---

9 I want to thank Julie Crawford, who answered a Facebook appeal and deciphered a particularly illegible sentence in the handwritten statement. Social media is a new resource for theatre historians that gives new life to Raphael Samuel's observation that "[e]ven as a form of literary production, history is the work of a thousand hands" (18).

If military records can be seen as expressing sympathy, they do so for Atkinson. There was nothing remarkable about his actual combat service but he did his job ably and appears to have thrived in administrative duties.

Atkinson sailed from Liverpool and debarked in Québec on 27 September 1917, was examined once more by a medical board and pronounced unfit, and dispatched by train to Victoria, the home of the Seaforth Highlanders, one of the feeder regiments of the 16th Battalion. He was part of a contingent of 238 Western Canadian soldiers that met cheering crowds in Winnipeg on 3 October ("238 Heroes"), and along with fifty-nine others proceeded to Victoria, where he was again examined and sent to the military sanitarium at Halcyon Lake both as a patient and a staff NCO, and then to the Balfour military hospital unit until his discharge took effect in 31 January 1918. His wife remained in England until the war was over.

For most of the soldiers of the CEF, the discharge would be the end of the military service. But Atkinson appears again in uniform in 1919, rejoining the CEF just months before its official termination. Having been in and out of military hospitals for two years, he re-enlisted as a staff sergeant in the Canadian Army Medical Corps and was assigned as an administrator to the military unit in the Vernon Jubilee Hospital; he was discharged as medically unfit on 25 November. The CEF disbanded shortly thereafter, but Atkinson remained in Vernon and continued to work at the hospital; in the 1920 edition of *Wrigley's British Columbia* directory he is listed as "Sec. Jubilee Hospital." He and Edith lived in Vernon for the rest of his life. He built a career as an accountant, served as secretary of the school board for several terms, was twice provincial secretary of the progressive United Farmers of British Columbia, founded an income-tax consultancy firm, and wrote plays. The last entry in his official service file is a note from the Department of Veterans Affairs that word had been received from his wife that William Stabler Atkinson died in the Jubilee Hospital on 26 February 1963.

PRIVATE ATKINSON IN THE HOLE

Glory Hole is life writing/life staging, but it is not a re-enactment of what Atkinson did; rather it is a restaging of what he saw and heard. The play recreates his visual and aural fields with exactitude and is filled with scopic detail. The play is set in a dugout, a small room dug into the face of a traverse trench immediately behind the front line. The detail of his description is holographic:

> The dugout is a sandbag earth affair, with one step down into it from an entrance at rear. Dirty scraps of paper on the floor which should be of earth. Some loose sandbags and two bundles of new ones, also a couple of empty long ammunition boxes and old iron flat bottomed dish pan which can be used for candles as some pieces of wood stuck out from the walls as candle brackets. There is a small hole on the wall at LEFT with some metal lath in from to form a grate—this is for a charcoal fire—at right there is a hole in the wall which is a listening sap—a pile of earth to the side gives impression of the excavation. This sap is for listening in on enemy operations which consist at this time of a mine under this sector stretching along under a hundred yards or so of front line. (iii)

Atkinson includes a drawing that shows the listening sap—the glory hole—as a vertical shaft accessed through a hole dug into the wall; in his sketch we can see the top rung of a protruding ladder. The effect of the description is one of claustrophobic and wretched containment, which is intensified by the call for "an impression of heavy or drizzling rain" to underline "the misery of the mud and continuous downpour" (iii).

The action of *Glory Hole* never leaves that mud, and the plot is as spare and bleak as its setting. The play begins with a squad of soldiers settling into the dugout as they relieve British troops of the Durham Light Infantry. There are six men crammed into the dugout that is their home, and Atkinson is extremely specific about their appearance, their kit, their voices, and their manners. We are seeing what he saw:

Fig. 1. William Stabler Atkinson's manuscript sketch of the dugout.

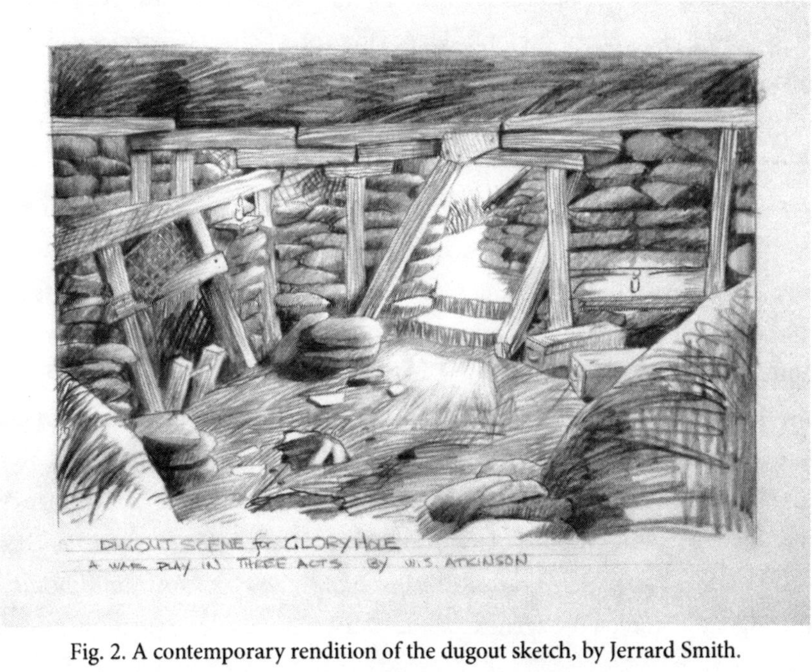

Fig. 2. A contemporary rendition of the dugout sketch, by Jerrard Smith.

> Private Monteith . . . 'Monty'
>
> Public school education—morose until gets his rum. Sort of ne-er-dowell [*sic*]. DRESS: steel helmet—usual pack and equipment—greatcoat—rubber sheet over shoulders. He is a middle aged man and a philosopher—a distinct type of remittance man. UNIFORM can be Seaforth kilt—gas helmet—khaki hose tops—has bottle of wine with and other sundries as may be referred to during action of play. (iv)

The specificity of the Seaforth Highlanders kilt is an authenticator that locates the play in time and place: these are men of the 16th Battalion, Atkinson's unit, and they have just moved into the Salient after a relatively quiet but miserably wet and muddy winter near Bailleul, twenty kilometres southwest of Ypres, rotating between divisional reserve and trench duty. In the nine months that Atkinson had been in the unit, the Canadian divisions had undergone extensive changes in tactics, training, organization, and weaponry, as they transformed into the professionalized fighting force that a year later would take Vimy Ridge. When they moved into the Ypres Salient—described by one historian as "the most miserable, dangerous place on earth"—in the spring of 1916 as part of the newly formed Canadian Corps, the 16th occupied the far right end of the Canadian trench sector (Zuehlke 6.1).

The stage reference to the steel helmet is equally significant because it enables us to pinpoint the exact date of the action. As noted in the battalion's war diary, the soldiers of the 16th Battalion had been issued steel helmets for the first time on 28 March, and moved into the Salient to relieve the British 50th (Northumbrian) Division (of which the Durhams were a part). This is the date of the action in the play, one day after British and Canadian sappers had blown a six-hundred-metre section of German trenches at St. Eloi, five kilometres south of the 16th's position; as described in the Canadian Army's official history, "the eruption blotted out old landmarks and collapsed trenches on both sides like packs of cards" (Nicholson 139). For the next three months the Salient would be the scene of some of the bitterest fighting in the war as both sides fought desperately to control the seven craters and the heights of Hill 60 and Mont Sorrel. In the time Atkinson had been in the unit, from July to March, the 16th lost 158 casualties out of a unit strength of approximately 1,200; in the ensuing five months they would lose another 653 (Urquhart 405).

The 16th remained in the Salient until August, when they moved south to the Somme front. But by that time, Atkinson was in England. From 11–22 March he was hospitalized with influenza and appendicitis. After a week in the trenches where *Glory Hole* is set, he was granted leave, fell sick on his way to England, and entered hospital in London. His leave was extended and two days later he was struck off service with the 16th and taken on by the CCAC. This was the nominal administrative assignment for all invalided soldiers, but Atkinson's clerical experience resulted in assignment as a non-commissioned officer on its staff.

In his nine months in France, Atkinson had a relatively easy war, compared to the horrors that the 16th would experience in the next two years. Between August 1915 and March 1916, the battalion spent a total of twenty-three weeks in the trenches. But the summer months at the Ploegsteert front had been quiet as both sides dug in to hold the line in a low-key war of attrition; the battalion historian, who served as a company commander, later referred to it as "the delightful summer of 1915" (Urquhart 123) and described the time as "the least trying of any fighting engaged in by the 1st Canadian Division" (117). As the soldiers of *Glory Hole* move into the Salient they are about to experience a new, bloodier war.

Much of the literature of the war by its veterans emphasizes the camaraderie of the trench, but in their muddy hole the six emotionally numb men of the section treat each other with rough disinterest. Half of them are British—two Englishmen and a Scot—and their lines are written in dialect. They crack jokes, insult each other, and argue. By the end of the play three of them are dead. The plot, which begins late in the procedural action of the play, focuses on a teenager, "about 16 or 17 years old," who has just arrived with a draft of reinforcements and remains in abject misery and terror throughout the play. The only man to comfort him is "Frenchy," a Métis lumberjack who is the butt of racist banter, particularly from their sergeant, who expresses contempt for ethnic diversity in a Highland regiment:

> You know—Corporal Rugg—ye've a hell of a mixed bunch in this section—(LOOKS THEM OVER)
>
> CORPL.
> I find them alright Sergeant.
>
> SERGT.
> Sae many nationalities—Sae many nationalities—
>
> FRENCHY.
> Dere is only wan nationality in dese battalions Sergeant and dat iss Canayen—say all come from Canadaw—eh?
>
> SERGT.
> (LOOKS AT HIM AND IGNORES THE REMARK) I'd like to know how they got intae it—it's a mystery to me. (I.II.11)

That diversity was a fact across the Canadian Corps but was particularly notable in a Highland regiment where the kilt was a talisman of ethnic tradition. Half of the battalion had been raised in Vancouver, and its complement was representative of the demographics of an immigrant frontier city.[10] The novelty

---

10 Urquhart writes that the initial complement of the 16th that sailed in 1914 comprised of

> natives of every province in Canada except the Yukon territory; of forty-seven of the counties in England, of the Isle of Man and the Channel Islands; of all but two of the counties of Scotland, of the Shetlands, the Orkneys and most of the Western Isles; of twelve counties out of all the provinces of Ireland; of four of the counties in Wales; of all the dominions and seven of the dependencies and crown colonies of the British Empire; of nine of all the states of the American Union; and of Mexico, Italy, France, Holland, Denmark and Sweden. (15)

of that diversity is captured in Eric Kennington's painting, *The Conquerors* (originally titled *The Victims* until protests by veterans forced a change), which depicts men of the 16th marching through a modernist landscape of ruin and desolation.

Kennington, a British war artist who was attached to the 16th in 1918, foregrounds the ethnic diversity of the troops: in the centre of the painting the

Fig. 3. Eric Kennington's *The Conquerors*. 1922, oil on canvas. Beaverbrook Collection of War Art, Canadian War Museum, CWM 19710261-0812.

eye is drawn to a man whose colour and features mark him as Southeast Asian; marching two ranks behind him is a man who appears to be Indigenous. Like the rest of the platoon, they are wearing the kilt, and it must have seemed exotic to the British, as it does to the sergeant, that the Canadian Scottish were, in fact, not.

For the men of *Glory Hole*, who have little in common and no shared identity, diversity is the subject of banter and bickering. When the routine of the play is established—quarrels over shifts down in the listening sap, the coming and going of work details—they hear a rumour that the Germans have planted explosives in a horizontal mine shaft beneath the trench and that according to a prisoner it is to be blown in three days' time. Mine warfare was an ongoing activity in the trenches, as both sides sought to take control of the ensuing crater to breach the enemy's front; in his study of mine operations, Simon Jones writes that in 1916 the British dug and blew 750 such mines and the Germans 696 (113).

The men of *Glory Hole* receive word that the battalion will be pulling back from the trench before it blows, but one section of each platoon in the company must leave a man to walk the trench and fire occasional shots so that the enemy will not suspect the line has been evacuated. They accept this brutal decision as just one more misery of the war, and draw lots for the doomed man and an alternate. Danny, the persistent cougher, loses the draw but he begins to hemorrhage shortly thereafter, exits to report sick, and dies before he can get medical aid. The onus then falls to Frenchy, who has been concealing a gut wound. As officers and NCOs come and go, issuing orders and threats, the men prepare for their withdrawal. Frenchy dies of his wound, and in the end the only one who can be left behind is Ross, "the Kid." The last moments of the play leave Ross alone, terrified and crying in the dugout with Frenchy's body:

> —an odd shot is heard—he looks up and the green light of the star shells—verify lights or flares—shine on his face—he wipes his eyes with his arms—another shot his heard—nearer—he looks at his rifle—takes off the cloth cover—comes back to Frenchy—takes

his hand—leaves dugout and a single shot is heard as if from Ross. (III.I.13)

Glory Hole is a play about conjuring an abject space, populating it with memory, and gradually emptying it. Contained in this space, the sparse plot functions not as narrative but as affective pressure. In the trenches, the men are always waiting—for the next work party, for the next explosive or gas shell, for the next to die—and the procedural routines of trench life are intensified by that waiting. In *Glory Hole* the countdown to the explosion is both an evocation of that pressure and the device that provides forward momentum in the plot. That plot is itself a re-enactment of the trench experience: nothing happens in the dugout except daily life and work; men come and go, to live another day or die, until the inexorable logic of war leaves a young teenager to die alone in the mud.

This skeletal plot, "based on hearsay," is the only obvious invention in the play. Its anti-sentimental minimalism is a remarkable theatrical achievement because it foregrounds the activities rather than the dramatic actions of the characters. We witness rather than feel, and in that way reoccupy Atkinson's visual and aural field of memory. We see and hear the action from the standpoint of a soldier coughing in the back of a dugout, as the war passes in and out of his vision. The play embodies that memory through ethnographic stage descriptions that recreate the rituals and patterns of trench life: how men watch each other closely as they take turns sipping rum from a tin cup; how they fold their kilts as bedding on the mud floor, "taking care to place seams just right with creases" (18); how they play soccer in the cramped dugout with a ball of muddy paper; the play of light from explosive shells and flares. At the same time, Atkinson recreates the aural field: the sound of incessant rain, intermittent artillery and machine-gun fire, the bits of doggerel the men recite to make conversation, their accents and the tempo of their speech.

More successfully than the other plays by returned soldiers, *Glory Hole* strips the artifice of genre and stage convention from restaged memory, because Atkinson was experienced enough a playwright to understand how minimal a plot can be to do its work. Elsewhere, another veteran of the trenches was inventing a new theatrical mode that could move beyond plot for similar reasons of re-enactment and documentation, but Erwin Piscator's political documentary theatre was an operation of cultural forensics in the service of revolution, and it developed in a crucible of artistic modernism. For William Stabler Atkinson, writing for theatre in a small town in the interior of BC, *Glory Hole* was a theatrical exorcism, and the only politics in it are the negotiations of men struggling to survive. "Once we began to look forward to the end of the war—now we don't even look forward to tomorrow," Monty says to Ross (II.II.10). Atkinson's notable innovation in the play is the testimonial affect of that trauma through precise re-enactment of the experience of living and witnessing it. As life writing its affective power recreates the author's sensorium in the (assumed) spectator so that memory is persistently re-embodied, and this may explain why Atkinson chose to write it as a play rather than a novel or a conventional memoir. Its theatricality may be subjunctive but *Glory Hole* stands today as an ethnographically dense cultural artifact of the war. It is also, despite its provisionality, a major contribution to Canadian theatrical modernism. Unnoticed and until now unremarked, it is a reminder that for the theatre historian the unproduced play is also the not-yet produced. The suspended and indeterminate space of the not-yet reminds us that the theatre-historical narratives we construct are themselves always provisional and temporary.

BEYOND PRIMARY SOURCES: USING DANCE DOCUMENTATION TO EXAMINE ATTITUDES TOWARD DIVERSITY IN THE MASSEY COMMISSION (1949–1951)[1]

ALLANA C. LINDGREN

What are the source texts that underpin the creation of primary sources? How can these documents help us to reconceptualize primary sources and the cultural narratives they construct? These questions are of increasing interest to researchers. For instance, scholars have recently reignited interest in Raphael Holinshed's *Chronicles of England, Scotland, and Ireland* by examining how the two editions of this book influenced Elizabethan perceptions of history, historiography, and politics, including—though extending beyond—attitudes detectable in William Shakespeare's history plays.[2] In so doing, they have re-emphasized the importance of Holinshed's *Chronicles* as an influential ur-source.

To transpose these questions to twentieth-century Canada, the Massey Commission Report is a rich and helpful case study. Tabled in 1951 as the culmination of the Royal Commission on National Development in the Arts, Letters and Science, which is more commonly known as the Massey Commission in recognition of its chairman, Vincent Massey, the report is key to understanding the history of cultural nationalism in Canada. It is arguably one of the most important federal documents related to Canadian culture.

---

1 I would like to thank Hayley Evans for her assistance in turning my archival sources into searchable text.

2 Most notably, see Kewes et al.

Yet parts of the report are based on earlier source texts: briefs that interest groups submitted to the commission as well as the transcribed testimony generated as the commission travelled across the country to hear directly from Canadians.[3] In other words, the report is a primary source that is informed by and in dialogue with other primary sources.[4]

The point here is not to dwell on how best to categorize the report, but to remind ourselves that the genesis of primary sources might have a material presence in the form of other sources, and these source texts should be consulted to determine if they augment or alter our understanding of the main subject.[5] In the case of the Massey Commission, an examination of briefs and testimony demonstrates how source texts sometimes illuminate, complicate, or even contradict the cultural narratives espoused in the report.

To explore this assertion more fully, this essay focuses on dance-related documentation to argue that reading the Massey Commission Report through one subset of its source texts foregrounds a debate about the role of diversity within the larger project of Canadian cultural nationalism—a plurality of opinions robustly presented to the commissioners, but largely muted in their report.[6] This process of reading means that researchers need to locate

---

3 The resulting archival material is now part of the Massey Commission's fonds at Library and Archives Canada in Ottawa.

4 It is also possible to argue that the report is simultaneously a primary source and a secondary source. It is a primary source when the commissioners' views are promoted and a secondary source when the commissioners comment on the briefs and testimony generated during the duration of the Royal Commission.

5 The issue of source texts needs more scholarly attention. For a more general discussion of primary sources and historiography, see Dobson and Ziemann.

6 To be clear, the concept of diversity within the context of the Massey Commission extended primarily to the ethnicity of European groups coupled with largely paternalistic concerns for the country's Indigenous population. Commentary about religious diversity and the tensions between English and French Canada are also present in the archival documentation related to the Massey Commission, but do not feature in the dance-related documentation.

and analyze testimony that was omitted from the report by training the eye to notice gaps and exclusions in the text.

There were, of course, many different interest groups that participated in the Massey Commission and created source texts that influenced the writing of the Massey Commission Report. Many of the related documents also offer insight into views about diversity in Canada. This essay, however, focuses specifically and exclusively on contributions that referenced dance as a means to demonstrate how this art form—often a neglected source of historical evidence in Canada—can be used as an analytical tool when pursuing cultural history topics. In so doing, this article invites a reconsideration of dance sources as vital and instructive to Canadian performance history while simultaneously noting that dance sources exemplify constitutive, but underanalyzed, elements that have factored in the creation of documents of political as well as cultural importance.

THE MASSEY COMMISSION

Before delving into specific examples, it is helpful to understand the Commission's mandate. In 1949, the Massey Commission was tasked with advising the federal government about how best to engage with post-secondary and cultural institutions.[7] Specifically, the Massey Commission was to provide recommendations about "the principles upon which the policy of Canada should be based, in the fields of radio and television broadcasting" as well as how to manage the following national institutions: the National Film Board, the National Gallery, the National Museum, the National War Museum, the Public Archives, the Library of Parliament, and the creation of a National Library (*Report* xvii–xviii). In addition, the commissioners were asked to make

7 The other commissioners were Arthur Surveyor, a civil engineer from Montreal; Norman A. M. MacKenzie, the president of the University of British Columbia; Georges-Henri Lévesque, the dean of the Faculty of Social Sciences at Laval University; and Hilda Neatby, a professor of history and the acting head of the Department of History at the University of Saskatchewan.

recommendations about how Canada should engage with UNESCO as well as national voluntary organizations involved in the areas the commission had been directed to examine. Although these parameters were the main focus, the Commission of Appointment granted latitude to the commissioners "to examine and make recommendations, without limiting the general scope of their inquiry" (*Report* xvii). One year into the Massey Commission, Prime Minister Louis St. Laurent requested that the commissioners also comment on methods for internationally disseminating information about Canada and suggest ways to preserve historical documents (*Report* xxi).

The Massey Commission received briefs and met with stakeholders as it travelled across the nation. The commissioners visited a total of sixteen cities in the ten provinces, holding public hearings at which over 1,200 witnesses provided testimony. The commission also received approximately 460 briefs from a wide range of stakeholders, including interested arts groups, government institutions, volunteer organizations, universities, businesses, private broadcasters, and private citizens (*Report* 8). To supplement their cross-country consultations, the commissioners requested forty "special studies" related to a variety of subjects.

Previous writers have noted that the Massey Commission Report, which helped to shape early federal cultural policies and advocated for financial support for the arts, perpetuated an elitist and colonialist aesthetic twinned with a nationalist impulse that appears to align with Massey's personal suspicions of mass culture and the influence of the United States as well as his anglophile aspirations. Other aspects of the Massey Commission that have been of interest to scholars include the political genesis of the commission and its critical reception, the report's prescriptive attempt to initiate remediation through government involvement in cultural activities, the commission's comments about UNESCO within the context of the Cold War, and the Arnoldian and Methodist influences that thread through the report's pages.[8]

The commission's engagement with diversity, however, has not been fully explored. This omission is unfortunate because, although the report is

---

8 See, for instance, Litt; Finlay; Upchurch; and Edwardson.

largely viewed as espousing an orientation to British ideals, it also contains numerous direct and indirect indications that the commissioners respected diversity. Notably, Part One of the report provides an overview of the briefs and comments shared with the commissioners while they were gathering evidence. As a result, there are sections that address the performing arts, folklore, traditional handicrafts, and "Indian" arts, in addition to other topics. Acknowledging the significance of traditional cultural practices, for example, the commissioners wrote, "Canadian folklore forms an important though neglected part of our history and of our traditions" (*Report* 232). Immigrants from Central and Eastern Europe were validated in the report in a section outlining handicrafts in Canada. A passage quoting a brief submitted by the Canadian Handicrafts Guild in Montreal was included:

> Handicrafts—the practical arts, like other forms of art, can be a great force in the integration of a national culture in society in fostering mutual appreciation, co-operation and unity of spirit between widely diverse age groups, social groups and newly arrived racial groups. (237)

Despite their apparent support for the potential for handicrafts to facilitate understanding and national harmony, the commissioners demurely claimed that handicrafts fell under provincial jurisdiction (*Report* 237).

Similarly, more than once the report praised Indigenous cultures, framing their importance in national terms:

> We have been frequently reminded that Indians by tradition are craftsmen of a very high order; and that to allow their traditional excellence in technique, their taste and originality in design, and their power of adapting their skills to the use of new materials and to the production of new types of articles to die out for want of encouragement would be to do an injury to all Canadians, Indian and white alike. (241)

These two examples, which are representative of the tenor of Part One of the report, often echo statements presented to the commission, but do not illuminate the wider social contexts of the concerns and ideas about race and ethnicity that were presented to the commissioners. Moreover, this section often simply and selectively paraphrases assertions espoused in certain briefs and testimonial statements without considering the aggregate importance of these perspectives.

The only mention of diversity in the report's formal recommendations—Part Two—reflects an attempt to be sensitive to French-language interests in the broadcasting sector and the National Film Board (297 and 313). In other words, this section, which arguably was more important than Part One since it offered a plan of action for the federal government, was largely silent on the issue of diversity. As a result, further research is needed to address the tacit debate about diversity embedded in many of the briefs and statements made by witnesses who appeared before the commission, but which ultimately did not appear in the report.

THE NEGLECTED TESTIMONY OF DANCE SOURCES[9]

Dance might seem like a peculiar source of historical evidence for any topic beyond itself. Furthermore, within the context of the Massey Commission, the validity of the art form was questioned on more than one occasion. Though it is precisely this uneasy relationship with the commission that makes dance a particularly interesting—if unusual—way into the report.

9 I am proposing the phrase "neglected testimony" as a companion for American historian Henry Guerlac's concepts of the "intentional record" and "unwitting testimony," later recast slightly by British historian Arthur Marwick as "witting" and "unwitting" testimony. Whereas Guerlac's and Marwick's terms focus on intentional and unintentional information embedded in documentary sources, neglected testimony references historical evidence that is overlooked by the researcher. See Guerlac 799; and Marwick 172.

In 1948, Prime Minister Louis St. Laurent was approached about the possibility of a Royal Commission to study arts funding. Initially, he was not interested. Jack Pickersgill, an influential federal bureaucrat, remembers that the prime minister couched his reluctance in terms of dance:

> I knew the very idea of such a commission would have been rejected by Mackenzie King as ridiculous and I was not sure how St Laurent would receive it. I was not really surprised, however, that [Brooke] Claxton and [Lester B.] Pearson were able to persuade him that such an inquiry would be in the public interest as well as being good politics. He was persuaded largely because the Commission was to deal with broadcasting and federal aid to the universities and his sympathy for aid to the arts was, in the early stages, very limited. He once said to me he was not very enthusiastic about subsidizing "ballet dancing." (139)

The reason for St. Laurent's alleged aversion to funding ballet is not clear. Perhaps he thought ballet was trivial and supporting it would make his government look like its fiscal priorities were skewed. Perhaps his comment was a reflection of homophobic fears that the ballet world was a haven for gay men.[10] Or perhaps he felt that ballet was a "foreign" art form or too "high art" to be accessible for most Canadians. Whatever his concerns, St. Laurent only agreed to the Royal Commission when the mandate was expanded to include the issues of broadcasting in Canada as well as federal funding for universities (Pickersgill 139; Vance, *A History* 359).

Just over forty years later, historian Paul Litt published *The Muses, the Masses, and the Massey Commission*, a seminal study of the Massey Commission. Litt was clearly aware of the presence of the dance submissions. In his discussion of cultural diplomacy he cites Joseph Whitmore, the chairman of the Canadian Ballet Festival Association, who promoted the cultural

10 For a more detailed discussion about homophobia in Canadian ballet during the mid-twentieth century, see Lindgren, "The National Ballet."

diplomacy potential of ballet when he appeared before the commission. Yet in evaluating the effusive claims of the popularity of "high art" culture by groups that had submitted briefs and had appeared before the commission, Litt trivializes the art form by stating that "[d]espite the impression conveyed by such reports, Canadians were not yet donning tutus *en masse* and taking to the streets to prance and pirouette to the strains of the lute" (169). While Litt's depiction could simply have been an attempt at playful imagery, it is interesting that the other arts are not editorialized in the same belittling way that forecloses serious analytical engagement.

Litt's motivation perhaps can be explained by feminist epistemology, which provides a useful framework to help us think about dance as an under-accessed historical source. According to feminist philosopher Miranda Fricker, "identity prejudices" (27–29) can lead to "testimonial injustice," when individuals or particular demographics of people are dismissed by those in power because who they are is equated with a lack of credibility (9–29). Dance artists are rarely consulted as authorities on Canadian history or cultural nationalism. Indeed, no doubt many choreographers and dancers would vocally reject the expectation that they be anything but experts on their art form. Nevertheless, we should not conflate people who dance with the historical sources they generate. The latter inescapably can be placed in dialogue with the aesthetic, economic, and socio-political contexts of their formation and dissemination.

The ephemerality of dance performances possibly compounds the situation as scholarly rigour usually involves verifiable—and therefore retrievable—evidence. Yet, as I have argued elsewhere, this perceived disadvantage is a moot point:

> It's true that the exact moment of a particular dance event or activity or "enunciation," if you will, cannot be studied repeatedly in the same way that a play script or musical score or painting can. Similarly, while digital recordings of dance can be useful, they remain flawed and limited as research sources. That said, how do we study the Second World War or any historical event? Through their material remnants. Dance is no different. ("The Other")

This situation is unfortunate because the arguably marginalized status of dance in Canadian society, in general, and the academy, in particular, has contributed to the relative lack of scholarly attention this art form has received. The growing body of Dance Studies literature generated primarily by scholars in the United States and the United Kingdom, however, has repeatedly demonstrated how dance can function as a means to better understand identity politics, social trends, and the implications of political decisions. For scholarship in Canada, this idea—that dance research can provide access to past attitudes and values—has been slower to find acceptance.

In the case of the Massey Commission, dance-related documentation can help us to see the commission in a new light as a forum for mid-twentieth-century ideas about diversity. To this end, the remainder of this essay focuses on three categories of dance—folk dance, Indigenous dance, and ballet—represented in the Massey Commission fonds as a means to uncover the multiple and sometimes oppositional attitudes toward diversity voiced to the commissioners.

FOLK DANCE

It is not surprising that submissions from groups advocating on behalf of different ethnic groups often addressed the issue of diversity. These groups were not lobbying for dance directly, yet their opinions disclosed an assumption that dance, along with other artistic activities, was a vital marker of their traditional cultures and ethnicity, while simultaneously helping to create social harmony in Canada through intercultural engagement. The Association of United Ukrainian Canadians (AUUC) was a particularly articulate and assertive advocacy group. In the program for the 1946 Ukrainian-Canadian Folk Festival in Edmonton, which was included as a supplement to the AUUC's submission to the commission, Peter Prokopchak, the national secretary for the AUUC, claimed that his organization saw culture as the means to fostering goodwill and alliances among Canada's diverse ethnic communities:

> We feel that by nurturing and encouraging the development of Ukrainian songs, music and folk dance, and weaving these grand traditions into the pattern of Canadian cultural life, we are promoting richer and friendlier relations, understanding and co-operations with our fellow Canadians.

This mandate of intercultural unity was reinforced in June 1947 when the AUUC sponsored the participation of dancers in the Art Gallery of Toronto Folk Festival.[11] The program for the festival, which was also included in the AUUC submission, featured a greeting from then Prime Minister Mackenzie King that validated the concept of cultural diversity:

> The meeting together of groups representing many of the varied streams of culture which make up Canadian life should prove to be a striking demonstration of the richness of our cultural heritage. It is, as well, a visible sign of the development of the unity of Canada; a unity all the more unique because of the diversity of the interests it represents.

Within this context, group dances both symbolized and demonstrated that the kind of unity envisioned by the AUUC was inclusive and did not privilege the few performers who had achieved the highest technical and artistic mastery according to a hierarchical register in which rarity of ability equated with excellence. Specifically, the AUUC brief suggested that culture should not be reserved for the elite nor "high art . . . experts of the concert stage." Instead it ventured that "culture is the life expression of the people. Because it springs

11 This sentiment anticipates the tenor of comments espoused by Prime Minister Pierre Elliott Trudeau when he introduced Canada's official policy of federal multiculturalism in the House of Commons on 8 October 1971: "National unity, if it is to mean anything in the deeply personal sense, must be founded on confidence in one's own individual identity; out of this can grow respect for that of others and a willingness to share ideas, attitudes and assumptions."

from the people, is theirs by birthright." It advocated for "mass" performances in which participation, not technical excellence, was valued (Association).

This kind of inclusiveness was seen as antithetical to the aims of the ballet lobby groups and was a part of a debate that extended beyond the Massey Commission. In 1954, for example, the final Canadian Ballet Festival included folk dance ensembles as part of its program. Canadians with heritages from Finland, Denmark, Czechoslovakia, France, and Germany participated. None of the previous festivals had featured folk dance or any kind of dance beyond ballet and a few modern dance groups. The inclusion of folk dance in the final festival perhaps reflected the fact that the larger dance companies had moved on. The Royal Winnipeg Ballet, which had been a perennial favourite at the festival, did not participate in the 1954 gathering. Similarly, the National Ballet of Canada, which was only founded in 1951, but had already achieved critical success, opted not to attend. The advent of television also provided jobs for performers hired to dance on the variety programs. It appears that by 1953 the festival was contracting in response to the professionalization of theatrical dance in Canada—a success it had helped to create. Therefore, it is possible that the organizers of the festival realized that they needed to expand its scope.

Not everyone, however, approved of the appearance of folk dancers on the same stage as ballet dancers. When *The Globe and Mail*'s Herbert Whittaker reviewed the festival, he pronounced that ballet required sustained study and expertise while folk dance was simply recreation, and therefore did not belong on the concert stage ("Showbusiness" 12).

The Massey Commission Report was less harsh, voicing support for folk traditions:

> We are sympathetic to a point of view frequently suggested to us that folklore forms an essential part of Canadian culture; indeed, for many of our people, the traditions of folklore are stronger and more productive than the more formal type of Canadian history taught in our schools and colleges. It is, of course, true that in many parts of the world national culture has its strongest roots in and draws much of its

> sustenance from folk-music, folk-dances, folk-tales and, in general, from popular traditions; and it would seem to us an unfortunate and even a great national loss if the background in music, in art, in craft skills and in the popular traditions generally of our varied peoples in Canada should, through neglect and indifference, be forgotten. [. . .] It is suggested that means be found to make known the very considerable material that has been collected but not published. (233–34)

Tellingly, despite its words of encouragement, the report offered no concrete plans beyond repeating a call to disseminate folk culture through publications—a suggestion that had been introduced to the commissioners by Marius Barbeau, the influential Canadian anthropologist and folklorist ("The Fountain-Heads of Canadian Culture").

INDIGENOUS DANCE

Ethnic associations were not the only groups to use dance to advocate for diversity. Marginalized individuals and organizations attempting to assist these people used dance—along with the visual arts and theatrical performance—to highlight ongoing social injustice and to advocate for a more inclusive and culturally diverse Canada. Most pointedly, on 28 October 1949, the commission was in Victoria, British Columbia. One of the representatives of the Fraser Canyon Indian Arts and Crafts Society who appeared before the commission was George Clutesi, a member of the Tseshaht First Nation.[12] In his conversation with the commissioners, Clutesi stated:

> It has been proven time and time again that the Indian can rival the white artist in producing what is one hundred per cent Canadian Art. [. . .] Give him a chance to produce his own drama within his own surroundings. Today it is against the law for an Indian to go out

12 For more information about Clutesi, see "George Clutesi."

> there and dance his own dances. It is against the law to show what he can really do, and what he really believes in his heart. After all, it is what you people do today to show what your grandfathers did yesterday. Without that feeling in our hearts, we are going to be a lost race for the rest of our lives.

Clutesi's comments are part of a history of Indigenous activist practices in which dancing bodies functioned as sites of resistance to federal assimilationist legislation motivated by an entrenched belief in social integration through cultural erasure. Specifically, these governmental attempts at control included amendments to the Indian Act that outlawed certain traditional ceremonies and rituals such as "give-away" dances, which were part of the potlatch, and dances like the Sun Dance, which historically involved self-sacrifice and endurance in the form of corporeal mutilation. Instead of passively accepting the amendments to the Indian Act, several early-twentieth-century Indigenous leaders challenged the fairness and logic of these legislative changes and the authority of federal laws and Indian agents who represented the Department of Indian Affairs.

A small sampling of these responses demonstrates that Indigenous leaders' activism ranged from conciliatory to sharply critical. In June 1914, for instance, the *Daily Province* newspaper reported that several Vancouver Island chiefs protested the changes to the Indian Act that affected the potlatch, arguing that they should not be compelled to dispense with their celebrations any more than white people should be prevented from celebrating Christmas or other festivities ("Indians Want Their Potlatches to Stand"). In January 1915, three Indigenous men from the Duffield reserve wrote to the Department of Indian Affairs. Unwilling to accept the word of the local Indian agent, they requested official confirmation about laws that had been passed that prohibited dancing. They voiced their collective view that if a law had indeed been passed, it was unfair and should be repealed. "These dances are simple, innocent amusements—the only amusements the Indians have," they wrote. "Even the birds and mice have their forms of amusement and their liberty" (Michael, Cree, and Rabbitt). That same month, Chief John Rattlesnake of the Valley River reserve in Saskatchewan sent a letter to Ottawa. He stated that the local farm overseer had claimed that the Department of Indian Affairs wanted to stop Indigenous peoples from dancing. He wanted a direct answer from Ottawa—"I know I have the right to ask you anything like this"—and demanded a response immediately. Clutesi's 1949 comments to the Massey commissioners echoed these earlier Indigenous entreaties and reproaches, while also reflecting shifting social mores in Canada as the Indian Act was amended in 1951, repealing the wording related to the outlawing of dance practices.[13]

Clutesi's comments and the historical antecedents of resistance, as exemplified by Indigenous protests against the Indian Act's attempt to eradicate traditional cultural practices, remind us of what literary scholar Richard J. Lane has called "the complex powers of performance and of how such powers have been, or may be, utilized to counteract official, at times repressive, discourses" (268).

Clutesi was not the only individual to advocate for Indigenous peoples within the context of the Massey Commission. The British Columbia Indian Arts and Welfare Society also submitted a brief. This agency had been founded by a group of white citizens who wished "to encourage Pupils of Indian Schools and Tribal Experts in the revival of their latent gifts of Arts, Crafts and Drama, with a view to improve their economic position, to restore their self respect, and to induce more sympathetic relations between them and their fellow Canadians" ("British Columbia Indian Arts Society"). In speaking with the commissioners, Mrs. W.C. Cryer, the president of the British Columbia Indian Arts and Welfare Society, articulated the society's mandate:

> [T]o bring to the notice of the public the innate merit and deep rooted artistic talents of the Indian people by means of collections of

13 My emphasis on Indigenous activism as key to understanding the ultimate failure of the federal government's attempt to outlaw "give-away" dances as featured in the potlatch, as well as dances involving corporeal mutilation, including the Sun Dance, serves as a supplement to the large body of scholarship addressing the Indian Act. Three particularly helpful sources are Olive Patricia Dickason's *Canada's First Nations: A History of Founding Peoples from Earliest Times*, Jacqueline Shea Murphy's *The People Have Never Stopped Dancing: Native American Modern Dance Histories*, and E. Brian Titley, A *Narrow Vision: Duncan Campbell Scott and the Administration of Indian Affairs in Canada*.

> their arts and crafts, folklore, music, drama and dance, and through meetings, conferences, publications, radio broadcast and the press, to arouse the Indians themselves to a realization of their true place in the social organization of this country and to encourage them to work for and take advantage of the opportunities offered under the revised Indian Act and to prepare themselves for community service and full citizenship. (Testimony)

Dance was only one small part of the society's interest, but the reference to Indigenous dances and other traditional practices helped to demonstrate the simultaneity of paternalistic assimilationist attitudes and a desire to generate cultural pride. This apparent paradox seemed to coexist without compunction in the society's casting of Indigenous peoples as citizens, not wards of the state. Still, the society couched its hopes for Indigenous communities in terms defined by and acceptable to white people.

BALLET

The majority of the briefs and testimonies related to dance advocated for ballet. Some of the submissions were from dance organizations like the Canadian Ballet Festival Association, which oversaw the Canadian Ballet Festivals. Gweneth Lloyd, the founder of the Winnipeg Ballet (renamed the Royal Winnipeg Ballet in 1953) appeared in front of the commission as part of a contingent representing the Arts Council of Manitoba. Some of the briefs from non-arts groups, including the document submitted by the Association of Canadian Clubs, were in favour of the idea of public support for ballet and the professionalization of the art form through the creation of a national ballet company.[14] These groups and individuals repeatedly promoted ballet

14 The National Ballet of Canada was founded in 1951. There was a parallel push for professionalization in theatre, which was a factor in the establishment of the Stratford Festival in 1952.

as important to the nation while simultaneously and subtly conveying ideas about the kind of Canada they deemed desirable.

The ballet lobby and its supporters tended to minimize the benefits or possibilities of diversity, instead promoting the art form as a unifying agent. Referencing the Canadian Ballet Festivals, for instance, the Junior League of Toronto asserted that the arts, including dance, could strengthen national ties:

> The ultimate greatness and strength of a country lies in its national unity. Canada, divided geographically and by so many other factors, needs every means to promote national allegiance and pride rather than provincial. We must have more faith, understanding and development in a culture of our own—a liaison between east and west, French and English. We are prone to judge by the United States recognition of artistic talent rather than capitalize on our own. The recent Canadian drama, ballet and opera festivals have proven not only the high standard of talent available, but also the great interest of the Canadian people in our own cultural efforts.

This statement was representative of others that similarly framed the performing arts in utilitarian terms that proposed ballet—along with theatre, opera, and so on—had social efficacy because it could help unite the divergent characteristics and factions that threatened to fracture the country. Diversity, in this context, was potentially divisive. But by focusing on the so-called high arts, little room was left for other types of creative expression.

Ballet proponents further minimized diversity in Canada by promoting the art form as borderless and innately understood by all. Or, as stated in the brief submitted by the Canadian Ballet Festival Association, "The Ballet, as perhaps no other Art form, is a universal stage language." According to this universalist schema, dance was easily accessible because it did not rely on written texts or the spoken word; it was, in other words, inherently comprehensible. Dance scholarship has subsequently countered this stance, positing instead that dance, like all the arts, is culturally and historically situated.[15] The Eurocentric history of ballet and its definitions of excellence, however, were implicitly naturalized and recast as representative of all cultures.

Paradoxically, ballet advocates took care to stress that while ballet was respectable because it had ties to Europe, especially Britain, it had been adapted to become a Canadian art form. In particular, the Canadian Ballet Festival Association argued that ballet had been adapted into an art form that was wholly Canadian: "Ballet in Canada has been pioneered by dancers from Europe who have brought the training and the culture of the old world to the new. They have been joined and supported by native Canadians and they together are uniting the best of both the old traditions and the dynamic new strength that typifies Canada, to create a Canadian dance form."

To further develop ballet as a national and nationalist art form, the Ballet Appreciation Club of Ottawa, under the direction of Nesta Toumine, voiced its desire to create "purely" Canadian ballets (Ballet Appreciation Club of Ottawa). This designation signalled a desire to produce ballets that had been choreographed by Canadian choreographers, set to music by Canadian composers, designed by Canadian designers, and performed by Canadian dancers. However, it also betrayed a denial of the inherently global nature of influences on ballet.

The issue of the intrinsic Canadianness of ballet was of interest to the commissioners. When she appeared before the commission as part of the Arts Council of Manitoba delegation, Gweneth Lloyd claimed that Winnipeg was a good centre for ballet because it had many immigrants and that, in particular, Central European men were not afraid of ballet. In October 1949, Jury Gotshalks, a Lativian-born dancer who, with his wife, Irene Apinée, had co-founded a ballet school associated with the Conservatory of Music in Halifax as well as the Gotshalks Halifax Ballet, appeared before the commission. Gotshalks was asked if Canadian children were good at ballet since the commission had heard from Lloyd that the new Canadians, specifically Ukrainians, were easier

15 The majority of contemporary dance scholarship is premised on the importance of cultural specificity. That said, a few sources have been particularly helpful in forming my understanding of this approach over the years. See Desmond; Garafola; and Manning.

to train because of "their background and experience and their lack of inhibition." Before Gotshalks could answer, Mr. Merritt, a representative of the Ballet School and Halifax Conservatory of Music, interceded and refocused the conversation back on the excellence of teaching in Canada. "I think that could best be answered a month ago," he said, "when Sadlers Wells were [*sic*] in New York. One of Mr. and Mrs. Gotshalks' pupils was there, and made an audition, and [the auditioner] said this little girl was the best trained ballet dancer he had seen in North America" (Merritt). This concern about whether dance was suitably Canadian was, at its core, a debate about immigration. Post-war prosperity had caused workforce shortages, which in turn necessitated increased immigration, though the hierarchy of desirable ethnic groups now reads as a register of mid-twentieth-century racism.[16]

Ballet interest groups assuaged suspicions of foreignness by holding up the Sadler's Wells Ballet, based in London, England, as the epitome of ballet excellence. Massey pushed the issue when he noted his surprise to Gotshalks that a high-quality company like Sadler's Wells would develop in Britain as "one does not associate ballet with the Anglo-Saxon" (Massey). Despite this misgiving, the commissioners clearly agreed with equating ballet with Britishness. In outlining the conditions necessary for the development of ballet in Canada, the Massey Commission Report implied that Britain was the standard by which to measure Canadian success by presenting British examples as a model: "[T]here is nothing to prevent the growth in Canada of a national ballet comparable to that of Sadler's Wells, which beginning from almost nothing, in twenty years has become one of the world's great ballet companies" (202).

In this regard, the report reflects the views of Massey, who was wary of North American continentalism (read: American cultural imperialism) and whose aesthetic preferences were calibrated to British taste and models—an orientation no doubt influenced in part by his tenure as Canada's High Commissioner to Britain from 1935 until 1946, during which time he had

16 For more information about the history of race-based immigration policies in Canada, see Walker; and Kelley and Trebilcock.

been associated with a coterie of affluent arts supporters who were actively engaged in shaping arts institutions in Britain.[17]

Curiously, the report expressed surprise that ballet could succeed in anglicized settings while also acknowledging that past moral judgments were changing:

> Ballet has been a late-comer among the arts in Canada, but in little more than ten years it has made astonishing progress. Rather to our surprise we have discovered, as was found in Great Britain, that classical ballet for so long thought exclusively indigenous to Russia, Italy and France, can be successfully transplanted; and, still somewhat self-consciously, with other English-speaking people, we are beginning to discern the fallacy in the ancient maxim, "no sober man ever dances", on which our attitude toward the dance has for so long been based. (201)

In addition to providing a glimpse into moral anxiety about dancing bodies, this statement is also an utterance of colonial loyalty: it uses dance to align Canada with Great Britain and "other English-speaking people." In this way, ballet helps us to understand that a type of nationalism, which simultaneously embraced Canada and its imperial British heritage, was still present even though it had been waning in the decades preceding the Massey Commission.

FINAL THOUGHTS

These examples of folk dance, Indigenous dance, and ballet are not the only instances of racial and ethnic diversity that emerged during the Massey Commission. Yet, as this chapter has suggested, source texts related to dance illuminate important social issues and can provide a snapshot of attitudes

---

17 For a more detailed discussion of Massey's affinity for British culture and his tenure as Canada's High Commissioner to Britain, see Upchurch and Finlay.

within the focused context of one art form. Specifically, the folk dance proponents promoted a vision of diversity that valued multiplicity as a national asset. In so doing, these groups anticipated the 1971 federal Multicultural Policy and the 1988 Canadian Multiculturalism Act. Indigenous representative George Clutesi used dance to denounce continued legislated race-based discrimination, highlighting the social inequality that hampered any potential twinning of the terms "diversity" and "equality." For white advocates wishing to help Indigenous people through the promotion of traditional Indigenous customs, including dance, diversity was desirable, but remained within the control of white Canadians. Finally, the discussions of diversity that emerged within the source texts of the ballet lobbyists asserted a fidelity to a form of nationalism that used ballet to orient Canadian cultural aspirations toward Old World ideals. Together these examples offer a fuller picture of how diversity was defined and positioned within the larger issue of cultural nationalism in Canada.

As this essay has suggested, primary sources are not necessarily the starting point when searching for historical evidence. Indeed, without looking beyond primary sources, we might end up with a limited understanding of the range of opinions voiced about a topic at a particular historical moment. Moreover, placing a primary source in conversation with its source texts has the potential to produce alternate or even counternarratives. We also need to remember that in looking to find marginalized voices and experiences, marginalized historical sources like dance-related documentation can be illuminating. In short, we are wise to consult dance source texts when examining primary sources like the Massey Commission Report, which has been foundational for the project of nation-building in Canada. In doing so, we not only learn more about the multiplicity of views about diversity that were present in the mid-twentieth century, we also better position ourselves to resist the ossifying effect of primary sources, particularly those assuming the authority to speak on behalf of all Canadians.

UN/DISCIPLINED RE/COLLECTIONS: TOWARD AN ARCHAEOLOGY OF NONPROFESSIONALIZING THEATRE PRACTICES

ROBIN C. WHITTAKER

Michel Foucault begins his fourth section in *The Archaeology of Knowledge* with a methodological discussion that may help to unearth a broader theatre historiography, one that is reflective and inclusive of more theatre practices, including those outside the restricted, and restricting, theatre profession. The broad discipline Foucault terms "the history of ideas" is distinct from the familiar disciplines. It is "imperfect," includes "those shady philosophies that haunt literature, art, the sciences, law, ethics, and even man's [*sic*] daily life," "never crystalize[s]," is "tangential," "transient," and replete with "temporary successes," "anonymous authors," "insidious thought," and "crumbling soil." In all, it is "difficult [. . .] to fix precise limits for it" (153). It is the sort of history that radically transforms the stringent boundaries and codified orthodoxies of the inherited disciplines. Similarly, a historiography that includes nonprofessionalizing theatre practices must be attuned to the anonymity of collaborative creativity, the "temporary," the "tangential," the "transient," and the "imperfect" because all performance—professionalized and nonprofessionalizing—is, by definition, each of these.

This study draws on primary sources to review one moment in 1972, in which Toronto's all-female-run Alumnae Theatre Company, Canada's second-oldest theatre, created and premiered the first translation of Anne Hébert's *Le Temps Sauvage*. In doing so it challenges the flawed anthropomorphic narrative that has come to define Canadian theatre history as a history of professionalizing practices maturing from amateur theatricals. It considers how Alumnae has been excluded from a pivotal chapter of Canadian theatre—the "originary" moment in which Toronto's professionalizing alternative theatres introduced francophone scripts in English translation—as a result of professional bias. It re-examines the maturation discourse that weaves together double-biased conclusions about nationalization and professionalization at the moment of examining the "document" with a view to offering an alternative archaeological approach that does not necessitate a misleading hierarchical relationship between nonprofessionalizing practices and the profession. And it shows that when sticking close to original documents, researchers may avoid vague biases about aesthetic "quality" that assume nonprofessionalized practices are inferior to contemporary professionalized practices. Play reviews, costume and set designs, flyers, posters, press releases, and other collected documents provide material for intertextual readings of the detritus of past productions and illuminate the broader context of the work of Alumnae's women and men.

Among nonprofessionalizing theatre companies, Alumnae makes an ideal case study because it both predates and runs contemporary and proximate to the early work of Toronto's alternative theatres. That its members recognized the importance of translating and producing Québécois plays in translation at the same moment as the alternative theatres speaks to the undervalued awareness of the women who ran Alumnae at a time when male leadership and ingenuity was most valued in theatre. Critic Gillian Pritchard highlighted this geographical and ideological proximity to the professionalizing alternative theatres when she called Alumnae "Toronto's original alternate theatre" (10). The careful study of Canada's long-standing nonprofessionalizing theatres tells us much about various performance practices and their wider value to the discipline.

This is not, of course, how the discipline of theatre studies has traced the histories of Canadian theatre. Starting from the view that today's English-Canadian theatre is dominated and disciplined by two legitimated professional associations and an arms-length funding body, one might imagine that Vincent Massey and Robertson Davies had their way. The Canadian Actors'

Fig. 1. Costume designs, *Le Temps Sauvage.* Reproduced courtesy of Alumnae Theatre Archives.

Equity Association (CAEA), the Professional Association of Canadian Theatres (PACT), and the Canada Council for the Arts discipline a professionalized national theatre ecology considerably removed from Massey's and Davies's mid-century musings. "Our Dominion Drama Festival" (DDF), postulated Davies's character Trueman in his fictionalized contribution to the 1951 Massey Commission Report, "proves to us every year that there is the raw material of a professional theatre in Canada which might rise to very great heights" ("The Theatre" 380). Thirty-eight years later, Herbert Whittaker's 1989 entry in *The Oxford Companion to Canadian Theatre* on "Little Theatre and Amateur Theatre" whisked away the final chalk dust from a decades-long erasure of amateur production by a professionalizing discipline:

> Just as the amateurs had filled the vacuum created by the departure of the touring companies in the 1920s, so the burgeoning Canadian professionals filled the vacuum created by the cessation of the DDF activities between 1939 and 1947. [A decade later, the] Canada Council agreed and the pattern was set—cultural funding would go to the professionals. (309)

Both Davies and Whittaker were heavily invested in the DDF as governors (and, respectively, playwright and director). And both are on record as supporting the professionalization of a Canadian "national theatre." To some this might seem paradoxical, even counterproductive. Davies himself wrote in his foreword to Betty Lee's *Love and Whisky* that the DDF "was an artistic venture dedicated to destroying itself in the cause of art" (x).

These utterances—Davies's from 1951 and 1973 and Whittaker's from 1989—form nodes between which a great deal of narrativizing took place in and around the field of "Canadian theatre history." This narrative frames nonprofessionalizing, or amateur, theatre as pre-professional, and therefore a relic of an historical past away from which Canadian theatre has progressed. Promoting this narrative are professional associations which, from the mid-sixties on, have sought to nationalize theatrical professionalization on their terms on behalf of theatre artists who dream of an acceptable profession in which to work. Many amateur companies have also contributed to this narrative. Theatre scholars have averted their gaze from nonprofessionalizing theatre in favour of professionalized fare.

Yet this narrative is fundamentally vulnerable. In a spring 1974 piece in *Canadian Theatre Review*, when describing the effect of the brief but significant impact of federal LIP (Local Initiative Program) grants on the emergence of Canada's professionalizing "alternative" theatres, Peter Hay wrote that "one sometimes feels in Canada that the only difference between amateurs and professionals is money" ("Cultural" 11). Here, Hay modestly questions any simple conduit between amateur and professional practices (is the difference just salary?), thus questioning the exclusivity of the terms' definitions.

Taken as signposts, Davies's, Whittaker's, and Hay's writings inherit a language and a perspective about the relationship between amateur practices and the concomitant emergence of a "profession" in the twentieth century, one that at once acknowledges the profession's indebtedness to what was variously—in 1951, 1971, 1974, and 1989—a view of static, sometimes fondly remembered, past amateur practices. Each use the word "amateur" only insomuch as it provides a foil to the maturation of the "professional" artist, company, or nation.

UNSETTLING MASTER NARRATIVES OF THEATRE'S PROFESSIONALIZATION

During the last four decades, parallel to this rich narrative of erasures, scholars have traced the history of the field of theatre in Canada as though it were inherently organized through birth, childhood, adolescence, and maturity. Where Alan Filewod has argued that the mechanisms of empire-building in Canada followed an "anthropomorphic fallacy" and a "Victorian zoomorphic determinism" during the last century as Britain parented the Dominion of "Canada" before Canada nationalized its identity and cultural practices into adulthood (58), the critics, policy-makers, practitioners, and scholars of theatre have framed Canadian theatre within a similarly resonant maturation myth. "Canadian theatre," says Filewod, "has been formed by imperial experience" ever since the nineteenth- and early-twentieth-century touring productions and annual patriotic pageants that were purpose-built to perform the nation (of Britain or America) (56). He argues that during and since Massey's influence, the "notion of public funding" for theatre is more an "ideological strategy" than a "national imperative" wherein the acceptable forms of professional theatre under Massey were based on the parent British model, while the acceptable forms of professional theatre since the market-driven 1980s—large for-profit musicals and small for-profit Fringe plays—have been influenced by America's Broadway and Edinburgh's Fringe

Festival respectively. Publicly funded professional theatre in Canada, Filewod concludes, exists to "satisfy those who see the arts as nothing more than a showcase of national 'maturity' " (69). Indeed, publicly funded theatre is seen by fewer audiences and participated in by still fewer theatre professionals—who, in many small- and midsize locales, may be both audience and professional artist in one. With its parent (Britain) and cousin (America) ever (re)embedded in its psyche, Canada's theatre profession is always-already a "decentered text" ("Erect Sons" 69) that echoes past and imported policies and practices.

Implicit in this discourse is that the maturation of a theatre ecology is analogous to its professionalization and that as a nation matures its practices "grow up" from amateur to professional. This logic implies that to remain amateur, to not professionalize, is for an artist, a theatre company, or a nation to arrest "natural" growth. It ignores the immensely forward-thinking, creative, and participatory practices of dozens of contemporary nonprofessionalized theatre companies in Canada.

Canada's longest-running, most enduring theatre companies are its nonprofessionalizing companies, those that have eschewed assimilation with the emerging profession and its dual disciplinary trappings of management associations and unionized labour. Ottawa Little Theatre (1911–present), Toronto's Alumnae Theatre Company (1918–present), Regina Little Theatre (1926–present), and the Victoria Theatre Guild (1929–present) at Langham Court Theatre are among more than one-hundred-and-fifty companies listed on provincial "community theatre" organization websites. Audiences, critics, and participating artists variously refer to these companies as "amateur," "community," or "volunteer" theatres. In doing so they appropriate a set of inclusive terms that are as highly contested under capitalist and neo-liberal labour doctrines as the unpaid cultural practices they describe. These companies are often dismissed by professionalized artists and researchers who see them as operating outside of the disciplined cultural labour force, and therefore outside of modern artistic orthodoxy. Yet their artistic work often has grounding relevance for certain of its professionalizing participants: professionalizing artists often participate in nonprofessionalizing theatre companies early in their careers, and nonprofessionalizing companies often "train" new audiences (see R. Whittaker, "Walterdale").

There is scant scholarship on postwar (or "post-adolescent") nonprofessionalizing practices, that is, companies that do not seek to professionalize or operate within a defined profession. Says Claire Cochrane, the professional historian shuns amateur theatre as an "*ersatz*" theatre excluded from "real" theatre practice while "sitting as audience in her own favoured performance environment" (170). By synecdoche, the researcher of amateur theatre risks being called "amateur" herself and therefore studies only the profession. Drawing from the anthropomorphic discourse of the Massey Commission, in which a nationalizing theatre is one that must also professionalize over time, scholars have treated the mid-century building of the Stratford Festival and the regional theatre system as fundamental dispersions of geographical professionalization that render local nonprofessional production irrelevant, or at least unworthy of attention. Though Canada's oldest theatre companies did not professionalize, for the most part they have been ignored in historical discourses of Canadian theatre.

CASE STUDY: ALUMNAE THEATRE COMPANY'S *LE TEMPS SAUVAGE*, BY ITS OWN RE/COLLECTION

Within the received discourse of Canadian theatre history rests the emergence of francophone theatre in English translation, particularly the impact that the 1970s alternative theatres had on the production of Québécois plays in translation. As English Canadians became increasingly fascinated by Québec culture, Tarragon Theatre founder Bill Glassco, as Denis W. Johnston puts it, began "broadening Toronto's understanding of what a Canadian playwright was" by introducing Toronto audiences to Québec plays in translation (155), especially the works of Michel Tremblay. Louise Ladouceur places into context the significance of this activity by explaining that following the nationalist fervour of Canada's Centennial celebrations, Anglo-Canadian theatre artists built new spaces for new, nationalistic plays and sought to produce already-proven francophone plays in English (188). She says that forty francophone plays were produced in English during the 1970s: twelve written by Michel Tremblay, ten of which were translated or co-translated by John Van Burek (27). Tremblay's plays in particular fulfilled English-Canadian drama's "need for innovation at a critical moment of its evolution" (190), even as those translations, Ladouceur argues, stripped those plays of much of their political efficacy (28). But whereas Denis W. Johnston concludes that "[t]he introduction of Québec playwrights to Anglophone audiences became one of Tarragon Theatre's signal, and continuing, achievements" (155), what is hidden from the received discourse is that within two weeks of Tarragon's first French-to-English translation, Alumnae Theatre Company was already premiering its second.

Founded at the University of Toronto as the Dramatic Club of the University College Alumnae Association in 1918, and for much of the 1950s and 1960s popularly known as the "Coach House Theatre" (owing to one of its mid-century, post-campus locations), Alumnae Theatre Company is a not-for-profit, nonprofessionalizing theatre company that currently produces four plays each season along with its New Ideas Festival that has featured over a dozen original short plays every year for the past twenty-five years. Not including the New Ideas Festival, Alumnae has produced over sixty local or national premieres (about half of these are world premieres). Today, Alumnae states that it "is dedicated to the production of adventurous, high-quality theatre not readily seen elsewhere, and to the promotion and skill development of women in theatre" ("About Alumnae"). It promotes a threefold mandate "to produce works that offer strong roles for women; to produce works that are not often seen in Toronto; and to produce works that are written by Canadians" ("About"). Since 1972 the company has been located in the former Firehall No. 4 at 70 Berkeley Street near Adelaide Street in Toronto's residential Corktown neighbourhood. Each year, plays are suggested for production by the production committee to the eleven-member board of directors, each elected from a company membership numbering about one-hundred-and-fifty. All paying members are, by definition, active participants in the production of plays and/or the running of the company. Men who work on Alumnae productions are considered "guests"; all "members"—as has been true since Alumnae's founding nearly a century ago—are women.

On Thursday, November 23, 1972, Alumnae Theatre Company opened its second production at its current location, the then newly renovated "Firehall Theatre." It was a two-and-a-half week run for the English-language premiere of Anne Hébert's *Le Temps Sauvage*, translated by longtime company member Elizabeth Mascall, produced by Shelagh Hewitt, and directed by John Van Burek. (To procure Van Burek's services, Alumnae received one-time funds from Theatre Ontario, the Ontario Arts Council, and the Ontario Department of Education.) The play had premiered in French in Québec City in 1966, produced by Théâtre du Nouveau Monde. This was Alumnae's second premiere of a French-Canadian play in translation, having premiered the English translation of Jacques Languirand's *Le Gibet* in May 1964. In fact, it was Alumnae's third new translation: in October 1971, at a previous venue on Maplewood Avenue, Alumnae premiered, in English, *Pablo Neruda's Lives of the Poet*, translated from the Spanish by Keith Ellis of the University of Toronto's Hispanic Department and Linda Landróne de Guevera, directed by de Guevera, and assistant directed by Mascall (actor Michael Polley played one of script's three "Nerudas").

Le Temps Sauvage—which is set in a remote and unidentified area of Québec and features the matriarch, Agnès, isolating her family from "the evils and pollutions of urban life" by preventing their freedom (Firehall)—is the product of one of Québec's most acclaimed writers, though Hébert was far less known to English Canadians at the time. She had already won the Governor General's Award in Poetry for her collection *Poèms* (1960) and would later win the Fiction award twice (1975 and 1982). *Le Temps Sauvage* plays symbolically on Québec's past/present, rural/urban, and church/family conflicts.

Alumnae's archives include a number of documents pertaining to its production of *Le Temps Sauvage*. These include original costume designs for the show by Alumnae's long-time costume designer Margaret Spence; material mounted for a lobby display featuring a biography and chronology of Hébert's life with accompanying photographs; several production photographs by John Bloom; Alumnae's press release, flyers, and posters for the show; the show's program; press clippings (previews, reviews, listings) from several newspapers, as well as the text of a radio review; and the sound operator's production copy (with sound cues) of the Mascall translation.[1] The extant production photographs all feature close-ups of one or two actors. They reveal a clear intensity of acting, but the close framing makes it difficult to visually determine the overall production design. They do, however, show that Margaret Spence's rustic, warm, dark-hued costume designs were carried through. Here is evidence not of gawky, haphazard, "amateurish" production conditions but rather premeditated attention to performance aesthetics.

Fig. 2. Production photograph of *Le Temps Sauvage*. Reproduced courtesy of Alumnae Theatre Archives.

The collected press clippings are also revealing. Appearing just two years after the "October Crisis," the play inspired the city's anglophone reviewers to

1 Like the material collected in the company's other production files, these documents have been gathered in an ongoing effort from the board, their archivist Catherine Spence, and previous archivist Agatha Leonard.

emphasize the production's political significance. The *Globe and Mail*'s Herbert Whittaker, the *Toronto Star*'s Urjo Kareda (Hewitt's husband), the *Toronto Citizen*'s David McCaughna, and the *Canadian Tribune*'s Martin Stone (the reviewing pseudonym of playwright Oscar Ryan) each argued that the production was important not only for its portrayal of "an old Québec in willful isolation" and for being "a new play by an internationally celebrated Canadian poet and novelist," as the production's publicity poster accentuated, but also for appearing just ten days after Tarragon Theatre opened the English-language premiere of Van Burek's translation of Michel Tremblay's *Forever Yours, Marie-Lou.*[2] Importantly, the production of the Hébert and Tremblay plays that month, said Whittaker in his review, "gives us a chance to learn about fellow Canadians and what they respond to in their more advanced theatre" ("*Le Temps*"). Stone argued that "the two plays reveal only a hint of the rich vein of Québec culture of which the rest of Canada sees all too little." Kareda and Whittaker cited Catholicism, the family, the household, and rural isolation as deeply resonant themes in Hébert's writing, themes they thought would resonate with Toronto's anglophone audiences. Said Whittaker, "If the rest of Canada is to accept Quebec as an equal partner in the country's life, it must learn to know its differences, to understand Quebec's background and motivations. This is where our national theatre, like our literature, can serve the nation well" ("*Le Temps*").

Though many reviewers shared a compulsion to situate Alumnae's *Le Temps Sauvage* in its timely political context, there was disagreement regarding its success. Much of this disagreement centres on the "professional-ness" (as opposed to the more vocation-laden term "professionalism") of the production's aesthetic accomplishments. Consideration of responses to the production's aesthetic elements through its archival traces reveals much about the relationships between an emerging theatre profession and those companies who fall outside of it.

2 *Forever Yours, Marie-Lou*'s translation, Ladouceur says, found success because "it had a comforting effect on a Toronto public anxious to understand what was shaking up Quebec playwriting," though it did not (or could not) represent to a "unilingual Anglophone audience" much of Tremblay's linguistic and cultural voice (28).

While Whittaker and McCaughna praised Susan Morgan's performance of Lucie as "vividly alive" (H. Whittaker, "*Le Temps*") and bringing "a gust of fresh air" (McCaughna), Kareda, Whittaker, and Stone faulted Van Burek for a "limp, unfocussed production" (Kareda, "*Le Temps*"), a "low-key monotony" (H. Whittaker, "*Le Temps*"), and a "somber mood which tends to subdue the actors" (Stone). Yvonne Helwig on *Radio York* deemed the production "on the whole disappointing and uncomfortable." Kareda pointed to a distracting set design and Van Burek's lack of attention to the play's "naturalistic" acting. Frequently preoccupied with the alternative theatres' handling (or not) of naturalism, Kareda wrote that the "actors often seemed to be struggling against mannerisms which didn't fit them" ("*Le Temps*"). Conversely, Sandra Souchotte in *The Varsity* suspected the tension lay between the "realistic backwoods depiction" and the poetic drama of the writing. Whittaker, an accomplished set designer himself, approved of the large burlap "Hessian batik" backdrop and "attractive Quebec furniture, here seen properly as background to the kind of people for which it was created—people close to the earth and their church." Said Helwig, the set is "surrounded by a continuous burlap swathe, aluminum spray-painted to represent the winter scene which permeates the dwelling in every sense." Kareda provided a final summation of the event that is ultimately provocative: "*Le Temps Sauvage* was most certainly worth doing. I only wish it had been a stronger production, strong enough to prove that point" ("*Le Temps*"). His judgment belies at once the centrality of Alumnae as a relevant producer of important theatre, even as it radiates an uneven aesthetic. Notably, the same statement could be, and frequently was, made by the same reviewers about Alumnae's professionalizing counterparts, further underscoring Alumnae's relevance to its theatre milieu.

The directing and design were not the production's only sites of contestation for critics. Some suggested that Hébert's original may have been well written, but was not adequate material for performance. Helwig called Hébert's work "more of a lyrical poem than a play." Whittaker deemed the script insufficient for the stage, saying, "Its text provides an undeniable interest that is not entirely theatrical" and lacks depth. Souchotte agreed, offering that, "Perhaps Anne Hébert should be read and not seen." And Kareda said that Mascall's translation made a "fair stab [. . .] at Mme. Hebert's baroque style" ("*Le Temps*").

These reviews are notable for the earnestness with which they treat the nonprofessionalizing company and its significant production. Here there is no fond or whimsical reminiscence of an amateur theatre of the past. They provide evidence that Alumnae was very much of its time in an early 1970s that saw nationalistic plays proliferate at alternative theatres. In his characteristic manifesto-like voice, Kareda declared in a preview feature about Van Burek that, "Since the spring, a new and distinct coloration of French-Canadian drama has started to make itself felt in Toronto" ("Giving"). He listed no less than five English-language premieres of French-Canadian plays in Toronto in the previous six months, each of which Van Burek had a hand in bringing to the stage. This "inconceivable pitch of activity" at which Van Burek was operating occurred with various theatre companies, including his own Le Théâtre du P'tit Bonheur (at the time Toronto's only French-language theatre), Tarragon Theatre, the Multi-Cultural Theatre Association, and Alumnae Theatre Company (Kareda, "Giving"). Indeed, during the 1970s, Kareda, Pritchard, and others situated Alumnae Theatre not only within the same context as Tarragon, Factory Lab, and Toronto Free, but as something of their godmother. Wrote Kareda of Alumnae,

> [T]his is the group, more than any other, which has reworked Toronto's theatrical atmosphere. [. . .] Their achievements are legion. [. . .] Over the half-century-and-a-bit of their existence, they have taken the first steps in so many directions. [. . .] The Alumnae is a stunning, startling example of a mass collective, unified will, modified by ambition, intelligence and the utter inability to understand rejections. ("Our")

Taken together, the publicity and press material, the visual evidence of design, and Mascall's translation suggest that Alumnae's *Le Temps Sauvage* shared with contemporary professionalized theatre productions a cultural significance and an aesthetic force. Mixed reviews (similar to those of the alternative theatre companies) and a handful of production photographs that lack wider angles of the set suggest that more might have been made of Hébert's drama even as some acting and design successes gratified the importance of producing the work in Toronto during the early wave of francophone plays produced in English translation.

Despite the significance of Mascall's translation, when Louise Forsyth's important *Anthology of Québec Women's Plays in English Translation* printed *Le Temps Sauvage*, among other English translations that carved a place among emerging feminist discourses, it was not Mascall's translation that opened the three-volume series. Instead, a new translation by Pamela Grant and Gregory Reid appeared, expressly commissioned for the anthology. Says Forsyth of Hébert's work:

> It was such an early play in the history of Québec theatre and, in particular, the Théâtre de Nouveau Monde (before it even had a home in Montréal). This was an important moment in both Montréal and Toronto theatre that could have changed the course of Québec and Canadian theatre history had critics and cultural activists not been so blown away by Tremblay. (Forsyth, Email)

Forsyth explains that because the Mascall translation received no further publication, production, or even adequate discussion after the premiere, she was unable to assess the impact of the Alumnae production, or even track down the script (Forsyth, Email), which in fact exists in its entirety. This situation is as significant as it is commonplace. On the one hand, Mascall, a decades-long member and leader of the company—her name now graces its upstairs studio theatre—died "suddenly" just four months after her translation opened (Alumnae, "Maxim"), no doubt contributing to the translation's eventual obscurity. On the other hand, to include a translation from a non-professionalizing theatre company would be to play against the maturation narrative underlying both the growth of a Canadian theatre and its entanglement with the performance of a growing, professionalizing nation. Just as the professionalization of theatre practices in Toronto served to marginalize

Alumnae's work, so too did the fact that Alumnae was (and is) a company run by women, in sharp contrast to all four of the major alternative theatres that were run by, in Kareda's words, "young men" ("Giving"). Whereas Tremblay's arrival in anglophone Canada coincided with Hébert's arrival, the former ultimately eclipsed the latter with the rise of the popular narrative of the professionalizing, male-dominated alternative theatres. What is implied, of course, is that professional space would be male space within this nationalization maturation mythology. That Hébert's *Le Temps Sauvage* was translated and produced by a nonprofessionalizing women's theatre company with an explicit mandate to involve women in leadership roles in theatre no doubt added to the silencing effect.

TOWARD AN ARCHAEOLOGY OF THEATRE HISTORIOGRAPHY

A history of nonprofessionalizing performance practices can be read as a *mise en abyme* of Foucault's history of ideas, both imbedded within it and a structural and hermeneutic reflection of it. Such a history, by definition, would be distinct from both the familiar professionalizing practices of theatre history's cunning actor-managers and for-profit moguls and syndicates, and from its modern version of these, the union-styled equity associations with their controls and restraints; yet it would also reflect the values it shares and the practices and practitioners it lends, borrows, trains, and trades with emergent professions. Such a history would revalue those aesthetic tastes that audiences are trained to see as either "perfect" or "imperfect" and "expert" or "dilettantish," abjure hand-me-down regulations when it needs to (or borrows from and in some cases redefines them), and remain fluid to contemporary conditions. Its boundaries are indeterminate but flexible. Its judgments are not prefigured by disciplinary regulations.

Conversely, a theatre profession, as it emerges and protects that which it has "gained," seeks to discipline and define *all* practices and statements (scripts, production schedules, performances, etc.) that lie both inside and outside of its borders. Those *within* the profession fall under professional documents such as collective and cross-institutional reciprocal agreements and professional work contracts; those *without* are left for chaff and stamped "amateur," a term that seeks to conflate a range of performance practices as inferior and dilettantish, from student productions and "community theatre" to Fringe Festival productions, street theatre, and burlesque. In unchecked examples of this longing to discipline and exclude nonprofessionalizing practices—among the most participatory of art forms—a profession may say that if you, or your company, are not a member of a professional association, you are "amateur," at once tainting the work with premature assumptions of poor quality. In doing so, a profession attempts to influence not only the widest breadth of contemporary practices, but also, even more broadly, the researching and telling of theatre histories by claiming aesthetic and structural superiority over nonprofessionalizing practices.

In the case of Mascall's translation of Hébert's *Le Temps Sauvage*, Alumnae Theatre Company had already positioned itself outside of the emerging profession. Yet the show's hired director, Van Burek, was very much active within the profession. Production photographs and costume designs do not suggest dilettantism or a lack of aesthetic quality. And half-a-dozen theatre critics gave convincing, honest judgments on the production that in no way bracketed off the company as "amateur" either by dismissing the play's, the production's, or the company's significance, or by ignoring their faults. In contrast, professional theatre historians have followed the lead of professional theatre artists who dismiss the importance of nonprofessionalizing productions like this one. This choice has served to further alienate women in the record of Canadian theatre and has given a distorted, or even absent, resonance to many of the discipline's signpost events, such as new francophone plays produced in English.

Neither professionalizing nor nonprofessionalizing practices are static. Both are fluid, emerging, and subject to internal redefinitions over time. And their interconnections are themselves fluid. As a profession's practices respond to and change with the emerging needs of its artists (for example, relatively recent developments in the CAEA's handling of independent member contracts), it collaterally impacts its relationships to its nonprofessionalizing "others." This latter set of vast and underconsidered practices comprises substantial, sometimes foundational, cultural activity.

An archaeology of theatre historiography, then, would equate found and archived utterances without pre-weighting their importance based on proximity to a profession. As both a cultural artifact and an unfixed trace of past practices, the reviewed document contributes to a broader conversation about performance created by career specialists, skilled hobbyists, and practitioners who may be professionals in other vocations but who create theatre for reasons other than regenerative job creation. This approach takes into account historical circumstance without being trapped in teleological arguments of building a maturing vocation.

The ways in which nonprofessionalizing theatre practices were recorded and narrativized (and not) in English Canada during the twentieth century are worth revisiting. Doing so forces us to rethink inherited teleological narratives of Canadian theatre's "evolution," which recorded a maturation from an amateur past to a professionalizing present and an even more professionalized future toward which a "growing" nation must strive. This rethinking reframes nonprofessionalized theatre practices as not only present and active in contemporary times, but also as more than foils to the professionalizing institution of a nationalized Canadian theatre scene. This reframing has functional and aesthetic repercussions, not the least of which influence critical reception. This approach critiques documented narratives of nonprofessionalizing theatre, such as those of the DDF and the Ottawa Little Theatre, as examples of a discourse of fond reminiscence too deeply beholden to the reductive *amore* of "amateur." It offers a more refined critique of their practices and productions in concert with professionalizing practices.

The re/collection of Alumnae Theatre Company's production of *Le Temps Sauvage* constitutes a history from a set of practices and statements. And due to the company's position outside of the emerging profession (and outside of script publication), the practices and statements related to the production are "recomposed in a new way" (Foucault, *Archaeology* 153–54). They no longer fall into delegitimized historical obscurity—tangential, transient, or temporary—but are reframed as foundational practices and statements within a broader discourse of theatre practices. Thus, the paradox is laid bare for the scholar of theatre: If a maturation myth, deaf to nonprofessionalizing practices, is allowed to relegitimize itself as a national discourse, how could we more fully account for its constitutive and defining nonprofessionalizing practices? The vague aesthetic notion of "quality," and its even vaguer relationship to the profession, haunts the history, and history-telling, of theatre.[3]

3 As with my other research into Alumnae Theatre Company's practices and productions, for this essay I am indebted to the company and their archivist, Catherine Spence, for allowing me ongoing access to their collections.

INVISIBILITY AND EARLY NEW PLAY DRAMATURGY: BILL GLASSCO'S DEVELOPMENT OF DAVID FREEMAN'S *CREEPS*

JESSICA RILEY

David Freeman's *Creeps* holds a position as a landmark in Canadian theatre history. The premiere, directed by Bill Glassco, garnered unprecedented attention for the newly opened Factory Theatre Lab in February 1971. Months later, *Creeps* served as the inaugural production of Glassco's own Tarragon Theatre. Having played a key role in the rise of two of the most prominent Toronto theatres of the so-called "alternate theatre movement," *Creeps* was also the first winner of the Floyd S. Chalmers Canadian Play Award and attained a place in the nascent canon of English Canadian drama, appearing in two foundational anthologies published in the 1980s (Plant, *Modern*; Wasserman, *Modern*). More recently, the play has been recognized for its significance as an early work of disability theatre (Lewis; K. Johnston, *Stage Turns*).

Examining extant drafts of *Creeps* illuminates not only Freeman's work on this historic script but also Glassco's unrecognized role in the writing process. From the early 1970s to his death in 2004, Glassco was a major force in Canadian theatre. As founding artistic director of Tarragon (1971–1981) he was a passionate advocate of Canadian drama, playing an instrumental role in the emergence of many celebrated playwrights, including most famously David French.[1] Before Tarragon, however, Glassco got his start in new play development at Factory, where he first directed *Creeps*. Notes in the margins of surviving drafts reveal that Glassco offered substantial feedback on the

1 Equally famous is Glassco's introduction (as director and co-translator) of the work of Québec playwright Michel Tremblay to English-Canadian audiences.

script, not only during rehearsals for the premiere, but also in the early stages of Freeman's writing.[2] Today, we would describe such sustained developmental consultation as dramaturgical. In the 1970s, however, the word *dramaturgy* was just coming into use among the alternate theatres in Canada[3] and it was common for the development of new scripts to be seen as an extension of the director's role.[4] By closely examining this early instance of developmental dramaturgy, this essay will analyze how Glassco's feedback contributed to the emergence of key features of the script, most notably its representations of disability and of sexual violence against women. Demonstrating how the values and approaches exemplified in Glassco's work on *Creeps* shaped Freeman's play, this essay sheds new light on Glassco's earliest contributions to Canadian theatre and invites further analysis of the underexamined influence of dramaturgs and dramaturgy in the 1970s.

---

2 Six of the surviving drafts are preserved in the Bill Glassco collection at the Toronto Reference Library and there is also an early, marked-up script among David Freeman's papers, housed at McMaster University. Although these drafts are undated, careful reconstruction of multiple trajectories of revision confirms that six of these seven drafts date from the Factory phase of the script's development. Considering that nearly all accounts of *Creeps*'s production history are careful to mention that the Tarragon production presented a *revised* version of the script, it is unfortunate that scant record of the changes undertaken between the Factory and Tarragon productions has been preserved. In this essay, I cite the published script and two of the earliest surviving drafts, both of which are found among Glassco's papers at the Toronto Reference Library, in files 13 and 14 of box 2.

3 Extant press releases dating from as early as 1973 suggest the operations of a "Dramaturgical Department" at Factory Theatre Lab. For the most part, however, dramaturgy remained—to borrow Peter Hay's 1975 phrase—"an Unborn Profession" in Canada until the 1980s ("Dramaturgy"), when *Canadian Theatre Review* dedicated a special issue to "Play Development" (1986), the Literary Managers and Dramaturgs of the Americas gained its first Canadian member (1988), and dramaturgy emerged as a more widely discussed profession in Canada.

4 In the early years at Factory, founder Ken Gass recalls that the work of reading script submissions was conducted by "various people," but that "it was really more the professional directors" who engaged in script development, including the kind of early, "one-on-one feedback" examined here ("re:").

Freeman wrote *Creeps* from his own lived experience with cerebral palsy. The play is set in the men's washroom of a "sheltered workshop" for the disabled, where an ensemble of five male characters escape not only their female supervisor, Miss Saunders, but also their demeaning and meaningless workshop labours, sanding blocks and weaving rugs. Sam is the angry young man of the group, giving voice in the loudest terms to his frustrations with the workshop, his parents, and society at large. Joining him are the largely silent Michael, whose disability is mental as well as physical, and Pete, a veteran of the workshop program, who expresses an attitude of defeated dependency on the institution. Rounding out the ensemble are Tom and Jim, whose aspirations to become a professional visual artist and writer, respectively, fuel the climax of *Creeps*. As the play draws to a close, Jim is very nearly persuaded to join Tom in his determination to leave the security of the sheltered workshop; the two men plan to find an apartment and pursue their ambitions together. In the final moments, however, this dream is thwarted by the arrival of Miss Saunders and her superior, Mr. Carson. With condescending paternalism, Mr. Carson succeeds in dissuading Jim—though not Tom—from pursuing independence. This outcome for Jim serves as a final illustration of the social construction of disability critiqued in *Creeps*. As an early work of disability theatre, the play is significant both for its staging of these disabling social systems and for its depiction, through the ensemble, of the frustrations and complexities of disability as a lived experience.

However, there is one disabled character in *Creeps* whose experience is strikingly underexamined in the script—and in the range of published responses to the play: the offstage character of Thelma, whose plaintive cry, "I need a priest!" is heard in the opening and closing moments of *Creeps*. Although she utters this line eleven times throughout the play, Thelma never appears on stage. The sanctuary of the men's room is unavailable to Thelma and her repeated cries are initially ignored (1, 4, 14) or treated as a source of irritation (2). Only once do the men discuss Thelma in any detail, when a concentrated repetition of her haunting plea prompts the group to tease Sam about the origins of her distress. The exchange culminates with Sam's reluctant delivery of the following account:

> Look I didn't mean for anything to happen that day. What do you think I am, stupid? . . . I just wanted to talk. She started fooling around, trying to grab my cannon and everything. Naturally I get a hard-on. What am I supposed to do? Silly little bitch! We were just going real good when she changed her mind. That's one helluva time to exercise her woman's prerogative, isn't it? Anyway, we . . . she fell out of bed. In a few seconds in come Mommy and Daddy. They thought I'd fallen out of my chair or something. Well, there I am in bed with my joint waving merrily in the breeze and Thelma's on the floor minus her P.J.'s, and all hell broke lose. You'd have thought they'd never seen a cock before. The old man, he bounced me out of bed along the floor and into the hallway. The old lady, she dragged Thelma up behind. Then they held us up in front of a little Jesus statue and asked it to forgive us 'cause we didn't know what we were doing. (17)

Reading *Creeps* from my subject position as a woman in 2016, I am disturbed by Sam's resentful reference to Thelma's "woman's prerogative" and by the intimations of rape in his elided description of how the "silly little bitch" came to end up on the floor. Given her repeated, desperate cries for a priest, it is clear that the incident has had a lasting and devastating effect on Thelma. For the onstage characters, however, Thelma's story is less a cause for concern than a source of mirth. They describe the drastic changes in Thelma's dress (which has become sombre and modest) and behaviour—"She used to laugh a lot, too" (18)—merely as a means to agitate Sam. The exchange ends when Michael's recitation, in a mocking "sing-song" voice, of "Thelma needs a priest, Thelma needs a priest" (18) drives Sam to incite a brief but riotous skirmish. When the fight ends, Thelma is forgotten.

The characters' indifference to Thelma's suffering strikes me as a strange—and troubling—authorial choice. Also surprising is the marked inattention to Thelma in critical responses to the play. Many accounts of *Creeps* ignore

Thelma altogether, while others refer to her only briefly.[5] When Thelma's recurring cries are acknowledged, the disturbing implications of her experience with Sam are left unexamined. Thus, Victoria Ann Lewis describes "the unseen Thelma's disembodied cry for help" as merely "providing the opening flourish and the closing coda" for the play (xxiv), while for Urjo Kareda the "tortured screams of a female patient" are reduced to vague thematic significance: "This is the unseen Thelma," he writes, the men's "link with ultimate mortality" ("New Theatre").[6] Eugene Benson and L.W. Conolly come closest to expressing my discomfort with the treatment of Thelma's experience in *Creeps*. Describing the incident explicitly as a rape, they acknowledge that "Freeman's handling of Thelma . . . is problematical" (90). For them, however, the problem is restricted to a perceived breach of dramatic plausibility; if she's been driven "mad" by the rape, they argue, "her continuing presence in the workshop seems improbable" (*English-Canadian* 90). Ann P. Massinger expresses a similar "quibble," finding Thelma "somewhat improbable" at "the realistic level of the play" (102). For Massinger, too, this objection is restricted to the realism of Thelma's presence in the sheltered workshop. The haunting reality behind the offstage character's screams—as intimated in Sam's disturbing speech—is of little concern; instead Thelma's cries are understood to serve a symbolic purpose, "underscore[ing] the theme of spiritual death" (102).

In my own reading of *Creeps*, the power of Thelma's offstage presence defies reduction to a mere thematic or symbolic device. Moreover, the problem with Thelma lies not in the plausibility of her presence in the "real" world of the play, but rather in her unaccountable lack of impact on the men

5 Thelma is entirely unmentioned in early reviews of the play by Nathan Cohen and Herbert Whittaker, and in the analysis of *Creeps* in Wasserman's essay, " 'It's the Do-Gooders Burn My Ass': Modern Canadian Drama and the Crisis of Liberalism." She is also absent from Kirsty Johnston's discussion of *Creeps* in her book *Stage Turns: Canadian Disability Theatre*.

6 Similarly, while Mary Elizabeth Smith observes the unsettling affect of Thelma's cry—a "nerve-wracking, wearing wail"—she is undisturbed by the account of its cause. For her, Sam's "deflowering of Thelma" is merely one of the sexual "escapades which have earned him the most notoriety among his fellows" ("Freeman" 79).

who inhabit it. Why link Thelma's suffering—foregrounded so emphatically through her repeated offstage cries—to an onstage character, only to depict the connection as insignificant? Offstage characters have a long tradition of exerting profound influence over those on stage—and, by extension, over audiences. Consider, for example, the invisible instrumentality of King Laius in *Oedipus Rex*, or the weighty absence of Beckett's Godot. For Andrew Sofer, these unseen characters cannot be reduced to mere devices; because of his "gravitational effects, both within and beyond the world of the stage . . . Godot is not just a sign" (336). The haunting insistence of Thelma's offstage cries suggests a character that is (or could be) imbued with similar weight and influence. And yet, in *Creeps*, Thelma is denied gravity in both senses of the word. Her experience, as described by Sam, is treated with indifference, even levity, and her impact, both within and beyond the stage world, is minimal. Despite the potential gravity of her audible offstage presence, *Creeps* offers limited—and marginalizing—access to Thelma's experience. Why does the play treat Thelma this way?

Examining extant drafts of *Creeps*, I will trace the roots of Thelma's strange lack of impact to the development process, revealing the shaping influence of Glassco's dramaturgical feedback, particularly in its establishment of areas of emphasis—and, crucially, de-emphasis—for revision. Beyond the implications for Thelma's treatment in the script, this analysis will demonstrate the effects of Glassco's dramaturgy, for better and worse, on many aspects of the script. Through an analysis of the influence of Glassco's subjective tastes, priorities, and assumptions, this essay will offer unprecedented historical insight into Glassco's early dramaturgy as a key condition of production that shaped Freeman's *Creeps*, inviting a re-examination of the largely invisible history and legacy of new play development as it emerged in the 1970s.

THE "UNSEEN THELMA": DRAMATURGICAL EMPHASIS AND DE-EMPHASIS

Among the surviving drafts of *Creeps*, there exists a very early version of the speech in which Sam describes his encounter with Thelma, accompanied by a particularly salient example of Glassco's handwritten feedback: "This whole speech must be very funny, very grotesque, and very much in Sam's favour" (B2F13 16). Glassco's comment is not only indicative of how he would come to direct this scene in *Creeps* but is also evidence of his early input on the development of the script. Subsequent drafts reveal Freeman's efforts to address Glassco's feedback: the potential for humour is heightened through additions that include Sam's "joint waving merrily in the breeze" and an expanded description of the reactions of Thelma's parents, which becomes more farcical and "grotesque" in its exaggerated physical detail. The revised version of the speech includes the "old man" "bounc[ing]" Sam into the hallway, the "old lady . . . dragg[ing] Thelma up behind," as well as the added detail of the "little Jesus statue." Other additions, such as Sam's innocent claim

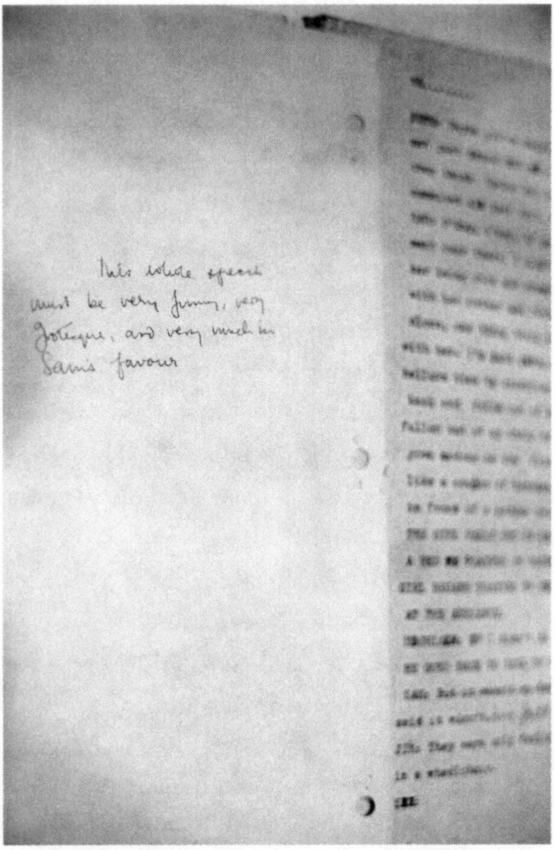

Fig. 1. Glassco's handwritten response to an early version of Sam's speech regarding Thelma. Photo by John Reed.

that he "just wanted to talk," and a new description of Thelma as the sexual initiator—"She started fooling around, trying to grab my cannon and everything. Naturally I get a hard-on"—contrive to render the account "in Sam's favour." However, as both Benson and Conolly's reading and my own response to the speech indicate, Thelma's consent remains disturbingly unclear in the revised, published version. If the speech was intended to be funny and sympathetic, why not seek to clarify this unsettling ambiguity?

There are no signs in the surviving record of any further dramaturgical feedback regarding Thelma's story; indeed, there are no further comments tied to the character of Thelma at all. This suggests that neither Glassco nor Freeman fully registered the disturbing intimations of Sam's account—or recognized the need to address them further, either by eliminating the potential of an assault (in the service of humour and audience sympathies for Sam) or by lending this experience (and Thelma) graver significance. Her potential, as a haunting offstage presence, was unrecognized and, consequently, undeveloped. Instead, the attentions of both playwright and director-dramaturg were focused elsewhere. The archive provides a record of several areas of dramaturgical emphasis informed by Glassco's personal set of dramatic tastes, assumptions, and priorities. Examining these wider areas of development will further illuminate Glassco's influence on *Creeps*, including the implications for Thelma, to which I will return.

Despite his inattention to the emotional interiority of the "unseen Thelma," Glassco's widely acknowledged taste for naturalism[7] is revealed in a marked preoccupation with the psychological realism of the male characters in *Creeps*. Perhaps unsurprisingly, Sam is the subject of much of this feedback. In the earliest extant draft, next to a speech which he finds not "quite believ[able]," Glassco expresses strong convictions regarding Sam's feelings about Jim, who works for Mr. Carson and is thus viewed as a traitor by others in the group. "Sam wouldn't hate Jim for disappointing him," Glassco writes,

7 Ric Knowles, for example, observes that Glassco's founding mandate for Tarragon "evince[s] a preference for . . . poetic naturalism" (*Reading* 135). As Kamal Al-Soylaylee has put it, Glassco's early taste for "variations of naturalism, including poetic naturalism," drew a lasting "blueprint" for Tarragon's house style (vi).

"He'd hate him for being false to himself." Alongside this assertion, Glassco suggests that "[p]erhaps Sam could put it [i.e. his criticism of Jim] differently," and even ventures to write his own alternative: "You're too smart to give in to them. You see through them and you know you do. You're lying to yourself" (B2F13 9). A few pages later, Glassco offers a similarly bold response to a line in which Sam appears to withdraw his critique of Jim's employment with Mr. Carson: "But if you've got a niche in the social whirl, why not do everything to hang on to it? Don't mind me. Everybody knows I got a big mouth" (B2F13 20). Despite Freeman's likely intention that this line be read as sarcasm, Glassco's note, recorded on the back of the opposite page, registers an earnest objection: "ugh!" he writes, "Sam *wouldn't* say this" (B2F13 20). Such strong responses register Glassco's investment in the character and illuminate his conviction that Thelma's story should be "very much in Sam's favour." Expressed very early in the script's development, these forceful opinions often exerted considerable influence; in the latter case, for example, the offending line is excised directly on the page, demonstrating the immediate impact of Glassco's feedback.[8]

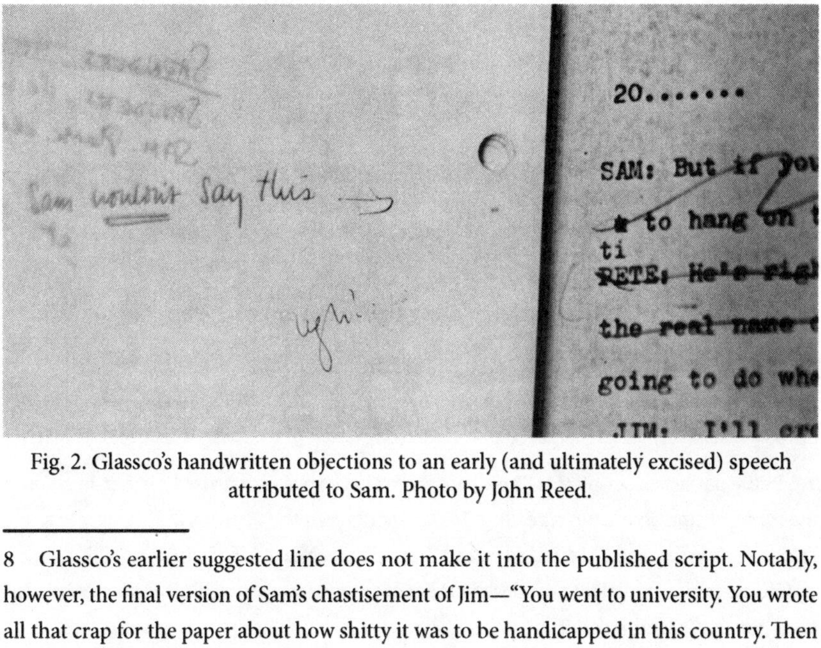

Fig. 2. Glassco's handwritten objections to an early (and ultimately excised) speech attributed to Sam. Photo by John Reed.

8 Glassco's earlier suggested line does not make it into the published script. Notably, however, the final version of Sam's chastisement of Jim—"You went to university. You wrote all that crap for the paper about how shitty it was to be handicapped in this country. Then

In addition to ensuring the psychological believability of the characters' utterances, Glassco also pursued a realist imperative to develop and distinguish each member of the ensemble through dialogue. In the earliest draft, for example, after flagging the word "shithead" with the assertion that it is "too strong for Jim," Glassco asks: "[H]ow much does each character swear? Who swears the most? The least?" (B2F13 22). Writing in 1978, Freeman recalls these questions: "[O]ne of Bill Glassco's criticisms was that all the characters sounded the same. He asked who swore the most? Who swore the least? Who was most witty? Who was most serious? . . . Everybody has a way of saying certain phrases, using and pronouncing certain words over and over again, that is unique to him" (Untitled 259). The surviving drafts show Glassco's role in shaping this aspect of the script, revealing in particular his own assumptions regarding which character ought to "swear the most." Against the observation that "shithead" is "too strong for Jim," Glassco suggests the replacement of several of Sam's tamer profanities, such as "bloody" and "blasted," with alternatives like "fuckin." Likewise Sam's "I just came in to see what you guys were shooting the bull about" is revised on the page to the much coarser "I just came in to see if you guys were jerking off together" (B2F13 2).[9] The archives confirm the lasting impact of Glassco's suggestions. In future drafts Sam is increasingly distinguished by his liberal use of expletives, a development that supports his emerging status as the group's most outspoken critic of the social constraints and infantalization he describes succinctly as "pityshit."

Indeed, the archives reveal that this potent expression is itself a product of Glassco's dramaturgical feedback. In the published script, it appears in the following speech: "You can always throw real shit at a black man or an Indian,

---

what do you do? You come running down here and kiss the first ass you see" (10)—incorporates Glassco's preferred subtext, i.e. that Sam "hate[s] him for being false to himself."

9 In the published script, this line—Sam's third in the play—is revised further, becoming the sarcastic and character-revealing, "No, I wanna join the circle jerk" (3). Significantly, Freeman later distances himself from the "foul language" used in the play, notably citing a realist imperative underlying the development of *Creeps*: "the very subject matter demanded such honesty" (Untitled 259).

but at us [i.e. the disabled] you're only allowed to throw pityshit. And pityshit ain't visible" (6). Surviving drafts show Glassco's role in developing this speech from its earliest incarnation, which reads: "You can always pelt a Negro or an Indian with a rock but, with us, all they've got to pelt us with is pity. It's quite a trick to hate and not be seen." In the margin, Glassco flags the entire speech as "awk" (i.e. awkward) and suggests cutting the final sentence (B2F13 5). In the next draft, the speech is revised: "You can always throw shit at a black man or an Indian. That's easy. But, with us, all they're allowed to throw is pity" (B2F14 6). With this revision, Freeman not only responds to Glassco's editorial feedback but also the directive to distinguish Sam's character through the use of coarse language. Unsurprisingly, it is Freeman's replacement of the original "rock" with the much stronger "shit" that prompts further development; recorded on the page in Glassco's handwriting is another "shit" appended to "pity," forming the thematically central neologism, "pityshit." In addition, Glassco records variations on a new closing line for the speech, "[a]nd pityshit is invisible," which is revised immediately to the final "[a]nd pityshit ain't visible" (B2F14 6). Unlike other instances of Glassco's handwritten notes, which quite clearly register his own observations (e.g. "Sam *wouldn't* say this"), it is likely that these markings represent acts of transcription, particularly in light of Freeman's restricted ability to write by hand. Whether "pityshit" sprang from the mind of Freeman or Glassco is a mystery the archive cannot definitively resolve. Nonetheless, it is clear that Glassco's handwriting records the outcome of a conversation to which he contributed in formative ways. In the case of Sam's "pityshit" speech, Freeman's negotiation of the combined realist and editorial imperatives of Glassco's dramaturgy produces a concise and potent articulation of the insidious oppression critiqued in *Creeps*.

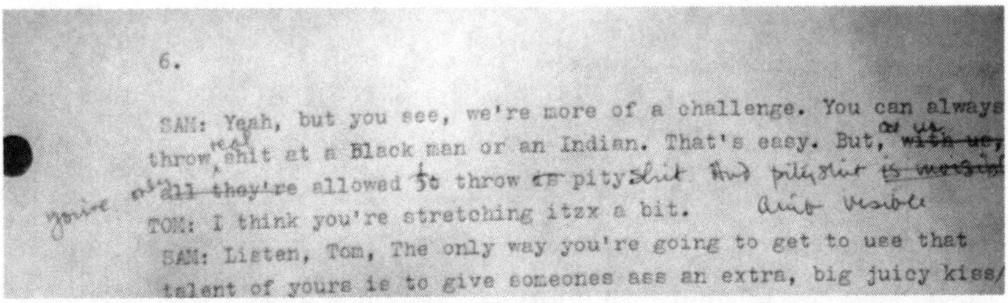
6.

SAM: Yeah, but you see, we're more of a challenge. You can always throw shit at a Black man or an Indian. That's easy. But, with us, all they're allowed to throw is pity.

TOM: I think you're stretching itzx a bit.

SAM: Listen, Tom, The only way you're going to get to use that talent of yours is to give someones ass an extra, big juicy kiss/

Fig. 3. Revisions recorded on the page in Glassco's handwriting. Photo by Jessica Riley.

Surviving drafts thus reveal the considerable influence of Glassco's dramaturgical feedback. Shaped by his personal preoccupations with naturalistic character psychology, realistic dialogue, and the refinement of unclear or "awk[ward]" writing, Glassco's responses to the script establish areas of emphasis that contributed substantially to ongoing revisions. In the process, however, other areas for development are de-emphasized, or overlooked. The "unseen Thelma" represents one such dramaturgical blind spot. In the case of Sam's speech, Glassco fails to push for revisions that fully address the disturbing implications for Thelma, absorbed instead with the development of humour and with maintaining audience sympathy for Sam. Elsewhere, Glassco ignores Thelma altogether—overlooking the potential for this off-stage presence to exert more meaningful impact within and beyond the world of the play.

A final example of Glassco's extant feedback further illuminates how the normalizing values underlying his dramaturgical emphases could render invisible not only elements of the play linked to violence against women but also its representation of disability; together these suggest Glassco's emphasis on respecting realistic conventions over advocating for social justice. In the published script, an important exchange concerns the events and programming offered by the "Spastic Club" where Jim is employed. Arguing against the magic shows and finger-painting contests typically organized by the club, Pete and Sam unsuccessfully advocate for more substantive—and less infantalizing—initiatives. Pete asks, "What about my idea of having that psychologist down from the university?" only to be told that Mr. Carson has vetoed the suggestion, "afraid the members would be bored." Likewise, Sam's inquiry, "What about my idea for installing ramps in the subway?" is met with Jim's claim that such a project is beyond the purview of the organization (22). This exchange offers a powerful illustration of the paternalistic disregard shown by the Spastic Club for the needs and ideas of its members, contributing meaningfully to the critique of such institutions for which *Creeps* is celebrated. Initially, however, this crucial dialogue was flagged by Glassco for excision; in the margin he writes "necessary?" An accompanying note reveals the priorities and preoccupations that informed this query: for Glassco, "[t]his page should be building more to Jim's outburst" later in the scene (B2F13 21).[10] Overlooking the significance of articulating the intellectual and architectural barriers that affect people with disabilities, Glassco's attention is instead focused on adherence to the dominant conventions of naturalistic character motivation. For him, establishing a preparatory psychological or emotional throughline for Jim is more "necessary" than the social and political critique expressed in the exchange between Sam, Pete, and Jim. Fortunately, in this instance, Glassco's advice fails to prompt a revision; Freeman retains this dialogue as an essential component of the representation of disabled experience in the script.

Despite Glassco's blind spot regarding disability politics, observable in his sense of what was "necessary" to the script, developments arising from his feedback carry considerable implications for *Creeps* as it came to be celebrated as an early work of disability theatre. Understanding this indirect but significant dramaturgical impact necessitates a brief turn from the archival analysis of the surviving drafts of *Creeps*. Examining the script's potential for production and reception as a work of disability theatre demonstrates how the emphases and de-emphases of Glassco's dramaturgy contributed both to important representations of disabled experience in *Creeps* and, in the case of Thelma, to the limitations of these representations.

10 The "outburst" in question is a confessional monologue (ultimately excised) in which Jim articulates both his hatred for and dependence on Mr. Carson and the institution that gives him support.

ANGER, SEX, AND (IN)VISIBILITY: DRAMATURGICAL IMPLICATIONS FOR *CREEPS* AS DISABILITY THEATRE

In her anthology of contemporary plays by disabled playwrights, Victoria Ann Lewis praises *Creeps* for its presentation of "a variety of disabled character types," arguing that the play "broke new ground in the gritty realism with which it depicted life for disabled people" (xxv). As the above analysis demonstrates, Glassco's character-driven feedback helped shape this feature of the script. Specifically, the coarse, angry language in the play, expressed with force by Sam, informs not only the "gritty realism" of *Creeps* but also its challenge to homogenizing and marginalizing conceptions of disability. As Kirsty Johnston has recently observed, one of the chief markers of disability theatre is the "dismantling [of] stereotypes," including that of the "sweet, innocent and morally deserving 'charity case' " (*Stage Turns* 5, 12). As early as 1973, reviewer Richard A. Watson (himself a person with cerebral palsy), identifies the "harsh language" in *Creeps* as crucial to its demonstration that "physically handicapped people are not as pure, innocent, and vacant of mind as people seem to think." Moreover, as Lewis argues, the coarseness of Freeman's language enacts an important disavowal of what disability studies scholar Irving Zola has identified as "denial of anger," "one of the major contributing factors to the invisibility of disabled identity in the modern era" (xxv).

Making visible the anger expressed by Sam and, to a lesser extent, the rest of the male ensemble in *Creeps*, can be read as a powerful act of resistance to stereotypes of purity and innocence. Denial of sexuality has similarly been part of the marginalizing social construction of disability. Indeed, Watson's early praise for the realism of the script and its power to undercut assumptions about disabled people singles out not only the "harsh language" in *Creeps* but also its "pornographic detail." Many moments in the script contribute to this aspect of *Creeps*. In one scene, the men read aloud from a pornographic novel. Elsewhere, assertions of sexuality emerge in the dialogue, frequently in lines delivered by Sam, such as his joke about "jerking off." Tellingly, many of the lines that serve as expressions of sexuality in *Creeps* also serve as expressions of anger; they are also frequently directed at women. Sam's frustrated account of the tasks assigned by his physical therapist—"she keeps making me do [i.e. sand] the same blocks over and over"—ends with: "(Pointing to his crotch) Take a bite out of this" (3). Likewise, Miss Saunders's earliest intrusion—"If you boys aren't back to work in five minutes I'm reporting you to Mr. Carson" (8)—prompts Sam to rally Tom and Pete into a cry of "Suck my boundingy!" (9). In this way, the characters' frustrated responses to the demeaning labour of the workshop and the infantalizing treatment of the institution often take the form of outbursts that, while valuable as depictions of lived experience and as challenges to dominant stereotypes about disability, also contribute to the normalized misogyny in the world of the play.

This brings me back to Thelma. While Sam's account of his experience with Thelma may be read, on one level, as part of the challenge posed by the script to stereotypes of disabled people as asexual or "innocent," this reading does not account for the disturbing intimations of rape in the story. Again, I find myself wondering why they are there. Imagine, for a moment, a version of Sam's speech without the ambiguities around consent and the disturbing misogyny of his reference to Thelma as a "stupid little bitch." The story would then be one of desire, awkwardness, and shame—at the hands of Thelma's villainous parents—for both parties. The heightened humour and "grotesque" details encouraged by Glassco might then have contributed to the effect Kirsty Johnston has identified in more recent examples of disability theatre: that complex depictions of "sexual desire, shame, esteem, and awkwardness . . . buil[d] public space for investment in disabled bodies as subjects, rather than simply objects, of emotion" ("Whose" 170). As written, however, Thelma is denied the agency to be either an enthusiastic participant in the encounter Sam describes or to express a rage of her own that meaningfully affects the other characters in the play. If the experience was to be understood as non-consensual, a stronger choice would have been to grant Thelma her anger, agency—and gravity. Denial of both her sexuality and her anger serves to reinforce her invisibility and to refuse her subjectivity. Dramaturgically, Thelma remains an object—a symbol of immortality, as Kareda sees her, or of the "spiritual death" of systemic oppression, as in Massinger's reading—acted upon but not active.

Ultimately, the unsettling ambiguity and indifference of Sam's account of his experience with Thelma, like the wider misogyny in *Creeps*, is the result of the dramaturgical emphases—and de-emphases—that informed this script development process. In other words, while Glassco and Freeman were focused on making the speech "very much in Sam's favour," pursuing the comedic potential of the scene, they failed to see—or to consider significant—the disturbing ambiguities around Thelma's consent. Likewise, the troubling intimations of Sam's description of Thelma as a "stupid little bitch" are rendered almost invisible both by the dominant imperative to heighten the coarseness of Sam's language and by a pervasive misogyny in the world of the play that was viewed, evidently, as merely a part of its "gritty realism."

WHO IS DOING THE SEEING? UNEXAMINED VALUES AND DRAMATURGICAL PATERNALISM IN EARLY NEW PLAY DRAMATURGY

I would like to suggest that the misogyny in *Creeps* is not only an underacknowledged feature of the script but is also broadly symptomatic, revealing how the development of a play depends in great measure on what is recognized as important—what is *seen* by those involved in the development process—as well as what remains unseen. This, of course, depends on *who* is doing the seeing. It is possible to speculate, for example, that if a woman had been positioned to offer early feedback, she might have asked different questions, offered different imperatives for revision, and shaped a different *Creeps* with a different Thelma. To be clear, it is not my contention that the misogyny in the script is a reflection of Glassco's or Freeman's deliberate intentions for *Creeps*. Rather, it is an indirect consequence of the dramaturgical emphases and de-emphases generated by their subjective assumptions, preoccupations, and priorities. While the agendas pursued by these two white men—Glassco's for polished writing in the tradition of realism, and Freeman's for representing the experience of disability—shaped some of the most celebrated features of the script, they also produced significant blind spots, including the potential for Thelma's role in the play. In this section, I will discuss the implications of unexamined dramaturgical subjectivity, tracing the legacies of some of the values and assumptions that have informed Canadian new play development since the early dramaturgy of Glassco and others in the 1970s.

Glassco's feedback was demonstrably informed by such factors as gender and ability, as well as a set of personal assumptions and priorities taken for granted as dramaturgical "common sense." As dramaturgs have observed in recent years, there is considerable room, in the spontaneous moment of feedback and revision, for the values embedded in the development process to be invisible to both playwright and dramaturg. To address this, Brian Quirt advocates a dramaturgy of "informed subjectivity," openly acknowledging the ways in which his approaches to and opinions about a developing work are "infused with [his own] preferences about theatre, storytelling, and form (among many other things)" (qtd. in Orr 244). Nonetheless, the potential for unexamined influence persists in contemporary dramaturgy. As Maureen Labonté observes in a recent guide to dramaturgical practice: "It's amazing how much we miss when reading a play. How much subjectivity causes us to not see what is actually there." For Labonté, the danger lies not only in failing to recognize these limitations, but in imposing them on playwrights during the development process: "Often in Canada we have a tendency to be paternalistic with our writers, and that is most unfortunate. We spend a lot of time telling them how they should work, what they should write" (qtd. in Trencsényi 93–94). Likewise, in *Theatre of the Unimpressed*, Jordan Tannahill observes the pervasive "desire to 'fix' plays that don't adhere to [a] formula" of inherited dramaturgical convention (51).

Such critiques are not new. Elliott Hayes, writing in 1986, cites a prevailing attitude of "disrespect for the living playwright, who is treated like a Victorian child, seen and not heard." Underlying this paternalism, Hayes finds, is a "masterpiece mentality" pervading play development practices in the 1980s: "the 'masterpieces' are worth producing or watching; other (i.e. original, Canadian) plays 'need work' " (1). Looking back, this attitude may be traced to the practices and assumptions that informed new play development in the 1970s. Part of the self-generated mythology surrounding the alternate theatres was the idea that they were creating original Canadian drama in a "vacuum, without roots, and, indeed, without playwrights" (Gass, Introduction). While the fallacy of this claim has been persuasively demonstrated in Canadian theatre scholarship,[11] the perception of a vacuum produced the conditions for the dramaturgical labour undertaken in these years by directors like Glassco. More importantly, this development work was often conceived as necessary due to the (real or imagined) inexperience of emerging playwrights and the assumed incompleteness of their scripts: "Sure we lack good Canadian plays," observed Gass's co-founder, Frank Trotz, in 1970, but existing "playwriting potential" was there to be developed by "help[ing] writers analyze their mistakes" (qtd. in D. Johnston 82).

Tellingly, Glassco's founding mandate for the Tarragon similarly asserts that "there are many exciting playwrights in Canada," but also that they "need to learn more about shaping a play, or how to write for actors" (qtd. in D. Johnston 149). An indication of the nature of this work—and a striking manifestation of the "masterpiece mentality" that informed it—appears in a 1974 newspaper article on Glassco, who was then on a break from the Tarragon and directing Ibsen in Vancouver. "[A]fter working so hard on making original plays work," Glassco observes,

> it is wonderful to be working on something so good. Let's face it. David Freeman's plays are meaningful and immediate, but they don't have the density of texture of *A Doll's House*. I think he will eventually get into that sort of subtlety. He knows that if he writes a flawed play, I will do it. I'll try and make it as good as possible because we have that connection and that responsibility to him. He has to be

11 See, for example, Alan Filewod's "Named in Passing: Deregimenting Canadian Theatre History" and Scott Duchesne's "A Golf Club for the Golden Age: English Canadian Theatre Historiography and the Strange Case of Roy Mitchell."

> produced so that he has an object lesson of what's right along with what's not right. (qtd. in Allen)

Tracing the evidence of Glassco's work on *Creeps* reveals the effects—both positive and negative—of attending to the perceived "flaws" in the work of a novice playwright. Significantly, however, those positioned in the1970s to undertake such work were themselves inexperienced in developing "playwriting potential." Glassco's dramaturgy at Factory, including his work on *Creeps*, marked his first ever involvement with new plays (D. Johnston 82, 145), and he wasn't alone; in the words of Bob White, another early Factory dramaturg, "everyone who has succeeded at being a dramaturg in this country has, in fact, made it up as they went along" (qtd. in Rudakoff and Thomson 60). White's admission suggests the potential for unexamined assumptions to have informed this early dramaturgy. Evolving an ad hoc process for developing new scripts, Glassco pursued his development of *Creeps* according to the needs of the script *as he saw them*, apparently with little reflexivity concerning his own assumptions or blind spots. This often meant offering bold suggestions (regarding, for example, what Sam would say or feel), prescribing line revisions, and uncritically privileging his own assumptions about what is "necessary." In later years, Freeman would critique the potentially damaging notion that "I couldn't work on the final draft of a play without somebody looking over my shoulder constantly giving me feedback" (Untitled 264). During the process itself, however, the inhibiting potential of Glassco's paternalism, like the shaping effects of his subjective preoccupations and preferences, remained largely invisible to the participants. Often, in the spontaneous moment, that pityshit ain't visible.

THE GRAVITY OF THE UNSEEN DRAMATURG: TOWARDS A HISTORIOGRAPHY OF DRAMATURGICAL INFLUENCE

The role of the dramaturg is often distinguished by its obscurity, described in terms of its peripheral or invisible functions. For Judith Rudakoff, the dramaturg is a "shadowy" figure in the development process, "a type of ghost presence" (Rudakoff and Thomson 3); for Emma Tibaldo, the dramaturg is a "secret, behind-the-scenes resource of support" (qtd. in Radz). In light of this, it is perhaps unsurprising that the history of dramaturgical practice has been largely unexplored in Canadian theatre scholarship. Although scholars like Ric Knowles have identified "the current practices of dramaturgy" among a list of factors contributing to a canon of Canadian drama marked by "aesthetically and therefore ideologically conventional structures" ("Voices" 106), dramaturgy remains historically overlooked. In particular, the early, ad hoc dramaturgical work undertaken among the alternate theatres has been largely invisible in the established histories of Canadian theatre.[12] Among the published accounts of the alternates, there is very little description of the dramaturgical practices employed in the period and no analysis of its implications or effects on individual scripts.

This marked de-emphasis on dramaturgs and dramaturgy in the histories of the alternate theatre may be partly attributed to the ways in which the leaders of the alternates perceived themselves and their work. As many have observed, the dominant narrative of the alternate theatres is a "self-generated history" (Duchesne 140), shaped by the conscious mythmaking of key figures in the period, for whom the project of promoting Canadian playwriting also

12 Of the two book-length histories specific to the alternate theatres, Renate Usmiani's *Second Stage: The Alternative Theatre Movement in Canada* and Denis Johnston's *Up the Mainstream: The Rise of Toronto's Alternative Theatres*, only Johnston's book includes explicit (though passing) reference to dramaturgs or dramaturgy. Likewise, the chapter devoted to "The Alternate Theatre" in Eugene Benson and L.W. Conolly's influential historical survey, *English-Canadian Theatre*, refers specifically to the profession of the dramaturg only once (105).

served the advancement of their careers as theatre directors (and, often, artistic directors). If new play development was initially conceived as a necessary, but incidental, extension of this primary directorial role, it is unsurprising that a peripheral conception of dramaturgy is reproduced in the dominant and "self-generated" histories of the alternate theatre, and even in the ways we conceive of the dramaturg as a "secret behind-the-scenes resource of support" today.

Like the most powerful offstage characters, however, the invisible presence of the dramaturg can be detected by his or her "gravitational effects," to revisit (and adapt) Sofer's theory of "*[i]nvisibility [as] the dark matter of theatre*" (332; emphasis in original). Through a process he terms "spectral reading," Sofer's aim is to "trace the gravitational effects of invisible forces at work in the world of the play or performance, such as characters [like Thelma] who never appear" (333). To uncover the hidden contributions of dramaturgs and dramaturgy, I propose a historiographical extension of this process, one that uses the archives to reconstruct the weighty influence of that "ghost presence" in new play development, the dramaturg. As demonstrated by my analysis of the surviving drafts of *Creeps*, tracing the gravitational effects of dramaturgy illuminates what would otherwise remain obscure, revealing the unexamined values that inform dramaturgical feedback and demonstrating the shaping contributions of the dramaturg to the development of the script.

Further research into early new play development will enhance our understanding of both Canadian theatre history and dramaturgical practice. By attending to his contributions *as a dramaturg*, for example, this analysis expands and reassesses Glassco's undeniable significance as a shaping force in Canadian theatre. Beyond this, evidence of Glassco's dramaturgical influence presents a challenge to received histories that construct collaboration, among the Toronto alternates, as the exclusive province of Theatre Passe Muraille, inviting new ways of conceiving of the processes of play creation at the Factory and Tarragon—two companies discursively and historically constructed as the "home[s] of the Canadian playwright" and of text-based, single-authored plays.[13] Moreover, Glassco's case suggests the possibility to trace the historical origins of many of the values and practices that continue to inform new play dramaturgy in Canada. For example, Glassco followed the script-based, "table work" model of playwright-dramaturg consultation that would proliferate in later decades. The case of *Creeps* offers a new way to understand—and affirm—recurring critiques of this approach as inherently logocentric and "skewed toward naturalism," "emphasizing dialogue [and] emotional throughline" (Flaherty 22). Likewise, Glassco's work on *Creeps* points to the historical significance of gendered subjectivity as a shaping influence on early dramaturgy at the alternate theatres—work which was undertaken predominantly by male directors and artistic directors. Amanda Hale recalls of a 1974 theatre conference featuring "all the pioneers of Canadian alternate theatre" that "[t]he male voices were loud" (81). Certainly, the gendered biases exposed in Glassco's process—which reduced the potential power of Thelma's voice in *Creeps* to an "impotent cry" (Wasserman, *Modern* 84)—suggest some of the challenges historically faced by women playwrights in Canada. Writing decades later, Margaret Hollingsworth observes the high number of Canadian women playwrights told in the processes of development and production that "they had produced a monster," highlighting the inhibiting potential of dramaturgical paternalism, particularly when "the rigorous principles of playwriting [are] applied by men" (16).

Crucially, too, the dominant "principles of playwriting" are informed by our national dramatic canon. Inherited ideas about what constitutes a "Canadian play" operate as what Knowles has described as a regulating "dramaturgical unconscious" (*Theatre of Form* 25).[14] Uncovering assumptions about

---

13 It was the Factory Theatre Lab that explicitly dubbed itself "Home of the Canadian Playwright." From its earliest press release Tarragon established its "primary aim" of "nurtur[ing] Canadian playwriting talent" (qtd in D. Johnston 150) and was thereafter discursively constructed as "a playwright's theatre."

14 In addition to *Creeps*, Glassco's early dramaturgy contributed to several other canonical plays, including most famously David French's *Leaving Home* (shortly after his work with Freeman on *Creeps*), as well as many of French's subsequent scripts. As Ric Knowles has argued, "the poetic naturalism of the Davids French and Freeman" (along with

literary value and theatrical form embedded in the development of canonical works invites a reassessment of the dramaturgical "common sense" that continues to exert gravitational force in Canadian theatre. Finally, it is important that a historiography of dramaturgical invisibility involve not only tracing development processes as they unfolded in the past, but also imagining what *might have been*. This, too, is a form of gravity. In the case of *Creeps*, while the developmental imperatives pursued by Glassco shaped key features in the script, including its celebrated "gritty realism," they also carried a cost for Thelma and limited the potential meanings generated by the play. Exposing the historical effects of new play dramaturgy can thus change the way we read canonical works and understand the conditions that informed their writing. Although largely unacknowledged and unexamined in the received historical narrative, early dramaturgs and dramaturgy have helped shape the development of Canadian theatre. There is much to be learned from attending to this weighty absence, making the unseen contributions of the dramaturg more historically visible.

---

neo-Aristotelian and Oedipal dimensions discernable in the works of both playwrights) has been one of the cornerstones of the dominant dramaturgical inheritance of the drama emerging from the 1970s and from the Tarragon Theatre in particular (*Theatre of Form* 53).

PART 3: RETHINKINGS

INTERVENTIONS INTO THE MAW OF OLD WORLD HUNGER: FROG MONSTERS, KINSTELLATORY MAPS, AND RADICAL RELATIONALITIES IN A PROJECT OF REWORLDING

JILL CARTER, KARYN RECOLLET, AND DYLAN ROBINSON[1]

The chapter that follows is an edited transcript of a round table that took place on 30 May 2016 at the Canadian Association for Theatre Research conference, held at the University of Calgary, located on the traditional territories of the Blackfoot and the people of the Treaty 7 region of Southern Alberta, which includes the Siksika, the Piikuni, the Kainai, the Tsuu T'ina, and the Stony Nakota First Nations. The questions that initially prompted this seminar were: How are theories for understanding the past encoded in performances that emerge from oral history? How can performance historians recognize and address the grounded contexts of culturally and spatially specific Indigenous critical theories and research methodologies; in other words, what are the potentials and pitfalls of international, that is between Indigenous nations, or trans-Indigenous applications of Indigenous methodologies and theories? What historiographical assumptions—about time, place, and space; genres of performance; and transmission of knowledges of the past—are challenged when Indigenous world views are explicitly brought to bear on the performances of the past?

---

1 With special thanks to Phay Gagnon for recording and transcribing the seminar proceedings.

DYLAN: Ch'itolétsel, Treaty 7 ó:wqw'elmexw. ch'ítolétsel, kw'as xólhmetelep ye tém:éxw íkw'elò. My name is Dylan Robinson. I'm Canada Research Chair in Indigenous Arts at Queen's University in Kingston, on the lands of the Haudenosaunee and Anishinaabe. I am Stó:lō, on my mother's side of the family. We have many nations up and down the Fraser River and Stó:lō is the word that seems to have stuck, to refer to all of our nations along the river. I also like to say that Stó:lō is the word that settlers—xwelítem—kept hearing again and again and I imagine the first newcomers to our lands kept hearing the word Stó:lō and assumed that was the word we used to call our people. But "Stó:lō" actually translates to river, and it was and is said so much because everything is oriented toward the river, everything that we do.

KARYN: My name is Karyn Recollet and I teach at the University of Toronto in the Women and Gender Studies Institute. I want to extend my appreciation for the caretakers of this Treaty 7 territory, and for all of the relationships with human and non-human relatives that are maintained, for providing the visions of futurity, in such a generative/imaginative space within which we relate our ideas and share thoughts today. I am Cree, originally from Sturgeon Lake First Nation, which is north of Prince Albert in Saskatchewan, so as I breathe the air here in Calgary I'm reminded of the air that I breathe back at Sturgeon Lake and Prince Albert and Saskatoon and all those spaces. I share mothering a five-year-old baby girl named Gracie with a wonderful community of aunties and nurturing folks in Toronto. I recognize those who are behind you and the work, and the caretaking that you do within your lives too. The thoughts and activations that I carry forward are centred on urban Indigenous spaces. Some of my research is on Indigenous hip hop, exploring cultural production in urban places, and the complex Indigeneities that are happening everywhere at all times. I have the honour and privilege of working in the same space as Jill Carter; I see her beautiful presence on campus maybe once a month and I'm always happy to see her. Dylan and I share cyberspace and I feel his support across territories. Thank you for bringing us all together and I'm quite happy to be here.

JILL: My name is Jill Carter and I work at the University of Toronto, within Indigenous Studies; the Transitional Year Programme; and the Centre for Drama, Theatre and Performance Studies. I'm a mixed-blood Anishinaabe woman. My bloodlines travel from Manitoulin Island and Ekaterinburg, Russia, to meet in me in Takaronto where I was born and raised. Takaronto is Treaty 13 territory, and it has been a space of meeting, commerce, and celebration for tens of thousands of years, stewarded alternately by the Erie, the Petun, the Wendat, the Haudenosaunee, and, most recently, the Anishinaabeg of Mississauga New Credit First Nation. It is a great privilege to be here to see and converse with two profoundly beautiful colleagues, and I echo them as I extend my thanks to Heather Davis-Fisch for bringing us together, to Phay Gagnon for supporting this work, and to all of you for being here to share this conversation, and, of course, to the original caretakers of this land whose good work continues each day, so that we are able to gather today in this beautiful place.

DYLAN: I have been thinking a lot about the practice of acknowledgement. CAUT—the Canadian Association of University Teachers—has launched a document in the spring of 2016 that outlines the appropriate ways to acknowledge the people whose lands universities are situated on. I am a little skeptical of a number of initiatives such as this that take place within what I've been calling the "bureaucratization of protocol." So I want to thank my colleagues here for modelling a different kind of acknowledgement; it's grounding to hear you talk about the ways in which it's meaningful to be here on these lands and what it means for you to be working in different Indigenous territories.

This CAUT document makes me think about the different ways in which Indigenous people acknowledge our relationships, our connections to the lands we are from and those we are visitors in. Because it's quite easy of course to announce those written-out acknowledgements CAUT has crafted—to say the names of the nation whose lands you are on (or butcher the pronunciation of the name as the case may be)—and while acknowledgement is an important thing to do, we have to recognize that acknowledgement is an irreducibly relational and situational protocol. Everything changes depending on who you are and to whom you're speaking to. It's really interesting to me, the kind of massive uptake of acknowledgement in Vancouver of being on "unceded Coast Salish territories." We need to ask what work bureaucratized acknowledgement does; in what ways does this kind of acknowledgement act as what Sara Ahmed calls "non-performative."

I just organized a gathering in Vancouver called "Doing Sovereignties," which was about the ways in which sovereignty is a practice that we do, particularly—from my perspective—through our protocols, through our songs. Sovereignty isn't just the official modes of governance, of written law, but something that we do every day in various ways. Thinking about that form of doing sovereignty, not just exclusively related to songs and dances and our traditions, but also walking—what is the practice of sovereign walking through our territories and breathing the air? This gathering brought to my attention the fact that with all the Indigenous artists and scholars that we brought together for three days, Indigenous scholars across the arts haven't, until relatively recently, had many chances to gather. It illuminated the fact that we have a lot to talk about and we have a lot of history to share between ourselves that we don't know. Coming here has reinforced for me that I know very, very little about this land here and need to do a lot to educate myself about the history. This is something that we have not had the opportunity to learn. I think many of us in the room are in this situation. Through curriculum, through high school, through university, you think about all the courses on European politics; we could—we should—have similar courses on all of our nations' histories and cultures and these things should be integrated fully within all educational curriculum, not just for settler students but for Indigenous students.

These are some things that have been on my mind recently and I hope to come back to them through some of what I'm going to talk about today. I'd like to frame the next part of the presentation with the title "Stop Indigenizing your Methodologies."

I'd like to begin today with a small admission: when Heather first invited me to this round table my first reaction was one of wariness. Since Len Findlay's first call to "Always Indigenize," many scholars across the humanities have sought to learn how Indigenous methodologies might be activated within their research, artistic practice, and teaching. This work has proceeded by affirming values of reciprocity, responsibility, and accountability, and particular models based upon nation-specific values, place-specific knowledge, and language-specific concepts.

Reciprocity, considering what it means to be responsible for knowledge, and having accountability to those who you learn from, are of course foundational not just for Indigenous methodologies, but to a more generalized ethics of research. Similarly, thinking through how histories of place and cultural specificity are connected to the work we do as artists and scholars is not just part of becoming better acquainted with the land which you occupy, but part of a larger critical reflexivity. Our research and artistic practices should be situated in relationship with these values not as an exceptional choice, but an everyday fact.

So I was, and remain, wary. In reading work by non-Indigenous scholars who have participated in the recognition and foregrounding of Indigenous knowledge that is often called "Indigenizing the academy," I have come to feel that, more and more frequently, Indigenization acts as a form of extraction that parallels resource extraction upon the lands and waters of Indigenous peoples across Canada. The knowledge economy we participate in is governed by extractivist principles where our knowledges, world views, languages, and cultural practices have become resources. This is not an Indigenous economy of trade, but rather a situation where we hear our words spoken through structures and grammars of settler logic. I am increasingly aware in this reconciliatory time and space that privileges forms of coming together that there is an increasing amount of work that shifts the terms just enough *not* to unsettle. To take seriously Glen Coulthard's call for "grounded normativity," that is, for Indigenous "place-based practices and associated forms of knowledge" (13) is also to understand that such work is inextricable from Indigenous experience, not in speaking *for* such experience, and not from speaking to someone about such experience and then redescribing it. To return to my feeling of wariness, this feeling did not result from Heather's lovely invitation to join this forum, but rather from an accumulative weariness of witnessing extraction, and of recent experiences being subject to what I think of as "extractive inclusion."

I have come late to the common experience of having work and knowledge extracted as a resource; I have come late to being a "native informant." I want to also be clear here that I'm not talking about practices of citation and referencing, but instead about a desire or hunger to know. Amongst Indigenous colleagues, this is certainly not an experience that is unfamiliar. In fact, historically, this state of hunger is at the heart of historical encounter between Stó:lō people and settlers, or those who we call "xwelítem" in Halq'emeylem.

"Xwelítem" means much more than the equivalent term for "settler"; more accurately, the word "xwelítem" means "starving person." As I understand it, the word came into use because, when settlers first arrived in our territories, they were starving. They were starving literally, for food; but starving also for gold. It is an understatement to say that this hunger for resources has not abated with time. Xwelítem hunger has long existed for the rocks, the trees, the water, and the land itself. Each has been thirsted after, each has been consumed. Much has been written since the word "appropriation" was first used to define one form of this hunger. Today we witness new forms of hunger that may seem more benign, forms that invite Indigenous people to join the conversation at the table of recognition and inclusion, to join together in hunger. Indigenizing work by xwelítem scholars, I'd like to suggest, is what we might think of as a "steady state" of hunger: hunger to do the right thing, to fit the Indigenous into one part of the multicultural mosaic, to understand and make accessible Indigenous "issues" through settler logics.

The methodological framework I would like to describe today firmly refuses structures of reconciliation, the imperative for settler scholars and Indigenous scholars to come together in intercultural harmony. I'm looking at methodologies of sovereignty that are multiple, that refuse Indigenizing as the mere application of Indigenous methodologies at a distance from lived experience, and instead demand that settler researchers and Indigenous scholars do some work together apart. This is very much inspired by David Garneau's work on "irreconcilable spaces of aboriginality" (26), which calls for separate spaces of doing work as Indigenous people, both that is nation-specific—for instance gatherings of Stó:lō people to discuss the next steps of Indigenous resurgence, or of Indigenous artists from across nations to think of what kind of international work we must do—and so it's a practice that's quite diverse.

To provide an example of this, for the next few minutes, I'd like to speak primarily to tel siyam q'ó:ltheteq, my friends here—Karyn Recollet, Jill Carter—that I return to think together with, as well as xwelmexw sí:yáye tl'ócha íkw'elò, other Indigenous scholars and respected friends that I hope to work with:

el siyam sí:yáye, I'd like to pose questions of sovereign methodologies for Indigenous scholars. Selchí:mcha: How shall it be? How should it be? How shall we define for ourselves sovereign methodologies; how shall we stand the ground of methodology to create benefit for our future generations? How shall we advance methodologies that re-embody sovereign forms of sensing the world of shxwelí—life around us? How shall we create sovereign spaces for our work to take shape; resurgent structures for viewing, returning to and affirming forms of gathering, ways of listening that are grounded in our nation- and community-specific forms of perception? How shall we acknowledge and explore intercommunity forms for coming together, of trade, that honour and affirm kinship ties between communities that have become fractured? How might we think more expansively of how the spaces we use, and how the structures of presentation might change to allow us to speak in different ways, and to listen in different ways? I name such normative structures of presentation here with the full knowledge that we have done much work already that seeks to transform the gallery, the theatre, the classroom. Sometimes we need new rooms and sometimes these spaces are the right ones for our work. But we must also redefine our structures of presentation and engagement because these structures set the terms of engagement. We are responsible not just for thinking about the work, but for thinking about the ways in which the work is situated: How would we like it to be read, listened to, viewed, or witnessed by each other? Rethinking structures is not simply an exercise to create spaces defined by Indigenous logics, but a necessity for intervening in unmarked forms of perception—colonial scopophilia, hungry viewing, and the "collecting gaze" desirous of Indigenous content and objects. How do we move beyond feeding the hunger for only certain kinds of stories (stories of trauma, of healing, of transformation)? How might we more explicitly demand new structures, new contexts that require a listening not driven by the desire to consume knowledge? To what extent can this be achieved through creating works that demand new structures of perception that are not starving, and to what extent does this need for new structures of perception result through shifting the presentational frame?

Many of our academic spaces for gathering, and our artistic places for viewing and listening, remain unmarked; the acts of viewing and listening remain shxwelítemelh: they remain hungry. These spaces situate the norms of looking and listening, norms that participate in allowing starving sight and hungry listening to continue. We sit in such a space right now. The form of the round table is shxwelítemelh, as is the structure of our associations, our journals, our books, as is the structure of the Congress of the Humanities and Social Sciences. I'd like to ask that we reconsider the very concept of methodology, the English word "methodology," as an overarching system for knowledge gathering and acquisition and who this concept serves. And what other concepts might we need to bring into the discussion that serve our communities in different ways?

KARYN: While you were speaking, Dylan, I was thinking through these practices of hunger, consumption, and their implications for Indigenous life and process. For instance, within a settler colonial context, people are encouraged and rewarded for how they consume land, territories; this gets expanded to the consumption of ideas, words, and processes, and this becomes intermeshed with the desire and hunger for Indigenous methodologies. Practising an active and ongoing refusal of such erasures and dispossessions, overflowing the boundaries of lands, bodies, and consciousnesses, Ashon Crawley's 2016 "Otherwise Movements" embodies these activated refusals. Intervening in these systems of thirst and hunger are Indigenous desirous futurities, and the creation of processes and possibilities for imagining worlds (Crawley). In Crawley's article, gesturing Otherwise is a process of dreaming new worlds into being, a refusal of being stilled, and the activation of a radical imagination whereby social change is created through different forms of nuance and style. If we can consider this in terms of radical relationalities in Indigenous gathering spaces (houses that are citied), there is process, methodology that is enacted in the everyday. Consumptive behaviours have no space here because these forces are constantly reactivating and rejuvenating themselves in a constant flow—creative intimacies forever creating "otherwise"—of surgent spaces. Settler colonialism entrenches a hoarding approach to Indigenous process, without the ethical awareness toward how these are held and carried to move within our bodies across territories. Western notions of love and settler colonial intimacy encourage us to perceive the worlds around us through the lens of possession and ownership, encoding these situated forms of love and intimacy with land, territories, and each other. In shifting these processes and structures, we desire worlds Otherwise and this desire can come from a place that is not about consuming bodies, or knowledges, and still remain intimately tied to land and land spaces at the urban scale(s). I was thinking about Mohawk scholar Audra Simpson's *Mohawk Interruptus* and the ideation processes she engages in critiquing the nation-state's consumptive desire and murderous intent as a hunger for Indigenous women's bodies as embodiments of Indigenous governance systems. Settler colonial consumption and hunger have brought about the crisis that we're in right now, in terms of missing, murdered, and disappeared women, queer, two-spirit, and trans lives.

Our collective hunger can manifest in so many ways. Diaspora, exile, and motion as a choreography of survival across territories have been legacies of movements for brown and black bodies. I remember being very hungry for "home"—a very complex and nuanced concept—within my own experience of dislocation as a Cree adoptee. I don't mean to tell this as a story as a way of narrating victimization or damage (Tuck 413); I think that we have to be cognizant of the ways in which stories have been and continue to be taken up by the academy in really harmful ways. In my twenties I was teaching at an urban Indigenous educational institute in Prince Albert, Saskatchewan, when my mooshom (grandfather), according to Cree understandings of kinship, was invited to share knowledge of Cree epistemologies. After his talk I came up to him and he looked at me and he said, "you were scaring me . . . just the way you were looking at me was scaring me." I carry that moment with me into adulthood as a reminder of my own hunger where his very being was home, territory, space—an Otherwise that I had only imagined. I was hungry in a way that I had to come to terms with and it took me a long time to find Cree epistemology in the everyday, the motion, the ways that ideas flow, choreographies of motion.

I think about process and methodologies as the activations of Indigenous layers and scales, such as the celestial, and the underground waterways. I'm really interested in thinking about the stories of the celestial. We have our own stories in Cree about the celestial and the star maps as part of critical Indigenous land pedagogies that are overflowing their own boundaries of being rooted rhizomatically downwards. Thinking about traditional territories as including the celestial really opens up how I think about kinstellatory relationships that are based upon our reciprocity and radical relationalities with multiple Indigenous scales.

Dylan, you had mentioned acknowledgements. I think that acknowledgements are multiscalar too and disrupt the fragmentation that we have toward lands and bodies. Constellatory relationality generates thinking about the human and the non-human within those acknowledgements to consider how we are in kinstellatory relationality. What can star knowledge tell us about being in radical kinship with each other? Of course there is so much knowledge in Indigenous intelligence and cosmologies: this is not new thinking. These sites of knowledge share important ideas about how we relate to space and place—so kinship is grounded and spatially specific—in multiscalar flows.

Anishinaabek and Nehiyawak (Cree) activations of decolonial love, as expressed by Michi Saagig artist/scholar Leanne Simpson (*Islands*) and Cree artist/scholar Billy-Ray Belcourt, propels deep consideration toward processes of futurity building emerging from spaces of decolonial love.[2] These conversations inform processes we then mobilize in holding and creating spaces, in movement building. When you enter into a relationship with somebody, you acknowledge their process. You acknowledge, "You are a water carrier, and/or a fire keeper—I don't want to take your fire—you need that." These types of protocols we practise in our everyday, determining how we construct our homes, and how we think about how we think about our movements and gestures within specific territorial spaces. These everyday kind of sovereignties are rooted in forms of decolonial love with the human and the non-human. I think that our perceptions of those spaces and places honours this sort of remembrance, honours ancestors, but also honours futurity, a continuing survivance (Vizenor, *Manifest* vii). I think about some of the ways in which Indigenous artists hold space for each other within and across territories, embracing all of the messiness and moments of synchronicity that surge forward.

I think this is what our ancestors have always done—held spaces for each other across territory—because as Indigenous folks we are born into motion. We have relationships with land and spaces but we also have relationships with the water, which is constantly moving. We have relationships with wild rice: in some territories, when you actually pick the wild rice you are reseeding. I learned this from the inspiring Anishinaabe activist/artist/futurity-builder Melody McKiver. We are born into constant motion and if we are activating methodologies and processes, then its important to centre this decolonially loving movement as constant reworlding motion. Why not think about mirroring constellations: if you're going to mirror something, mirror constellations, like the movement Idle No More, born of the principle

2 My thinking of decolonial love draws upon, and is in conversation with, both Simpson's (*Islands of Decolonial Love*) and Belcourt's (nakinisowin.wordpress.com) articulations of decolonial love whereby radical decolonial love is an urgent matter of Indigenous survivance. Radical decolonial love and creative intimacy are Indigenous forms of holding spaces for each other through, within, and despite the rapturous interstices of settler colonialism. Radical decolonial love presents itself in all of its flaws, inconsistencies, imperfections, ruptures, releases, gorgeousness, and brilliance.

of love in our actions to activate the territorial, radical relationalities that are bringing what is traditional into the future.

The founders of the Idle No More activations (Sylvia McAdam Saysewahum, Sheelah McLean, Nina Wilson, and Jessica Gordon) encouraged activating the territory from which you are situated—this is what the movement has always been about. The gestures and choreographies of the round dance revolution, the formulation and reinscription of concentric circles at Yonge and Dundas Square in Toronto, for instance, remind me of the multiple scales that are being activated. There are also celestial things going on that mirror the motion and the movement of folks who are trying to transform and create other worlds in this realm. This shapes the trajectories of stories. These activations are happening, folks are gathering, producing these inspiring movements and "creative solidarities" (Gaztambide-Fernandez 56)—movements are coming together in creative solidarity, for instance between Black Lives Matter and the movement to resist the Dakota Access Pipeline at the Sacred Stone Camp in North Dakota.

Dancer/choreographer Starr Muranko's collaborative performance *Spine of the Mother* was brought to Native Earth Performing Arts's Weesageechak Begins to Dance Festival in 2015. The choreography has dance artist Tasha Faye Evans gesture outward to grasp stars from the constellatory scrim behind her, stars which manifest into small rocks that Evans then places on top of dance-maker Andrea Patriaus, who is lying on the dance floor with her legs bent as if in a semi-fetal position. Positioning outwards to mirror star worlds and constellations, this activation gestures toward considering choreography as writing or glyphing bodies, to reworld and reshape the ways in which we radically relate to each other, as though producing constellatory "theories of change" (Tuck 413). In Michelle Thrush's conversation about *Making Treaty 7*, she reminded us of the value in listening deeply and witnessing, in attenuating to the layering of the land.[3] I don't want to make assumptions, but I believe

---

3 Earlier on 30 May 2016, *Canadian Theatre Review* sponsored a plenary panel on "Indigenous Practice/Making Treaty 7," featuring Michelle Thrush, Troy Emery Twigg, and Andy Curtis. The artists discussed their experience working on and performing the

Michelle was talking about those Indigenous scales that exist not only above and below but also outwardly. I thought that was really interesting: How do we gesture futurity, how do we gesture toward being rhizomatically rooted this way? [I gesture outwards and above toward what exceeds the limits of terrestrial.] The reach for land pedagogies needs to spill over—"spinning us out beyond the terrains as well as we are in the terrains" (J. Gray). Isn't decolonization just activating spaces by unearthing stories and scales as spatial trajectories toward futurity? We need to remap the fluidity and collapse of time/space to consider our future ancestors. Originally we weren't thinking about these binaries, we were thinking about the past-present, and the future-past. "Our future ancestors" acknowledges these scales, as Tahltan artist/scholar Peter Morin discusses. We need to reframe the language through which we speak about our worlds, our realities, and I think that we can do that through listening and witnessing.

Choreography is interesting to look at as a way of reworlding. I've been thinking about Ashon Crawley's work a lot. I've been watching the Beyoncé video "Formation" to consider how these choreographies can be seen as spatial maps to futurity making. I think that the work of stars' choreographies—how they move and shape future/ancient possibilities—can be seen as mappings; these are mappings to futurity. This also extends to Starr Muranko's choreographies as "writing" stars through movements. We build a relationship to the lands through activating it, in similar ways to how we build radical relationalities through radical love with each other as human and non-human beings. I believe that this activation can come in the form of choreographic fugitivity, as a process of glyphing, an ancient futurity practice of imprinting futures on rock—as territories that hold spaces as acts of remembrance (Recollet 91). Black expressions within popular culture can also be seen as vehicles capable of glyphing remembrance of leaders, such as the X formation glyphed by the dance artists, and the counter-hegemonic anti-violent space produced by the young dancer who situated their body against the line

multidisciplinary piece, which explored historical events at Blackfoot Crossing in 1877 and their consequences today.

of the state in Beyoncé's video. Similarly hoop dancers such as Cree dancemaker James Jones are shaping worlds in A Tribe Called Red's performances all across Turtle Island and beyond.[4] The technologies of the remix in these instances actually illuminate the scales that are already present, including the intentionality of presence that has yet to come fully into light.

I think of love and hope as futurity projects inspiring motion. I think that worlding sometimes requires that we make these shifts in the way that we speak—to transcend the limitations of language. Let's talk about what makes the hairs on the back of your neck stick up, let's use that as a language or gesture to build our futures and to reworld.

JILL: Anishinaabe Elder Eddie King from Wikwemikong tells a delightful story about hunger that is as cautionary as it is empowering. Based upon traditional teachings of the Odawa Midewiwin Lodge, it has been re-worked by Elder King with the Debajehmujig ("storyteller") Theatre Group into a contemporary play—*The Gift*. First produced in 2003 in the Mission-ruins in Wikwemikong, it continues to be performed across Turtle Island in a giant, portable tipi. Here, a single storyteller, flanked by two musical muses, takes the stage, not as an authority, but as one who is searching for his place as an Anishinaabe who has been given a story to tell and tasked (by Elder King) with its telling. Our storyteller spends much of his time evading his task, which is to recount this origin story of the Frog Monster. He hesitates, prevaricates and rationalizes: "Oh wait, are [we] ready"? What if he tells the "wrong story"? He has nowhere to sit! What if he picks the "wrong stump" upon which to sit and tell his story (De-ba-jeh-mu-jig 176)?[5]

4 A Tribe Called Red, made up of three members—2oolman, DJ NDN, and Bear Witness—produces music layering house, electronic, and pow wow dubstep, with Indigenous expressions of sonic sovereignty. The collective's third album, *We Are the Halluci Nation* connects ATCR with artists such as Tanya Tagaq, Black Bear, and Yasiin Bey, a.k.a Mos Def.

5 "You see, traditionally storytellers sat on stumps when they told stories" (De-ba-jeh-mu-jig 176). But in the space we share for this performative event, the storyteller, his musical muses, and the witnesses all sit on stumps. We are all responsible to the story. We are all

Eventually, the evasions cease. And our reluctant storyteller, Joe Osawabine, begins to tell the story of a monstrous frog who has sprawled himself across the mouth of a river, blocking the flow of water to hoard it for himself, so that the Anishinaabeg living downstream begin to perish of thirst. At last, an unnamed hero—unnamed, as many of the protagonists of our stories are—takes it upon himself to travel up the dry riverbed to discover the source of the drought. Embedded in the "archive" (the story) and in the "repertoire" (its telling) are seven Odawa values: "Love, Honour, Respect, Truth, Trust, Compassion, and Patience" (De-ba-jeh-mu-jig 180). This is the story of one who is willing to sacrifice himself so that others might live, who will not lie to spare himself hardship, and who exercises great compassion to uphold the teachings (through action) that define the Anishinaabe—the exceedingly good ("nishin") human being ("naabe"). This culture hero will achieve no personal fame or lasting glory; his name is lost to history; only the deed is remembered. Its benefits (or consequences) constitute the legacy that outlives the man himself and the memory of even his name.

When our unnamed hero encounters the source of his people's misery, he is offered a deal. The Frog Monster will release the water (the lifeblood of creation) and allow it to flow down to the people if this young man will offer him "unconditional love" in exchange (De-ba-jeh-mu-jig 180). Our hero has too much respect and honesty to dissemble; he's not unloving, but he's also not a liar. He knows love is reciprocal and cannot be purchased through extortion, so he rejects the bargain. They do battle then, and our hero defeats the Frog Monster. And out of the chaos of their mythic battle—out of the devastating impact of their superhuman collision—creation occurs: Manitoulin Island with all its medicines is created, as are seven great bodies of water—the five Great Lakes plus Lake Saint Clair and the Hudson Bay. And those bodies of life coincide with the seven Odawa values that we encounter in this story. As the Frog Monster, finally, lies beaten and broken on the ground, the creator instructs the nameless man to "go ahead and kill the Frog Monster for what

---

responsible for the teachings we take from it and for how we will carry those teachings in our attitudes and behaviours.

he [has] done." But the nameless man cannot bring himself to do this because such action would run counter to the Odawa value system, which he upholds. So, the creator transforms the fallen monster's destructive power (through the creature's descendants) into a multitude of little blessings—the generations of frogs who control the wetlands' mosquito populations and who alert us of the coming rains in cheerful song (De-ba-jeh-mu-jig 180).

The Anishinaabe storyteller in *The Gift* lives out, in corporeal performance, a structural tenet of Indigenous storytelling and provides a way into this paradigm for researchers and critics as we seek to engage with this work, to enrich ourselves and to benefit our communities by sharing what we have encountered and what we have learned through the encounter. For this storyteller, the theory (the cognitive structures underpinning a people's lifeway) that manifests itself within this performative encounter is "personal"—and this is, as Leanne Simpson reminds us, as it has always been and as it should continue to be (*Dancing* 39; fn 57). The storyteller does not stand apart from the creation story he is recounting; rather, he weaves himself into it; he wrestles with the questions it inspires; and he personalizes them. Who is he as "researcher?" Who is this one who mines an ancient treasure, sifting through it to make and disseminate its meaning? Do his process (played out before us in real time) and the product of his labours reveal him to be, in essence, a frog monster or a culture hero? The repertoire (Joe Osawabine's performance), here, somatically discharges a theory of being and, in so doing, assiduously preserves it in the archive.[6] It models and instructs us in the humility, transparency, and self-reflection that must accompany all research endeavours. Debajehmujig has not extracted an ancient story and offered it up to be consumed; rather, through artful dissemination, this ancient story has been rendered into something that *consumes the contemporary witness*—an agent of transformation that carries in its telling the power to reworld.

6 Anishinaabe creation stories, as Leanne Simpson and Edna Manitowabi remind us, are not simply speech acts upon which we are invited to theorize. Rather, our creation stories "set the 'theoretical framework,' or give us the ontological context from which we can interpret other stories, teachings, and experiences" (280).

Often when I encounter non-Indigenous people working in any sort of research partnership, there is an eschewal of heuristic practice and a hesitancy or outright refusal to reflect upon and share the researcher's personal journey. This very well may be a consequence of humility: a desire to listen rather than speak, a desire to learn rather than teach. But humility is not passivity. And passivity—when it manifests itself as a refusal to personally engage in encounter—is not humility. Such passivity, manifested in silence, will bring our peoples no closer to conciliation than did the outright contempt for and forceful silencing of Indigenous peoples that characterized Canada's relationship with its treaty partners. In the political arenas, in research partnerships, and in social interactions, it may begin to manifest itself in the same "disease" that American director Anne Bogart fears in the rehearsal studio:

> The process of collaboration is a road littered with real and tangible obstacles. Passivity is one of the most predominant problems because collaboration is too often misunderstood as agreement. But collaboration is emphatically not agreement. With too much agreement, too little happens. "The disease of agreement" engenders passivity and even worse *passive aggression*. (n.p.; emphasis added)

As we listen to the stories about which we will tell stories, or as we bear witness to the testimony of experience, we are charged with the responsibility to engage with these things *personally*—to hike up the riverbed and battle the frog monster (within or without) and through the endeavour to ask and begin to answer, "Who am I in all of this?"

During the discussion on the making of *Making Treaty Seven*, it was such a gift to hear Andy Curtis (from One Yellow Rabbit) share how he as a non-Indigenous theatre worker explored these questions during his partnership with that show's creative team. "What does it mean to know who you are and where you are from?" he asked. Because he recognized that, as a product of Canada's culture of forgetting, he does "not own [his] story in the same way as they [his Indigenous colleagues] do" he began with the exercise of really "listening." As he began to encounter and understand "different ways of holding stories," and as he became more comfortable working within hitherto unfamiliar processes, he was able to weave himself into these stories and processes—to recognize himself and acknowledge himself personally accountable to them: "Who am I *now* in this place?" he asked. What, he was asking, is my responsibility to *this* Story? What are the actions I must pursue to live out my duty to this encounter in this historical moment? This strikes me as a mode of conversing that has been undertaken in the spirit of true collaboration and out of a desire for true conciliation. Curtis's testimony models the courage and generosity of a soul that *hungers* for transformation. It offers possibilities of reworlding through engaged collaboration within which the stories *to and for* which we are accountable are recognized, acknowledged, and shared. Curtis's words resonate with me as healthful and loving manifestations of hunger—a hunger for truth, a hunger for honour exercised through the ownership of responsibility, and a hunger for life-affirming and life-sustaining relationships.

Hunger and thirst, in and of themselves, are inescapable conditions governing fleshly existence. Our nameless hero and the Frog Monster he battled were both driven by these cravings. We are all hungry. We all thirst. These are "first things," part of the bundle with which we were born. The processes through which we choose to sate ourselves determine whether we play out our stories as equal partners in creation or as Frog Monsters, as "xwelítem," as bloated agents of destruction.

I've been experimenting with my own intervention into the maw of hunger, as I have experienced it in the classroom, in the rehearsal hall, and in the interventions I have organized or participated in with Indigenous Performing Arts Alliance, *Talking Treaties*, and First Story, Toronto. In 2014, there were 84,556 students enrolled at the University of Toronto. Approximately three hundred students identified as Indigenous (to Canada), and if we take into account those who choose not to identify, we could safely estimate their numbers at five hundred to seven hundred students. Obviously, then, in most classes that I teach, settler students far outnumber Indigenous students. Their openness to and hunger for the truth are wonderful. But, unchecked and misdirected, this hunger can also overwhelm, frighten, and sadden. There is beauty here, but it is a "terrible beauty" (Yeats)—a frog monster—born of forgetting and fattened on mourning, requiring a firm hand and compassionate address to forestall the destruction that it promises.

British-Canadian researcher Natalie Chambers has demonstrated, after years of research with immigrant and refugee peoples, that Canada's "collective amnesia" has arisen not simply out of malice or negligence but as a "survival strategy [. . .] to protect [newcomers to these shores] from [the] chaos—created by guilt, grief, insecurity, and dislocation" (260–61). But, as she observes, this survival strategy has not ordered the chaos; rather, it has produced an inchoate disconnect, rupturing the relationships between guest and host, between humans and their biotas, and between mind and heart. When Jeannette Armstrong (quoting her father) characterizes non-Indigenous Canadians as "dangerous," as "insane," as "people without hearts [who] are wild and scatter anywhere" (qtd. in Chambers 261), she holds up a mirror to all Canadians, allowing them to view themselves, momentarily, through the eyes of their Indigenous neighbours and to see clearly just what this "survival strategy" has cost all of us: we are, all of us (in our different ways and for different reasons), *hungry*. We are, all of us, afflicted by the disease of the colonial project, a dis-ease, which has grievously disrupted our treaty relationships with each other and with the natural world, and we all share the responsibility to fully engage ourselves in a project of reworlding.

To intervene upon this dis-ease in myself and in the lecture hall, seminar room, or rehearsal studio, I have been working with a model proposed some years ago by Hawaiian scholar Poka Laenui. Laenui presented his model of decolonization as a socio-political model to be undertaken by the collective (community, state, nation). For me, it is a model that has proven itself as efficacious in the personal and familial realms as it has in the theatre (as a dramaturgical model) or in the classroom (as a "container" through which to deliver content). This processual model realizes itself in five stages that spiral back upon each other, forcing us to cycle back repeatedly as we move ourselves forward. It presents itself as an effective intervention on the profound hunger and mourning that afflict many who grapple with the legacy of colonization and that have led (and may continue to lead, if left unaddressed) to grievous acts of self/destruction. This hunger, born of loss and sharpened on the whetstone of grief, is unavoidable in any class that seriously wrestles with Indigenous history on this continent. It is, Laenui reminds us, a necessary stage in the process of reworlding (152), and it is treacherous. Grief turned Wiitigo will swallow us whole, and so we must push past it. Preceded by Recovery/Rediscovery, it must carry us through the stages of Dreaming, Commitment, and finally Action (Laenui 152) into full recollection and recovery of what it is to be a human being exercising human agency within the ongoing processes of creation.

In the classroom, we begin with the *recovery and rediscovery* of traditional epistemologies, languages, and ceremonial life. As we begin to take stock of what has been recovered, *mourning*, for what has been lost or broken, sets in. But while we must face painful truths here, we must not stay mired in the outrage or paralysis such grief engenders. To move us out of the mourning phase (without denying or repressing it), we begin to *dream* a way forward through which the works that we create will bring lasting benefits, not harm, to all of those who share these lands. From here, we interrogate works that strengthen our *commitment* to that dream, while workshops and embodied praxis introduce practicable strategies with which to *act* upon that commitment (see Carter 82).

This is a structure through which to filter Story. It requires the settler student to take ownership of the story. It requires the settler student to "world" with us, to decolonize with us—on a separate road than I or my Indigenous students walk, but in solidarity and moving in the same direction. It takes account of settler grief (of the "survival strategy" that has become a destructive way of life), requiring settler students to research *themselves*, to recover themselves, and then to share that bundle—that gift of self—and say, "Here I am." Here is where conversation truly begins and where hunger, so directed toward the creation of reciprocal relationships, finds mutual satiation therein.

Here, too, is a process with which to engage as we structure our research endeavours. As non-Indigenous researchers invest time and energy into sating a hunger to know the Other and to disseminate the knowledge they have extracted, how much time and energy have been invested in locating and mining their own hearts—in re-membering themselves? *What has brought you to this moment? From what "boat" did you (or your ancestors) disembark on these shores? On what shore did you first arrive? From what nations? What has been left behind? What languages, spiritual beliefs and practices, attitudes, lifeways, and knowledge systems have been forgotten, ignored, or discarded? Why? What may be worth retrieving and preserving and sharing with (not imposing upon) others? Why do your research questions concern themselves with Indigenous people? For what have you been hungering?* Through disciplined self-reflection, the process of intervening on a deep grief that has been numbed with studied amnesia, pernicious complacency, and a rapacious certainty of entitlement begins. To what extent might our work engineer those spaces in which every Canadian may, at last, converse truthfully, restore functional relationships with our biotas, and begin the process of conciliation with the original stewards of these biotas? Certainly, as culture workers who "midwife," nurture, and interpret the Stories that build communities and nations, we play a key role in these processes.

DYLAN: Thinking about those structures of storytelling, of research, of stories, Thomas King's *The Truth about Stories* is a model of telling that teaches us something about our relationships to knowledge and responsibility, but also, as Karyn mentioned, the trajectories of stories. The basic Western model of academic scholarship is introduction, body, conclusion, argument, support, prove the argument. It's teleological, it's a goal-oriented progression, it's a model of progress. I'm not saying we throw out all those structures of how to progress through something and lead and care for a reader, those are very important, but I'm reminded in what you're saying that this is a standardized, normative form, that we don't really consider how our own positionality and histories and relationships impact those structures. What we want to achieve through doing that writing, how that impacts the structure: I think that's a much harder thing to teach graduate students or ourselves because these questions challenge those firm rules we so easily slip into. In our condensed lives, we say, "This is my time for writing, this is my time for marking," and it's a problem, this sense of time. This idea of time, the time it takes to do things, not just in collaborative theatre practice but also in scholarship, in the writing that we do, we don't have time. We're constantly battling against pressures of time that doesn't necessarily fit with the time it might take to do a different kind of work.

JILL: I am in absolute agreement! I know this sounds facile and it happens in slow steps but I think it's a way of beating back the academy. I find myself talking to graduate students who seem to be claiming space to take their time, saying, "Well, that's the nature of the game." They're not going to do this research in a year; they have to take two or three because they have to have the time to build; the first year's just building a relationship. Every little victory opens things up more and brings others on board. Allowing our settler students in, at least to work with some of these methods, we begin to ignite a shift: I hope to inspire a new generation of scholars to push back against the pressures of time (imposed by the institution) by just saying, "no," because the process matters. We all know that. The process matters, and if our work takes a little longer, will catastrophe ensue? (The Davin Report took only forty-five days to "research," write up, and submit. Consider the catastrophic effects it wrought! Consider the catastrophic effects it continues to wreak on the generations of Indigenous children who continue to wrestle with the ill-starred legacy of their parents' and grandparents' residential-school experiences.)

KARYN: I'm just gonna offer some ideas here that will hopefully house some kind of decipherable flow. Some questions that come to mind in all of this are: What is the reverb of stories, the soundscapes and patterns that stories are creating orally? What are the vibrations that are created, and the nature of the embodied transference; what are the tones and the formations of storytelling in terms of all of these different considerations? I think that stories are shaping space as they are being shaped by space, and I think that bodies are being shaped by story as much as they are shaping story. What is an Indigenous story, when we talk about Indigenous storytelling? Are they stories of dislocation, are they stories of rupture, are they stories of being specifically rooted to a particular territory? What is a story; what constitutes a story? What are the gestures of remapping through storying? In my understanding of creation—or recreation—stories it is the fall or the jump. The muskrat coming up from below bringing forward this piece of land creates Turtle Island. It's all about jumping scale.

What does a woman look like as she's falling? What kind of body gestures and positionings are being taken? How is Skywoman shaping the space around her in creating these worlds? What are the gestures of muskrat and how can we look to those gestures as storying, as reworlding? We have always reworlded; our elders are the original virtual-reality holders—they are the original VRers—that's what they did. In ceremony they time-travelled, so our people have always been time travellers, worlders, reworlders. Complex ideas of quantum mechanics, multiverses, these are ancient practices and processes. Jumping scale into other worlds, other realms, has always been knowledge. I like to think, in terms of the trajectory of story, what is the reverb of the story; how does this story bounce off bodies; how does this story bounce off objects; how is this story creating itself as it's being told in various ways that are not necessarily about a verbal telling as much as a story as I think you were gesturing toward?

I love Jill's embodied process of storytelling; [Gesturing toward Jill] I can see the shape of your story, the contours of your stories just based upon your gestures. They're so important, sometimes even more important than the verbal telling, because you are engaging the worlds around you and shaping the contours of the lands and the worlds in which you are operating at the same time, and also shaping the contours of the relationality that you're building with others as well. It might look like you're offering a gesture for another to reciprocate and reworld with you. I think that that's what our elders knew when they were telling these stories, as they would always gesture, and I think that knowledge of reworlding was a part of that. We do shape our reality, we do shape our worlds, and we do that collectively by listening and witnessing and participating.

DYLAN: And yet at the same time I worry about the reduction of stories to useful, "teachable" content. I think that what you're saying is really important about the embodiments and the sound and the way that we feel and experience this work. I worry about it because I feel like stories are another thing that have been hungered after, particularly with the Truth and Reconciliation Commission, as a machine that gathers stories, that gathers testimony. All of those testimonies are now at the National Research Centre in Manitoba and accessible online, all of them except for the private ones and the ones that have restrictions placed upon them. We were explicitly called to witness by Justice Murray Sinclair and that means a very specific thing for xwelmexw and other nations on the northwest coast—a heightened listening, a heightened engagement with the work that's happening there. But what this also means for me is that I am attendant to *whatever* is said by survivors and intergenerational survivors. However they choose to structure this time, whatever they need to say, the off-topic-ness and the tangents and whatever else is said. These are the important things I need to listen to—*especially* when they might not seem "relevant." So now that survivors' experiences are available online through the National Research Centre people can pause and fast-forward and stop and say, "No, that's not the story I want to hear," or, "This one doesn't seem relevant, I'm going to go to the next testimony." So there's a change in witnessing, in a sense, where the listener has full control and I think to a certain extent may not even have to witness what's going on because they can be selective about time, with time. It's so essential to consider, what takes place as we listen and witness, how time shifts during testimony. The temporality, the space, the embodiment—these are things we also need to remain aware of when we think about bearing witness. What our elders and families shared disrupted the basic teleological drive to conclusion of story because you don't know, you have no idea when something is going to conclude and you're just there to be present to the time that that takes—that's how I understand it at least. And to the unsettling aspect of that being maybe an excruciating bit of time or a very short bit of time or moving between those two.

KARYN: That's like the first visit. When we visit each other, we put things in our cellphones: "I'm going to visit from this time to this time," but the actual visit never works like that. You're automatically on your sixth cup of tea and you didn't even realize you just drank six cups of tea, so the visit takes its time, it's time-less. As is reciprocity. You don't know when things are said that needed to be said, you don't know when that's going to be, you don't know when that reciprocity has come to—not a conclusion, because it never really is, but a pause until I see you again.

DYLAN: There is a different use of time in the reciprocity of visiting, and in the instrumentalization of story and instrumentalization of knowledge. To approach visiting and learning from "I only have so much time" makes us act quickly to determine what is relevant, what we can use quickly. My wariness comes from seeing and feeling this kind of instrumentalized approach to extracting Indigenous content from the ways in which we gather and visit. My call for non-Indigenous and settler scholars to stop Indigenizing your methodologies is a way to say: stop instrumentalizing Indigenous world views, language, or stories for what they help you say, treat them as the incommensurable things that they are rather than things that might be easily applied to your work.

JILL: Diane Glancy, a playwright of Cherokee ancestry, speaks of "written language [as] a costume the repertoire wears." So, in performance, as a storyteller, I am illuminating embodied existence within the spoken word.[7] As scholars and critics who write stories about the stories, we witness—we *costume*—the performative events that we're writing about with our language . . .

There is a particularly potent moment, during Spiderwoman's recent production of *Material Witness*—a moment of corporeal witnessing when this truth exerts itself on our hearts and minds and convicts us with the knowledge of our responsibility. Penny Couchie (Anishinaabe) recounts an exciting period in her life when, finally, after many years of training as an actor and a dancer and too many years of playing "too many trees and too many whores," she receives the opportunity to dance as an *Indigenous woman in an Indigenous story*. As she quips, she "danced genocide, danced smallpox, and danced Indigenous reclamation." During the rehearsal period, the choreographer tells her that she must lose weight to fit into the costume. But throughout her telling (in the present moment of performance), Couchie keeps dancing, demonstrating the power, beauty, and grace with which she was originally able to illuminate the story she had been hired to tell. As the pressure to lose weight mounts, her movements become more panicked and inchoate. The scene peaks as Couchie dances herself to the ground, madly shimmying to get into an unseen costume, while a chorus keeps time by madly chanting, "Go fatty! Go fatty! Go fatty!" Once the

7 This is not the same thing as performing a script where, as a Method or Epic actor, I "costume" the word with selections from my repertoire of embodied expression.

beautiful dancer's body has been squeezed into the unsuitable costume, Couchie struggles to her feet, constricted and hobbled, her natural grace and dignity stifled. "F@#k, why didn't you just get me a bigger costume? Like, seriously, how hard was it?" she asks (Spiderwoman).

This is a crucial lesson: the fabric and cut of these "costumes" (our words) and the linguistic and narrative frameworks through which researchers embark upon research, engage in relationship with Indigenous peoples and Indigenous knowledge systems, and disseminate our findings will either distort the works we seek to know, to share or to celebrate, or they will *illuminate* them. Is this not what we, as theatre scholars, are called to do? To deepen the experience for others? To build bridges between multiple communities and Indigenous artists? And to facilitate and deepen conversations between artists and fellow artists by facilitating authentic, unhindered expression?

As an Anishinaabe theatre worker, I find myself uncomfortably occupied by a series of questions, posted by Sioux Lakota playwright Larissa FastHorse on a 2015 blog post: "Do white playwrights ever think about this? Do they worry about losing jobs for white actors? Do they question if they are writing about enough white issues? [. . .] Do they fear [their work may somehow prove itself to be or be reimagined by the dominant culture into a tool that facilitates] the genocide of their race?" As an Anishinaabe researcher and educator, I find myself preoccupied (and my work occupied) by similar concerns: Do non-Indigenous researchers experience the same anxiety around harming those about or for whom they write, whether they are doing research within their own communities or within communities to which they are outsiders? Do non-Indigenous researchers (and their funders) privilege the needs and aspirations of the communities in and with which they work over the demands that are made upon them either to produce and publish or to languish irrelevantly? Why do we do the work that we do? Of what value are our questions, explorations, and theories to the artists with whom we engage (if we actually do engage) and to the audiences for whom they create? Does our work support the work of Indigenous theatre workers? Does it misrepresent that work, obfuscate that work, dismiss or erase that work? Do we regard our own work as a sacred trust? Do we handle each story with which we engage gently, as we would a vessel that contains the life and essence of a people?

"The truth about stories is that that's all we are" (King 2), and the truth about the stories that *we tell* about stories is that *they contain power*: the stories we tell can lift up the artists, their works, and their communities or they can silence, denigrate, and destroy. The stories we tell can open up spaces of fruitful encounter between Indigenous artists, their communities, and non-Indigenous peoples, or they can engender disaffection, distrust, and disengagement. The stories we tell are the fruits of our engagement—of our commitment to engage and to facilitate engagement. But engagement, I believe, is, in itself, not enough. It is the *process* we employ that shapes the character of our engagement with Indigenous art workers and their works. And it is this process, mindfully undertaken, that will determine the extent to which our engagement and the fruit it bears will ultimately stimulate dialogue rooted in the spirit of true respect and the desire for conciliation—dialogue that brings Indigenous peoples and settlers together and moves us forward in a good way towards the "eighth fire."[8]

---

8 The Anishinaabeg once lived on the shores of the Atlantic Ocean. Long before the first European ever came in sight of North America, the prophecy of the Seven Fires was delivered to the Anishinaabeg. The colonial encounter, our prophets told us, would unfold in seven stages (through seven eras, represented by seven fires). To reduce the impact of first contact (i.e. disease and/or outright attack), the Anishinaabeg were instructed to migrate west and north away from the sea to where food (wild rice) grows upon the water. As it was prophesied, the agents of colonization have visited greater and greater destruction on the land and peoples with each new era. Today, many Anishinaabeg believe that we are now in the time of the seventh fire: in this historical moment, the dominant culture has the opportunity to consult Indigenous peoples and to respectfully integrate our ancient knowledge systems into their own practices at every level of existence. If this is done, the prophets promised, both peoples will enter the time of the eighth fire together—a time of peace and good life for all. If the disrespect and disregard for Indigenous knowledge continue in this era, we were told, then all will be lost, and all life will end.

THEATRE IN THE NEW WORLD: TROUBLES IN MODERNITY

YVES JUBINVILLE

TRANSLATION BY DOUGLAS BUCHANAN, IN COLLABORATION WITH STÉPHANE ZAROV

If the history of Québec theatre today appears to be a fragmentary narrative, the result of the hard work of dedicated researchers who have toiled in a disorganized fashion, it is nevertheless one that offers readers a fairly consistent understanding of the evolution of theatrical activity in Québec. Considering works published since the emergence of scholarly expertise in the field, one can see that the diverse approaches that characterize research on Québec theatre over the last forty years have not radically altered the dominant historical view that has emerged in academic discourse during this period. This is made evident by a "common horizon of justification" (Létourneau 767–68) that allows one to identify the prominent historical figures, works, and forces that have ordered theatre's institutional development and its aesthetic evolution.

Special conditions may explain the relative homogeneity of Québec theatre historiography, the main one being that it was developed over a relatively short period by a generation of researchers who, beyond their divergent theoretical and political positions, shared an ideological climate and the idea that their primary mission was to make theatre a legitimate object of research. The result is not a single version of history but a field of well-marked possibilities that define the framework within which the discipline of theatre studies in Québec has developed and provide its practitioners with a number of key ideas, heuristic models, and argumentative dispositions to carry out the necessary "synthesis of the heterogeneous" (qtd. in Dubied 49) called for by any historical approach.

It is within this framework that discussion can take place. Over time a number of problems and recurring themes, reflecting the changing nature of theatrical and dramaturgical practices in Québec, resulted in different readings and interpretations; these, however, did not hinder but rather allowed for the formation of a global narrative thread explaining Québécois theatre. Many of these themes belong to a well-established historiographical tradition that prescribes the conditions for understanding the development of theatre in a national context. In Québec, as in France, Norway, or the United States, theatre history in the nineteenth and twentieth centuries is inseparable from the impact of emerging industrial capitalism and the establishment of the nation-state. The same is true of issues relating to repertoire, the status of actors and the development of professional practice, and architectural infrastructures. Although Québec's cultural specificity and unique historical experience must be taken into account, they can nevertheless be seen as unfolding within an established narrative that operates according to categories, tropes, and topoi, not to mention a model of periodization, inherited largely from European historiography.

In my previous work on the origins of theatre in Québec, I discussed how the dominant narrative of European theatre can distort and misrepresent Québec's theatrical past ("Un Théâtre"). Here, I am concerned with yet another *problematic* chapter of this history, namely the entrance into modernity, following in the line of a comparative survey with two other historiographical traditions that share common concerns for nation formation in the New World (Bouchard 220). Apart from analyzing the contrasting rhetorical and narrative strategies used by scholars in Canada and the US, this essay takes the opportunity to investigate the particular conditions that led to the development of theatre studies in North America and shed light on the epistemological shakeup the discipline has gone through in recent years.

The "modernity" I discuss here is neither homogeneous nor uniform, despite the current notion of it as a clear historical break. For Jean Baudrillard, Alain Brunn, and Jacinto Lageira, modernity cannot be reduced to the idea of rupture, and still less to an event that would introduce, in the fabric of time, a before and an after. In dialectical terms, modernity remains paradoxically "traditional" in that it aspires (albeit in the mode of protest) to exert a form of regulation. Its *modus operandi*, though variable depending on the circumstances and contexts, can be defined in terms of a logic of permanent instability of the forces governing the social, cultural, technical, and economic spheres. Tracing the genesis of the term, Baudrillard, Brunn, and Lageira affirm that "everywhere on earth does not have a 'modernity': that is to say, an historical and political structure of change and crisis. This modernity is recognizable in Europe from the sixteenth century, and only takes on its full meaning from the nineteenth century onward." They add that the term "only takes strength in countries with long-standing traditions. *To speak of modernity has little meaning when it comes from a country with neither a tradition nor any Middle Ages, like the United States*, and conversely, modernity has a very strong impact in Third World countries, with strong traditional cultures" (emphasis added).

QUÉBEC THEATRE: THE HAUNTING MIRROR OF MODERNITY

In all the literature reviewed in this study, Québec certainly offers the most striking evidence of an ongoing debate on the issue of modernity. Steadily, since the 1980s, researchers in the field of theatre studies, like their colleagues in literature, art history, and philosophy—not to mention historians of all stripes—have made it a compulsory figure in their research. This movement corresponds with a general overhaul of the standard discourse disseminated by the elites of the Quiet Revolution, according to which Québec happened onto modernity all at once, drawing a line separating the old times from the new times. This refutation of the "the ideology of catching up" (Rioux 118)[1] sought in part to situate the debate over Québec's modernization within a

1 "[I]déologie du rattrapage."

longer historical process while also identifying the different loci and multiple modalities of a properly modern dynamic in the social, cultural, and aesthetic fields. The terminology used since 1980 is significant in this regard. We read of the *emergence*, the *domestication*, the *formation*, and *learning* of modernity: terms that describe a graduated sequence of operations covering a wide range of practices and discourses, and showing the development of society (according to the classical rhetoric of personification) as a way of achieving self-awareness and subjectivity.

This approach completely contrasts with that of the Quiet Revolution's reformers who had forged the myth of a "technocratic" modernity for whom the state apparatus would complete Québec's transformation into a "normal society" (Létourneau 783). Conversely, the revisionist discourse of the 1980s (and beyond) places more emphasis on the idea of modernity as the fulfillment of both individual and collective sovereignty, thus describing a journey that culminated in the 1960s but which was predated by, and only realized because of, changes in the social framework and in how actors interacted and interpreted these changes. After the first referendum on Québec independence in May 1980, one can easily understand how and why the question of modernity reappeared and was re-evaluated. The theatre discipline, and critics and artists alike, did not escape this injunction.

MODERNITY / MODERNISM

André G. Bourassa (1936–2011) devoted much of his research career to tying Québec's scenic and dramaturgical practices to the European avant-garde movement, as embodied by the figure of painter Paul-Émile Borduas. Author of a thesis on surrealism and literature in Québec, Bourassa based his subsequent work on theatre on research in the field of art history. As articulated by the heroic narrative of the *Automatistes*, art had, during this same period, helped shape the myth of a modern Québec (Gagnon), originating in the spirit of contestation and emancipation expressed by the *Refus Global* (1949). Around this pivotal time, Bourassa picked out seminal works

(*Bien-être* [1947], *Le Vampire et la Nymphomane* [1949]) as well as leading figures (Claude Gauvreau, Alfred Pellan, Françoise Sullivan, and Jeanne Renaud) in the movement to examine under the light of his accumulated knowledge of the art world itself. His object of study was the networks of acquaintances and friendships between artists who were privileged agents in the circulation and transformation of ideas, forms, and aesthetic sensibilities. The portrait that emerges is of a movement necessarily breaking with contemporary domestic production at the time,[2] but suffering from perplexed critics and the indifference (if not disapproval) of the elites, and would have no significant meaning or resonance until the 1960s and 1970s.

What unfolds here is an infra-history that squares with the canonical narrative of modernity emergent in the sixties and seventies in France,[3] which hinged upon a number of assumptions. Chief among these was the importance of actor training as a key condition for renewing and diversifying forms of representation. Following the work of Odette Aslan, Bourassa identified places, people, and training practices that allowed for a modern theatre practice to emerge as best it could, despite the lack of a well-established theatre school in French Canada. Bourassa also questioned the means by which European theories of acting, dramaturgy, stage design, and directing found their footing in Québec. Having traced how the writings of naturalists (Antoine, Zola) and French Symbolists (Lugné-Poe, Copeau) were made available in Québec in the first third of the twentieth century, Bourassa also followed the trail of François Delsarte, whose *Cours d'Eloquence Parlée* introduced modernity to many French-Canadian practitioners.[4] For Bourassa, Delsarte, who mentored Rudolf

---

2 Theatrical activity in Montreal in the 1940s favoured light comedies, popular entertainment, and religious theatre. The experimentations of Father Émile Legault (Compagnons de St-Laurent) and Pierre Dagenais (L'Équipe), on the side of classical or contemporary theatre, are the exception, despite the enthusiastic echo of the press of the time.

3 Especially under the leadership of the Centre national de la recherche scientifique (CNRS) and the research team gathered around Denis Bablet. Another important influence was Andre Veinstein, head of the Performing Arts Archive at the National Library of France from 1953 to 1971 and author of *La mise en scène théâtrale et sa condition esthétique* (1955).

4 See Hamel.

Laban and Isadora Duncan, inaugurated an "American" vision of modernity, for it was through the United States that Delsarte's thinking made its way into Québec. Despite the European framework of his historical analysis, Bourassa thus tried to embrace the many expressions of modernity rooted in a distinct geographical and cultural territory.

In the end, the picture of modernity that emerges from Bourassa's work is not all clear. Faced with the repeated failures, timid statements, and self-confessed compromises of Québécois theatre artists in the modern era, one must ask if the demands of modernity have had any real impact upon these artists at all. This doubt might even bring us to ask why modernity formed a central theme of Bourassa's historical reflection for no less than twenty-five years. In fairness, however, we should remind ourselves that the discipline of theatre studies in Québec, emerging as the 1970s turned into the 1980s, undertook its review of the theatrical past in light of recent but profound aesthetic and institutional developments, with which it had been grappling for no more than a decade. The need to mitigate the impression of an absolute break with the past (supposedly introduced by the 1960s), and to fill the void of memory that had resulted from the narrative of that break, was interpreted by many as an invitation to unearth the premises of modernity, to go back to its source, so that Québécois theatre could appear on the "right side of history" and worthy of consideration. Seen within this context, the critical work of Bourassa provides a fairly accurate overview of the academic orthodoxy of his time. His analysis of modernity (1930–1965) has allowed for the establishment of a consensus on periodization, which, if we can judge by the theatre histories available to the general public,[5] essentially holds to this day. On the other hand, it must be said that the formalistic approach privileged in all of his works, centred on the Automatist movement, raises many concerns. They have contributed little of note to contemporary scholarship.

5 There are few books for the general public dealing wholly or partly with Québec's theatre history. Note, however, two publications: Sabourin and Greffard; and Biron et al.

CULTURAL MODERNITY

The scholarly effort to revisit Québec's theatrical past in the 1980s was made possible by researchers whose main task was to produce documentary tools cataloguing theatrical activity, through a systematic review of private and public archives as well as periodical sources. The team behind the *Dictionnaire des Œuvres Littéraires du Québec* (1980–2011), which included theatre specialists, sought to reopen the past using a different interpretive grid than that of the pioneering generation of literary and theatrical historians. Shifting away from the cultural divisions established by post-war elites,[6] the *DOLQ*'s mission was to reveal the submerged portion of Québec's literary and cultural iceberg. In the field of theatre, this project would lead to the first attempts to synthesize the dramatic and scenic activity of the eighteenth and nineteenth centuries (Hare), the relationships between theatre and the Church (Laflamme and Tourangeau), between theatre and the state (Burger), and the establishment of professional theatrical activity in Montreal (Larrue, *Le Théâtre*; *L'Activité*). In the same spirit, studies on popular forms and practices highlighted a theatre rooted in a society marked by rapid urbanization and the advent of mass culture (Hébert, *Le Burlesque*; "Sur le burlesque"; Tourangeau). The problem of modernity rose to the surface again, this time at an embryonic stage before disciplinary boundaries were fixed and where the question of sensibility was more clearly understood as one that concerned not only the producers of cultural capital, but all social actors.

Lucie Robert employs an eloquent formula to describe this phenomenon. For her, Québec's modernity comes into focus when it is put "to the test of the heterogeneous." She speaks of heterogeneity of discourse and practices, but also of collective representations. Therefore her comprehensive approach does not lead to a viewpoint inspired by the history of ideas

6 In the field of literature, the influence of Pierre de Grandpré and Roger Duhamel, both authors of literary textbooks, was decisive. For theatre, the pioneers of historiography are Léopold Houlé, Jean Béraud, and Jean Hamelin.

(European) nor of cultural studies (American), which tends to dissolve artistic activity in the practices of everyday life, but rather consists in "reconstructing the conception that the actors of the time themselves possessed of modernity" ("Le Moderne"). In works that span nearly two decades—starting with those she produced for *La vie littéraire au Québec* (which she has co-directed since 2010)—Robert considers performance practices as well as dramatic texts and stage works within the realm of possible forms of artistic creation, considering both individual and collective strategies without passing judgment on their immediate success, far less their legacy. A definitive locus of heterogeneity, the city of Montreal emerges as the haven of this modernity: a modernity that is lived, explored, and performed before becoming an object of study, insofar as it represents something shifting, uncertain, and unfinished that is associated with a deep sense of uncertainty (Robert, "La Vie Culturelle"). Blurring fixed boundaries between literature and theatre, Robert's analysis reports on the constant circulation not only of actors, authors, and designers, but also of the public, moving between music, the lyrical arts (including opera and song), dance, and theatre, not to mention their constant interaction with emerging media (cinema and radio).

As an example of this approach, we might consider Robert's study of the career of Jeanne Maubourg ("Jeanne Maubourg"). This daughter of a conductor and an opera singer, born in Namur (Belgium), had a brilliant career in London and New York before moving to Montreal in 1916 in order to found her own singing school with her husband, Albert Roberval. With Yvonne Audet and Eugene Lassalle (founder of the eponymous Conservatory), she became one of the first generation of trainers of dramatic and musical talent in Québec. As her subsequent performing career shows, there was no impermeable barrier between the arts at this time, nor does there appear to have been one between professional and amateur circles. Active in the Société des arts lyriques and the Société nationale d'opéra, Maubourg joined the Barry-Duquesne theatre troupe in 1926; she also took part in several productions of the Théâtre Intime as stage director. This little-known fact goes against the canonical history of stage direction in Québec, founded, according to the established orthodoxy, by the two charismatic (male) figures of Émile

Legault and Pierre Dagenais. But it also bears witness to an underground activity that, though poorly documented, could be connected with some of the challenges facing Québécois modernity: the role of women, the development of artistic careers, the question of training, and the notion of art as labour. By taking these backroads, Robert's research shows us a modernity that has been, in her own words, an "*apprentissage discret*" (a hidden learning process) ("Jeanne Maubourg" 182): one that we encounter today as though we are hearing distant music.

Robert's is a work of historical restoration, not to be confused with that of rehabilitation, which so often characterizes research on vernacular scenic forms and practices. Her approach shows a constant concern for the social, cultural, and ideological conditions surrounding theatrical activity. In the introduction to her anthology of one-act plays from the Belle Époque to the Great Depression (*Apprivoiser la Modernité Théâtrale*), she conjures the image of a theatrical modernity that demands to be interpreted from a dual historical context. On the one hand, the body of texts in this anthology presents itself as a distant, North American echo of the social and ideological crisis that gave birth to modern European drama: a drama that portrays isolated subjects who confront their own inner worlds as opposed to confronting each other. Robert shows how, in the context of early-twentieth-century Québec, the modern malaise operated differently on the dramatic form—hence the need for a second historical reference point. The brevity of the plays collected in the anthology, she argues, must be understood in relation to the canonical form practised by the previous generation of French-Canadian playwrights: historical drama. To break with this norm, both formally and thematically, meant breaking with "*l'esprit national*" (the national spirit). It also meant pushing away a dominant narrative that strove to wed theatre to collective memory by associating the sources of national drama with the Defeat of 1759 and the Patriots' Rebellion of 1837–38. Finally, it repudiated the notion, promoted by the American touring companies that had long monopolized theatrical life in Montreal, of theatre as a purely commercial and professional venture.

It should be added that, though "rescued from oblivion," this collection of one-act plays didn't withstand the test of time in spite of its modernity (or perhaps because of it). An essentially literary phenomenon, without notable impact on the theatrical practices or criticism of its time, this collection of plays did not appeal to subsequent generations either. Robert does not say otherwise, nor does she explain why this was so. It is as if her project of memorial restoration aims, in the end, to describe what can only be called a circumstantial modernity.

POPULAR MODERNITY

Another lost world, the tradition of burlesque—otherwise known as "*théâtre des variétés*" (variety theatre)—benefited from scholarly research during the close examination of Québec's cultural modernity in the 1970s and 1980s. In the historical narrative that developed at the time, the idea of the new Québécois theatre appears inseparable from its "popular" sources.[7] Up until this point, these popular origins had been embodied in such figures as Gratien Gélinas[8] (the Father) and Marcel Dubé[9] (the Son), upon whom was built the patriarchal lineage of national dramaturgy. Henceforth, however, they found more authentic resonances in the irreverent language, mocking tone, and comic gesture of actors and actresses whose stage names clearly reflect the familiar rapport they maintained with their public: Tizoune, La Poune,[10] Baloune, Pic-Pic, Macaroni, Pizzi wizzi. It was Chantal Hébert, who

---

7 See Bélair 62.

8 In 1949, just after the triumph of his *Ti-Coq*, Gélinas delivered, at the University of Montreal (which awarded him an honorary doctorate) a speech entitled "For a national and popular theater."

9 The "popular" qualifier denotes the first pieces of Dubé: *Zone* (1953) and *Un simple soldat* (1957), depicting the working-class environment in which the author grew up.

10 On the first page of the first version of *Les Belles-Sœurs*, dated 1965 but never published, Michel Tremblay acknowledges that the character Rose Ouellette's surname is a direct reference to the burlesque actress and groundbreaking female theatre director (Théâtre Cartier, Théâtre National) who called herself La Poune. At the premiere of the play in 1968, the author chose the name of Rose Ouimet, but the figure still reflects the influence

published *Le Burlesque au Québec, un Diverstissement Populaire* in 1981, who was responsible for opening up this territory:

> Burlesque, however, while it got no respect from the gods of high culture, was born, grew and prospered here; no doubt because it met the expectations of many Québecers . . . whatever their taste. Therefore, it was able to inform us, as well could as any other significant cultural event, about a slice of our history. Is not that reason enough to encourage us to look at it more closely, even if the realm of the "comic," despite its undeniable popularity, was rarely selected as an object of study, as noted by le Théâtre Euh! (*Le Burlesque* 20)

The reference here to Théâtre Euh!, a troupe whose lifespan marked the heyday of collective creation, is not trivial by all accounts. At the time, it indicated to researchers that the legitimacy of their object of study would be measured on the scale of artists' historical consciousness of their own practice. At the very least, this factor had to be considered in the same way as that which dictates, from the point of view of popular theatrical memory, the need to make room for forms that, resonating through the whole social body, helped to shape the national identity.

Hébert addressed the burlesque from this perspective, seeing in the comic actor and his relationship to the public an attitude of defiance and resistance to social norms, including those of theatre, and hence the expression of a typically popular modernity. This approach reappears in a recent book by Germain Lacasse examining the figure of Alexandre Sylvio, a huckster, silent-film narrator, actor, and writer of reviews during the golden age of popular entertainment in Québec (1900–1930). With great brio, this study places the conceptual arsenal of cultural history in the service of a rather binary vision of Québec's past, as represented by two antagonistic entities: the elites and the masses. Lacasse's goal is "to understand how the

---

of popular comedy on the play. It also suggests a female (and indeed, feminist) origin of Québec theatre, in contrast to the male lineage with which Tremblay wished to break.

masses represented [modernity to themselves] and how they appropriated it" (54). His analysis, comparing the views of the masses to the elites' view of them, takes up where the reformers of the Quiet Revolution left off, in that it amplifies the conservatism of the ruling classes in order to celebrate the liberating potential (Lacasse 38) of the urbanized culture embodied by the wicked Sylvio.

Whether one adheres to this representation of the past or not, it should be noted that it proceeds from a reformulation of the heuristic framework according to which theatrical historiography had, to that point, addressed the question of modernity. Strictly speaking, *Le Diable en Ville* (*The Devil in the City*) lies at a crossroads of scholarly research on popular scenic practices and the early days of cinema at a time when disciplinary lines were not only shifting but when the notion of *spectacle* or entertainment, in the ambient social discourse, described a type of collective experience that was not exclusively theatrical. Drawing upon the work of three major modern writers (Baudelaire, Benjamin, and Brecht), Lacasse retraces the path of Sylvio and analyzes the form of the topical revue by evoking such archetypal figures as the *flâneur* and the onlooker (Benjamin and Baudelaire), whom he associates with the urban reality of speed and distraction (Benjamin, *L'Œuvre*) that the bourgeois and clerical elites sought to repress. At the time, according to Lacasse, dramatic and cinematic revues were implicated in the social logic of nascent consumerism, which made use of such proven strategies as the exhibition of miscellanea and the montage of discontinuous narratives (Benjamin, *L'Œuvre*). Both forms also embraced a new conception of space and time, inaugurated by mass media (newspapers and radio), which tends to make the here and now the seat of impulses, sensations, and collective imaginations. Ultimately, this vernacular modernity—broadcast on stage and screen, lived by the stroller on the streets (Brecht 856), and inspiring the revue writer's creations—is best understood as a sensory experience rather than a discursive one.

This vision is perfectly aligned with Benjamin's understanding of modernity as a human *sensorium*,[11] a hostile urban environment orchestrating the collision of differences and affecting thereby the cognitive and perceptual frameworks of individuals. In Lacasse's work, this analysis is echoed in the characterization of a French-Canadian social environment that is "semi-colonial and closed off by the political authority of the British Empire and the ideological influence of traditionalist Catholic clergy" (Lacasse 47), but that manages, through the dislocation effected by industrial capitalism, to rend the veil of traditional society. This positive interpretation of popular modernity speaks well of the American context of Québécois culture. In this interpretation, it was through the popular classes, and not the elites who disapproved of them, that modernity achieved its most lasting transformation of French-Canadian society, blurring the uniform and homogeneous representation it had created of itself and establishing a public space characterized by the free flow of bodies and images and thus a certain kind of democratization. For the spectators of public shows and entertainments, this became evident in the fact that Montreal lived more and more under American influence, especially once it began to share its "star system"—under which local celebrities competed with American icons—and to adhere to its models of mass consumption and communication.

This rehabilitation of popular cultural practices goes against the grain of an analysis of modernity founded upon Enlightenment ideals whose main agent was literate high culture. Indeed, addressing modernity in these terms sidelines the familiar model of interpretation that explores the processes of empowerment and individuation normally associated with modern art, literature, and philosophy. Perhaps this explains the lack of interest that this perspective has aroused in theatre studies. The gap between Lacasse's work and that of his scholarly colleagues seems to reflect not only their divergent understandings of phenomena, but also the radically different questions that

11 Developed primarily in his book *The Work of Art in the Age of Mechanical Reproduction* (*L'Œuvre*). Siegfried Kracauer endorses this approach in his work on the city and the cinema.

underlie their contrasting forms of investigation; it is as though the questions and issues raised by the one simply do not interest the other, and vice versa. Nevertheless, it should be noted that this type of cultural history, fascinated as it is by the cleavage between popular classes and elites, provides the elements for a critical reflection on the gradual decline and marginalization of theatre in Québec's cultural life in light of the prevailing dominant discourse on "a national and popular theatre," to use Gratien Gélinas's expression, capable of producing social connections and rallying collective memory.[12] This myth appears antithetical to the notion, promoted by the canonical narrative of modernity, of art as a critical tool and vehicle of progress that considers public approval (and its corollary, stardom) as suspicious and depreciates any practice based on collaboration and communality (Shepherd-Barr 64). It is this contradiction, which contributes to theatre's exclusion from the grand narrative of modernity, that cultural history seeks to resolve.

THE OTHER AMERICA

After this overview, inevitably biased and partial, of Québécois writing on the subject, it seems appropriate to examine the body of research on the history of theatre produced in Canada and the United States. In the historiographical discourse of these two nations, the theme of modernity has not reached the same levels of controversy and polemic as we have observed in Québec's scholarly output. A search by keyword in different databases, although it reveals the recurrence of the term (i.e. "modern" or "modernity") in a significant number of theatre history works, displays a more neutral employment of the concept. In this regard, two preliminary remarks are in order to underline the difference from historical research in Québec.

The word "modern" is most often used in Canada and the United States in reference to a literary or dramatic canon as opposed to the broader designation embracing all theatrical practices (directing, acting, and stage design).

12 See Jubinville, "Du théâtre populaire au Québec."

According to this conventional view (much contested in recent historiography) modernity is recognizable through its characteristic textuality, based on the idea that the modern work, like the great European repertoire, is one that manages to transcend the conditions of representation. In works of historical synthesis, the term "modern drama" appears more or less as a label referring to a body of works circumscribed in time and identified by relatively loose aesthetic criteria. Though such criteria necessarily imply a standard of judgment, they—at least in the majority of publications we have surveyed—do not necessarily infer a *problematization* of the concept of modernity. This concept appears to be implicitly understood and requires no specific interpretation adapted for the North American context. One must also note that the use of the term *modern* in Anglo-Saxon academic research significantly declines throughout the 1980s and 1990s. The term is mostly used to designate a set of dramatic works belonging to a separate national repertoire as distinct from the *contemporary*, the *mainstream*, or the *popular*. This means that in addition to securing an historical period or genre, the label also begins to underline a schism within the discourse of theatrical historiography itself, which has entered a period of radical overhaul that treats the question of modernity as obsolete or "irrelevant," along with all the aesthetic, social, and ideological issues that had previously motivated the term's widespread use.

The following survey, which deals with the theme of modernity in Canadian and American theatre studies, unfolds under the shadow of this disappearance. Of course, we must emphasize from the outset the limits of this analysis, based on a far from exhaustive consultation of Anglo-Saxon scholarly output in the field of theatre history. Initially, our choice of materials was dictated by the particular light or understanding they seemed to shed on those epistemological questions that had mobilized practitioners on both sides of the border. Our attention then turned toward those works of historical synthesis or theory that, despite their relative silence on the question of modernity, somehow reflected ongoing discussions in Québec on the subject. Finally, we should also note that in the limited set of writings we consulted, we favoured those works and authors whose position within their respective disciplinary fields was made clear through both their critical enunciation and meta-discursive content.

THE USA: MODERNITY UPDATED

The canonical narrative of American theatre recorded in a number of monographs and works of synthesis produced during the 1960s and 1970s generally draws a continuous line that connects the forms and popular practices of the nineteenth century, emblematic of an industrial entertainment system that was set up in major cities, with a modern theatre movement from the Little Theatres, whose European source appears as a token of progress. In this evolutionary narrative, the point of rupture or division signifying the entrance of theatre into the age of maturity usually occurs in the 1920s (Toten-Beard 11–31) with the redevelopment of an American drama that acquired the virtues of realism, the appearance of major institutions (such as the Actors' Equity Association) that promoted the professionalization of the actor, and the establishment of a training tradition that facilitated the development of stagecraft. These factors, in the economic context of the Great Depression, prompted the US government to set up the Federal Theatre Project (1935–1939), which contributed to the legitimization of theatre in American society. In a short span of time, theatre—which in the eyes of the elites had had little or no value—acquired the status of a respectable, if not noble, profession.

In the 1980s and 1990s, several researchers openly opposed this linear and heroic storyline of American theatre either by deconstructing it or by providing parallel narratives that took into account the experiences of women, blacks, Indigenous peoples, gays and lesbians, amateur performers, or immigrant populations. Plotting such alternative paths undermined the logic of a unified historical process, replacing it with a polyphonic narrative written mostly in the margins of a hegemonic and normative cultural space. Many recent inquiries take this path in search of unexplored historical genealogies and affiliations.

For example, in his introductory essay to Volume 2 of *The Cambridge History of American Theater*, entitled "The Hieroglyphic Stage: American Theater and Society," theatre historian Thomas Postlewait offers an in-depth rereading of American modern theatre beginning with a new periodization

(1870–1945) that refuses the usual demarcation of the 1920s as signalling a new era. The modernity addressed here has little to do with the metaphysical or aesthetic modernity inherited from the Enlightenment. In the tradition of a sociology based on cultural practices and forms, Postlewait shows how the theatre not only participated in the process of modernizing American society but also helped to define the conditions of its emergence. Postlewait's analysis hinges on theatre's ideological, technological, and cultural interactions with a society that thinks itself as a *spectatorium*. At the heart of this social configuration, derived from industrial capitalism and mass culture, theatre appears as a central element of an American modernity where distinct social realities and temporalities all converge through spectacle to shape new myths and new representations of national identity:

> [. . .] The history of American entertainment from the mid-nineteenth century to the present can be understood, then, not only as a struggle between Europe and America, melodrama and realism, lowbrow and highbrow, stage and screen, country and city, natives and immigrant, men and women, whites and blacks, but also, and more tellingly, as an overall process whereby a democratic or mass culture enters into a new kind of spectatorship, an optical culture defined by the reign of the eye and the seduction of images[.] (Postlewait 188)

CANADA: BEYOND MODERNITY

To our knowledge, English Canada has not yet seen an undertaking comparable to Postlewait's, seeking to take up anew the question of modernity in the theatre. The impression given by recent work in the field of historiography seems to suggest discomfort with, if not indifference to, this notion. This impression is further reinforced by those who concede, albeit with disappointment, that a unified global outlook on the theatrical past has become an impossible undertaking. In "The Trades of T.R.I.C.: There Are No Macrohistories Here," Robin C. Whittaker laments that, since 1987, all projects of historical synthesis of theatre in Canada have been abandoned. The reference to 1987 clarifies the debate that seems to have taken place in academic circles, as this was the year that Eugene Benson and L.W. Conolly's *English-Canadian Theatre*—the last such synoptic attempt (to date)—was published. For Whittaker, it also marks the beginning of an *aggiornamento*, which would profoundly transform the discipline of theatre studies in Canada. He argues that the

> absence of Canadian macrohistory is a product of long, extended, hard fought, and ongoing efforts to erase the act of narrativizing historical events in our increasingly pluralistic, polyvocal, fragmented discipline. For decades the "story" was the nationalizing, professionalizing project of Anglophile Canadians. To tell the story, even *a* story, of Canadian theatre is a dated notion that, for some, threatens to monologize the plurality of voices engaged in the practice and research of drama, theatre, and performance. ("The Trades" 250–251)

In the same spirit as that which swept the United States in the same period, this transformation called into question the very idea that there was only one possible Canadian theatre history.

The strength of the criticism wielded against the generation of researchers who built the framework of a unified and unifying Canadian theatre history seems, to an outsider, disproportionate, but it becomes understandable if one takes into account the efforts provided, the resources mobilized, and the ideological reasoning that led to what many now call the "myth" of Canadian theatre. As in the United States, the canonical narrative of the Canadian theatrical past, patiently constructed between 1950 and 1970, appears inseparable from the national project that was developing at that time. Theatrical activity came to be seen as the vector or agent of a collective identity moving toward self-affirmation; modernity—a positive term for that generation—was then linked to the project of *nation building*. The key figures responsible for this construction included Vincent Massey, the Dominion Drama Festival, the Stratford Festival, and the Canada Council for the Arts. In the conventional historiography, Canadian theatre is then presented as a state matter,[13] the result of a collective and political will expressed across regional or linguistic divisions in reaction to the cultural hegemony of the British Empire and the United States. This communal narrative, based on the idea that the theatre can embody or exalt the spirit of the nation, would (with the 1980 Referendum, the Meech Lake Accord, and the rise of First Nations resistance) soon break up against the selfsame reef of political realities from which it had drawn its initial momentum. According to the scholarly output of today, Canadian theatre resembles the body politic itself: fragmented into a plurality of communities in relative peace with each other, each legitimately aspiring to build its own memory in the gaps (or blind spots) that the Grand National Narrative left behind.

The tide of performance and cultural studies that swept through the Anglo-Saxon academic world and defined its scholarly dynamic from 1990 to 2000 supports the above diagnosis, especially with regard to the question posed by modernity. The norms and hierarchies imposed by modernity are inadmissible within the theoretical and epistemological framework espoused by many Canadian scholars today. The idea of an aesthetic modernity assumes that theatre takes place away from everyday life, in a world that defines its

13 In an essay that examines the essential elements we just mentioned, the historian and critic Alan Filewod identifies the source of that historical interpretation in the person of Don Rubin, founder of *Canadian Theatre Review* ("Undermining" 179).

rules by and for itself. Conversely, the idea of performance involves a radical shift in the principle and power of representation, which has allowed the discipline to extend its field of expertise to objects (phenomena, activities, events) lying beyond the aesthetic and cultural spheres. Arguably, under the regime of performance, theatre as a field of analysis and inquiry yields to practices whose effectiveness is no longer evaluated via their dialogue or conflict with a self-reflexive cultural tradition, but through the manner in which they include concrete data situated in reality. If a new history of Canadian theatre were to be written under the aegis of performance studies, one can guess that it would not incorporate the evolutionary pattern that belongs to modernist theatre historiography. The project of such a history, though as yet un-conceived, is perhaps not inconceivable.

THE END OF MODERNITY?

At the end of this journey, it seems appropriate to affirm the necessity of further pursuing the kind of critical inquiry that has been broached here: the necessity, that is, of reading still more deeply into the history of theatre in Canada, the United States, and Québec. The importance of this task is clear at a time when the field of theatre studies is at a crossroads. In Québec, the opportunity is all the more to be seized now that the will to produce such a historical synthesis has been revived after years of lying fallow.[14] In this context, comparative analysis of historiographical traditions is particularly welcome, since a close critical examination of epistemological and ideological postures available to scholars is a condition of its realization. Any comparative operation that forces neighbouring scholarly traditions to confront one another cannot help but be beneficial in enabling each to make more enlightened choices. The present study has helped to point out certain themes that

14 Under the framework of the project *Régimes socio-esthétiques du théâtre au Québec* funded by the Conseil de recherches en sciences humaines (CRSH), a team of eight researchers (led by David Gilbert) has been working, since 2014, on the first synthetic history of theatre in Québec from 1945 to the present.

deserve to be (re)addressed, such as the questions of text and author, of historical periodization, and of the emergence of *mise en scène*. Further topics appear on the horizon: criticism, theatre's audience, the status of the actor, and the importance of mass media. Each of these could be the object of further analysis, helping to identify the narrative and discursive processes that, in the memories of various communities, work to create the artistic, social, economic, and political stories of theatre.

With this in mind, we should attempt some concluding remarks on the topic of modernity in theatre research in Québec as compared to its treatment in Canada and the United States. Within the limits of an analysis based on a rather small body of writings, we can fairly say that Québec is a "distinct society" in terms of theatre research. The question of modernity allows us to uncover issues of culture and identity that remain unresolved in Québec, while it is precisely these issues that mark at the present time a breaking away from the old order of discourse in the Anglo-Saxon world. There are many reasons for this state of affairs, some of which relate to the place and role that theatre now plays in these three societies. Theatre remains central to Québec's cultural dynamics, in part because of an institutional development that has no equivalent in the rest of North America and that is based on a public support system expressing a collective will for cultural affirmation. In Québec, theatre receives a larger share of public resources than dance, music, literature, and the visual arts. This tells us something of the high regard in which the theatrical tradition is held, but it also reveals its function as a symbolic cultural marker, despite Québécois theatre's conflicted relationship with its European heritage.

The consensus on which this system has been established seems threatened, however. That theatre and "national culture" are one and the same is no longer a given, especially when we observe the gap between the recent demographic trends, marked by increased diversity, and the current state of theatrical and dramaturgical creation. Theatre's slow relegation to marginality is doubly evident: first through the eyes of the younger generations who no longer connect with its horizon of meaning; and second with regard to the development of interdisciplinary artistic practices that overtly oppose dominant structures and advocate for alternative modes of production.

Québec's theatre studies are gradually taking the measure of all this. Shaken by the rise of interdisciplinarity, the field now seems to be going through a transformation similar to that which occurred elsewhere on the continent, rising against the hegemony of the theatrical model in the analysis of performing arts. However, some resistance to change is quite obvious, and leads us back to the question of modernity, which appears paradoxically in Québec's theatre histories as both a *foundational* and a *bygone* moment (Nardout-Lafarge 297). The term's constant recurrence reflects scholars' ongoing search for an element that provides a kind of narrative cohesion, a guiding principle that holds together the pieces of the puzzle of theatre's collective memory. While the choice of terms (modernity, modernism, modernization), time markers (1900, 1930, 1965), or lines of descent (European or American) varies, it is precisely Québec's theatrical past that remains an open question, one that tells us how uncomfortable Québec's position remains in the political and cultural landscape of the continent. If theatre studies today embraces the diversity of theatrical practices and of individual and collective trajectories that have shaped their development, the field remains essentially committed to questioning a cultural heritage that no longer serves as the benchmark of today's society, but still says something about its particular historical experience.

"SHIELD US FROM THIS BASE RIDICULE": THE PETITIONS TO CENSOR BLACKFACE CIRCUS CLOWNS, TORONTO, 1840–43

STEPHEN JOHNSON[1]

For four years, from 1840 through 1843, a group of Toronto's citizens, for the most part members of its black population, submitted petitions to the council of the newly incorporated city of Toronto, requesting that it forbid the performance of certain songs and acts on the stages of the city, because such performances would cause distress to the petitioners and disrupt the peace of the community. The originals of these four documents can still be read in the archives of the City of Toronto; taken together, they provide a testament to the power of performance, in this case (unfortunately) to move audiences toward a more demeaning and violent treatment of others. This essay will examine these documents, not to settle on a single "true" narrative history (if only there were such a thing!) but to examine the range of narratives that they might generate. It takes a microhistorical approach toward the documents themselves, considering how and why they were created, the immediate context for their creation by local culture, and the immediate effect they had on that local culture. It is a narrative of questions rather than answers. What performances were these citizens protesting against? Who was protesting? What was the relationship between the performances and the offended citizens? Where were these performances taking place? To whom were these

1 My thanks to Seika Boye for sharing archival research, Matt Jones for assistance gathering illustrations, and Heather Davis-Fisch for sharing her work on popular protest in Western Canada.

citizens protesting? What power was assumed or appealed to that might have been used to stop the offending performances? And, finally, what was the outcome—in the short and the long view of history?

Such questions are not extraordinary in and of themselves; the documents, however, are extraordinary in a number of ways. That they exist, well preserved, is already no small thing.[2] They were created by, and articulate the opinions of, a disenfranchised population: "coloured citizens" were seldom given voice in any community in North America at any time in the century, let alone this early. These documents uniquely preserve a protest that seems as desperate and as angry to the reader today as the day they were written. "Listen to us!" they by turns plead and demand. "We are in danger! Don't let this 'thing' into our city!" There are few documents in existence that provide this immediacy, not from this population and about this particular "danger"—the blackface performer. And this reference, too, is unusual in the documents, for they protest a form of entertainment that became, but was not yet, a powerful and popular performance idiom (see Cockrell, *Demons* and "Of Soundscapes"; Lhamon; Lott; Johnson, "Time" and *Burnt Cork*). It is a protest *avant la guerre*, and that provides insight into the growth—the "triumph," really—of nineteenth-century North America's most popular and most troubling entertainment, the "Minstrel Show." How often do historians find such fodder from the dispossessed, articulating their needs and their fears, not one, but four times?

It will be no *spoiler* to alert the reader, in advance, that these petitions failed in every respect. They failed to stop the entertainments they protested. They failed to convince the broader population of Toronto to turn away from this kind of demeaning, segregationist, racist entertainment. And they failed to make their way into the narrative history of theatre and performance in Canada; for although the petitions are mentioned on occasion, the events they represent have remained peripheral, indicative only of the racism inherent

2 The Metropolitan Toronto Archives holds the petitions for 1840, 1841, and 1843 as part of the recorded Minutes of Toronto City Council. The petition for 1842 is missing from that archive, but available as a photocopy in the Schomburg Collection, New York Public Library, in the Robin Winks collection.

in the more "popular" forms of entertainment, a sign forbidding entry. The battle that these petitions represent is thus all but invisible in our history; this is not the failure of the petitioners, but of ourselves.

THE DOCUMENTATION OF DESPERATION: FOUR PETITIONS

The four petitions, taken together, read as a desperate warning against an imminent danger. The first alludes to the presentation of "American" actors that "ridicule" and "hold up to contempt" the character of the petitioners, causing, among other things, violence against them.

> July 20, 1840
>
> To his Worship the Mayor and the Corporation of Toronto
>
> The Subscribers of this humble petition represent to his Worship the Mayor, and the Corporation, that they have remarked with sorrow that the American Actors, who from time to time visit this City, invariably select for performance plays and characters which, by turning into ridicule and holding up to contempt the coloured population, cause them much heart-burning and lead occasionally to violence. They therefore respectfully entreat His Worship, and all those to whom the right pertains, to forbid in future the performance of plays likely to produce a breach of the public peace.
>
> Your petitioners are, in all dutiful respect to you, Her Majesty's devoted and loyal Subjects.

The second refers to the way the petitioners' own characters are made "contemptible" and "ridiculous," leading to insults and worse. It is also more specific about the nature of the genre and performance venue; they are not "actors" but "Circus actors" who must be stopped.

Oct 14, 1841

To His Worship the Mayor of Toronto

The Petition of the undersigned, People of Colour, residing in the City of Toronto, Humbly Sheweth; That your Petitioners are informed that a Company of "Circus Actors" from the United States (now travelling in this Province) are shortly to visit this City for the purpose of performing etc.

That Your Petitioners from the general and almost invariable practice of such Actors in their Performances, have good reason to apprehend annoyances and insults, in the manner they endeavour to make the Coloured man appear ridiculous and contemptible in the eyes of their audience.

Your Petitioners would humbly prey that Your Worship would be pleased to prevent the occurrence of such annoyances and insults, as Your Petitioners believe that such attempted exhibitions of the African Character are not at all relished or approved of by the sensible and the well-thinking Inhabitants of this Community.

And Your Petitioners as in duty bound, will ever pray.

The third petition is different in appearance, abbreviated in length, with numerous spelling and grammatical errors (if the other petitions are used as the comparative model). It seems more hastily written but it is in a way more precise, naming the offending characters—"Jim Crow" and "Aunt Dinah"—as individual performers in "Yankee" amusements. These petitioners appeal to the city, as "loyal subjects," that it "shield us from this base ridicule." The petition exudes a sense of desperation, as if real violence were about to take place.

May 9, 1842

May it please your worship

To his worship the Mayor and counsol [*sic*] of this City of Toronto we the colored citizens of this City do pray that your worship May be pleased to have this our petition. Feeling assured That in the insuering [*sic*] Season many Applications will be made For Licens to perform in amphitheatre and circus thair by contamennating [*sic*] the wholesome air of our City with yankey amusement of comic Songs known by the Name of Jim Crow and Aunt Dinah we as Lawal Subject [*sic*] of British North America and true to our gracious Sovereign do pray that in granting such licins thair May be [*sic*] on the part of your worship Such Restriction as will Sheild us [*sic*] from this base ridicule we the undersigned to approach you in humble Submission to all the Laws and Regulation and for which we ever pray,

We The Committee appointed by the people

The fourth and last of these entreaties specifies, for the first time, just what offence is being committed: they are being "taken off," that is, parodied or mocked. This petition then offers us the distinguishing feature that sets this performance apart from all others; for while other groups are "taken off" as well, they "go no farther," implying that for these petitioners there are real consequences outside of the performance venue, "broils"—that is, violence. In this case, clearly and with some confidence, this petition both directs the council to the bylaw they may have forgotten when reading over the past three petitions, and a precedent for taking action from another city.

April 21, 1843

To His Honor the Mayor, the Aldermen, and Councilmen of the City of Toronto

We Her Majesty's colord [*sic*] subjects, residents of the City of Toronto, having found by reference to an act passed in 1834 that your honorable body have the right to license or refuse the request for the exhibition of shows etc in this City—and we also find that your body have the power to make such laws, as will tend to the peace, welfare, and safety, of the inhabitants of this city. And as the season for the exhibitions of plays, shows, etc is now approaching, we anticipate that our city, will as usual be visited by such persons, and as certain acts, and songs, such as Jim Crow and what they call other Negro Characters, performed by them has heretofore been productive of many broils and suits between the white and colord [*sic*] inhabitants of this city. We your humble petitioner prays that your honorable body will act as have been done by the authorities of Kingston, to wit, refuse to license such exhibitions, unless the exhibitors pledge themselves under a penalty, not to exhibit such songs or plays. Your petitioners are well aware that other persons are taken of[f] in those plays, but they are also aware that these take offs go no farther, which is not the case with us. They serve to degrade us as well as involve us in difficulties.

Respectfully Yrs

There is a consistency in these petitions regarding the shock value of the performance being protested; but there are also telling differences. The first is brief and formal, and the signatories do not identify themselves as the "colored citizens"; this petition includes by far the longest list of names, so many that an additional page had to be glued onto the first to accommodate them. This is certainly a list created by anti-slavery sympathizers, on behalf of and in solidarity with their black colleagues in business and society, as well as in sympathy with the fugitive population then pouring into the city. Some of these names, though in a smaller list and with a less intense tone, also appear in the 1841 petition. The second two petitions, from 1842 and 1843, are quite different. They are less carefully written and more extreme in tone; but in a way they seem better and more directly informed, naming the characters (Jim Crow, Aunt Dinah) and the venues (the Circus) that are promulgating these negative sentiments, and providing practical advice on how to prevent such performances. The petitions grow increasingly precise in their identification of the offence. The complaint is against a particular kind of performer, the Blackface Clown, closely associated with a particular kind of venue, the Circus, a combination that resulted in race-related violence. I find no other evidence of such violence in Toronto at this time. And yet here it is, forcefully and emotionally presented in writing, by the people who were most affected, and who normally would not write. They are afraid of something. But who were they, and what was it they were afraid of?

THE "COLORED CITIZENS" AS PETITIONERS

There is nothing simple in the statement that these petitions were presented by the "colored citizens of this city," as they characterize themselves in 1842. First of all, there were a number of points of origin for any "colored citizens": long-standing residents who had come up to Ontario from the United States during the American Revolution as Loyalist sympathizers; the descendents of slaves who had been freed in Upper Canada earlier in the century; as well as a large and continuing influx of runaway slaves who at this point saw Upper Canada as "The Northern Star," a haven of freedom (Winks 142–77). This last group in particular—who we should imagine as refugees constituting a visible minority—created a social unease in a white population that was already divided on the subject of slavery. Not everyone was an abolitionist, after all, and there was considerable sympathy for the status quo of slave ownership in the southern United States. We should consider the possibility that the sudden influx of a new and very differently acculturated black population altered the way the long-resident and settled black population was treated. Indeed, I would suggest that the petitions constitute evidence of this, because they are written during a sudden increase in the black refugee population, and because their tone expresses a real sense of surprise, as if those composing the petitions were being treated differently, suddenly and for reasons that they did not foresee (Winks 233–35).[3] These suggestions, however tentative, reinforce the idea that it was the long-resident citizens who organized these petitions, and that they did so because attitudes changed toward them. This in turn testifies to the idea that the "thing" they were protesting, the "Jim Crow" figure, while well known to the refugee population from the United States, was new to the city, and to them.

THE CIRCUS AS VENUE FOR AN INVASIVE PERFORMANCE

The conduit for this performance was an old venue given new life on tour—the Circus. The "Circus" was not unfamiliar to audiences around North America at this time (Wittmann 18–40). It had been around for some decades, as an urban entertainment that emphasized equestrian expertise. The "circus" or circular configuration of the entertainment was entirely driven by this original performance; and for this reason, touring entertainments called "Circuses" were normally held out of doors in makeshift venues, in riding arenas or barns, and, finally, from the mid-1820s, in the newly invented canvas tent. But while the physical configuration remained relatively consistent, the nature of the entertainment had changed in several respects. Though equestrians remained essential to the structure of the Circus, organizers brought in a range of other entertainments to provide variety to the advertised bill: jugglers and acrobats, animals (other than horses), and, important to our purpose, the Clown.

The early 1840s Toronto newspapers carry very few advertisements for popular entertainments; a fortunate exception is the Circus, which made

3 Winks discusses the difficulties in determining the size of the black population during this period, because of inflated accounts of "fugitive slave" immigration and inaccurate census reports.

a point of advertising generously in print. For this reason, we can to some extent know what it was the petitions of 1840 to 1843 were protesting. Several entertainments calling themselves Circuses passed through town, including one of particular interest, the Bowery Amphitheatre Circus. It lists the dates of performance, location (the "green" next to the new market square), and sometimes the performers ("New York" 19–22 Aug. 1840; "New York" 19 Oct. 1841; "New York" 14–16 July 1842; "Great Western"; "Rockwell"). This information is crucial for an understanding of the existence of the petitions and their forceful tone, in part because this was the most successful and influential Circus of the time. It was no small thing, then, for it to appear in Toronto, and it would have had a reputation in advance of its arrival. Among other reasons for its fame, the Bowery Amphitheatre Circus was known as the single most influential conduit for the popularization of the blackface "negro" Clown called "Jim Crow" (Wittmann 13). The authors of the Toronto petitions, then, were not writing to their fellow citizens to express vague concerns. In this case the immediate danger was real, and on its way from New York City to Toronto.

If the presentation on tour with the Circus was similar to that of the New York venue, as is likely, then we can have a reasonable idea of what it was like to attend such a performance in Toronto. The audience would have been in some kind of tiered seating surrounding an open circle. It would have felt very close to the performers, perhaps dangerously close to the horses, and certainly close enough to see nuanced facial expressions, to hear any sound made, verbal or not, even to smell the sweat of animals and performers. The basic organizing structure of the bill of fare focused on trick horseback riding with acrobatics. In general a master of ceremonies would announce each performance in stentorian language describing the extraordinary feats that the audience was about to witness. The equestrian riders, the "stars" of the performance, retreated frequently off stage to prepare for their next trick, and other performers would take to the ring. In the brief bill of fare offered in the press when this Circus visited Toronto, we are given hints of the kinds of performances offered to the audience. In addition to equestrians, the bill included musicians (a violinist, "Green Mountain Boy," in 1841; a "Bugle Band

Leader," named Mr. Post, in 1843); exhibitions of the physically unusual (an "American Giant," Mr. Charles Freeman, in 1841; two "Strongmen," Mr. Hatch and Mr. Mynheer Leydon, in 1843); tableaux vivants (posed "living pictures") of "Adam and Eve, or The First Fratricide" in 1840; and in 1841 "The Indian Hunter" and "The Dying Moor," likely brief equestrian spectacles with exotic settings and costumes. The emphasis was on spectacle, novelty, and variety. The offending figure named in the petitions was not apparently among these entertainments, though it is telling that the list of characters for "The Dying Moor" includes "Ethiopian Characters" and "Clown."

The equestrians and the master of ceremonies were central characters in most Circuses, providing its primary attraction and its structure. The third significant member, the Clown, provided something quite different to the "bill"—intimacy. The Clown figure was particularly important to nineteenth-century British-inflected popular performance; in particular, he alone was permitted to mock everyone in the venue, performers and audience members alike. He wore grotesque makeup, by turns laughable and frightening, and dressed outrageously, in a mockery of the costumes of the equestrian and the acrobat. He talked and sang incessantly, in dialects, puns, and nonsense. And he involved himself in the activities of other people, in an endless round of impossible-to-document improvisation. In the Circus, the Clown would attempt whatever the equestrian was doing so well, and fail to do it, often spectacularly (and with as much skill, all things considered). And he would talk to the audience, singling out individuals for conversation and temporary ridicule, sometimes referring to local events in the process. In this last respect the Clown was the performer most directly involved with the audience, and most directly participatory in the local culture, wherever he was performing. If he was good, he would assess the audience—which, after all, would be very different depending on the community and the time of day, sometimes children and families, sometimes young men looking for their own personal *carnival*. Whether that very local culture was understood and addressed depended on the skill of the performer, no doubt; what is important for this discussion was the fact that the Clown specialized in individual confrontation and mockery (Wittmann 13; Towsen 105–39).

Fig. 1. Image, circa 1832, of Thomas D. Rice as "Jim Crow," the performer who originated the character of "Jim Crow." This image emphasizes one aspect of the original character, which was advertised as drawn from life, and emphasizes an authenticity in costuming. Elements of the Clown, and the extreme caricature imposed on this figure, are missing. See Figure 2 for a complicating, complementary image of this figure. From the cover of the sheet music for *The Original Jim Crow* (New York, E. Riley, n.d.).

A "NEW" CLOWN: JIM CROW AT THE CIRCUS

For the Bowery Amphitheatre Circus, unlike other Circuses of these early years, "Clown" signified "blackface," and "blackface" had a particular connotation. The Bowery had for some time supported and encouraged the "blackface" entertainer, a strangely hybrid character that was part traditional Clown, part political commentator, and part purveyor of "authentic" slave culture from the plantations of the southern States and the streets of northern cities. This kind of performer is best represented by Thomas D. Rice, whose performances as "Jim Crow" were influential across the United States and Great Britain.

Rice purported to depict a character he had seen on the streets: an old, lame black slave, who wore tattered clothes and danced in a particular way because of his affliction. One "legend" suggests that he purchased the old man's clothes and performed an imitation of the dance he observed, spoke in his subject's local dialect, and sang the song he heard, "Jump Jim Crow," when he took this "new" act to the stage (Cockrell, *Demons* 62–66; Lhamon passim). This new act was extraordinarily successful, not because it was "authentic" imitation, but because it incorporated, seamlessly and confusingly, two other well-known kinds of performance. The first was that of the Clown described above, indulging in audience participation and dialogue, challenging and goading spectators, but always as a mocking character, and as someone the audience would and could, finally, themselves mock—as a lower-class and inept figure, something not quite human. The second, also related to the Clown figure but clearly foregrounded by Rice, was the political satirist and commentator. Rice's song was so simple (and nearly tuneless), that he could endlessly improvise on its lyrics, apparently with great skill, commenting satirically and with impressive humour on contemporary culture (Cockrell, "Of Soundscapes"). "Jim Crow" offered a strange amalgamated character, by turns a "real" individual, a quite savvy and aggressive political commentator, and a less-than-human, ridiculous-but-attractive Clown. The combination of these three aspects of performance had great and grave repercussions.

Rice's influence on what was evolving into a particular kind of clowning was powerful, and his imitators proliferated. During the 1830s individuals performed in blackface to all of these purposes, in some combination. Some emphasized the authenticity with which they could imitate southern plantation life, in song and dance, and in particular in the playing of an indigenous instrument (to the plantation, if not to Africa): the banjo. Some emphasized the political comment available through this particular character, in tortured dialect complaining about the world through the "stump speech." Underpinning both was the figure of the Clown, who worked to undermine both imitative and political intentions, through the presentation of a personal inability to speak effectively, or behave appropriately, or to "be human" in any kind of appropriate manner, mocking the persona. This was a figure out of control, and that was the attraction.

Although T.D. Rice had moved on from the Bowery by 1840, his legacy was well represented there. Among the regulars in the Bowery Circus was a master physical comedian, Dick Pelham, a significant figure in the organization and promotion of blackface performance in the United States and Great Britain from the 1830s until the 1870s (Nathan 127–56 passim; Johnson, "Death" 82–90).

Fig. 2. "The Virgina Serenaders," considered the first full evening's "Minstrel Show." The figure on the left, playing the tambourine, is Richard Pelham. The imagery effectively illustrates the way these characters were presented and received, as a pastiche of racialized, grotesque physical extremes, Clown-influenced costuming, and a grotesque, dangerous sense of movement. From the cover of the sheet music for *The Celebrated Negro Melodies, as Sung by the Virginia Minstrels*, arranged by Th. Comer (Boston, 1843).

I mention Pelham in particular because he appears—as R.W. Pelham—in the bill of the Toronto appearance of this Circus in 1840, the year of the first petition. I suggest that the object of fear in that first petition was quite specific. The goal was to stop Dick Pelham from performing in Toronto.

THE ACT OF "BLACKING UP"

The "blackface" makeup of the Rice-influenced Clowns had a long tradition off the stage and in the community; though as with so much of popular culture, the evidence is both pervasive and peripheral. This was part of an oral-performative culture that is often referred to by those who "document" the world around them, but rarely with an attention that brings it into the centre of the frame. "Blacking up" has been tied to the portrayal of the medieval devil ("black" the colour of sin), and to the *commedia dell'arte* character of Harlequin (commonly depicted in a "black" mask). Certainly the "blackface" figure was present—not dominant, perhaps, but one of many disguises—at Lenten Carnival celebrations, Christmas mummings, French charivaris, and at occasions across Europe of both ritual and real rebellion. Indeed, in both rural and urban working-class environments, "blacking up" constituted a commonplace disguise that mocked the status quo, often in a violent, if temporary, manner (Cockrell, *Demons* 30–61).

Though it is difficult to find evidence of this form in Upper Canada, its presence was bound to be as pervasive there as it was in Western Europe, the source of its cultural traditions, and in the United States, where its use and abuse were better documented. Two examples occurring in or near Toronto provide suggestive encounters. Accounts of a nighttime attack on William Lyon Mackenzie's newspaper office in 1826 describe the perpetrators as if they were Indians; but they are also described as having "a little lamp black on their faces" (qtd. in Davis-Fisch, "Lawless" 34).[4] More pertinent is an 1837 incident,

4 This argues for the non-specific nature of the carnival costume, that would mix-and-match cultures and historical periods to effect its grotesquerie and terror. Such

in which a mob of young men in Belleville (near Toronto) sang and danced as they hanged and burned the effigy of a local newspaper editor, apparently because he was thought to be Jewish. The report does not in fact mention any "blacking up"; but the song reported is clearly a variation on the tune always used by the character of Jim Crow, and the verses include the phrase "wheel'd about," directly quoting from the song's refrain.[5] If the first image indicates how rudimentary this makeup could be as a signifier of ritual violence, the second distills everything a group of Toronto's black citizens might want to keep out of the city: a mob burning an effigy of a reviled individual because of his "race"; a performance of ritual violence in front of that individual; and a violent mockery, while singing and dancing, all within the frame of a "Jim Crow" performance. Most audiences at any performance in Toronto would have recognized the "blacked-up" figure, however obscure or rudimentary. But in this single image—of Jim Crow, race, violence—all the elements are in place for the appearance of the Bowery Circus Amphitheatre. And it is feasible that most audience members recognized blackface, and that some at least had indulged in it (see Cockrell, *Demons* ix–xiv, 30–54).

The use of blackface on the professional stage doesn't seem to become a widespread phenomenon until performers at the Bowery Amphitheatre Circus incorporated it into the persona of the Clown, and combined it with

---

performances were not interested in a realist portrayal of any one group, unlike the commercial "Jim Crow" character. This example also suggests just how widespread this kind of violent carnival-like activity was, enacted here by the privileged. All members of society have a "popular culture." See also Wilton; esp. Burke, *Popular Culture*.

5 Dale Cockrell reports this 1837 event: "There a crowd attacked Mr. Benjamin, editor the *Belleville Weekly Intelligencer*, and burned him in effigy (a form of charivari). Motivated by political animosity, the crowd accused Benjamin (wrongly) of being Jewish. A report published shortly after the incident claimed that while the effigy burned the mob sang:

> Last Friday night some wicked boys
> Thought they would something do:
> So they turned out, and wheel'd about,
> And hung the Belleville Jew . . . "
> (*Demons* 74; *British Whig*, 27 Apr. 1837)

the "delineation" of the southern plantation slave. Beginning in the 1830s, audiences began to associate something that had not been an authentic portrayal of any particular group—the Clown, the "carnival" character—with a very particular group, perhaps in part coinciding with an influx of a southern black population, escaped from slavery or newly freed. There was, then, in Toronto, that confusion and conflation of the Clown, the satirist, and a fixed and clearly "delineated" class of humanity—those who were "black" (Cockrell, *Demons* 60–61). That conflation created a powerfully destructive character, as black audiences in Toronto attested to in their petitions.[6]

AN INVASIVE PERFORMANCE: JIM CROW MEETS "THE COLORED CITIZENS" AT THE CIRCUS

In addition to the unusual range of performances available to experience, the Circus had another unusual and disruptive attribute—it was accessible to a broad-based population. Prices tended to be lower than for other kinds of entertainments, in part because several performances were given each day, and in part because of the savings of the temporary (or open-air) venue. Long hours and low prices opened up the performances to women and children (Wittmann 13; Cockrell, *Demons* 25, 28). In addition, because the kind of entertainments available at the Circus might have been seen in the fairground or on the street corner, there was a certain familiarity that attracted

6 Blackface existed in many settings, as a part of variety acts, Circus, entr'actes in legitimate theatres, in large cities, and on tour. Performance pervades culture, and to become "popular," any kind of performance must be in some way recognizable to the audience when it is introduced to them as a "novelty." There is reference to "Circus riders" in York in 1833 (quoted in the *Christian Guardian*; see Mary Shortt 26–27), to "A Negro Extravaganza" circa 19 August 1839 (*Commonwealth Herald*), and performances of the Blackface Minstrel standard "Jim Along Josey" circa 7 September (*British Colonist*). See O'Neill 235, 237. See also Cockrell's work for this pre-history across North America.

people who otherwise would not have been found in the theatre.[7] And, finally, because this kind of temporary venue was not subject to the norms of society—that is, no one quite knew the rules of attendance for a "Circus"—it attracted a range of people who might not normally be present together at a performance, certainly not in a more "legitimate" theatre. Thus it happened that women, children, the working and middle classes might share the space, along with members of a black population (Wittmann 32; *The Knickerbocker*).

When the "colored citizens" of Toronto appealed to city council to stop the depiction of a certain kind of "character," they were experiencing something like the following:

A new kind of entertainment arrived in Toronto, one that uncharacteristically allowed the comingling of class, age, economic status, and cultural and geographic origin, if not into the same seating area of a performance, at least into the same venue, with the ability to witness the same entertainments. Into this environment came a segment of the black population of Toronto, enjoying, along with everyone else, equestrians, acrobats, musicians, and Clowns. Into the ring rushed the Clown; but instead of the usual and expected otherworldly grotesque, this "Clown" was also a "black man," a "southern plantation slave"—a "Jim Crow." He engaged with the audience in some aggressive mockery, indulged in some dialect humour, perhaps commented on the politics and social mores of the day in some manner, and, most of all, indulged in "self-mockery"—that is, an incompetence and absence of self-control whenever he tried to behave "as if" he were a civilized citizen—the main source of humour for this figure. The Blackface Clown engaged with different parts of the audience, at different times, in different ways. With children, he was the source of a foolish self-mockery only. With young men of the working class he tapped into a memory of the folk roots of this figure—and so, perhaps, into something violent.

And when this Blackface Clown turned his attention to the black citizens themselves—what then? He confronted them like a distorted mirror; and at

7 This was a fact not lost on those who, a few years later, began touring productions of *Uncle Tom's Cabin* "under canvas," circumventing theatre managers and touring circuits, and attracting audiences that would never enter a theatre to see a "play," which they considered immoral. See S. Johnson, "Time" 87–111.

that moment the rest of the audience turned to look. Some would have seen the insult. Some would have confused the mirror with the original. And some would have used the occasion of insult to reinforce pre-existing prejudice. In this case a segment of the population, having been ridiculed openly in front of their fellow citizens, took action against the insult, through petitions to their local government.

CITY COUNCIL AS (A VERY POOR) MORAL ARBITER

These petitions were submitted to Toronto City Council, which was newly incorporated in 1834, and busy reviewing all of its bylaws to improve the city's infrastructure. Even a cursory review of the 1840 minutes of the council serves as a reminder of just what such bodies did, on a day-to-day basis. It considered many "petitions," including—to select at random—one from a citizen asking "to be appointed a tax collector," another "praying to be allowed to drain a vault in the yard of the St James Church," and another from "various citizens approving of the proposed new gas and water systems." Infrastructure and appointment constituted the day-to-day business of this council; the only line item in the minutes for 1840 that stands out as exceptional is the one that drives this study: "Petition of various citizens, praying that performances by American actors will be forbidden when they turn to ridicule the coloured race. July 20, 1840." We can imagine the Council reading this aloud, and wondering just how to respond (Minutes, 20 Jul. 1840, list of submissions).[8]

Fortunately, we can do more than imagine; there is a further entry for this date, with a brief description of the head-scratching ambivalence that ensued after the reading of this petition:

8 The Bowery Amphitheatre Circus appeared in the city beginning 19 August, so that the petition was meant as a deterrent, and an advance strategy.

> A Communication from George Stewart and others praying the Council to prevent certain representations in the City was read. // Alderman Boulton seconded by Mr Young moves that it be Resolved that His Worship the Mayor be authorised to communicate to the coloured inhabitants of this City that under existing laws the grievances complained of in their communication cannot be put a Stop to and that this Council can hold out to them no hope of bringing in the Bill for such purpose without prohibiting such exhibitions altogether which at the present moment they are not prepared to do. // Alderman Monro seconded by Alderman Dixon in amendment moves that all after the word moves in the original Resolution be expunged and the following be inserted, "that the consideration of the communication of George Stewart and others be deferred which was carried." // Upon the Question that the original Resolution as amended be adopted it was carried. (Minutes, 20 Jul. 1840, recorded minutes)

This entry suggests that there was a real discussion as to what the council might do with this request, and a considered decision that they could do nothing—though not because there was no sympathy, evidenced by the extended and near-apologetic tone of the original motion. The fact that Alderman Boulton wanted the mayor to talk with these citizens is no small thing; it was so unusual a request, in fact, that Alderman Monro stopped it, proposing an amendment that the "communication . . . be deferred." Apparently Alderman Boulton was out of line in pointing out to the petitioners that the council could not help them; the resulting "communication" in fact established hope for some future action, and so provided a reason to submit further petitions.

They never did have this conversation with the "coloured inhabitants," at least so far as the public record relates (Minutes 1840–43).[9]

---

9 According to the recorded minutes, the 1841 petition was submitted only five days before the appearance of the Circus, and in 1843, three months prior. There is no record for 1842.

ON THE RELATIONSHIP BETWEEN PETITIONER AND PETITIONEE

The reticence of members of council to tell the "coloured inhabitants" that they could not help them might have been a product of guilt, or laziness. There is the chance, also, that there was a political motivation. Most of the black population were politically conservative, members of an all-black militia that had sided with the colonial administration during the divisive 1837 rebellion. They saw the queen as the defender of their freedom, the very antithesis of the reformers, who wanted to institute change—already problematic—but "republican" change, which from experience the black population would have seen as accommodating slavery (Winks 151). Almost certainly members of Toronto's city council had been involved in the rebellion, and would have viewed the petition in that light.

Of course there is no way to know why the city council behaved the way it did. It was relatively new, established when Toronto was fully incorporated in 1834, and still working its way through a revision of all of the bylaws. They had an enormous workload, much of it mundane, that would distract them from any significant discussion, and might encourage them to avoid any such. This was a period of Toronto's history when the population doubled, and when gas lines, sewers, and "planked streets" became a part of the infrastructure (Shortt 30–31). It was, conversely, a time of economic depression across the continent, all governments in recovery after a collapse in 1837 (O'Neill, *A History* 71–73).[10] The city council may have considered themselves utterly powerless in the face of their own local bylaws, their workload, and their lack of money. Still, we shouldn't put aside the prospect that local politics also played a role.

---

10 Among the "troubles" of this new community: an international economic depression since 1837; a cholera epidemic in the mid-1830s; a reformist rebellion in 1837; a ruling party, the "Family Compact," that was fast losing power after changes in the structure of colonial government, which had merged Upper and Lower Canada. Toronto was not, overall, seen as a vibrant community in the early 1840s, as indicated by the decision to overlook its prospects to become the capital of Upper Canada; it was passed over in favour of Kingston. See also Shortt; Careless.

THE DENIAL OF AUTHORITY; OR, BYLAW NUMBER 50

When the petitioners asked that the council stop the offending performances, to what authority were they appealing? When Council suggested in its 1840 response that there was nothing it could do, what authority, if any, was it denying? In fact, just at this moment, as the first petition was being written, a change was taking place in city law that may further explain the sense of powerlessness of the city council—or, more correctly, the renunciation of power, manifested in By-Law No. 50 (Toronto, By-Law No. 50).

This bylaw served to "Regulate Theatrical Performances and other Exhibitions" in the city. It is a document quite unlike anything Toronto had instituted before, though founded on similar documents in New York City (Fay 732–35). It is a foundational document of the "sin tax." For the first time, it provided for the control of a long list of entertainments, including "Theatres, Menageries, Exhibitions, [Various] Showmen, Mountebanks, Circus Riders, Jugglers, and other persons exhibiting any idle acts or feats for gain or profit in the City of Toronto . . . " It made only one demand, the payment of a licence fee in order to perform, and the process and repercussions are clearly stated: a licence is required to perform in the city in any capacity, indoors or out; that licence must be applied for through the mayor's office; the licence must be exhibited at all times during performance; if there is no licence, the city bailiff can and will arrest the individual, imposing a sizable (indeed, debilitating) fine; while the performer is under arrest, the bailiff has the right to take possession of the performer's material goods; if the fine is not paid promptly, these goods may be sold to pay the fine. It is a draconian set of rules for any itinerant performer, raising the prospect of losing freedom temporarily, and the means of earning a living forever, if the juggling balls or tightrope—or the horse—are confiscated.

On the face of it, this might seem to be just what the petitioners were appealing to; but an essential attribute of this document is that it carries no clause that allows for a judgment against the kind of performance, based on its effect on the audience. Perhaps in a general sense, the high cost of the licence and the rather frightening manner in which the bylaw describes what happens if this isn't paid, could be said to be "anti-theatrical" (O'Neill, *A History* 48, 62). But if the performer could pay the price and purchase the licence, there was no provision to say no; and it would be a loss of much-needed revenue for the city.

When the first petition was submitted to City Council, and first refused, this bylaw was just being written: the petition was submitted in July, the bylaw passed in August. But it may have been the reason, nonetheless, for the recorded discussion in the council chambers, where the mayor and aldermen were still assessing their "revised" authority. Certainly the petitioners became aware of the problem this bylaw created for their cause; they allude to it in the 1843 petition when, having clearly done their homework, they provoke the city council with reference to "an Act passed in 1834 that your honorable body have the right to license or refuse the request for the exhibition of shows etc in this City . . . " (Minutes, 21 Apr. 1843). This is a brazen move, to "call out" the government of the day, to tell them they are using the wrong law. The city provided no recorded response to this; but the petitioners were not wrong.

The bylaw to which they were referring was certainly No. 6, passed 31 May 1834, before the city was incorporated (Toronto, By-Law No. 6). It is a generic licensing bill, that applied to all "Retailers of the Beer and Cyder, Butchers, Cartmen, Showmen, and Keepers of Ordinances or victualling houses . . . " On first reading, it seems to be a far cry from what the petitioners would have required; except that, once the need for a licence is established, there is the following proviso: that the holder of the licence "shall not permit any riotous or noisy persons to be assembled in his house, store or cellar . . . "

Unlike By-Law No. 50, this law—signed by the reform-minded Mayor William Lyon Mackenzie—allows the mayor the option of shutting down any licensed establishments if they prove themselves a public nuisance. In this respect, it has similarities with other bylaws of the time that allowed local authorities to stop any activity that was disruptive of the norms of public practice—too many animals on the street, too much sewage in the yard, or too much noise in the beer garden. By-Law No. 6 pertained to any private establishment that involved either of two commodities to be sold—food or drink, and performance. It is likely that by 1843 it had been superseded by By-Law No. 50, and public performance, now described in rich detail, was separated out and designated with its own kind of licence, one that provided no room for censorship.

THE OPPOSITE OF INFLUENCE: POST-PETITION DISAPPOINTMENTS

The post-petition history of blackface performance in Toronto would not have pleased the petitioners. Around January of 1843, Dick Pelham and three other blackface performers mounted a performance at the Bowery Amphitheatre in New York City that was a stand-alone evening purporting to show the entertainments of the southern plantation slave, though in fact it was a kind of Blackface Clown show (Cockrell, *Demons* 149; Nathan 157–72; see Fig. 2). This is the first performance of the Minstrel Show, a distinct branch of entertainment that became the single most popular performance idiom across North America, including the British colonies, during the nineteenth century (Lenton-Young 176). The confusions created by "Jim Crow"—Clown, satirist, "negro"—through the Minstrel Show became a part of the fabric of American culture, as well as British imperial culture, in ways that are still evident.

At the same time, during the 1840s in Toronto, resentment grew against the fast-increasing visible minority now perceived, thanks in part to the blackface performer, as a "black" population, and segregation increased (Winks 142–77, esp. 148). Some sign of the results can be seen in Toronto's theatrical culture, as those who produced and licensed such entertainment worked to regain some control over the cultural landscape of the city. Most telling: in September of 1849, at the recently established Royal Lyceum Theatre, a troupe of minstrels from New York regaled the population of Toronto, oblivious to the earlier attempts to stop this kind of performance ("Playbill"). It was now thoroughly normalized, and thoroughly "legitimate," now truly part of the dominant culture of theatrical enterprise. But also, just a few months earlier in the same venue, a group called the "Toronto Coloured Men's

Amateur Theatrical Society" performed an all-black production of Thomas Otway's Restoration play *Venice Preserv'd*, along with "Several Scenes from Shakespeare."

The significance of these two performances cannot, I believe, be overstated in light of the subject of this essay. Nine years earlier, a group of black citizens, some long-time residents of Toronto, some newly arrived, were active in the politics of the city, and in some measure integrated into it. They attended the Circuses that promoted the well-known and much-hated "Jim Crow" character, progenitor of the Minstrel Show, in performances of a mockery and diminution of the black population. In the early 1840s, this population felt comfortable suing the city for protection against such entertainments. But here, at the end of the decade, an entire evening's "Minstrel Show" built around this kind of character was an accepted part of theatrical culture; and, segregated and assimilated in equal measure, members of the black population were performing Shakespeare. At last, under the umbrella of a theatrical licence and a purpose-built venue, there could be some semblance of control by the city council: over the presentation of the Blackface Clown; over the assimilation of the black population into English culture; and over the segregation of a community that had, less than ten years earlier, been sufficiently integrated into the civic life of Toronto to submit petitions to its city council, seeking redress from the insults of strangers.

THE AFTERLIFE OF POPULAR PERFORMANCE

The story of the afterlife of these petitions is very brief: they had no afterlife. They had no effect on the immediate decision regarding the performance of "Jim Crow" in Toronto. They had no effect on the performance of "Jim Crow" in its revised and expanded performance idiom, the Minstrel Show—an entertainment that became so deeply ingrained in North American culture that it has not wholly disappeared. And they had no effect, later, on the writing of the history of performance in this country.

As to this last statement—I would suggest that there is more for historians to examine here. A group biography of the signatories of each petition would give us a much better understanding of who and why these petitions were created, as would more work on the abolitionist organizations in Toronto at this time. A similar study of the men who were elected to council would help to understand the politics, the social dynamics, and the prejudices of an over-burdened group of inexperienced politicians. A closer look at the settlement of Canada West would no doubt elaborate on the relationship between old and new black populations in Toronto. There is much more to look for in the history of the petition, and theatrical licensing laws, which would have much to say about these local efforts to control performance. And, finally, it seems clear that folk culture predetermined the way audiences witnessed and interpreted commercial performances; a better understanding of this important influence would be a daunting but fascinating project.

There is certainly more to the story of these petitions, and to their role in the struggle for the rights of the individual over the power of performance. The primary narrative of Canadian theatre history has been based on the presence of purpose-built venues (that is, theatres), and the presentation of dramatic productions. The reasons for this are not difficult to understand. Unlike the performance of Jim Crow in a Circus, theatres and plays produce the ready-made documentation needed for study—architectural plans, set designs, and play scripts. They are direct and tangible evidence of the event, things we can collect, and from which we can make meaning. This other kind of performance—the rough music of the street performer and the stunt rider and the busker, the topical humour of the improvisateur/provocateur—cannot be documented in a way that reflects the performance satisfactorily, or easily. Understanding this kind of performance in any way that allows for reflection and analysis is time-consuming, and any "reading" is forever provisional. Such studies are often left for another day by the busy historian, in favour of a more "credible" event. Popular performances are not ignored, exactly; but they are not often made a part of the central narrative.

And yet, if we step away, climb to a higher altitude, and look back down on such events, we can see just how important they are to our understanding, not of the past, but of ourselves. At the time of writing this essay (2016), as I look at the history of these petitions from a distance, I see a new technology overwhelming a local community's social order, and disrupting the tentative peace. I see a sudden influx of refugees escaping a demeaning political system, but followed to their new home by the racist culture they were seeking to escape. I see an extreme ideology, in the form of a Clown-like figure, inciting hatred and violence and prejudice by ridiculing and vilifying one part of a population. And I see a government so overburdened by the minutiae of infrastructure and bureaucracy that it cannot acknowledge and cannot assist in any meaningful way the pleas of its citizens.

Seen from a height, this all looks terribly familiar.

THREE SENTENCES: A CHILD ACTRESS IN HALIFAX, 1833[1]

MARLIS SCHWEITZER

> At the close of the second season at the "Warren" we went to Halifax, Nova Scotia, to act with the Garrison amateurs twice a week during the summer. We saw a good deal of human nature there—all the petty strife of real actors without their ability. However, it passed the summer away very pleasantly.
>
> —Mrs. John Drew

A single sentence (or three) can crack a research project wide open. This happened to me while reading the 1899 memoirs of Mrs. John Drew (née Louisa Lane),[2] a doyenne of the nineteenth-century American stage. I was in the beginning stages of a project exploring the many hundreds of child performers who travelled along transatlantic theatre circuits in the early nineteenth

1 I presented a draft of this essay at the 2015 Canadian Association for Theatre Research conference. My thanks to the conveners of the Performance Historiography seminar, Heather Davis-Fisch, Roberta Barker, and Stephen Johnson, and to other participants for their feedback. The research presented in this essay is part of a larger Social Sciences and Humanities Research Council (SSHRC) Insight grant entitled "Ambassadors of Empire: Child Performers and Anglo-American Audiences." Special thanks to Julie Matheson for her research assistance.

2 Drew is celebrated for her lengthy stage career and her role as matriarch of the Drew family, one of the US's oldest surviving theatrical families. Her son John Drew was a matinee idol in the 1890s and early 1900s and her grandchildren, John, Ethel, and Lionel Barrymore, went on to become major stars of the twentieth-century stage and screen. Mrs. John Drew's legacy continues today with her great-great granddaughter, the film star and producer Drew Barrymore. For more on Drew, see R. Kelly; Kotsilibas-Davis; "Mrs. John Drew is Dead."

century. I was fascinated by Drew's account of her experiences as a young girl when she and her family toured the Caribbean and along the Atlantic coast, encountering excitement and boredom, friendship and obligation, discovery and loss along the way. Several pages after reading of her stepfather's death during the family's misguided trip to Jamaica, I came across her description of an 1833 visit to Halifax where she and her mother "act[ed] with the Garrison amateurs twice a week." Fourteen years old at the time, Drew recalls that "[w]e saw a good deal of human nature there [Halifax]—all the petty strife of real actors without the ability. However, it passed the summer away very pleasantly" (Drew 69). This description of a pleasant summer among "amateurs" surprised me, not only because I had assumed that garrison actors were exclusively male but also because I had read little about amateur actors performing alongside touring professionals in pre-Confederation Canada. How typical was this kind of engagement, I wondered? And what, if anything, did it have to do with her earlier experiences in the Caribbean and United States? Had I completely misunderstood Halifax's contribution to the formation of transatlantic, hemispheric, and imperial theatre cultures? If so, was it just me (how embarrassing!) or was my ignorance tied to other acts of historical forgetting?

Drew's three sentences about Halifax tripped me up and led me down a rabbit hole of historical (re)discovery that I retrace here. Such tripping offers a prime example of what Terry Eagleton calls the "symptomatic point," an "apparently peripheral" word, image, passage, or other fragment in a text that catches the reader's attention and in so doing threatens to unravel "or dismantle the oppositions which govern the text as a whole" (133). It's not that Mrs. Drew's memoir fell apart as I stumbled on her three sentences but that the stumbling exposed lingering blind spots in my own thinking, which in turn led me to question several assumptions that still dominate Canadian theatre histories. In particular, it led me to question traditional distinctions between amateur and professional performers and corresponding narratives that treat the rise of professional theatre as a critical marker in Canadian theatre's evolutionary development. Such social Darwinist accounts depict Canada as a nation "creeping"[3] toward culture and gloss over the contributions of non-professional or amateur players (Filewod, *Performing* 9).[4] As Robin Whittaker observes in his study of nonprofessional Canadian theatre:

> General practice has it that if you want to learn about the place of amateur theatre in Canadian history, you need look no further than chapters and articles dealing with Canada's theatre history up to and including "garrison theatricals," for example, of the eighteenth and nineteenth centuries before being thrust forward into the fifty years leading up to the establishment of the Manitoba Theatre Centre in 1958. (*Un/Disciplined* 10)

By turning explicitly to the period when garrison theatricals dominated theatrical entertainment in British North America, this essay extends Whittaker's assertion that " 'amateur' and 'professional' theatre practices are part of the same dynamic practice continuum" (*Un/Disciplined* 11). Indeed, Mrs. John Drew's three sentences complicate received histories about divisions between amateurs and professionals, men and women, and children and adults in 1830s Halifax, demonstrating that all participated in the formation of a distinctly transnational theatre culture.

Tripping over Drew's sentences further led me to reconsider the place of Canadian theatre scholarship within the so-called "hemispheric turn." This turn dates to the early-1990s when scholars in such disciplines as English, history, American studies, and theatre and performance studies rejected the myopia of national(ist) and imperialist narratives and began tracing the shared histories and circulation of objects, bodies, and ideas throughout the Americas (Parrish; Levander and Levine; Taylor, *Archive*). By offering an alternative to thinking along an east-west axis, hemispheric scholarship has illuminated "unsuspected social networks and flows of information," thereby

3 See, for example, Don Rubin's "Creeping Toward Culture."

4 Whittaker uses the term "nonprofessional" instead of "amateur" to avoid the negative connotations associated with the latter term (*Un/Disciplined* 12, 20).

complicating national histories or previous assumptions about local affiliations (Putnam 618), while "illuminat[ing] the shared historical experiences of North, South, and Central America—colonialism, slavery, independence wars, national formation, and new transnational identities" (J. Lane, "Keywords" 458). Such projects have also pushed hard against United States exceptionalism, recasting the relationship between the US and the rest of the Americas through an emphasis on shared histories and ongoing social, economic, cultural, and political dependencies (Bost 266; Moynagh 17). Yet Canadian scholars have been slow to adopt these methodologies, often arguing that the hemispheric turn merely reaffirms US cultural dominance and equates Canadian and US cultures. While acknowledging these concerns, this essay demonstrates that a hemispheric approach can open up new understandings of theatrical practices and challenge assumptions about hemispheric theatre culture itself.

In keeping with my revisionist goals, I take pains to emphasize my own rather awkward journey through primary and secondary sources. I do this not to annoy readers or to convince them of my ineptitude as a historian—though they may well leave with this impression—but rather to make transparent the complicated processes involved in making and unmaking histories. In other words, calling attention to my missteps, misinterpretations, blind spots, and biases is a critical part of my methodology. Admittedly, this essay asks more questions than it answers, but by acknowledging my personal relationship to the material I hope to model a way of doing history that is self-aware, critical, and distinctly performative. Writing now at a historical

Fig. 1. Louisa Lane as a young woman. TC 58 olvwork100850. Courtesy: Houghton Library, Harvard University.

moment when "truth" appears to have lost all meaning (if it ever had any) and evidence seems secondary to making bold assertions, I believe our job as historians is to investigate the stories that guide our lives as Canadians; to return with renewed vigour to the primary and secondary sources we *think* we understand; and to continue seeking lost, overlooked, or ignored material even though such quests may result in messiness, uncertainty, and even more unanswered questions.

FOLLOWING THE SOURCES

Let me start with three pesky questions that arise from Drew's account before zooming out to the larger historiographic concerns I've identified above. If, as previous accounts of garrison theatricals suggest, there was an "unwritten rule barring women from acting in garrison productions" (Boutilier 47), how did Drew and her mother end up playing alongside these men? And if women, and not just women but teenage *girls*, performed with the garrison troupe, why hadn't earlier historians ever acknowledged this as an anomaly—or had they? What led professional actresses like Drew and her mother to appear alongside garrison amateurs in the first place?

I first understood Drew's reference to the garrison amateurs to mean that she had performed in a garrison theatrical—a fairly logical assumption, I think, given most historical treatments of garrison theatre. I remembered first reading about such entertainments in Eugene Benson and L.W. Conolly's *English-Canadian Theatre* as an undergraduate, so I returned to this source and other histories of garrison theatre to learn more. These texts reminded me that military officers garrisoned in Halifax, travelling on naval vessels, or stationed elsewhere frequently staged productions of popular British dramas to amuse themselves and strengthen ties with the local community.[5] Such productions served as important tools of empire, inviting male officers and their

5 On shipboard theatricals, see O'Neill, "Theatre in the North"; Isbell; and Davis-Fisch, *Loss* 29–60.

predominantly male audiences to affirm their connection to British culture and to imagine themselves as part of a much larger "imagined community" of imperial theatregoers.[6] But where did girls like Mrs. John Drew and women like her mother fit into this homosocial culture?

Help came from Alex Boutilier and his 2005 thesis, "The Citadel on Stage." Although Boutilier confirms that "female parts were always played by male officers" (46), since Halifax society would have objected to the notion of women playing on stage, he acknowledges that "[f]rom time to time unmarried actresses from the United States would appear with professional troupes on the stages of Halifax" (47). Here was a significant piece of evidence. I realized that while women did not perform in garrison productions per se, they occasionally appeared alongside garrison actors *if* and when those men were needed to round out a professional acting company (54).[7] I came across further evidence of this practice in the online pages of the *Halifax Acadian Recorder*. For example, a June 1833 announcement for an upcoming production of *Paul Pry* and the farce *Soape Grace* informed readers that "[t]he principal parts in both pieces by the Gentlemen Amateurs, of the Garrison, who have kindly consented to appear on the occasion" ("Theatre"). This advertisement answered the question of the garrison amateurs—they had "kindly consented" to appear on stage with the professional company—but where was Mrs. John Drew in all of this?

I turned, as we all do at some point, to the *Oxford Companion to Canadian Theatre* and to Patrick O'Neill's entry on Nova Scotia theatre. I noted his paragraph on Halifax's New Theatre, a dynamic performance space that welcomed numerous professionals onto its stage between 1829 and 1844, including William Rufus Blake, who performed for "two years ending in 1833" (389). I flipped to O'Neill's entry on Blake in the same reverend tome and retraced

6 I gesture here toward Alan Filewod's use of Benedict Anderson's concept of "imagined community" to discuss the role of theatre in pre-Confederation Canada. See *Performing* 11–33.

7 For other work on Halifax theatre in the early nineteenth century, see Bains; Norris; and Williams.

the steps that led the actor-manager-playwright to Halifax, discovering that he had "managed the opening seasons at Boston's Tremont Theatre in 1827 and the renovated Walnut Street Theatre in Philadelphia, before returning to Canada in 1831" to perform in Québec (54). O'Neill then mentions that Blake "later managed his own company of American actors at The [New] Theatre, Halifax, for which he produced and probably wrote *FITZALLAN,* the first play by a Canadian-born author produced in Canada" (54). This led me to ask whether Mrs. John Drew and her mother knew Blake from earlier contracts. Had they, for example, played at the Tremont Theatre or the Walnut Street Theatre under Blake's tenure as manager? I returned to my PDF of Mrs. John Drew's autobiography and typed in Blake's name. Bingo. There he was on page 66, identified as a member of the acting company at Boston's "Warren" Theatre.[8] I read on and realized that Drew had visited Halifax after her second season at the Warren when she was fourteen years old (67). What Drew leaves out of her account, but which I'm now almost certain was the case, is that she and her mother travelled to Halifax at Blake's invitation for what would be his final season in the city. There, as members of Blake's professional acting company, they shared the stage with several garrison amateurs; and there, fourteen-year-old Mrs. John Drew observed "all the petty strife of real actors without their ability." Riddle solved.

I'll pause now to ask the inevitable academic question: So what? Why does Mrs. Drew matter? At first glance, the story of Drew's visit to Halifax and her encounter with the garrison amateurs seems relatively insignificant, an interesting trivia item. On closer examination, however, Mrs. John Drew's recollections pose key questions about the relationship between amateurs and professionals in pre-Confederation Canada that in turn might lead us to rethink how we draw our aesthetic, geographic, and temporal borders. Let's begin with Mrs. John Drew's own investment in professionalism . . .

---

8 Although O'Neill's entry on Blake doesn't include a reference to the Warren Theatre, his career, like that of his contemporaries, was highly mobile.

A PROFESSIONAL CHILD AMONG THE AMATEURS

Mrs. John Drew's brief but dismissive comments about the "Garrison amateurs" hint at ongoing tensions between "real" professional players and local performers. What is unclear is whether these comments represent *actual* tensions that Drew and her mother experienced in the 1830s or, rather (as I suspect), shifting attitudes toward professionalism in the 1890s when Drew wrote her memoirs. By the late nineteenth century, actors and actresses in the United States were finally gaining the respectability and social standing they had desired for decades. In an effort to perform their professional status, they established official clubs and associations, befriended society leaders, formalized actor training, and published articles and memoirs detailing the challenges of the acting life (MacArthur 85–122; also R. Whittaker, *Un/Disciplined* 45). As one of the most widely respected actresses and theatre managers in nineteenth-century North America, Mrs. John Drew epitomized "professionalism." More than documenting her career, then, her memoir participated in a larger cultural project designed to secure a better social standing both for herself and for her fellow professionals. Small wonder that she was so abrupt in her dismissal of the bumbling "Garrison amateurs."

In fact, for all its abruptness, Mrs. Drew's comment about the Halifax players is consistent with 1890s views of amateur actors. As Robin Whittaker has shown, the professionalization of acting in the late-nineteenth and early-twentieth century developed in tandem with the denigration of nonprofessional acting by emergent professionals (and critics). This insistence that professional players were superior to their amateur counterparts profoundly influenced later historians, many of whom accepted the characterization of amateurs as insignificant, incapable, and untalented. Such a perspective underpins the "maturation" narrative of Canadian theatre history, a narrative developed in the 1970s by Canadian theatre scholars who were, themselves, seeking greater professional standing (Filewod, *Performing* 9). These historians largely overlooked the complicated dynamics that shaped the relationship between nineteenth-century amateurs and professionals in local settings and dismissed the vital contributions of nonprofessional performers to local forms of cultural expression (R. Whittaker, *Un/Disciplined* 61).

Reading Mrs. John Drew's memoirs as a product of late-nineteenth century professionalization offers new insights into the relationship between amateurs and professionals in colonial Halifax. We learn, for example, that William Rufus Blake's professional theatre company often performed with amateur actors out of necessity and that this mixing gave a girl like Drew a new perspective on "human nature" and the "personal strife" the actors experienced, as much as it informed her opinions of their acting ability. This account further complicates assumptions about the homosocial nature of garrison theatre, suggesting that the actors who performed in male-only garrison productions might have received training or drawn inspiration from the professional actresses with whom they occasionally performed. Intriguingly, a May 1833 review of Blake's production of *Fitzallan* concludes with the critic's hope that the professional company will continue to collaborate with the amateurs in staging Shakespeare, alluding to an earlier production of *Romeo and Juliet* ("Great Novelty"). Further research might identify how frequently garrison actors played with Blake's company (among others) and investigate the extent to which such interactions influenced the amateurs' understanding of theatre. How "professional" were the garrison amateurs after all? Did their brief encounters with professional companies inspire dreams of becoming "real" actors? In what ways did the amateurs in turn shape touring actors' perceptions of local communities? What friendships, romantic liaisons, and other exchanges did this mixing of performers invite?

I'll leave these questions dangling in the hope that someone else might care to pick them up . . . or not.

HEMISPHERIC PERFORMERS

As I followed the bread-crumb-like clues left by Mrs. John Drew's three sentences, I found myself pulled back to earlier pages in her memoirs, where accounts of personal tragedy and forced mobility intermingled with character sketches of some of the era's most celebrated players. I realized that if I wanted to understand something of Mrs. John Drew's life touring along transatlantic and hemispheric theatre circuits, it wasn't enough to focus on her visit to Halifax. I had to pay closer attention to where she had come from, to the life experiences that had brought her to the colonial city. In so doing, I also hoped to learn more about Halifax's contribution to transatlantic and hemispheric theatre cultures. What follows then is a fairly typical biography of Lane's early years, but I recount it here as a way of getting at some of the complexities noted above.

Drew was born into a theatrical family in 1820 in London, England, and christened Louisa Lane. Her father, Thomas Frederick Lane, was "an actor of considerable provincial fame" and her mother, Eliza Lane (Trenter), was a "very pretty woman and a sweet singer of ballads" (Drew 5). Drew made her stage debut at twelve months of age, when her mother took her on stage to play the part of "crying baby" (5). Her earliest speaking roles at age five included the part of the "rightful heir" in the melodrama *Meg Murnock; or, the Hag of the Glen*, and the brother of Frankenstein in an adaptation of the Mary Shelley story (9). Drew's graduation to speaking roles coincided with the death of her father yet despite (or perhaps due to) this loss, mother and daughter continued to work in the theatre. When Drew was seven, John Hallam, the "accredited agent for Price & Simpson, of the old Park Theatre, New York," engaged mother and daughter to travel with him to North America along with other members of a newly formed acting company (17). Drew recalls that the four-week journey on board the packet ship *Britannia* was "exceptionally fine" and the company landed in New York in 1827, after which they travelled to Philadelphia for a stint at the Walnut Theatre (18). During this period, the Lanes performed alongside and came to know most of the major US stars of the day, notably Junius Brutus Booth and Edwin Forrest (21–26).

Not long after their arrival in the United States, Eliza Lane married her second husband, John Kinlock, "a stage manager, and a very capable actor and manager," who was always eager for new business opportunities (Drew 26). Noting the popularity of child actress Clara Fisher, Kinlock decided to

Fig. 2. Eight-year-old Louisa Lane in the five characters from the farce, *Twelve Precisely*. Original drawing by D.C. Johnston on 3 November 1828; later in the collection of actor John Drew. Courtesy Houghton Library, Harvard University.

promote his stepdaughter as a second "Clara" (28–29).[9] Drew made her debut as a "prodigy" in *The Spoiled Child*, a play that was an established part of Fisher's repertoire, and "from this time to the latter part of 1830 [she] played as a star with varying success (financially)" (29). In late 1830, the entrepreneurial Kinlock, "bitten with the idea of management" (32), partnered with a Mr. Jones with the goal of taking a company to Jamaica. But his dream of

9 For more on Clara Fisher, see Mullenix; Schweitzer, "Casting"; Varty.

theatrical gold quickly dissolved when the ship the company was travelling on struck a hidden rock, "a case of ignorant carelessness," Drew opines, "as it was a most beautiful moonlight night" (34). The boat was close enough to shore for the passengers to safely disembark but since they were nowhere near "any settlement," the company had little choice but to "settl[e] ourselves to stay for some time" (36), making strategic use of shingles and staves from the ship's deck. For six weeks, the company remained in their makeshift shelter while the captain and another crew member travelled approximately forty miles to San Domingo for help.[10] After a lengthy delay, the captain returned with aid and the company made its way to San Domingo and thence to Kingston, where they apparently delighted the audience. But success was short-lived. Not long after arriving in Kingston, both John Kinlock and Drew's infant sibling contracted yellow fever and died. Drew's mother Eliza also became very ill and the company retreated to Falmouth at the northern part of the island so she could recuperate. When "rumors of insurrection" in the region became "alarming" (38), Drew and her mother returned with the company orchestra leader to Kingston, and then continued on to New York.

After recovering from their disastrous time in Jamaica, mother and daughter returned to the stage. For several years they travelled along the Atlantic coast, performing with companies in New York, Boston, and Philadelphia out of financial need as well as (presumably) a desire for community and friendship. These needs and desires brought the two to Halifax in the summer of 1833 when William Rufus Blake hired them for his company (Drew 69).

Drew's account of her extensive travels—from England, to the United States, to Jamaica, back to the United States, and then to Nova Scotia—challenges still lingering tendencies to define historical projects along national, provincial, or urban borders. Her memoirs remind us that nineteenth-century theatre culture exceeded borders of colony and nation. This recognition in turn invites theatre historians, especially those working on histories of transatlantic theatre culture, to recognize Halifax's place within or along the evolving hemispheric touring circuit—to see it as one in a chain of colonial

10 Mrs. John Drew identifies the town as San Domingo, today known as Santo Domingo.

theatre cities that included Kingston (Jamaica), New Orleans, Charleston, Boston, and other major cities along the Atlantic coast.[11] Such recognition is important, not just for Canadian theatre history, but also for the history of transatlantic theatre culture more broadly. As historian Elizabeth Maddock Dillon observes of the Atlantic world, "[T]he circuits of transportation that were in full-fledged operation in the eighteenth century were those developed and fine-tuned by the economic systems that sustained the colonial Atlantic world, linking Charleston, for instance, to London, the Caribbean, and Africa" (57–58). Ironically, despite her sophisticated mapping of Atlantic theatre cultures, Dillon ignores Halifax entirely, neglecting any colony north of the US border. Dillon is hardly alone in her geographic oversight; as I argue below, such definitions of the Atlantic world are symptomatic of larger blind spots in hemispheric (and transatlantic) theatre studies. Nevertheless, Dillon's emphasis on viewing colonial cities as "nodes in a larger Atlantic/imperial network" (58) is incredibly valuable as it presents new ways to think about theatre's role in Halifax *and* Halifax's place within the Anglo-American world.

While previous research by O'Neill, Ed Mullaly, Denis Salter, and others has effectively traced the ebbs and flows of theatrical activity in Atlantic Canada,[12] new research might follow the hemispheric travels of those who visited Halifax, St. John's, and other Maritime towns and shed new light on the hemispheric circulation, transmission, and reception of performance repertoires.[13] For example, John Kinlock's decision to promote his young step-daughter as a new Clara Fisher points to the popularity of child performers, not just in the United States but along the Atlantic seaboard. Yet my research

11 Halifax is notably absent from many studies of transatlantic and/or hemispheric theatre culture. See, for example, Roach; Dillon; and Wilson.

12 The now-defunct Atlantic Canada Theatre Site (ACTS) was an incredibly valuable source. One of its features was a Theatre Playbill Archive, which extended back to the eighteenth century.

13 Maintaining a professional company in Halifax was extremely difficult in the 1830s, not least because the city's population was insufficient to support a permanent company longer than a season or two; by the 1840s Halifax regularly hosted touring companies (Salter).

on other child performers of the era has revealed startling differences in audience attitudes toward female "prodigies" (Schweitzer, "Unmanly"). Paying attention to such diverse responses might alert us to local anxieties, conflicts, and acts of resistance to imperialist hegemonies that we might otherwise miss (Bost). Did Halifax audiences embrace performers that other cities had rejected? If so, what does this suggest about the specific needs, desires, and anxieties of the city or Nova Scotia as a colony?[14] Intriguingly, the 1833 issue of *The Novascotian* that references the Blake company's production of *Romeo and Juliet* also alludes to the much-anticipated visit of the British actor Charles Kemble and his daughter Frances (Fanny) Kemble (*The Novascotian* 138).[15] How frequently were such visits planned, if not realized, and how did the fantasy of welcoming performers of the Kembles' stature shape Haligonian visions of Empire and their place within it?

A hemispheric focus on performers' movements might also take into account the extensive travels of the garrison amateurs themselves. As hypermobile subjects, both soldiers and actors experienced the hemisphere, and therefore the British Empire, in ways that settler-colonists did not.[16] Did this shared mobility encourage tighter bonds or other forms of communal feeling between soldiers and touring actors? Or is the disdain evident in Drew's memoirs typical of the way professional actors looked upon members of the British military who tried their hand at acting?

Finally, the account of Mrs. Drew's transatlantic travels challenges us to rethink how nations "claim" performers as *theirs*. Drew travelled extensively along the Atlantic coast throughout her early career yet she is frequently, if not exclusively, described as an American actress/manager.[17] What if instead

14 On Halifax within an imperial context, see Boyd; and McNairn.

15 These hopes did not materialize, although the Kembles did stop in Montreal and Québec City in July and August 1833. See Bains and Jenckes.

16 Writing about colonial Jamaica, Kathleen Wilson observes how "strolling players . . . hailed from diverse locations, all around the British isles and the world" (383). This was also true for the soldiers temporarily garrisoned in Halifax.

17 Although she does warrant a mention in Errol Hill's history of Jamaican theatre (85).

we identified her as a hemispheric performer, as an important player in the history of multiple nations, who shaped these nations (in varying degrees) even as she moved through/between them? This acknowledgement might lead us to rethink how we designate certain plays or actors as "Canadian" and, in turn, encourage us to celebrate the contributions of "non-Canadians" to the formation of local, national, and hemispheric theatre cultures.

CANADIAN THEATRE STUDIES AND THE HEMISPHERIC TURN

Thinking along hemispheric lines might also lead us to reflect critically on the reasons why Canadian theatre scholars have been slower than others throughout the Americas in following the "hemispheric turn." It is no surprise that US and US-based academics have been some of the loudest advocates of the hemispheric turn, perhaps none more so than NYU scholar Diana Taylor, founder and director of the Hemispheric Institute of Performance and Politics. For Taylor, the word "hemispheric" is an important alternative to "America" because it does not carry the same historical baggage and competing definitions of the latter term ("Remapping" 1418). She argues that "America" is a distinctly performative word that *does* something to those who hear or use it (i.e. inspires devotion, provokes anger), whereas "hemispheric" is an "antiperformative" word that means comparatively little to most people and "conjur[es] hazy images" ("Remapping" 1424; see also Taylor, *Archive*; and J. Lane, "Hemispheric America"). The word hemispheric, Taylor contends, opens up opportunities for scholars and artists throughout the Americas to work collaboratively, to identify points of connection and departure across borders of nation or ethnicity, and to rethink geographic affiliations in the interests of advancing shared political goals.

But the word "hemispheric" is more performative than Taylor allows, certainly outside the United States where many critics see it is a convenient cover for a neo-colonial academic project designed to reaffirm US political, economic, and cultural dominance within the Americas and thereby undermine nationalist work elsewhere (Adams and Phillips 7). In Canada, ongoing cultural nationalism, prompted by lingering memories of the struggles to establish Canadian-specific programs and disciplines in the 1970s and 1980s, offers a further explanation for scholarly resistance to hemispheric thinking (M. Smith, *Too Soon*; Adams and Phillips). Within Canadian theatre studies, this anxiety often manifests itself in conversations about association names, journal mandates, and graduate program profiles, when those advocating broader geographic perspectives are met with dire warnings of US cultural imperialism.[18] Some critics maintain that even *if* a hemispheric approach succeeds in decentring the United States, it runs the risk of reinscribing imperial hegemonies.[19] As Ralph Bauer observes in an essay on early American literature after the hemispheric turn, "One of the ironies of this declaration of independence from the proto-nationalist 'origins' model . . .

18 On these tensions, especially around the spread of Performance Studies in Canada, see Levin, "In Search."

19 Other factors explain the slow uptake of hemispheric approaches in Canada. Some critics point to a tendency within hemispheric studies to ignore Canada and focus on the relationship between the United States and its southern neighbours (Adams and Phillips 6; Sadowski-Smith 64). When scholars consider Canada, they often treat it as culturally equivalent to the United States, as the junior sibling in a mostly harmonious familial relationship, and therefore less interesting or worthy of study. In such instances, Canada's distinctive social, cultural, political cultures are ignored or effaced, lumped in with all things "American." This tendency to treat the United States as a synecdoche for all of North America was strikingly evident at the 1979 meeting of the International Federation of Theatre Research held in Toronto, when, as conference organizer Michael Sidnell recalls, "one of the bulletins carrying a notice of the conference transmogrified its title [from Theatrical Touring and Founding in North America] into 'Theatrical Touring and *Fund*ing in the *United States*,' an interesting pair of Freudian slips" (ix). Even when scholars or other public figures identify differences between the two countries, they often treat Canada as "a kind of fantasy land through which US Americans contemplate their own country's shortcomings and envision a simpler and more aesthetically satisfying world" (New, qtd. in Sadowski-Smith 64). Such tendencies become painfully obvious whenever US commentators use Canada to critique a US politician or social phenomenon. See, for example, Tina Fey's TV sitcom *30 Rock* (2006–2013), Michael Moore's *Bowling for Columbine* (2002), and Trudeaumania 2.0.

has been that early American literature has once again become British" (250). The same irony applies in the Canadian context, in that any study of hemispheric connections must necessarily take into account the colonizing actions of the British and French. Rather than seeing this as an irresolvable problem, however, I feel strongly that closer reflection on imperial politics and the dynamic interactions that shaped personal and communal identities can play an important role in larger decolonization projects.[20]

Thankfully (if paradoxically), historians looking to reframe Canadian theatre history along hemispheric lines can find valuable leads in the work of earlier Canadian theatre historians, notably those writing in the 1970s and 1980s. Indeed, while I've offered my reading of Mrs. John Drew's memoirs as a corrective to nationalist modes of history-making, this approach is hardly new. Such an observation may seem surprising, counterintuitive, or simply ironic, given the emphasis in this earlier period on excavating local, regional, and national theatre histories. Driven by questions such as, "Was there any theatre of significance in Saint John?" (M. Smith, *Too Soon* ix) and the firm belief that "truth [could] be found in the artifactual record" (Plant 4), historians dove deeply into the archives, developed city- or province-specific performance calendars in adherence to what Ron Vince called the "documentary imperative" (4), and wrote reader-friendly accounts designed to prove the existence and viability of Canada's theatre history. Yet while some scholars eschewed "an international context" in the interests of promoting cultural nationalism, others found it impossible to ignore the hemispheric (or global) movements of their research subjects.[21] For example, at the 1987 Atlantic Canada Symposium, an event dedicated to exploring four centuries of theatre in the Atlantic region, Denis Salter delivered a compelling paper on William Rufus Blake (yes, that Blake!), wherein he referenced the actor-manager's 1821 visit to Kingston, Jamaica, where he was called upon to "assume many of the leading roles"

20 Despite these anxieties, a growing number of Canadian theatre and performance studies scholars are undertaking hemispheric projects. See, for example, Alvarez, *Fronteras* and *Latina/o*; and Wasserman, "Transnational."

21 See Bains and Jenckes; Hughes; Lawrence; Lynde; Mullaly; Sperdakos.

after a "senior actor died of yellow fever" (74). While primarily interested in Blake's acting career, Salter's archival exploration of US and Jamaican newspapers and his observation that Blake spent some time following "the touring circuit along the Atlantic seaboard" (74) offer twenty-first century historians valuable clues about nineteenth-century touring practices. For my purposes, Salter's research raises the possibility that Blake felt a special affinity with Mrs. John Drew and her mother following their tragic losses in Jamaica given his own experiences in the Caribbean colony.

Salter's article offers but one example of what we might term a proto-hemispheric perspective. Patrick O'Neill similarly stressed the importance of asking how performers' movements along the Atlantic seacoast shaped their lives and informed their relationships with local audiences. For example, in a 2000 review of Yashdip S. Bains's *English Canadian Theatre, 1765–1826*, O'Neill faulted Bains for failing to read the 1768 Halifax appearances of the actor Henry Giffard against his earlier appearances in Jamaica (Review). While O'Neill stopped short of calling for the kind of hemispheric theatre history that many scholars are now working toward, he clearly understood the importance of thinking hemispherically. These examples remind me that my own assumptions about the hypernationalism of earlier theatre scholarship is in itself a kind of blind spot, one that I need to move beyond in order to develop a sharper understanding of the making and unmaking of Canadian theatre history.

I realize that I have posed more questions than I have answered here, but I do so with the goal of provoking deeper consideration of our (past) investments in national narratives. By this, I am not suggesting that we throw away our "old" histories—in fact, as I have argued above, our old histories offer vital clues for writing new ones. Rather, I encourage readers to continue undoing the "maturation" narrative of Canadian theatre history and to extend our analysis beyond Canadian borders. Indeed, if one of the central projects of the twentieth-century Canadian theatre historian involved knitting together neat and tidy histories that could be packaged into thin paperback volumes and transmitted to students via semester-long courses, then perhaps one of the central projects of the twenty-first century Canadian theatre historian should involve unpicking the threads of those old histories and encouraging students to reread old sources, to seek new ones, and to ask questions that will lead us down previously obscured, overlooked, or forgotten pathways.

"THE DEATH OF PERFORMANCE ART!" PERFORMING PERFORMANCE ART DOCUMENTATION

T. NIKKI CESARE SCHOTZKO

When I walk round my flat, the various aspects in which it presents itself to me could not possibly appear as views of one and the same thing if I did not know that each of them represents the flat seen from one spot or another, and if I were unaware of my own movements, and of my body as retaining its identity through the states of those movements.
—Maurice Merleau-Ponty, *The Phenomenology of Perception* (235)

I am sure that in this journey I will come across many distorted images of myself.
—Guillermo Gómez-Peña, "Culturas-in-extremis: Performing Against the Cultural Backdrop of the Mainstream Bizarre" (48)

I. STRANGE FRICTION

As *Corpo Insurrecto 3.2*, the final performance of La Pocha Nostra's residency at the University of Toronto in late October/early November 2014, neared its end, the audience jostled and jockeyed its way toward the stage at the back of the Centre for Drama, Theatre and Performance Studies's Helen Gardiner Phelan Playhouse. Artist-scholar and La Pocha Nostra founder Guillermo Gómez-Peña was directing the hot, sweaty, and mostly naked ensemble members into one last tableau vivant formed as part of the final piece, *Ways to*

Kill a Mexican. "Take more pictures!" Gómez-Peña roared over the crowd. "Take more pictures! Put them on Facebook! This is why we are doing this!" Would-be digital archivists thrust their cellphones forward and up; elbows were thrown; pregnant women were pushed out of the way. (I know this because I was one.) The performers held their ultimate, lurid pose, their expressions betraying no sense of the rabid audience, at this point just inches away from them. The air was heavy with the smell of bodies as Gómez-Peña barked, "You are witnessing the death of performance art!"

"Phenomenology posits that the world requires a consciousness to experience it," write Maaike Bleeker, Jon Foley Sherman, and Eirini Nedelkopoulou, following Maurice Merleau-Ponty, in the introduction to their collection *Performance and Phenomenology: Traditions and Transformations* (2). So too does performance—its consciousness indicated through audiences' physical, emotional response to it that opens, as Janelle Reinelt suggests, "a space for feelings, associations, impressions, and emerging values" (361). The application of phenomenology to performance allows not only for the consideration of that which is explicitly available to the audience, but also that which is inclusive of the implicitly unavailable: "what happens beyond or beneath the registers of human sense experience" (Bleeker et al. 2). Bleeker, Sherman, and Nedelkopoulou continue, "[Phenomenology] not only provides a perspective on the body and experience in how the world becomes available to us, but also acknowledges the body as the very possibility of having a perspective and therefore also a constraint to perceptual consciousness." Thinking through phenomenology as a methodology of performance, and, more particularly, of witnessing and documenting performance, allows for a broader analysis of "the relationship between action, perception, and environment" (6).

As there is a phenomenology of performance, there is also a phenomenology of its documentation. Performance's documentation exists in a space in the world alongside the performance it replicates, and in a temporality too that is alongside that of the performance. In *The Phenomenology of Perception*, Merleau-Ponty challenges the metaphor of time's passing or flowing, arguing that any event named as such is contingent not upon the objective event that happened but rather on the witnessing of it by an in-objective and spatio-temporally located (or "finite") witness: "the very notion of event has no place in the objective world." Rather, as he continues, "if I consider the world itself, there is simply one indivisible and changeless being in it":

> Change presupposes a certain position which I take up and from which I see things in procession before me: there are no events without someone to whom they happen and whose finite perspective is the basis of their individuality. Time presupposes a view of time. (477)

There is no time without the perception of it; there is no performance without the (conscious or unconscious) awareness of it. But, as performance, both in the mainstream and on the more experimental edges, seems to ask, what does the mode of perception do to the time of performance? And what happens to the future of performance when the simultaneity of the event of performance with its socially mediated documentation turns the present now into a concurrent historical event?

Gómez-Peña's call to social-networking action, a call to a certain mode of witnessing and documentation of experience, was very much informed by the ensemble's then-recent battles with Facebook's censorship policies—conflict with institutional authority endemic to La Pocha Nostra since its founding by Gómez-Peña and fellow artists Roberto Sifuentes and Nola Mariano as an ongoing and growing collective in 1993. According to the troupe's newer Facebook page *La Pocha Nostra 3.0*, their previous page was "shut down due to 'explicit nudity,'" causing them to lose six thousand virtual members (La Pocha Nostra, "La Pocha").[1]

---

1 This is, to be fair, somewhat misleading. As of April 2015, there remained the Pocha Nostra page dating from 2009, which features, according to my fast and entirely unofficial count, photographs of at least six naked breasts, accumulated from four different women, and one photograph of naked male buttocks; several pages created by the institutions at which Pocha Nostra was conducting workshops, including the U of T; and a few closed

Fig. 1. SHUT DOWN DUE TO "EXPLICIT NUDITY." La Pocha Nostra 3.0 censored Facebook page. 14 December 2014. Screen grab by T. Nikki Cesare Schotzko.

However, in its animation of the audience out of the present moment and into the immediate future-history of social-media broadcast through the forced simultaneity of the live event with its DIY documentation and distribution, Gómez-Peña's directive suggests not just a shift in the relationship between the well-worn pairing of performance and documentation but, more significantly, in the responsibility or imperative on the part of a performance's attendees to the maintenance of that event's future: an act not only of performative documentation but of performative archiving that is at once anarchistic in its methodology and staid in its ideology.

I am sounding out Gómez-Peña's call to La Pocha Nostra's audience on that sticky autumnal night at the Phelan Playhouse through two other performances I am considering here (and was present at). Each performance, like *Corpo Insurrecto 3.2*, was contingent not only on its audience's presence but also on its audience's willingness to document the act: performance artist Jess Dobkin's *How Many Performance Artists Does It Take to Change a Light Bulb*

groups as well as La Pocha Nostra Art Gallery. I can no longer, however, find the Pocha Nostra 3.0 page on which the troupe first posted notice of Facebook's censorship.

(for Martha Wilson), a durational solo (of sorts) performed on 16 April 2015 at Toronto's Images Festival; and visual artist Chun Hua Catherine Dong's *The Other Words*, performed with fellow artist Robert Black at Toronto's Katzman Contemporary on 30 January 2016, part of the west side gallery's two-day performance-art festival Duration and Dialogue. These performances put pressure on notions of linear narrative and history, as well as on how the notion of the "live" is contingent upon its digitally and socially mediated prosthetics; and so I am also sounding out Gómez-Peña's call through Molly Nesbit's eponymous pragmatism in art criticism, which seeks to redefine the notion of the historical through its dependence on (or, "punishing hunt for") the present; Alice Rayner's thesis on a "live/ness" that is as temporally as it is spatially marked; Shelley Liebembuk's challenge to the context in which a performance and its witnessing takes place when nationalist ideologies are at (the) stake; and Johanna Householder's take on Husserlian memory processes, with a couple of short treks in the direction of other calls to act and to action. These performances and theorists make increasingly evident not only the complex, phenomenological relationship between a performance event and its subsequent (or in these cases, concurrent) documentation—an old thesis in theatre and performance studies made new by these artists' forays into social media and collective, consensual documentation—but also the strange new friction between the real-time, or in situ, materiality of the performance and the ephemerality of the digital-virtual document. This friction is inextricable from the phenomenological in and of performance—performance both of the event, rendered objective by Merleau-Ponty's "finite" witness, and of its documentation by that witness, particularly when that documentation appears and disappears on social media. Ultimately, the fragmentary matter that remains of these performances enacts a performative intervention into the imperative of documentation by a performance genre that has always determined itself through disappearance.

II. HOW MANY PERFORMANCE SCHOLARS DOES IT TAKE . . .

For Jess Dobkin, documentation stands in less for the death of the event than for its persistent capacity to make us feel; affect and emotion equally untroubled by the medium of their provocation (Dobkin, "Untitled"). Her work has included both controversial and fun interventions into social and political constructions and expectations of gender and sexuality—being fisted as a "live puppet" by Lex Vaughn in her lip synch of "It's Not Easy Being Green" (2009); tending a breast-milk bar at Toronto's OCAD University in *Lactation Station* (2006); or inviting audience members to sharpen a pencil with a sharpener held within Dobkin's vagina in *Fee for Service* at Toronto's 2006 Nuit Blanche—and Dobkin brings to the performative fore issues prevalent in her private and public life. Dobkin's performance pieces necessarily reference her experience as a queer woman, performer, and mother (not necessarily in that order), as well as quite literally manifesting Merleau-Ponty's idea of the experiential body as both sensible (objective) and sentient (phenomenological), a means by which the body recognizes itself as both subject and object only in relation to others' subject- and objecthood. "The body," Merleau-Ponty writes, "unites us directly with things through its own ontogenesis, by welding to one another the two outlines of which it is made, its two laps: the sensible mass it is and the mass of the sensible wherein it is born by segregation and upon which, as seer, it remains open" (*Visible* 136). By putting her body in such vulnerable juxtaposition with her audiences' bodies, Dobkin makes us ever more aware of ourselves even as we become so intimately aware of her.

Dobkin originally intended to title *How Many Performance Artists Does It Take* . . . a "Rape Party," as she said in her final extended monologue, speaking of and to her own experience of sexual violence as a young girl that formed the conceptual ground of the piece. But she was afraid that if she did either no one would come, or those who did wouldn't be the people she wanted to party with. Instead, Dobkin placed both the subjecthood and subjection of her explicit body, to borrow the term from Rebecca Schneider (*Explicit*), in the hands of her audience—not to mention the authorship of her piece.

Figs. 2 and 3. Jess Dobkin, *How Many Performance Artists Does It Take to Change a Light Bulb (for Martha Wilson)*, Images Festival, Toronto, Ontario, 2015. Photos by T. Nikki Cesare Schotzko.

Throughout the more than four-hour long durational performance, one hundred official, volunteer documentarians formed, with the non-documentarian audience, a wide circle around a demarcated central space in the Enoch Turner Schoolhouse, as they photographed, Polaroided, video-recorded, sketched, and wrote, in prose and poetry, through Dobkin's autobiographical monologue. A single light bulb hung, unreachable, from the ceiling.

Chun Hua Catherine Dong extended the space of her intimate performance *The Other Words* into the less immediately intimate realm of the digital-virtual. In addition to the audience already present to the event, Dong, a visual artist born in China and currently based in Montreal, Québec, called on certain audience members to post new tweets, status updates, images, and videos of the performance to social media every five minutes of its three-hour-long duration. A group of young, mostly Asian artsters crowded in on the two performers as Dong sat, wearing a severe houndstooth jumper and white blouse, across a white table from the fully naked Robert Black. With excruciating patience, Dong offered Black spoonfuls of rice that she had just

Fig. 4. Chun Hua Catherine Dong with Robert Black, *The Other Words*, Duration and Dialogue Festival, Katzman Contemporary, Toronto, Ontario, 2016. Photo by Johannes Zits.

masticated, complicating the nurturing dimensions of her feeding of Black with the aggressively omnipresent nature of the social media feed.

Considering performance more an "attitude than a medium," Dong creates work that figures the body, most often her own, as a political and politicized site "to activate social commentary on immigration, race, and gender" (Dong, *Chun Hua*). The constructed dichotomies of "East/West" and "self/other" that inform her practice—which includes performance, photography, and video—play out in *The Other Words*, both through the explicit presentness of her body across from Black's and through the mild disruption the Asian youth created through their social-media record of the performance. Their documentation provided a supplement to the live event at the gallery that not only extended the space of the performance but also its time, even as much of the uploaded material disappeared, like the in-situ performance, after its conclusion. Though Dong and Black seemed to remain almost in a point of stasis through the extended time of their durational and di-gestational performance, they slipped away through the constricted and conscripted time of its documentation.

The digital-virtual archive—accruing through social media's uncurated ontology—generates a phenomenologically different mode of archival witnessing that is at once made more democratic *and* more exclusive via the corporate vehicles that control its existence as well as its dissemination. The incorporation of social media into the performance event suggests at once a shift in how we experience the social space that performance creates that is predicated on a parallel shift in how we express our sociality in the world—"sociality is interwoven with valued theatrical experiences," notes Janelle Reinelt (359)—and a concurrent shift in how value is determined through the aggregate of social media approval: shared posts, pics, links, and likes becoming the measure of accumulated cultural capital.

The CFP for a 2015 seminar on Performance History and Historiography at the annual Canadian Association for Theatre Research (CATR) conference asked, "What strategies do we employ in order to textualize the messy remains of the performative past, 'wrangling' disorderly events into coherent (and academically acceptable) narratives?" I ask, in concert, how might such performative archival processes *de*-textualize the potential remains of any live event, rendering the archive as intentionally and necessarily messy as—or even more so than—the performance? For instance, how to "cite" (and by "cite," to validate) the documentary fragments from Dong and Black's performance that no longer exist, yet in the act of their recording comprised a significant component of the live performance? To whom to grant authorial ownership in Dobkin's performance when the photographs and videos and sketches and texts are submitted by multiple witnesses to it? How might such fabulous incoherence reimagine our understanding of the "academically acceptable" narrative? Further, if the archive lives in Google, or on Twitter or Facebook, or, even more phenomenologically savvy, Periscope or Snapchat (there may be no more Husserlian interface than one that presumes its own disappearance), what random algorithm controls our access to it, and therefore our research of it? Especially as these algorithms are not so entirely random, emerging from our own digital-virtual peregrinations.[2] What happens when the documentation disappears? Or, put more simply, what happens when the light bulb . . . goes out?

III. THE PRAGMATISM OF PERFORMANCE DOCUMENTATION

In *The Pragmatism in the History of Art* (2013), Molly Nesbit extends Merleau-Ponty's views on time (and on time's views of itself). For Nesbit, time is still in motion, distinct from its modes of measurement, but in a motion that exists as a spatial and temporal counter that moves through and against the

---

2 Facebook, for instance, not only tracks its members' virtual footprint, but also uses this information to determine a means of categorizing users' personal interests and inclinations: from entertainment and media preferences to political views. While the former has a distinctly and immediately commercial application, the latter, too, is subject to more insidious advertising and marketing. As Jeremy B. Merrill writes in a 24 August 2016 *New York Times* article, "Donald J. Trump's presidential campaign has paid for its ads to be shown to those who Facebook has labeled politically moderate" (A13).

spatiotemporal objectivity of the world as Merleau-Ponty describes. Writing about Gordon Matta-Clark's 1971 May Day performance *Tree Dance* at Vassar College in Poughkeepsie, New York, in which Matta-Clark and members of the Vassar Dance Troupe climbed high into the branches of a tree bedecked with rope ladders and canvas cradles, alternately climbing, swinging, and dangling from them,[3] Nesbit posits the work of art not only as an object in its own right but also as one coexistent within time's multitudinous possibilities:

> The performance itself was unmarked: it had no time frame, no set beginning or end, no audience to speak of. It was an event infiltrated simply by the many shapes of time. The random minds looking up to the tree dance were full of other things, thoughts of fighting not only in Southeast Asia, but in the Middle East, in Ireland, in Bangladesh, the list was long, and thoughts of impending exams, maybe wondering about the survey of Andy Warhol's work that had opened at the Whitney Museum the night before. [. . .] The minds were full—remembering perhaps the last call for realism at the end of "Why?" (84)

Nesbit proposes an anti- or even meta-present within the archaeological process of mining the resources of recent art history, ultimately challenging how far back the historical project needs to extend to validate itself as, indeed, historical, and suggesting that the question of remembering is not only that of Why? but also, When? "It falls to history to study the nature of change and to chase the present's trail into time's grey ebb," she persuades. "It may take a while to realize that history is nothing less than an eternal, punishing hunt for the present—no matter when it happened" (24). Gómez-Peña's call to document during *Corpo Insurrecto 3.2* was embedded in a drive to

---

3 See P. Lee. To view the 1971 9:32 minute, black-and-white, silent, 16-mm film on video *Tree Dance*, visit https://vimeo.com/3308233 (though you'll have to turn the sound off on your computer, as the film has a sound track added). And, for the digitally adventurous, to view a 2011 version of *Tree Life* created by Michel Favre in the now virtual ghost world *Second Life*, visit https://vimeo.com/18972191.

re-establish presence in the present of the performance within its threatened social-media space; Dobkin, too, uses the performance, and performative, present to address a certain threat to presence—specifically, the presence of the queer woman's body and the violences that might be done to it—within history's narrowly defined parameters. But both the present and presence, in performance as in life, remain ever more elusive as the distinctions between the digital-virtual and the real or in situ overlap, in time and in memory.

Looking forward to a time in the future rather than in the past, or in history, Alice Rayner turns the Merleau-Pontian argument around in "E-Space: Performance in the Time of Cyberspace," framing the space of contemporary performance, and of "live/ness," as one marked not primarily by its spatiality—that is, by the here and now of spectatorial engagement—but by its temporality: the many heres of its (still singular) now. "Both cyberspace and performance, in utterly practical ways, materialize the 'now,'" she writes, comparing it to the "now" of theatre—a now that "must play in real time" (360).[4] That now, however, is contingent upon a "temporal collapse" that digital technologies enable via a simultaneity of the time of engagement. As Rayner continues:

> For both performance and cyberspace, "liveness" has much less to do with living bodies than with "live," meaning simultaneous, in real time. That kind of "live" may or may not have anything to do with mechanical reproduction or organic life. "Live" shifts the question of presence from its spatial sense of here to its temporal sense of now. (361)

The resignification of the "now" as a temporally based element of performance independent from spatial proximity creates a signifying shift, too, in

4 Rayner writes, alluding both to Thornton Wilder and, like Nesbit, Gilles Deleuze, "Performance, being always now, is a singularity that has no substitute. Not being a thing, performance must play in real time." She continues, "Both cyberspace and performance, in utterly practical ways, materialize the 'now.' Unlike theatre, however, they do not necessarily frame the now in some special aesthetic context" (360, 361).

the moment of encounter: it is no longer that bodies might interact within a space but rather that they intersect within time.[5] When the materialization of the now in the performance encounter extends into its simultaneous and often immaterial digital-virtual record, as it did, explicitly, in the audience members' posting of images and video to social media as part of Dong and Black's performance *The Other Words*, and in Gómez-Peña's socially mediated call to La Pocha Nostra's audience, the present not only rubs uncomfortably up against now, but also against a subsequent then: against the past, and against its history.

IV. THE UNFIXITY OF THE EVENT

To rub up against the past, even in the present moment, creates a bodily as well as a theoretical (and, still, strange) friction. When a performance exists simultaneously in the real—that is, the sensory world—and the digital-virtual, the very idea of the body in performance is strained by its own disappearance from the event, trying as it does to realize itself simultaneously in the actual and the intangible (or the visible and the invisible, to recall Merleau-Ponty). The politics at play in performance art's struggle for institutional and economic stability and validity re-emerge in these matters of documentation as well as in the performances themselves. It is no accident that I am bringing together in this chapter a Chicano artist-scholar whose work has long worried the boundaries of identity as a political act within the artistic frame; a queer performance artist who engages deeper questions of violence and sexuality through what might on its surface seem more colloquially fun; and a clothed

5 Examining the process-driven methodology in Anna Deavere Smith's work, and in particular *On the Road: In Search of American Character*, in which the significance of the performance hinges not in the space between the "real" of Smith's interviews and the "illusion" of her performance of them but rather in the movement between the two, Rayner writes, "Both performance practices and cyberspace technologies counteract such a metaphysics of substance in their chronic displacement, implying perhaps that the body and identity must be considered temporal intersections more than substances" (365).

Asian woman force-feeding a naked white man, both fully self-conscious of how they have embedded themselves in a contradictory matrix of feminist and colonialist discourses.[6]

Mark B.N. Hansen takes this up, shifting the notion of "phenomenological intentionality" to "implication." "Eschewing any phenomenological reduction designed to transpose worldliness into a content of consciousness," he writes, "implication involves the causal impact of worldly materiality on an experiential unity that cannot be reduced to a pure state of consciousness" (222–23). Hansen offers a counter to the relationship between phenomenology and performance by realigning the centredness of the body within the event:

> [T]he performing body shifts its role: no longer an object relative to a larger sensory distribution, the body instead becomes an element among others within a larger matrix of sensibility. Alongside this shift in the role of the body, we must revise our understanding of performance: no longer a capacity of the body, performance now designates an environmental event that involves but is not exclusively channeled through the body—an event that implicates the human through its robustly embodied contact with worldly sensibility. (227)

The body, for Hansen, becomes "a participant" rather than "an agent," privileging not the notion of presence but rather of expression of the total "environmental event" that is the performance (229). However, to reveal the body as no longer the agent of the event also obscures the capacity for agency within the event in which one is implicated as participant.

La Pocha Nostra creates an especially compelling case study here, fostering, as it does, "the creation of intercultural, cross-border collaborations with performance artists from many countries." The troupe's work is decisively

---

6 Both Dong and Black discussed, during the performance's talkback, the exchange of labour involved in *The Other Words*—chewing requiring, at least perceivably, more effort than swallowing—as well as the explicitly visible power dynamics Dong was both enacting and challenging in setting herself, an Asian woman, across the table from Black's naked white male body (Dong, *Other Words*).

predicated upon such trans-border and international collaboration, while also stimulating incisive critique of the nationalist and imperialist codes of identity and belonging that underlie any such actual or conceptual crossing of borders.

> As a direct response to the ironic global phenomenon that immigrants of the third-world live within and redefine the culture of the much touted first-world (and many times within the very country responsible for the hardships of their homeland), we have challenged ourselves to detect artists in other countries mapping parallel artistic territories and dealing with similar issues: artists who occupy the space between "homeland" and host country; between cultural memory and present politics; between gender and race. (La Pocha Nostra, "What is")

Gómez-Peña and the other members of La Pocha Nostra, unlike Dobkin or Dong, do not identify as Canadian artists, though neither are they especially American (as in from the United States or North America)—they may be Latin American, but even that demarcation is tenuous. Their art and their activism is at once global in its reach and local in its enactment: for the duration of their time Toronto, they became, in part, Canadian; the ephemerality of such nationalist designations implicitly demonstrating the shiftiness of any such categorization by self or institution.

Yet performing nationalism on the theatrical or global stage is no small thing; nor is it to think of performance as a life-or-death matter. The consequences of Gómez-Peña's call in *Corpo Insurrecto 3.2* in the broader context of La Pocha Nostra's performance of *Ways to Kill a Mexican* reflect a more complicated power dynamic at work between performers and audience. In her review of the performances and workshops that constituted La Pocha Nostra's visit to the University of Toronto, "Contextualizing the Image: La Pocha Nostra in Toronto," Shelley Liebembuk (who also co-organized the event) challenges the efficacy of the troupe's performance methodology that bares audiences' own political and personal vulnerabilities, even as it bares its performers' (and sometimes its audiences') bodies, without necessarily offering a concurrent space or context for such implicating prostrations. Speaking to the final tableau, Liebembuk writes,

> As [LPN member Jess] Balitrónica walked across the space, soliciting participants, I felt deeply unsettled by the political implications of the invitation, as well as by the strange dis-located position of Mexican American politics in a primarily Anglo-Canadian context. More disconcerting was the additional invitation for those participants who wanted to kill a Mexican to get naked while doing so: an invitation which seemed to create quite a lot more tension in the audience than the first. [. . .] What is at stake in creating these images here, at this time, with this audience? How much of the effect of these images is their ability to shock a prudish audience with nudity and sexualized imagery? (23)

The stakes in this performance are high for both performers and audience, and Gómez-Peña has commented on audiences' willingness to embrace a markedly (and unflatteringly) colonialist position in the deceptively safe zone of the performance event. In one exceptionally vivid example Gómez-Peña relates the experience, during LPN's international tour of *The Museum of Fetishized Identities*, of audience members whipping Mexican performance artist Juan Ybarra with the host country's flag. "Willing audience members immediately formed a line to carry out his instructions," Gómez-Peña recalls, "while others screamed, 'harder, harder!' " (63). Such performances, including that of *Ways to Kill a Mexican* in Toronto, Gómez-Peña suggests, "reveal a new relationship between performance artist and audience, between the exoticized 'foreign' body and the white voyeur" (64).

This new relationship, however, rather than heightening the political reality represented and reanimated within the aesthetic free-for-all, is instead "characterized by the lack of political or ethical implications" on the part of naively willing audiences (Gómez-Peña 64). Though the troupe's intention may be to offer its audiences an opportunity for critical reflection on these artistically motivated reproductions of historical violences perpetuated on the marked body of the Other, do such violent reproductions not yield more of a reflection of the audience's own willingness to exceed its personally rather than politically inflicted limits, and to celebrate the state of its own aestheticized body in excess rather than that of the racialized body in duress? Or, as Liebembuk asks, "Is the tableaux' potential for showcasing the problematic sexualization of violence and the reification of minority bodies as hypersexual being overshadowed by the audience participants' 'liberating' experience of public nudity?" (23). The re-, or, more accurately, de-politicized self-reflection on the part of La Pocha Nostra's audiences is doubled, then, as is the violence done to performers' bodies, through Gómez-Peña's call during the Toronto performance. It is not the performers' bodies, nor even the performance here, that matters; rather, this call to document is intentionally a call to distribute: the accounting of "shares" and "likes" racking up a value that exceeds a shared personal accountability.

Dobkin, too, asks her audiences not just to witness the event of her performance, but to take curatorial responsibility for the performance; the spectatorial role repurposed from watching to documenting, and, by documenting, also creating. In her earlier piece *Flowers*, performed and recorded in four takes at Toronto's Buddies in Bad Times, Dobkin recreates a lip-synched duet with herself of Barbra Streisand and Neil Diamond's 1978 hit "You Don't Bring Me Flowers," while certain members of the audience, invited by Dobkin via Facebook, photographed and digitally videoed each take.[7]

---

7 Streisand and Diamond's duet evolved from a strange set of circumstances in itself, as Sharon Davis describes in *'80s Chart Toppers: Every Chart-Topper Tells a Story* ("October 1980: Barbra Streisand"). According to Davis, and to pop legend, the program director of the Kentucky radio station WAKY-AM, Gary Guthrie, received both Diamond's 1977 album *I'm Glad You're Here With Me Tonight*, which included "You Don't Bring Me Flowers"—and which Diamond had co-written with Alan Bergman and Marilyn Bergman—and Streisand's 1978 album *Songbird*, on which she covered the track. Both singers, coincidentally, sang the song in the same key. Twenty years at least in advance of Girl Talk's huge success with his pop-music mashups, Guthrie spliced the two recordings together on air for, as the story goes, his wife, whom he'd recently divorced. After the rampant success of Guthrie's DIY version, Streisand and Diamond recorded the duet officially later in 1978.

Naked—except for fuzzy mules, a long brunette wig, and some fierce fake fingernails painted almost black—and prone atop a satin-covered double bed on the Buddies in Bad Times stage, with cameras live-streaming her face and nether regions in two separate, crookedly set square projections on a screen just above her, Dobkin begins her performance lip-synching Streisand's breathy introduction: "You don't bring me flowers / You don't sing me love songs." A close-up of Dobkin's face is projected first, highly done up and over-articulating the words. As Diamond's part begins, with his slightly harsh tenor—"You hardly talk to me anymore / When I come through the door / At the end of the day"—the second projection appears, shot from a camera directed between Dobkin's legs. Dobkin manipulates, with her artificially long nails, her labia, those lower lips synching with Diamond's voice as a pair of googly eyes, affixed to Dobkin's pudendum, goggle on. During the four takes, Dobkin gave instructions to the DIY documentarians for the type of shot she wanted, and the final performance film includes several shots of blue-lit cellphone screens high in the air, on which a tiny naked Dobkin is doubled and then doubled again, and again.[8]

How Many Performance Artists Does It Take to Change a Light Bulb (for Martha Wilson) maintained a similarly festive feel—truly a party if perhaps not the "Rape Party" Dobkin intended—though this was never meant to be a documentation of a performance but rather documentation as performance. Dobkin, as she notes on the event's Facebook page, takes her title from a joke in Martha Wilson's oral history of performance art:

> Q: How Many Performance Artists Does it Take to Change a Light Bulb?
>
> A: I don't know. I left after 4 hours. (Images Festival)

See Davis 2012. Guthrie also recounts his memory of this story on the blog *79 WAKY*: *http://www.79waky.com/garyguthrie.htm*.

8 To view *Flowers*, visit Jess Dobkin's homepage, www.jessdobkin.com/, or, directly, vimeo.com/31436314.

Dobkin's retort to this joke:

> Q: How Many Performance Artists Does it Take to Change a Light Bulb?
>
> A: One to change the light bulb and 40 to document it. (Images Festival)

For Dobkin, *How Many Performance Artists Does It Take* . . . is "at once a question, a joke and a reflection on the ways we see." Challenging the functional ubiquity of social media as a medium (and media) for documentation, Dobkin poses this performance as "an attempt to overwhelm the definitions and intersections of performance, documentation, the archive and image reproduction to investigate the nature of performance itself" (Images Festival). However, that Dobkin has yet to reveal the final performance document—its excess (there is so much!, as Dobkin has said) rendering it nearly impossible to corral into a functional whole—suggests that even intentionally troubling the distinctions between performance and its documentation exerts a potentially insurmountable weight on the performance.

I was an "extra" of sorts in both *Flowers* and *How Many Performance Artists Does It Take* . . . , having neither been asked nor volunteered to be an official documenter in either piece. This did not mean, however, that I did not have my cellphone out with its camera app at the ready; I too took pictures: of Dobkin, and of those photographing and digitally videoing Dobkin in *Flowers*—or, in *How Many Performance Artists Does It Take* . . . , of those sketching, painting, Polaroiding, and video- and audio-recording Dobkin, and those watching those sketching, painting, Polaroiding, and video- and audio-recording Dobkin. And in my own documentation of my experience of her work, and of others' experience of the experience of her work, I also took note, and took picture, if you will, of those moments that became part of her work through my distraction from it. For instance, the point at which I stopped watching Dobkin to breastfeed my one-month-old son during the performance.

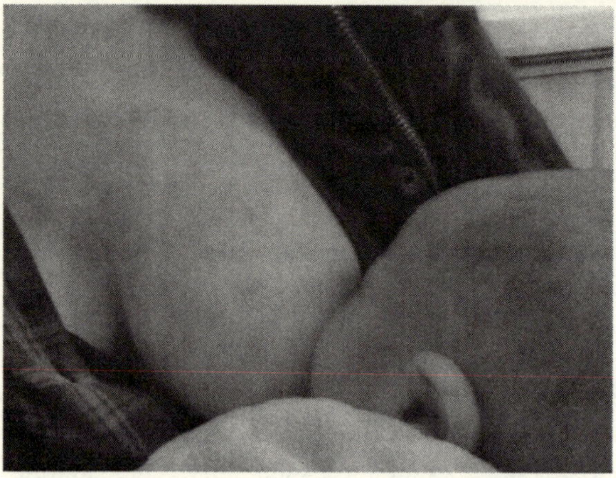

Fig. 5. Distracted, breastfeeding my son during the performance. Jess Dobkin, *How Many Performance Artists Does It Take to Change a Light Bulb (for Martha Wilson)*, Images Festival, Toronto, Ontario, 2015. Photo by T. Nikki Cesare Schotzko.

During the performance of Dong's *The Other Words*, the documentation was both more blatant and more banal—as Dong intended it to be. Dong and Black sat across a small white table, with a bowl full of white rice between them, the bowl set slightly closer to Dong than to Black. Dong would slowly and methodically draw a spoonful of rice from the bowl, insert it into her own mouth, chew it, then expel it, still with exquisite slowness, back onto the spoon, and feed it to the naked Black. Though from mid-thigh up Dong was fully dressed, and wearing, too, a pair of wonderfully dominatrix-esque shiny black kitten heels, her legs were bare, and sometimes touching Black's under the table. The table, marking the space between Dong and Black, also created a horizontal bifurcation within the performance, suggesting a different intimacy of skin beneath it than the more gastronomically informed intimacy above.

The audience members Dong had invited to document the performance and post their findings to social media at regular five-minute intervals generated a different energy in the audience than that felt by those of us on the outer, more analog circle. These predetermined documenters swooped in and out of the performance aura around the table, or moved in ellipses around it with their cameras held outward from their bodies, their in-the-moment videos live-streamed via the WebTV app Periscope (live-streamed then but now no longer available). They clustered at the edges, comparing shots and taking selfies, occasionally giggling quietly among themselves and disrupting the otherwise contemplative silence of the room. The piece was a metaphor for translation—the "nutrition" of the original, to quote Dong, that is lost but replaced with the "taste" of the translator when "eaten" by the reader (Dong, *The Other Words*). As Dong writes in the notes accompanying images from the piece on her website,

> Translation is political, and translating a text is like chewing up rice and then feeding it to somebody else. It refers [*sic*] that the sense of authenticity, integrity and beauty of resource language get lost in translation. The rice in this performance is a metaphor of text. I am sitting on a desk, translating a big plate of text to my reader who is devouring this plate in its translated form. My reader may understand the subject, but the quality of what he has consumed is definitely not the same as the original once [*sic*]. In fact, translating a text is like chewing up rice and then feeding it to somebody else. In performance, what I feed to people is still rice. However, this transformed rice has already lost its flavour and nutrition. (Dong, "The Other Words")

That Dong invited mostly young Asian youths to document the piece on social media suggested, as Dong discussed in the talkback after the performance, a cultural translation as well, replicating the paparazzi-like behaviour expected of audiences to performances in China, for example (*The Other Words*).

The documenters were respectful, but, whereas without them (and, at times, even with them) the performance could have taken on the more sombre affect that attends many performance-art events, their presence added a playfulness that warmed up, figuratively at least, the otherwise austere environment Dong had intentionally created. During other performances included in the Duration and Dialogue Festival, the lights were dimmed and the audience were offered pillows on which to sit; Dong denied the audience any such little comforts. The lights were set high, the concrete floors were bare, and, perhaps most cruelly to Black, the heat was turned very low—if on at all. Despite our unusually temperate winter, it was still January in Toronto, and the warehouse gallery space was decidedly chilly. By the time the talkback immediately following the performance began, both performers were visibly trembling from cold, even though Black was fully dressed and both were wearing their downy winter coats and sipping hot tea. (In an especially kind moment during the talkback, an audience member took off his own coat to wrap around Black when Black's shivers were interfering with his ability to respond to comments from the audience.)

These distractions from the performance event, these infiltrations of the many shapes of time, to recall Nesbit, shape too the memory of these performances, and in doing so reconstruct a history that is both fixed in its recorded permanence and malleable in its incorporation of these moments that otherwise would be left at the unmarked margins of each performance's time. Such distractions, then, become unwilling or even unwitting additions not just to the in-situ performance but to performance in its documentary perpetuity. However, even as such unintentional interventions create a mixed-media narrative of the performance event, this narrative is only available to those with access to the documentation itself, pointing to the performative rather than evidentiary nature of such documentation. And these performances are connected within a narrative for me, as audience to each of them, that is as much about the technologically and socially mediated space-time dimensions as that of the other spatiotemporal and intensely personal dimension of my second son as he progressed from avocado-sized fetus during La Pocha Nostra's *Ways to Kill a Mexican*, to hungry newborn in *How Many Performance Artists Does It Take . . .* , and finally to enthusiastic toddler running up to me just as *The Other Words* concluded. These distractions happen within moments that became at once fixed and unfixed, at once a memory of what the performance was and of what else it might have been, too.

V. PERFORMANCE IS DEAD; LONG LIVE PERFORMANCE

Toronto performance-art scholar-superstar Johanna Householder, who moderated the talkback after Dong and Black's performance, discussed the give and take of Dong and Black's exchange of rice in *The Other Words*, addressing the interrelated phenomenological processes of retention (simply put, consciousness of an act having happened, or "primary memory") and protention (anticipation of an act to happen, or "primary expectation" [Husserl 41]), re-enacted as it was in Black's bodily anticipation for or potential rejection of each spoonful (Householder). Black related how his heart would begin to beat faster as Dong prepared the rice, and how these physiological responses were predicated as well on Dong's affective demeanour toward him: whether she was meeting his gaze, focused as it was entirely on Dong throughout the performance, or surveying the gallery; whether she was allowing him enough time to swallow and digest each spoonful of rice; whether she was actually, physically there or not. When Dong stood up and left the table to retrieve more rice from the back room of the gallery, Black felt, as he said, abandoned.

For Edmund Husserl, retention is "a comet's tail that attaches itself to the perception of a moment" (37), and protention is that "which leaves open the way in which what is coming may exist" (309). Contingent upon an "impression"—"a corresponding perception, or a corresponding primal impression, [that] precede[s] the retention" (35)—retention and protention are differentiated from memory and apprehension in that while retention and protention demand a certain passivity on the part of the perceiver in relation to the event or object being perceived, memory and apprehension demand action and thereby act upon the event or object perceived (M. Kelly). As Michael R. Kelly clarifies,

> Memories occur faster or slower and can be edited or reconstructed, retention occurs "automatically" and cannot be varied at one's whim. [. . . R]emembering re-produces a completed temporal object,

> whereas retention works at completing the consciousness of a temporal object, unifying its presence and absence.

Merleau-Ponty, influenced at least in *The Phenomenology of Perception* by Husserl's phenomenology of temporality (if not in Merleau-Ponty's later work *The Visible and the Invisible* [see M. Kelly]), notes further how, through the accrual of perceptions, the now accrues experience. "I do not pass through a series of instances of now, the images of which I preserve and which, placed end to end, make a line," Merleau-Ponty wrote. "With the arrival of every moment, its predecessor undergoes a change: I still have it in hand and it is still there, but already it is sinking away below the level of presents; in order to retain it, I need to reach through a thin layer of time" (484).

Such unfixity of experience and of perception is dependent upon a singular temporality; the condition of possibility for a phenomenological "extended now" (see Rodemeyer 128) is that there must be only one elemental "now," whether that now is spatially or temporally situated. When the "thin layer of time" through which Merleau-Ponty reaches thickens with the aggregation of images, it is no longer levels of presents but an explosion in which each retention or primary memory is fragmented from context and from the event itself. Which, in many ways, seems to be exactly what these artists are intending: a fragmentation of the very idea of the historical wherein history is, still, "nothing less than an eternal, punishing hunt for the present—no matter when it happened" (Nesbit 24).

The question of the historical, when it comes to performance, is, essentially, a question of memory. In " 'When This You See': The (anti) Radical Time of Self-Surveillance," Sarah Bay-Cheng considers the means by which these now-ubiquitous digital technologies allow us to capture and record memories—both those we are aware of and those we otherwise—that is, without the benefit of the apparatus—miss. "These technologies become increasingly necessary to comprehend moments of experience that strain the resources of human temporal reception," she writes. "But," she asks, "at what cost?" (49). How many performance artists will it take?

Modes of documentation, digital or otherwise, having been placed, by the artists, quite literally in the hands of the audience in these performances render the present moment of performance immediately and legitimately historical through the simultaneity of its documentation and (digital) distribution—even as such historicization of the event, with all its presences and distractions from them, reaffirms the immediately present now. Such documentation and distribution—or, as it becomes via social-media's machinations, documentation as distribution—cedes the present to the past even as this present is happening, and "presence" risks becoming something a little less present, though no less live. With each uploaded image, as La Pocha Nostra ensemble members' stilled bodies saturated social media even as they were, still, shifting from one pose to the next in real time, as Dobkin's prostrate body is lit by the uncanny glow of so many cellphone cameras or sketched into being on an anonymous audience member's tablet, and as videos of Dong feeding Black fed the social-media feed, we were not only witnessing but actively and ecstatically participating in the many small deaths of performance.

WORKS CITED

"238 Heroes Cheered on Return Home." *Winnipeg Tribune*, 4 Oct. 1917. *Newspapers.com*, www.newspapers.com/image/44203985/.

"About." *The Alumnae Theatre Company's Blog*, 15 Apr. 2015, alumnaetheatre.wordpress.com/about/.

"About Alumnae Theatre Company." *Alumnae Theatre Company*, 15 Apr. 2015, www.alumnaetheatre.com/about-us.html.

"About Us: Margo Kane." *Full Circle First Nations Performance*, www.fullcircle.ca/margo-kane.

"About Us: Mission & Philosophy." *Full Circle First Nations Performance*, www.fullcircle.ca/mission-philosophy.

Adams, Rachel, and Sarah Philips Casteel. "Introduction: Canada and the Americas." *Comparative American Studies: An International Journal*, vol. 3, no. 1, 2005, pp. 5–13. *Taylor and Francis Online*, doi: 10.1177/1477570005050946.

Ahmed, Sara. *On Being Included: Racism and Diversity in Institutional Life*. Duke UP, 2012.

Allen, Bob. "He Set Our Theatre Afire." *The Province* [Vancouver], 9 Feb. 1974, p. 55.

Al-Solaylee, Kamal. "Alternative to the Alternative: A Short and (Mostly) Unbiased Critical History of the Tarragon Theatre." *Tonight at the Tarragon*, edited by Al-Solaylee, Playwrights Canada, 2011, pp. iii–xi.

Alumnae Theatre Company. "Maxim Gorky's *The Zykovs*." Program.

Alvarez, Natalie, ed. *Fronteras Vivientes: Eight Latina/o Canadian Plays*. Playwrights Canada, 2013.

---. "How Can Theatre and Performance Studies Thrive in the Corporatized University?" *Canadian Theatre Review*, vol. 161, 2015, pp. 74–75.

---, ed. *Latina/o Canadian Theatre and Performance*. Playwrights Canada, 2013. New Essays on Canadian Theatre 3.

"Amusements." *The Globe* [Toronto], 19 Nov. 1892, p. 15. *ProQuest Historical Newspapers: The Globe and Mail (1844–2011)*, search.proquest.com.proxy.ufv.ca:2048/docview/1648033226?accountid=10969.

Anderson, Kim. *A Recognition of Being: Reconstructing Native Womanhood*. Second ed., Women's Press, 2016.

Appleford, Rob, editor. *Aboriginal Drama and Theatre*. Playwrights Canada, 2005.

---. "The Desire to Crunch Bone: Daniel David Moses and the 'True Real Indian.'" *Canadian Theatre Review*, vol. 77, 1993, pp. 21–26. *Proquest*, search.proquest.com/openview/a8295eb6a6c558da08f14dcbfe91b4ef/1?pq-origsite=gscholar&cbl=47044.

Arsenault, Marc. "La relève." *L'idéArt: célébrons la littérature acadienne*, 1997, p. 12.

Ashcroft, Bill, Gareth Griffiths, and Helen Tiffin. *The Empire Writes Back: Theory and Practice in Post-Colonial Literatures*. Routledge, 1989.

Aslan, Odette. *L'Acteur au XXe Siècle. Évolution de la Technique. Problème d'Éthique*. Seghers, 1974.

Association of United Ukrainian Canadians, Manitoba Section. "Submission to the Massey Commission." Circa 1949, Royal Commission on National Development in the Arts, Letters and Sciences Fonds, PAC, RG 33, 28, vol. 3, nos. 27–39 [CD1 C-1999, 725].

Atkinson, William Stabler. *Glory Hole: A Play of the Great War of 1914-18*. Mount Saint Vincent University, Canadian Drama Collection, C.D.Coll 19.13.

Babineau, Jean. *Bloupe*. Perce-Neige, 1993.

Bains, Yashdip S. *English Canadian Theatre, 1765–1826*. Peter Lang, 1998.

Bains, Yashdip Singh, and Norma Jenckes. "Fanny Kemble and Charles Kemble: As Canadians Saw Them in 1833." *Theatre Research in Canada*, vol. 5, no. 2, 1984, pp. 115–31. *Theatre Research in Canada*, journals.lib.unb.ca/index.php/TRIC/article/view/7436.

Ballet Appreciation Club of Ottawa. "Brief to the Royal Commission." 1949, Royal Commission on National Development in the Arts, Letters and Sciences Fonds, PAC, RG 33, 28, vol. 4, nos. 40–53 [CD1 C-1999, 828].

Bank, Rosemarie K. *Theatre Culture in America, 1825–1860*. Cambridge UP, 1997.

Barbeau, Marius. "The Fountain-Heads of Canadian Culture." Circa 1949, Royal Commission on National Development in the Arts, Letters and Sciences Fonds, PAC, RG 33, 28, vol. 25, nos. 295–96 [CD2 C-2012, 684-685].

Baudrillard, Jean, Alain Brunn, and Jacinto Lagiera. "Modernité." *Encyclopædia Universalis*, www.universalis.fr/encyclopedie/modernite/.

Bauer, Ralph. "Early American Literature and American Literary History at the 'Hemispheric Turn.'" *American Literary History*, vol. 22, no. 2, 2010, pp. 250–65. *Project Muse*, doi: 10.1353/eal.2010.0015.

Bay-Cheng, Sarah. "'When This You See': The (anti) Radical Time of Mobile Self-surveillance." *Performance Research*, vol. 19, no. 3, 2014, pp. 48–55.

Bélair, Michel. *Le Nouveau Théâtre Québécois*. Éditions Leméac, 1973.

Belcourt, Billy-Ray. *Billy-Ray Belcourt*, nakinisowin.wordpress.com.

Benjamin, Walter. *Illuminations*. Edited by Hannah Arendt, translated by Harry Zorn, Pimlico, 1999.

---. *L'Œuvre d'Art à l'Epoque de sa Reproductibilité Technique*. Translated by Frédéric Joly, Petite Bibliothèque Payot, 1939.

Benjamin, Walter, and Charles Baudelaire. *Un Poète Lyrique à l'Apogée du Capitalisme*, Payot, 1979.

Benson, Eugene, and L.W. Conolly, editors. *English-Canadian Theatre*. 1987. Oxford UP, 2002.

---. *The Oxford Companion to Canadian Theatre*. Oxford UP, 1989.

Béraud, Jean. *350 Ans de Théâtre au Canada Français*. Le Cercle du Livre de France, L'Encyclopédie du Canada Français, no. 1, 1958.

Bessai, Diane. "The Regionalism of Canadian Drama." *Canadian Literature*, no. 85, 1980, pp. 7–20.

Bial, Henry, and Scott Magelssen, editors. *Theater Historiography: Critical Interventions*. U of Michigan P, 2010.

Biron, Michel, et al., editors. *Histoire de la Littérature Québécoise*. Boréal, 2007.

Black, Malcom, et al. *Report of the Committee of Inquiry into Theatre Training in Canada*. Canada Council for the Arts, June 1977.

Bleeker, Maaike, Jon Foley Sherman, and Eirini Nedelkopoulou, editors. *Performance and Phenomenology: Traditions and Transformations*. Routledge, 2015.

Bogart, Anne. *What's the Story: Essays About Art, Theater and Storytelling*. Routledge, 2014.

Bossé, Paul. *Empreintes*. Collectif Moncton-Sable, Moncton, 2001. Play script.

---. *Traces*. Translated by Glen Nichols, St. Thomas University, Moncton, 2004. Play script.

Bost, Suzanne. "Doing the Hemisphere Differently: A Response to Ralph Bauer." *American Literary History*, vol. 22, no. 2, 2010, pp. 266–70. *Project Muse*, muse.jhu.edu /article/382099.

Bouchard, Gérard. "Le Québec et le Canada comme collectivités neuves. Esquisse d'étude comparée." *Recherches sociographiques*, vol. 39, no. 2–3, 1998, pp. 219–48.

Boudreau, Annette, and Raoul Boudreau. "La littérature comme moyen de reconquête de la parole. L'exemple de l'Acadie." *Glottopol*, vol. 3, 2004, pp. 166–80.

Boudreau, Annette, and Françoise Gadet. "La situation sociolinguistique de l'Acadie du Nouveau-Brunswick." *Francophonies: recueil d'études offert en hommage à Suzanne Lafage*, edited by Antoine Queffélec, Didier Erudition, 1998, pp. 55–61.

Boudreau, Raoul. "L'hyperbole, la litote, la folie: trois rapports à la langue dans le roman acadien." *Les langues du roman: du plurilinguisme comme stratégie textuelle*, Presses de l'Université de Montréal, 1999, pp. 72–85.

---. "La poésie acadienne depuis 1990: diversité, exiguïté et légitimité." *Itinéraires de la poésie: enjeux actuels en Acadie, en Ontario et dans l'Ouest canadien*, edited by Robert Yergeau, Le Nordir, 2004, pp. 83–97.

Bourassa, André G. "Premières Modernités, 1930–1965." *Le Théâtre au Québec, 1825–1985*, edited by Renée Legris, Jean-Marc Larrue, Bourassa, and Gilbert David, VLB/SHTQ/ Bibliothèque nationale du Québec, 1988, pp. 89–140.

---. "Scène Québécoise et Modernité." *L'Avènement de la Modernité Culturelle au Québec*, edited by E Trépanier and Y. Lamonde, Institut Québécois de Recherche sur la Culture, 1986, pp. 139–71.

---. *Surréalisme et Littérature Québécoise*. L'Étincelle, 1979.

---. "Texte Dramatique et Modernité (1906–1955)." *Protée*, vol. 15, no. 2, winter 1987, pp. 134–45.

---. "Vers la Modernité de la Scène Québécoise: Les Contre-Courants (1901–1950)." *Pratiques Théâtrales*, no. 14–15, 1982, pp. 3–31.

---. "Vers la Modernité de la Scène Québécoise: Influence des Grands Courants du Théâtre Français au Québec (1898–1948)." *Pratiques Théâtrales*, no. 13, 1981, pp. 3–26.

Bourque, Denis. "Théâtre de libération et théâtre carnavalisé: quelques réflexions sur l'évolution et la carnavalisation du théâtre acadien." *Les littératures d'expression française d'Amérique du Nord et le carnavalesque*, edited by Bourque and Anne Brown, Éditions d'Acadie, 1998, pp. 91–116.

Boutilier, Alex D. "The Citadel on Stage: The Rise and Decline of Garrison Theatre in Halifax." Saint Mary's U, 2005. M.A. dissertation.

Boyd, Michelle. "An Angel of Lucknow, the Hero of Halifax: A Nova Scotian Musical Response to the Indian Mutiny of 1857–58." *Nineteenth-Century Music Review*, vol. 11, no. 2, 2014, pp. 195–217. *Cambridge UP*, doi: 10.1017/S1479409814000342.

Brecht, Bertolt. "La Scène de la Rue—Modèle Type d'une Scène de Théâtre Épique (1938)." *Écrits sur le Théâtre*, Gallimard, 2000, pp. 856–66.

"British Columbia Indian Arts Society." *Memory BC*, www.memorybc.ca/british-columbia-indian-arts-society-fonds.

Burger, Baudouin. *L'Activité Théâtrale au Québec (1765–1825)*. Parti Pris, 1974.

Burke, Peter. *Popular Culture in Early Modern Europe*. Third ed., Ashgate, 2009.

Butler, Judith. "From Gender Trouble: Feminism and the Subversion of Identity." *Performance Analysis: An Introductory Coursebook*, edited by Colin Counsell and Laurie Wolf, Routledge, 2001, pp. 72–77.

Canada. 1911 Census of Canada. *Library and Archives Canada*, www.bac-lac.gc.ca/eng/census/1911/Pages/about-census.aspx.

Cardinal, Cliff. *Huff & Stitch*. Playwrights Canada, 2017.

Canadian Ballet Festival Association. "Brief to the Royal Commission." 1949, Royal Commission on National Development in the Arts, Letters and Sciences Fonds, PAC, RG 33, 28, vol. 9, nos. 102–107a [CD1 C-2002, 1259].

Canadian Expeditionary Force Study Group. "16th Battalion." *Canadian Expeditionary Force Study Group*, cefresearch.ca/matrix/Army%20Corps/Divisions/1st%20Division/3rd%20Infantry%20Brigade/16th%20Battalion.htm.

Careless, J.M.S. "The Cultural Setting: Ontario Society to 1914." Saddlemyer, pp. 18–51.

Carter, Jill. "Towards Locating the Alchemy of Convergence in The Native Theatre Classroom." *Canadian Theatre Review*, vol. 149, 2011, pp. 82–84.

Chambers, Natalie. "Reconciliation: A 'Dangerous Opportunity' to Unsettle Ourselves." *Response, Responsibility, and Renewal: Canada's Truth and Reconciliation Journey*, Aboriginal Healing Foundation, 2009, pp. 257–78.

Chiasson, Herménégilde. *Pour une fois*. Moncton, 1999.

Chiasson, Zénon. "Itinéraire d'un parcours difficile ou l'émergence d'une dramaturgie acadienne." *Dalhousie French Studies*, vol. 15, 1988, pp. 69–82.

Clutesi, George. "Testimony." 28 Oct. 1949, Victoria, BC, Royal Commission on National Development in the Arts, Letters and Sciences Fonds, PAC, RG 33, 28, vol. 19, nos. 204–25 [CD1 C- 2008, 903-904].

Cochrane, Claire. "The Contaminated Audience: Researching Amateur Theatre in Wales before 1939." *New Theatre Quarterly*, vol. 19, no. 2, 2003, pp. 169–76.

Cockrell, Dale. *Demons of Disorder: Early Blackface Minstrels and Their World*. Cambridge UP, 1997.

---. "Of Soundscapes and Blackface: From Fools to Foster." S Johnson, *Burnt Cork*, pp. 51–72.

Cohen, Nathan. "A Ferociously Funny Play." *Toronto Star*, 6 Feb. 1971, p. 61.

Coleman, Daniel. *White Civility: The Literary Project of English Canada*. U of Toronto P, 2008.

Collett, Anne. "Fair Trade: Marketing 'The Mohawk Princess.'" *Economies of Representation 1790–2000: Colonialism and Commerce*, edited by Leigh Dale and Helen Gilbert, Ashgate, 2007, pp. 157–68.

---. "Red and White: Miss E. Pauline Johnson Tekahionwake and the Other Woman." *Women's Writing*, vol. 8, no. 3, 2001, pp. 359–74. *Researchgate*, doi: 10.1080/09699080100200140.

Collombat, Isabelle. "Traduction et variation diatopique dans l'espace francophone: le Québec et le Canada francophone." *Arena Romanistica, Journal of Romance Studies*, vol. 10, 2012, pp. 28–55.

Conolly, L.W., editor. *Theatrical Touring and Founding in North America*. Greenwood, 1982.

Cooper, Cynthia. "Dressing Up: A Consuming Passion." *Fashion: A Canadian Perspective*, edited by Alexandra Palmer, U of Toronto P, 2004, pp. 41–67.

Coulthard, Glen. *Red Skin, White Masks: Rejecting the Colonial Politics of Recognition*. U of Minnesota P, 2014.

Crawley, Ashon. "Otherwise Movements." *The New Inquiry*, 19 Jan. 2015, thenewinquiry.com /essays/otherwise-movements.

Cryer, Mrs. W.C. "Testimony." Circa 1949, Royal Commission on National Development in the Arts, Letters and Sciences Fonds, PAC, RG 33, 28, vol. 5, nos. 54–66 [CD1 C-2000, 695].

Daigle, France. *Petites difficultés d'existence.* Boréal, 2002.

David, Gilbert. "Quebec, Theatre in (French)." Benson and Conolly, *Oxford*, pp. 444–50.

Davies, Robertson. Foreword. *Love and Whisky: The Story of the Dominion Drama Festival and the Early Years of Theatre in Canada, 1606–1972*, by Betty Lee, McClelland and Stewart, 1973, pp. ix–xi.

---. "Mixed Grill: Touring Fare in Canada, 1920–1935." Conolly, pp. 41–56.

---. "The Theatre: A Dialogue on the State of Theatre in Canada." *Royal Commission Studies: A Selection of Essays Prepared for the Royal Commission on National Development in the Arts, Letters and Sciences.* Edmund Cloutier, Printer to the King's Most Excellent Majesty, 1951, pp. 369–92.

Davis, Sharon. *'80s Chart Toppers: Every Chart-topper Tells a Story.* Mainstream, 1999.

Davis, Tracy C. "Performative Time." *Representing the Past: Essays in Performance Historiography*, edited by Charlotte Canning and Thomas Postlewait, U of Iowa P, 2010, pp. 142–67.

Davis-Fisch, Heather. "Complicated Feelings: *Tecumseh* as Literary Land Claim." *Theatres of Affect*, edited by Erin Hurley, Playwrights Canada, 2014, pp. 129–51. New Essays on Canadian Theatre 5.

---. "Lawless Lawyers: Indigeneity, Civility, and Violence." *Theatre Research in Canada*, vol. 35, no. 1, 2014, pp. 31-48.

---. *Loss and Cultural Remains in Performance: The Ghosts of the Franklin Expedition.* Palgrave Macmillan, 2012.

" 'Dawn in Heaven' to be Played at Auditorium Concert Hall May 12, 15." *Winnipeg Tribune*, 4 May 1934. *Newspapers.com*, www.newspapers.com/image/39309729/.

De-ba-jeh-mu-jig. *The Gift. Stories from the Bush: The Woodland Plays of De-ba-jeh-mu-jig Theatre Group*, edited by Joe Oswawabine and Shannon Hengen, Playwrights Canada, 2009, pp. 169–88.

Deleuze, Gilles, and Felix Guattari. "Introduction: Rhizome." *Interconnected*, interconnected.org/home/more/2005/06/1000Plateaus00Rhizome.pdf.

"Delightful Programme Presented by Miss E. Pauline Johnson and Mr. W. McRaye." *The Daily Examiner* [Peterborough], 20 May 1903. McMaster University, William Ready Division of Archives and Research Collections, Pauline Johnson Archive, box 4, file 8.

Dening, Greg. *Mr. Bligh's Bad Language: Passion, Power, and Theatre on the Bounty.* Cambridge UP, 1992.

---. *Performances.* U of Chicago P, 1996.

Denison, Merrill. "Nationalism and Drama." Rubin, *Canadian*, pp. 90–93.

Desmond, Jane C., editor. *Meaning in Motion: New Cultural Studies of Dance.* Duke UP, 1997.

Devries, Laura. *Conflict in Caledonia: Aboriginal Land Rights and the Rule of Law.* U of British Columbia P, 2011.

Dickason, Olive Patricia. *Canada's First Nations: A History of Founding Peoples from Earliest Times.* Third ed., Oxford UP, 2002.

Dickeson, Robert C. *Prioritizing Academic Programs and Services: Reallocating Resources To Achieve Strategic Balance.* Revised and updated ed., John Wiley & Sons, 2009.

Dillon, Elizabeth Maddock. *New World Drama: The Performative Commons in the Atlantic World, 1649–1849.* Duke UP, 2014.

Dobkin, Jess. *Jess Dobkin: This is My Work*, www.jessdobkin.com.

---. "Untitled." Centre for Drama, Theatre and Performance Studies, University of Toronto, 9 Oct. 2014. Lecture.

Dobson, Miriam, and Benjamin Ziemann, editors. *Reading Primary Sources: The Interpretation of Texts from Nineteenth- and Twentieth-Century History.* Routledge, 2009.

"Dominion Theatre, 'The Man From Saskatchewan.'" *Winnipeg Tribune*, 31 Jan. 1931. *Newspapers.com*, www.newspapers.com/image/37274077/. Advertisement.

Dong, Chun Hua Catherine. *Chun Hua Catherine Dong*, chunhuacatherinedong.com.

---. "The Other Words." *Chun Hua Catherine Dong*, chunhuacatherinedong.com/portfolio/the-other-words-3/.

---. *The Other Words.* Moderated by Johanna Householder, Katzman Contemporary, Toronto, 30 Jan. 2016. Audience talkback.

Doyon-Gosselin, Benoit. "Éloge en chiac au coin des rues." *Liaison*, vol. 142, 2008, p. 55.

Doyon-Gosselin, Benoit, and Jean Morency. "Le monde de Moncton, Moncton ville du monde." *Voix et Images*, vol. 29, no. 3, 2004, pp. 69–83.

"Drama Studies." *Academic Calendar*, 2016–2017. *Mount Allison University*, www.mta.ca/academic_calendar/16-17c/Drama.html.

Drennan, Barbara. "Theatre History-Telling: New Historiography, Logic, and the Other Canadian Tradition." *Theatre Research in Canada*, vol. 13, no. 1–2, 1992. *The Centre for Digital Scholarship Journals*, journals.lib.unb.ca/index.php/tric/article/view/7244/8303.

Drew, Mrs. John (Louisa Lane). *Autobiographical Sketch of Mrs. John Drew.* New York, 1899.

Dubied, Annik. "Une définition du récit d'après Paul Ricœur." *Communication*, vol. 19, no. 2, 2000, pp. 45–66.

Duchesne, Scott. "A Golf Club for the Golden Age: English Canadian Theatre Historiography and the Strange Case of Roy Mitchell." Filewod, *Theatre Histories*, pp. 140–54.

Duhamel, Roger. *Manuel de Littérature Canadienne-Française*. Éditions du Renouveau Pédagogique, 1967.

Eagleton, Terry. *Literary Theory: An Introduction*. Blackwell, 1983.

Edwards, Murray. *A Stage in Our Past*. U of Toronto P, 1968.

Edwardson, Ryan. *Canadian Content: Culture and the Quest for Nationhood.* U of Toronto P, 2008.

"Emily Pauline Johnson." *Library and Archives Canada Website*, 28 Feb. 2015, www.bac-lac.gc.ca/eng/discover/aboriginal-heritage/first-nations/Pages/pauline-johnson.aspx.

Fagan, Kristina, et al. "Canadian Indian Literary Nationalism? Critical Approaches in Canadian Indigenous Contexts—A Collaborative Interlogue." *The Canadian Journal of Native Studies*, vol. 29, no. 1, 2009, pp. 19–44. *Brandon University*, www3.brandonu.ca/cjns/29.1-2/04Collaborative.pdf.

Fairhead, Wayne. "Drama in Education." Wagner, pp. 236–44.

FastHorse, Larissa. "Do White Playwrights Think About This?" *Howl Round*, 27 Feb. 2015, howlround.com/do-white-playwrights-think-about-this.

Fay, Joseph D. *Digest of the Laws of the State of New York*. New York, 1876.

Fee, Margery. *Literary Land Claims: The "Indian Land Question" from Pontiac's War to Attawapiskat.* Wilfrid Laurier UP, 2015.

Filewod, Alan. *Committing Theatre: Theatre Radicalism and Political Intervention in Canada.* Between the Lines, 2011.

---. "Erasing Historical Difference: The Alternative Orthodoxy in Canadian Theatre." *Theatre Journal*, vol. 41, no. 2, 1989, pp. 201–10.

---. "Erect Sons and Dutiful Daughters." *Imperialism and Theatre*, edited by J. Ellen Gainor, Routledge, 1995, pp. 56–70.

---. "Named in Passing: Deregimenting Canadian Theatre History." *Writing and Rewriting National Theatre Histories*, edited by S.E. Wilmer, U of Iowa P, 2004, pp. 106–26.

---. "National Battles: Canadian Monumental Drama and the Investiture of History." *Modern Drama*, vol. 38, no.1, 1995, pp. 71–86.

---. *Performing Canada: The Nation Enacted in the Imagined Theatre*. Textual Studies in Canada, 2002.

---. *Theatre Histories*. Playwrights Canada, 2009. Critical Perspectives on Canadian Theatre in English 13.

---. "Undermining the Centre: The Canon According to *Canadian Theatre Review*." *Theatre History in Canada*, vol. 11, no. 2, 1990, pp. 178–85.

Findlay, Len. "Always Indigenize! The Radical Humanities in the Postcolonial Canadian University." *Ariel: A Review of International Literature*, vol. 31, no. 1, 2000, pp. 307–26.

Finlay, Karen. *The Force of Culture: Vincent Massey and Canadian Sovereignty*. U of Toronto P, 2004.

Finn, Patrick. "The Steamroller." *Canadian Theatre Review*, vol. 161, 2015, pp. 88–90.

Firehall Theatre. "First English Production of Anne Hébert's *Le Temps Sauvage*." Nov. 1972. Poster.

Flaherty, Kathleen. "Table Stakes: Gambling with New Play Development." *Developing Nation: New Play Creation in English-Speaking Canada*, edited by Bruce Barton, Playwrights Canada, 2009, pp. 18–22.

Forsyth, Louise, editor. *Anthology of Québec Women's Plays in English Translation, Volume I (1966–1986)*. Playwrights Canada, 2006.

---. Email received by Robin Whittaker, 16 Jun. 2015.

Foucault, Michel. *The Archaeology of Knowledge*. 1989. Routledge, 2006.

---. "Nietzsche, Genealogy, History." *The Foucault Reader*, edited by Paul Rabinow, Pantheon, 1984, pp. 76–100.

Freeman, Barry. "Rethinking the Virtues and Values." *Canadian Theatre Review*, vol. 161, 2015, pp. 80–82.

Freeman, David. *Creeps*. Bill Glassco Collection (1966–1988), Toronto Reference Library Special Collections, box 2, files 13 and 14. Draft manuscripts.

---. *Creeps*. U of Toronto P, 1972.

---. Untitled contribution. *Stage Voices: Twelve Canadian Playwrights Talk about Their Lives and Work*, edited by Geraldine Anthony, Doubleday, 1978, pp. 255–72.

Fricker, Miranda. *Epistemic Injustice: Power and the Ethics of Knowing*. Oxford UP, 2007.

Friedlander, Mira. "The Enduring Vitality of Community and Grass Roots Theatre." Wagner, pp. 227–35.

Gagnon, François-Marc. *Paul-Émile Borduas (1905–1960): Biographie Critique et Analyse de l'Oeuvre*. Fides, 1978.

Gallagher, Kathleen. "A Foothold in the Margins: Theatre Studies and Education." *Canadian Theatre Review*, vol. 161, 2015, pp. 83–84.

---. *Why Theatre Matters: Urban Youth, Engagement, and a Pedagogy of the Real*. U of Toronto P, 2014.

Garafola, Lynn. *Diaghilev's Ballets Russes*. Oxford UP, 1989.

Garneau, David. "Imaginary Spaces of Conciliation and Reconciliation: Art, Curation and Healing." *Arts of Engagement: Taking Aesthetic Action in and Beyond the Truth and Reconciliation Commission of Canada*, edited by Dylan Robinson and Keavy Martin, Wilfrid Laurier UP, 2016, pp. 21–42.

Gass, Ken. Introduction. *The Factory Lab Anthology*, edited by Connie Brissenden, Talonbooks, 1974, p. 7.

---. "re: Historian inquiry: dramaturgy at Factory in the 1970s." Received by Jessica Riley, 8 Dec. 2015.

Gauvin, Lise. *Langagement: l'Écrivain et la Langue au Québec*. Boréal, 2000.

Gaztambide-Fernandez, Ruben A. "Decolonization and the Pedagogy of Solidarity." *Decolonization: Indigeneity, Education & Society*, vol. 1, no. 1, 2012, p. 56. *Decolonization: Indigeneity, Education & Society*, decolonization.org/index.php/des/article/view/18633/15557.

Gélinas, Gratien. "Pour un Théâtre National et Populaire." *Amérique Française*, vol. 3, no. 3, 1949, pp. 32–42.

"George Clutesi." *Tseshaht First Nation*, www.tseshaht.com/history-culture/influential-figures/george-clutesi.

Gerson, Carole, and Veronica Strong-Boag, editors. *E Pauline Johnson Tekahionwake: Collected Poems and Selected Prose.* U of Toronto P, 2002.

Gilbert, Reid, editor. *Theatre Research in Canada; Special Issue on Marie Clements*, vol. 31, no. 2, 2010.

Gilroy, Paul. *The Black Atlantic: Modernity and Double Consciousness.* Verso, 1993.

Glancy, Diane. "Scene I: Bowling." *Writings on the Process of Writing Native Theater*, Alexander Street, 2012.

Gómez-Peña, Guillermo. "Culturas-in-extremis: Performing Against the Cultural Backdrop of the Mainstream Bizarre." *Ethno-Techno: Writings on Performance, Activism, and Pedagogy*, Routledge, 2005, pp. 45–63.

Gotshalks, Jury. "Testimony." 1949, Royal Commission on National Development in the Arts, Letters and Sciences Fonds, PAC, RG 33, 28, vol. 19, nos. 204–25 [CD2 C-2009, 78].

Goupil, Laval. *Le Djibou: Pièce en deux actes.* Éditions d'Acadie, 1975.

---. *Tête d'eau.* Editions d'Acadie, 1974.

Grandpré, Pierre de, et al. *Histoire de la Littérature Française du Québec.* Four volumes, Beauchemin, 1967–69.

Gray, Charlotte. *Flint and Feather: The Life and Times of E. Pauline Johnson, Tekahionwake.* HarperCollins, 2002.

Gray, Jack. "Indigenous Dance Inside and Outside of Institutions: What is Needed? Problems and Possibilities." Indigenous Choreographers at Riverside (ICR) Gathering, Nov. 2016.

"Great Novelty." *The Novascotian*, 9 May 1833, p. 139. Toronto Metro Reference Library Collections.

"Great Western Amphitheatre." Mr. S. H. Nichols, Proprietor; no location given; *Mirror* [Toronto], 25–28 Jul. 1842. Advertisement.

Gressler, Thomas H. *Theatre as the Essential Liberal Art in the American University.* Edwin Mellen, 2002. Studies in Theatre Arts 16.

Guay, Hervé. "Training an Audience for the Arts." *Canadian Theatre Review*, vol. 161, 2015, pp. 85–87.

Guerlac, Henry. "Some Historical Assumptions of the History of Science." *Scientific Change: Historical Studies in the Intellectual, Social, and Technical Conditions for Scientific*

Discovery and Technical Invention, from Antiquity to the Present, edited by Alistair Cameron Crombie, Heinemann, 1963, pp. 797–812.

Guthrie, Gary. "Gary Guthrie's WAKY Thoughts." *79 WAKY*, www.79waky.com /garyguthrie.htm.

Guthrie, Tyrone. "A Long View of the Stratford Festival." Rubin, *Canadian*, pp. 204–15.

Hale, Amanda. "A Dialectical Drama of Facts and Fiction on the Feminist Fringe." *Work in Progress: Building Feminist Culture*, edited by Rhea Tregebov, Women's Press, 1987, pp. 77–99.

Hamel, Thomas-Étienne. *Cours d'Éloquence Parlée d'Après Delsarte.* L'Événement, 1906.

Hamelin, Jean. *Le Renouveau du Théâtre au Canada Français*. Éditions du Jour, no. D4, 1961.

Hamilton, Michelle. "Borders Within: Anthropology and the Six Nations of the Grand River." *Lines Drawn Upon the Water: First Nations and the Great Lakes Borders and Borderlands*, edited by Karl S. Hele, Wilfrid Laurier UP, 2008, pp. 191–204.

Hansen, Mark N.B. "Performance as Media Affect: The Phenomenology of Human Implication in Jordan Crandall's *Gatherings*." Bleeker, Sherman, and Nedelkopoulou, pp. 222–44.

Hare, John. "Panorama des Spectacles au Québec: de la Conquête au XXe siècle." *Le Théâtre Canadien Français*, edited by H. Beauchamp, B. Julien, and P. Wyczynski, Fides, "Archives des Lettres Canadiennes," no. 5, 1976, pp. 60–107.

Hay, Peter. "Cultural Politics." *Canadian Theatre Review*, vol. 2, 1974, pp. 7–15.

---. "Dramaturgy: Requiem for an Unborn Profession." *Canadian Theatre Review*, vol. 8, 1975, pp. 17–26.

Hayes, Elliott. "Stasis: The Workshop Syndrome." *Developing Nation: New Play Creation in English-Speaking Canada*, edited by Bruce Barton, Playwrights Canada, 2009, pp. 1–4.

Hébert, Chantal. *Le Burlesque au Québec: Un Divertissement Populaire*. Hurtubise HMH, 1981.

---. "Sur le Burlesque: un Théâtre 'Fait Dans Notre Langue.' " *Jeu: Revue deTthéâtre*, vol. 18, no. 1, 1981, pp. 19–31.

Helwig, Yvonne. "*Le Temps Sauvage*." *Radio York*, CHRY, York University, Toronto, n.d.

Highway, Tomson. *The Rez Sisters*. Fifth House, 1988.

Hill, Errol. *The Jamaican Stage, 1655–1900: Profile of a Colonial Theatre.* U of Massachusetts P, 1992.

Hollingsworth, Margaret. "Collaborators." *Canadian Theatre Review*, vol. 69, 1991, pp. 15–19.

Holt, Ardern. *Fancy Dresses Described; or, What to Wear at Fancy Balls.* Fifth ed., London, Debenham and Freebody, 1887. *California Digital Library/Internet Archive*, archive.org/details/fancydressesdesc00holtrich.

Homestead file for William Stabler Atkinson. Saskatchewan Archives, Saskatchewan Homestead Index, file no. 1829099, Part NW, Section 27, Township 51, Range 27, Meridian W2.

Hotte, Lucie. "Littérature et conscience identitaire: l'héritage de CANO." *Produire la culture, produire l'identité?*, edited by Andrée Fortin, P de l'U Laval, 2000, pp. 53–68.

Houlé, Léopold. *L'Histoire du Théâtre au Canada.* Fides, 1945.

Householder, Johanna, moderator. *The Other Words.* Katzman Contemporary, Toronto, 30 Jan. 2016. Audience talkback.

Hughes, Alan. "Historical Facts: The Charles Kean Company in Victoria." *Theatre Research in Canada*, vol. 9, no. 1, 1988. *Theatre Research in Canada*, journals.lib.unb.ca/index.php/TRIC/article/view/7348.

Hunt, Russ. "Traces ('Empreintes')." *Russ Hunt's Reviews*, 2004, www.stthomasu.ca/~hunt/reviews/traces.htm.

Husserl, Edmund. *On the Phenomenology of the Consciousness of Internal Time (1893–1917).* 1905. Edited by John Barnett Brough, Kluwer Academic, 1991.

Images Festival. "How Many Performance Artists Does It Take to Change a Light Bulb? (for Martha Wilson)." *Facebook*, www.facebook.com/events/339784929553003/.

"Indians Want Their Potlatches to Stand." *Daily Province*, 23 June 1914, n.p. Department of Indian Affairs Fonds, PAC, RG 10, vol. 3826, file 60, 511-3 [C-10145, 102].

Isbell, Mary. "P(l)aying off Old Ironsides and The Old Wagon: Melville's Depiction of Shipboard Theatricals in White-Jacket." *Leviathan: A Journal of Melville Studies*, vol. 15, no. 1, 2013, pp. 6–30. *Sage Journals*, doi: 10.7227/NCTF.38.2.8.

Jauvoish, Simon. *Dawn in Heaven.* Mount Saint Vincent University, Canadian Drama Collection, C.D.Coll 24.13.

Johnson, Evelyn. "Chief John Smoke Johnson." *Ontario Historical Society Papers and Records*, no. 12, 1914, pp. 102–13.

Johnson, Pauline. "The Iroquois Women of Canada." Gerson and Strong-Boag, p. 203.

---. "A Red Girl's Reasoning." *The Dominion Illustrated Monthly*, vol. 2, no. 1, 1893, pp. 19–28. *Early Canadiana Online*, eco.canadiana.ca/view/oocihm.8_06471_13.

---. "A Strong Race Opinion: On the Indian Girl in Modern Fiction." Gerson and Strong-Boag, pp. 177–83.

---. "To Sir Wilfrid Laurier." Letter to Sir Wilfred Laurier, 27 July 1900. *National Archives of Canada*, Mikan no. 449658, collectionscanada.gc.ca/ourl/res.php?url_ver=Z39.88-2004&url_tim=2017-0103T21%3A42%3A20Z&url_ctx_fmt=info%3Aofi%2Ffmt%3Akev%3Amtx%3Actx&rft_dat=449658&rfr_id=info%3Asid%2Fcollectionscanada.gc.ca%3Apam&lang=eng.

Johnson, Stephen, editor. *Burnt Cork: Traditions and Legacies of Blackface Minstrelsy*. U of Massachusetts P, 2012.

---. "Death and the Minstrels: Race, Madness, and Art in the Last (W)Rites of Three Early Blackface Performers." S. Johnson, *Burnt Cork*, pp. 73–103.

---. "Time and the Tom Show: Familiarity and Shorthand in the Performance Traditions of Uncle Tom's Cabin." *Performing Adaptations: Essays and Conversations on the Theory and Practice of Adaptation*, edited by Michelle MacArthur, Lydia Wilkinson, and Keren Zaiontz, Cambridge Scholars P, 2009, pp. 87–111.

Johnston, Denis W. *Up the Mainstream: The Rise of Toronto's Alternative Theatres*. U of Toronto P, 1991.

Johnston, Kirsty. *Stage Turns: Canadian Disability Theatre*. McGill-Queen's UP, 2012.

---. "Whose Awkward Moments?: Affect, Disability, and Sex in *The Book of Judith*, *Time to Put My Socks On*, and *The Glass Box*." *Theatres of Affect*, edited by Erin Hurley. Playwrights Canada, 2014, pp. 154–70. New Essays on Canadian Theatre 4.

Jones, Simon. *Underground Warfare 1914–1918*. Pen & Sword Military, 2010.

Jubinville, Yves. "Un Théâtre du Nouveau Monde: Regards Croisés sur l'Écriture de l'Histoire du Théâtre. Le Cas des Collectivités Neuves." *Revue d'Historiographie du Théâtre*, no. 1, autumn 2013, pp. 8–18. *Société d'histoire du théâtre*, www.sht.asso.fr/revue_histoire_theater_numerique/numero/7/lecriture-de-lhistoire-du-theater-etsesenjeux-memoriels.

---. "Du Théâtre Populaire au Québec ou la Généalogie d'un Mythe Moderne." *L'Annuaire Théâtral*, vol, 49, spring 2011, pp. 113–28.

Junior League of Toronto. "Development of Suggestions for a Canadian Arts Festival and Background of our Proposal to the Royal Commission on National Development in the Arts, Letters and Sciences." 1950, Royal Commission on National Development in the Arts, Letters and Sciences Fonds, PAC, RG 33, 28, vol. 21, nos. 241a–272 [CD2 C- 2010, 16].

Kadar, Marlene, editor. *Essays on Life Writing: From Genre to Critical Practice.* U of Toronto P, 1992.

Kadar, Marlene, et al., editors. *Tracing the Autobiographical.* Wilfrid Laurier UP, 2005.

Kane, Margo. *Moonlodge. Singular Voices: Plays in Monologue Form*, edited by Tony Hamill, Playwrights Canada, 1994, pp. 83–107.

---. "Re: Full Circle, Talking Stick Festival & Margo Kane seeks support!" Received by Michelle La Flamme, 31 Mar. 2016.

Kapuscinski, Kiley. "Negotiating the Nation: The Reproduction and Reconstruction of the National Imaginary in Margaret Atwood's *Surfacing*." *English Studies in Canada*, vol. 33, no. 3, 2007, pp. 95–123. *Academic OneFile*, muse.jhu.edu/article/265232.

Kareda, Urjo. "Giving a French Accent To Theatre in Toronto." *Toronto Star*, 11 Nov. 1972.

---. Introduction. *Leaving Home*, by David French, Stoddart, 1985, pp. v–ix.

---. "New Theatre's First Production Beyond Praise." Review of *Creeps*, by David Freeman. *Toronto Star*, 6 Oct. 1971, p. 34.

---. "Our Most Creative Theatre Group Opens in a New Home Thursday." *Toronto Star*, 14 Oct. 1972.

---. "*Le Temps Sauvage* Needs More Shape." *Toronto Star*, 24 Nov. 1972.

Keller, Betty. *Pauline Johnson: First Aboriginal Voice of Canada*. XYZ, 1999.

Kelley, Ninette, and Michael Trebilcock. *The Making of the Mosaic: A History of Canadian Immigration Policy*. Second ed., U of Toronto P, 2010.

Kelly, Michael R. "Phenomenology and Time-Consciousness." *Internet Encyclopedia of Philosophy*, www.iep.utm.edu/phe-time/.

Kelly, Rivka. *The Duchess: An Analysis of the Life and Legacy of Louisa Lane Drew*. Paper 23, U of Vermont, 2014. Senior dissertation.

Kennington, Eric. *The Conquerers*. 1922, oil on canvas, Canadian War Museum, Ottawa.

Kewes, Paulina, Ian W. Archer, and Felicity Heal, editors. *The Oxford Handbook of Holinshed's Chronicles*. Oxford UP, 2012.

Kindelan, Nancy. *Artistic Literacy: Theatre Studies and a Contemporary Liberal Education.* Palgrave MacMillan, 2012.

King, Thomas. "Godzilla vs. Post-Colonial." *World Literature Written in English*, vol. 30, no. 2, 1990, pp. 10–16.

---. *The Truth About Stories: A Native Narrative*. House of Anansi, 2003.

The Knickerbocker. Vol. 13, no. 1, Jan. 1839, pp. 67–76. Wittmann, pp. 184ff.

Knowles, Richard [Ric] Paul. "Alternative Pedagogies, Cultural Studies, and the Teaching of Drama and Theatre." *Theatre Research in Canada/Recherches théâtrales au Canada*, vol. 19, no. 2, 1998, pp. 158–76.

---. General Editor's Preface. Nolan and Knowles, pp. v–vii.

---. "Otherwise Engaged: Towards a Materialist Pedagogy." *Theatre History in Canada*, vol. 12, no. 2, 1991, pp. 193–99.

---. *The Proceedings of the Theatre in Atlantic Canada Symposium*. Centre for Canadian Studies, 1988. Anchorage Series 4.

---. *Reading the Material Theatre*. Cambridge UP, 2004.

---. *The Theatre of Form and the Production of Meaning*. EWC, 1999.

---. "Theatre/Research/Canada." *Theatre Research in Canada*, vol. 35, no. 2, 2014, pp. 226–29.

---. "This Discipline Which Is Not One." *Theatre Research in Canada/Recherches théâtrales au Canada*, vol. 16, no. 1–2, 1995, pp. 82–91.

---. "Voices (off): Deconstructing the Modern English-Canadian Dramatic Canon." *Canadian Canons: Essays in Literary Value*, edited by Robert Lecker, U of Toronto P, 1991, pp. 91–111.

Kotsilibas-Davis, James. *Great Times, Good Times: The Odyssey of Maurice Barrymore.* Doubleday & Co., 1977.

Kovacs, Alexandra. *"I May Act Till the World Grows Wild and Tense": The Performances of E. Pauline Johnson.* U of Toronto, 2016. Dissertation.

Kracauer, Siegfried. *Le Voyage et la Danse. Figures de Ville et Vues de Films.* Laval UP, 2008.

Kuokkanen, Rauna. "Sami Higher Education and Research Toward Building a Vision for Future." *Indigenous Peoples: Self-determination, Knowledge, Indigeneity*, edited by Henry Minde, Eburon, 2008, pp. 267–82.

Lacasse, Germain, et al. *Alexandre Silvio et l'Émergence de la Modernité Populaire au Québec.* U of Montréal P, 2012.

Ladouceur, Louise. *Dramatic Licence: Translating Theatre from One Official Language to the Other in Canada*. Translated by Richard Lebeau, U of Alberta P, 2012.

Laenui, Poka. "Processes of Decolonization." *Reclaiming Indigenous Voice and Vision*, edited by Marie Battiste, U of British Columbia P, 2000, pp. 150–59.

La Flamme, Michelle. "(re)animating the (un)dead." Nolan and Knowles, pp. 214–45.

Laflamme, Jean, and Rémi Tourangeau. *L'Église et leTthéâtre au Québec*. Fides, 1979.

Landau, Emily. "Double Vision." *The Walrus*, 12 Sept. 2002, thewalrus.ca/double-vision/.

Lane, Jill. "Hemispheric America in Deep Time." *Theatre Research International*, vol. 35, no. 2, 2010, pp. 111–25.

---. "Keywords in Latin American Performance." *Theatre Journal*, vol. 56, no. 3, 2004, pp. 456–59. *Project Muse*, doi: 10.1353/tj.2004.0108.

Lane, Richard J. "Performing History: The Reconstruction of Gender and Race in British Columbian Drama." *Performing National Identities: International Perspectives on Contemporary Canadian Theatre*, edited by Sherrill Grace and Albert-Reiner Glaap, Talonbooks, 2003, pp. 265–77.

La Pocha Nostra. "La Pocha Nostra." *Facebook*, www.facebook.com/La-Pocha-Nostra-102383088598/?fref=nf.

---. "What is Pocha?: la pocha ex-centris." *La Pocha Nostra*, www.pochanostra.com/what/.

Larrue, Jean-Marc. *L'Activité Théâtrale à Montréal de 1880 à 1914*. Université de Montréal, 1987. Dissertation.

---. *Le Théâtre à Montréal à la Fin du XIXe Siècle*. Fides, 1981.

Latour, Bruno. *Reassembling the Social: An Introduction to Actor-Network-Theory.* Oxford UP, 2005.

Lawrence, Robert G. "Lillie Langtry in Canada and the U.S.A., 1882–1917." *Theatre Research in Canada*, vol. 10, no. 1, 1989. *Theatre Research in Canada*, journals.lib.unb.ca/index.php/TRIC/article/view/7323.

Leblanc, Gérald. "L'alambic acadien: identité et création littéraire en milieu minoritaire." *L'Acadie plurielle: dynamiques identitaires collectives et développement au sein des réalités acadiennes*, edited by André Magord, Université de Moncton/Centre d'éudes acadiennes, 2003, pp. 517–22.

Leclerc, Catherine. "De Bloop à Bloupe, de Moncton à Monckton: L'énonciation de la ville dans Bloupe de Jean Babineau." *Lieux propices: L'énonciation des lieux, le lieu de l'énonciation dans les contextes francophones interculturels*, edited by Simon Harel and Adelaïde Russo, Presses de l'Université Laval, 2005, pp. 281–93.

---. "Ville hybride ou ville divisée: à propos du chiac et d'une ambivalence productive." *Francophonies d'Amérique*, vol. 22, 2006, pp. 153–65.

Lee, Betty. *Love and Whisky: The Story of the Dominion Drama Festival*. McClelland and Stewart, 1973.

Lee, Pamela M. *Object to be Destroyed: The Work of Gordon Matta-Clark*. MIT P, 2001.

Lenton-Young, Gerald. "Variety Theatre." Saddlemyer, pp. 166–213.

Létourneau, Jocelyn. "Le Québec Moderne. Un chapitre du grand récit collectif des Québécois." *Revue Française de Science Politique*, no. 5, 1992, pp. 765–85.

Levander, Caroline F., and Robert S. Levine, editors. *Hemispheric American Studies*. Rutgers UP, 2008.

Levi, Giovanni. "On Microhistory." *New Perspectives on Historical Writing*, edited by Peter Burke, Cambridge, 1991, pp. 93–113.

Levin, Laura. "In Search of PS North: Performance Studies in Canada." *Canadian Theatre Review*, vol. 149, no. 73, 2012, pp. 74–76. *Project Muse*, doi: 10.1353/ctr.2012.0002.

---. "It's Time to Profess Performance: Thinking Beyond the Specialness and Discreteness of Theatre." *In Defence of Theatre: Aesthetic Practices and Social Interventions*, edited by Kathleen Gallagher and Barry Freeman, U of Toronto P, 2016, pp. 161–77.

Lewis, Victoria Ann. Introduction. *Beyond Victims and Villains: Contemporary Plays by Disabled Playwrights*, edited by Lewis, Theatre Communications Group, 2006, pp. xiii–xlv.

Lhamon, W.T., Jr. *Raising Cain: Blackface Performance from Jim Crow to Hip Hop*. Harvard UP, 1998.

Liebembuk, Shelley. "Contextualizing the Image: La Pocha Nostra in Toronto," *alt.theatre*, vol. 12, no. 1, 2015, pp. 18–23.

Lindgren, Allana C. "The National Ballet of Canada's Normative Bodies: Legitimizing and Popularizing Dance in Canada During the 1950s." *Contests and Contestations: Bodies and Nation in Canadian History*, edited by Patrizia Gentile and Jane Nicholas, U of Toronto P, 2013, pp. 180–202.

---. "The Other D Keynote Address: Disciplinarity and the Future of Dance in Canadian Universities." *Performance Matters*, vol. 2, no. 2, 2016, pp. 84–94. *Performance Matters*, performancematters-thejournal.com/.

Litt, Paul *The Muses, the Masses, and the Massey Commission*. U of Toronto P, 1992.

Lloyd, Gweneth. "Testimony." 11 Oct. 1949, Royal Commission on National Development in the Arts, Letters and Sciences Fonds, PAC, RG 33, 28, vol. 34, Public Hearings [CD3 C- 2017, 618].

Lonergan, David. "Une histoire du théâtre acadien en cinq pièces, pourquoi pas?" *Tintamarre: Chroniques de littérature dans l'Acadie d'aujourd'hui*, edited by Lonergan, Prise de parole, 2008, pp. 329–38.

Lott, Eric. *Love and Theft: Blackface Minstrelsy and the American Working Class*. Oxford UP, 1993.

Lynde, Denyse. "Sir Peters and Lady Teazles of Montreal's Theatre Royal, 1829–1839." *Theatre Research in Canada*, vol. 4, no. 1, 1983, pp. 57–72.

Lyon, George. "Pauline Johnson: A Reconsideration." *Studies in Canadian Literature / Études en littérature canadienne*, vol. 15, no. 2, 1990. *Centre for Digital Scholarship Journals*, journals.lib.unb.ca/index.php/SCL/article/view/8124.

MacArthur, Benjamin. *Actors and American Culture, 1880–1920*. U of Iowa P, 2000.

Mackenzie King, William Lyon. "Greeting." *Art Gallery of Toronto Folk Festival Program*, 1947, Royal Commission on National Development in the Arts, Letters and Sciences Fonds, PAC, RG 33, 28, vol. 2, nos. 18–26 [CD1 C-1999, 261].

Mailhot, Laurent. "Laval Goupil, fabulateur et fabuliste, jeune et vieux renard." *Si Que*, vol. 4, 1979, pp. 47–55.

Mair, Charles. *Tecumseh: A Drama. Dreamland and Other Poems and Tecumseh: A Drama*, U of Toronto P, 1974, pp. 1–127.

"Making Treaty Seven: A Panel with Michelle Thrush, Troy Emory Twigg and Andy Curtis." Annual Meeting of the Canadian Association for Theatre Research, Calgary, 30 May 2016. Live Presentation.

Malaborza, Sonya. "But c'est live du Dance-a-Rama! La Batture, ou comment est née une traduction en chiac pour le théâtre acadien." *Circuit, le magazine de l'Ordre des traducteurs, terminologues et interprètes agréés du Québec*, vol. 9, 2006, pp. 9–10.

Mallet, Janie. *Les modalités de transformation du roman à l'adaptation théâtrale: l'exemple de* Sans jamais parler du vent *de France Daigle*. Université de Moncton, 2013. M.A. dissertation.

Manning, Susan. *Ecstasy and the Demon: The Dance of Mary Wigman*. Second ed., U of Minnesota P, 2006.

Marion, Michael-Allan. "Chiefswood Celebrates Life of E. Pauline Johnson." *Brantford Expositor*, 20 May 2013, www.brantfordexpositor.ca/2013/05/20/chiefswood-celebrates-life-of-e-pauline-johnson.

Martin, Sandra. "The Persistence of Pauline." *The Globe and Mail*, 19 Aug. 2000, theglobeandmail.com/arts/the-persistence-of-pauline/article18425117/?page=all.

Marwick, Arthur. *The New Nature of History: Knowledge, Evidence, Language*. Lyceum Books, 2001.

Massey, Vincent. "Commentary during Commission Session." 1949, Royal Commission on National Development in the Arts, Letters and Sciences Fonds, PAC, RG 33, 28, vol. 19, nos. 204–25 [CD2 C-2009, 82].

Massinger, Ann P. "In Sickness and in Health." *Canadian Literature*, vol. 59, 1974, pp. 101–03.

Masson, Alain. "Étranglement étalement." *Lectures acadiennes : articles et comptes rendus sur la littérature acadienne depuis 1972*, edited by Alain Masson, Perce-Neige, 1994, p. 5184. [NN]

---. "Une idée de la littérature acadienne." *Revue de l'Université de Moncton*, vol. 30, no. 1, 1997, pp. 125–132.

McCaughna, David. "Quebec Imports." *Toronto Citizen*, 14 Dec. 1972.

McNairn, Jeffrey L. "'Everything Was New, Yet Familiar': British Travellers, Halifax and the Ambiguities of Empire." *Acadiensis: Journal of the History of the Atlantic Region*, vol. 36, no. 2, 2007, pp. 28–54. *JSTOR*, www.jstor.org/stable/30303188.

Merleau-Ponty, Maurice. *The Phenomenology of Perception*. 1945. Translated by Colin Smith, Routledge, 2005.

---. *The Visible and the Invisible*, edited by Claude LeFort, translated by Alphonso Lingis, Northwestern UP, 1968.

Merrill, Jeremy B. "Liberal, Moderate or Conservative? See How Facebook Labels You." *New York Times*, 23 Aug. 2016, p. A13.

Merritt, [first name unknown]. "Testimony." 1949, Royal Commission on National Development in the Arts, Letters and Sciences Fonds, PAC, RG 33, 28, vol. 19, nos. 204–225 [CD2 C- 2009, 79].

Michael, Chief Joseph, Joseph Cree, and Joseph Rabbitt. Letter to Department of Indian Affairs, 19 Jan. 1915. Department of Indian Affairs Fonds, PAC, RG 10, vol. 3826, file 60, 511-3 [C-10145, 155].

Minutes of Toronto City Council. 20 Jul. 1840. Metropolitan Toronto Archive, 1840, typescript copy of list of submissions, p. 48.

---. 20 Jul. 1840. Metropolitan Toronto Archive, 1840, typescript copy of recorded minutes, 20 Jul. 1840, item 177.

---. 14 Oct. 1841. Metropolitan Toronto Archive, 1841, typescript copy list of submissions, p. 64.

---. 21 Apr. 1843. Metropolitan Toronto Archive, 1843, typescript copy list of submissions p. 84.

"Miss E. Pauline Johnson." *The Globe* [Toronto], 23 Sept. 1893.

"Miss E. Pauline Johnson: Canada's Indian Elocutionist." *Ottawa Citizen*, n.d. McMaster University, William Ready Division of Archives and Research Collections, Pauline Johnson Archive, box 4, file 4.

"Mission." *The Hemispheric Institute of Performance and Politics*, hemisphericinstitute.org/hemi/en/mission.

"The Mohawk Poetess." *The Evening Journal* [Ottawa], 2 Nov. 1892, p. 1.

"Mohawk Princess. Of Royal Indian Blood and Native Indian Eloquence." *Grand Rapids Democrat*, 18 Nov. 1896. McMaster University, William Ready Division of Archives and Research Collections, Pauline Johnson Archive, Performance Clippings, box 4, file 3.

Mojica, Monique. *Princess Pocahontas and the Blue Spots*. Women's Press, 1991.

Mojica, Monique, and Ric Knowles, editors. *Staging Coyote's Dream: An Anthology of First Nations Drama in English*. Vol. 1., Playwrights Canada, 2003.

---. *Staging Coyote's Dream: An Anthology of First Nations Drama in English*. Vol. 2, Playwrights Canada, 2009.

Monture, Rick. " 'Beneath the British Flag': Iroquois and Canadian Nationalism in the Work of Pauline Johnson and Duncan Campbell Scott." *Essays on Canadian Writing*, vol. 75, 2002, pp. 118–41.

Morton, Desmond, and J.L. Granatstein. *Marching to Armageddon: Canadians and The Great War 1914–1919*. Lester and Orpen Dennys, 1989.

Moses, Daniel David. *Almighty Voice and His Wife*. Playwrights Canada, 2009.

Mount Saint Vincent University. *Catalogue of the Canadian Drama Collection*. Mount Saint Vincent U, 1984.

Moynagh, Maureen. "Eyeing the North Star? Figuring Canada in Postslavery Fiction and Drama." *Comparative American Studies: An International Journal*, vol. 3, no. 1, 2005, pp. 15–27. *Research Gate*, doi: 10.1177/1477570005050947.

"Mrs. John Drew is Dead." *New York Times*, 1 Sept. 1897, p. 7. *ProQuest Historical Newspapers*.

Mulcahy, D.G. *The Educated Person: Toward a New Paradigm for Liberal Education*. Rowman & Littlefield, 2008.

Mullaly, Edward. *Desperate Stages: New Brunswick Theatre in the 1840s*. Fiddlehead Poetry/ Goose Lane, 1987.

Mullenix, Elizabeth Reitz. *Wearing the Breeches: Gender on the Antebellum Stage*. St. Martin's, 2000.

Murphy, Colleen. *Pig Girl*. Playwrights Canada, 2015.

Nardout-Lafarge, Élisabeth. "La Valeur Modernité en Littérature Québécoise: Notes pour un Bilan Critique." *Constructions de la Modernité au Québec*, edited by Nardout-LaFarge and Ginette Michaud, Lanctôt Éditeur, 2004, pp. 285–91.

Nathan, Hans. *Dan Emmett and the Rise of Early Negro Minstrelsy*. 1962. U of Oklahoma P, 1977.

Nesbit, Molly. *The Pragmatism in the History of Art*. Periscope, 2013.

"New York Bowery Amphitheatre, Circus." H. Rockwell, Manager; June Titus, Angevine, and Co., Owners; Mr. Pelham, Performer; in Market Street; *Mirror* [Toronto], 19–22 Aug. 1840. Advertisement.

---. Messrs. N. B. and T. V Turner, Managers; in Market Street; *Mirror* [Toronto], 19 Oct. 1841. Advertisement.

---. Rockwell, Stone and Turner, Proprietors; in Market Street; *Mirror* [Toronto], 14–16 Jul. 1842. Advertisement.

Nichols, Glen. "Bard of Acadie: The Theatre of Herménégilde Chiasson." *Port Acadie: revue interdisciplinaire en études acadiennes*, vol. 2, 2001, pp. 25–42.

---. "Building Bridges: English & French Theatre in New Brunswick." *Theatre Research in Canada / Recherches théâtrales au Canada*, vol. 26, no. 12, 2005, pp. 4–18.

---. "Collectif Moncton-Sable: New Visions of Acadian Theatre." *alt.theatre*, vol. 5, no. 1, 2007, pp. 9–11.

Nicholson, G.W.L. *Canadian Expeditionary Force 1914–1919: The Official History of the Canadian Army in the First World War*. The Queen's Printer, 1962.

---. *Seventy Years of Service: A History of the Royal Canadian Army Medical Corps.* Borealis, 1977.

Nicholson, Helen. *Theatre and Education*, edited by Jen Harvie and Dan Rebellato, Palgrave Macmillan, 2009.

Nolan, Yvette, and Ric Knowles, editors. *Performing Indigeneity*. Playwrights Canada, 2016. New Essays on Canadian Theatre 6.

Nolette, Nicole. *Jouer la traduction. Théâtre et hétérolinguisme au Canada francophone.* U of Ottawa Press, 2015.

Norris, William. "Forum—An Unrecorded Glimpse of Halifax's Theatre Journal." *Theatre Research in Canada*, vol. 5, no. 2, 1984. *Theatre Research in Canada*, journals.lib.unb.ca /index.php/TRIC/article/view/7444.

"NotaBle Acts Prepares to Take the Stage." *Fredericton Daily Gleaner*, 24 Jul. 2004, p. B6.

The Novascotian. 9 May 1833. Toronto Metro Reference Library Collections.

O'Neill, Patrick B. "Blake, William Rufus." Benson and Conolly, *Oxford*, p. 54.

---. "Carroll Aiken's Experiments in Playwriting." *BC Studies*, vol. 137, 2003, pp. 65–92. *BC Studies*, www.bcstudies.com/issues/item/bc-studies-137-spring-2003.

---. "*Fitzallan*." Benson and Conolly, *Oxford*, p. 212.

---. *A History of Theatrical Activity in Toronto, Canada: From its Beginning to 1858.* Volumes 1 and 2, Louisiana State U and Agricultural and Mechanical College, 1973. Dissertation.

---. "Nova Scotia, Theatre in." Benson and Conolly, *Oxford*, pp. 388–94.

---. Review of *English Canadian Theatre, 1765–1826*, by Yashdip S. Bains. *Theatre Research in Canada*, vol. 21, no. 1, 2000. *Theatre Research in Canada*, journals.lib.unb.ca/index.php /TRIC/article/view/12655/13542.

---. "Theatre in the North: Staging Practices of the British Navy in the Canadian Arctic." *Dalhousie Review*, vol. 74, no. 3, 1994, pp. 356–84.

Orr, Shelley. "Critical Proximity: A Case for Using the First Person as a Production Dramaturg." *Theatre Topics*, vol. 24, no. 3, 2014, pp. 239–47.

Paré, François. "Acadie City ou l'invention de la ville." *Tangence*, vol. 58, 1998, pp. 19–34.

---. *La Distance habitée*. Le Nordir, 2003.

Parkin, Andrew. "The New Frontier: Toward an Indigenous Theatre in British Columbia." Conolly, pp. 101–12.

Parrish, Susan Scott. "The 'Hemispheric Turn' in Colonial American Studies." *Early American Literature*, vol. 40, no. 3, 2005, pp. 545–53. *Project Muse*, doi: 10.1353/eal.2005.0054.

Pattison, Stephen. *Shame: Theory, Therapy, Theology*. Cambridge UP, 2000.

Pauline. Created by Margaret Atwood, music by Tobin Stokes, directed by Norman Armour, City Opera Vancouver. The Cultch Theatre, 23 May 2014, Vancouver.

Peacock, Gordon. "Education and Training." Benson and Conolly, *Oxford*, pp. 191–93.

Perkyns, Richard. "Nova Scotia." Wagner, pp. 106–11.

Perrot, Marie-Ève. "Statut et fonction symbolique du chiac: analyse de discours épilinguistiques." *Francophonies d'Amérique*, vol. 22, 2006, pp. 141–52.

Phelan, Peggy. *Unmarked: The Politics of Performance*. Routledge, 1993.

Pickersgill, Jack W. *My Years with Louis St Laurent: A Political Memoir*. U of Toronto P, 1975.

Plant, Richard. "Chronology: Theatre in Ontario to 1914." Saddlemyer, pp. 288–346.

---, editor. *Modern Canadian Drama*. Penguin Books, 1984.

"Playbill." Royal Lyceum Theatre; Mr. C. K. Mason, Manager; King Street; Sept. 1849. Collection of the Toronto Public Library.

Pollock, Sharon. *Walsh*. Talonbooks, 1973.

Postlewait, Thomas. "The Hierogliphic Stage: American Theater and Society." 1999. *Cambridge History of American Theater*, vol. 2, Cambridge UP, 2008, pp. 107–95.

Pratt, Mary Louise. *Imperial Eyes: Travel Writing and Transculturation*. Routledge, 1992.

Pritchard, Gillian. "Down From the Pedestal: On the Eve of Its 60th Birthday, The 'Alum' Is Shedding Its Elitist Image. There'll Be Some Changes Made." *Scene Changes*, 1978, pp. 10, 19, 27.

"Productions & Events: Past Productions, Moonlodge (1990–2000)." *Full Circle First Nations Performance*, www.fullcircle.ca/past-productions.

"Productions & Events: Past Productions, The River-Home." *Full Circle First Nations Performance*, www.fullcircle.ca/past-productions.

Prokopchak, Peter. "A Message from the National Secretary, Association of Ukrainian Canadians." *Ukrainian-Canadian Festival Program*, 1946, Royal Commission on National Development in the Arts, Letters and Sciences Fonds, PAC, RG 33, 28, vol. 3, nos. 27–39 [CD1 C-1999, 747].

Putnam, Lara. "To Study the Fragments/Whole: Microhistory and the Atlantic World." *Journal of Social History*, vol. 39, no. 3, 2006, pp. 615–30. *Project Muse*, doi: 10.1353/jsh.2006.0010.

Radz, Matt. "Offstage, A New Sense of Direction." *The Gazette* [Montreal], 15 Sep. 2007, p. E8.

Rak, Julie. "Double-Wampum, Double-Life, Double Click: E. Pauline Johnson by and for the World Wide Web." *Textual Studies in Canada*, no. 13–14, 2001, pp. 153–70.

Rattlesnake, Chief John. Letter to Department of Indian Affairs, 25 Jan. 1915. Department of Indian Affairs Fonds, PAC, RG 10, vol. 3826, file 60, 511-3 [C-10145, 157-160].

Rayner, Alice. "E-Space: Performance in the Time of Cyberspace." *Land/Scape/Theatre*, edited by Una Chaudhuri and Elinor Fuchs, U of Michigan P, 2002, pp. 350–70.

"Recital: Literary, Musical, Dramatic." Association Hall, Hamilton, Ontario, 20 Dec. 1892. *Hamilton Public Library*, www.archive.org/details/cihm_36329. Program.

Recollet, Karyn. "Glyphing Decolonial Love Through Urban Flash Mobbing and Walking with Our Sisters." *Curriculum Inquiry*, vol. 45, 2015, pp. 129–45.

Reinelt, Janelle. "What UK Spectators Know: Understanding How We Come to Value Theatre." *Specatorship*, special issue of *Theatre Journal*, vol. 66, no. 3, 2014, pp. 337–61.

Report of the Royal Commission on National Development in the Arts, Letters and Sciences, 1949–1951. Edmond Cloutier, C.M.G., O.A., D.S.P., printer to the King's Most Excellent Majesty, 1951.

Rifkind, Candida, and Linda Warley, editors. *Canadian Graphic: Picturing Life Narratives*. Wilfrid Laurier UP, 2016.

Ringwood, Gwen Pharis. *Lament for Harmonica (Maya)*. *The Collected Plays of Gwen Pharis Ringwood*, edited by Enid Delgatty Rutland, Borealis Press, 1982, pp. 339–53.

Rioux, Marcel. "Sur l'Évolution des Idéologies au Québec." *Revue de l'Institut de Sociologie*, no. 1, 1968, pp. 95–124.

Roach, Joseph. *Cities of the Dead: Circum-Atlantic Performance*. U of Michigan P, 1996.

Robert, Lucie. *Apprivoiser la Modernité Théâtrale: La Pièce en un Acte, de la Belle Époque à la Crise: Anthologie*. Éditions Nota Bene, 2012.

---. "Jeanne Maubourg (1875–1953): L'Apprentissage de la Modernité Théâtrale." *Jeu: Revue de Théâtre*, vol. 123–24, 2007, pp. 173–82.

---. "Le Moderne à l'Épreuve de l'Hétérogène ou Du bon Usage des Catégories Lexicales dans les Études Littéraires." Colloque Annuel de l'Association des Littératures Canadiennes et Québécoises, 31 May 2015, Université d'Ottawa.

---. "Pour une histoire de la dramaturgie québécoise." *L'Annuaire théâtral: Revue québécoise d'études théâtrales*, vols. 5–6, 1988, pp. 163–69.

---. "La Révolution du Temps au Théâtre." *Voix et Images*, vol. 41, no. 2, winter 2016, pp. 57–66.

---. "La Vie Culturelle et Son Histoire. Quelques Remarques sur la Notion de Vie." *Globe: Revue Internationale d'Études Québécoises*, vol. 15, nos. 1–2, 2012, pp. 231–42.

Robichaud, Anne-Marie. "Entretien avec Herménégilde Chiasson." *Si Que*, vol. 4, 1979, pp. 65–78.

"Rockwell and Stone's Circus." Messers. Rockwell and Stone, Managers; in Market Street; *Herald* [Toronto], 17–19 Jul. 1843. Advertisement. [Note: Though not listed as "New York Bowery Amphitheatre," the management is the same].

Rodemeyer, Lanei. "Developments in the Theory of Time-Consciousness: An Analysis of Protention." *The New Husserl: A Critical Reader*, edited by Donn Welton, Indiana UP, 2003, pp. 125–56.

Rogers, Janet. "Why Mohawk poet Pauline Johnson should be on Canadian money." *CBC News*, 4 Dec. 2016, www.cbc.ca/news/indigenous/why-mohawk-poet-pauline-johnson-should-be-on-canadian-money-1.3875336.

Rubin, Don, editor. *Canadian Theatre History: Selected Readings*. Copp Clark, 1996.

---. "Creeping Toward a Culture: The Theatre in English Canada Since 1945." Rubin, *Canadian*, pp. 318–31.

---. "Training the Theatre Professional." Wagner, pp. 284–92.

Rudakoff, Judith, and Lynn M. Thomson. *Between the Lines: The Process of Dramaturgy*. Playwrights Canada, 2002.

Ryga, George. *The Ecstasy of Rita Joe*. Talonbooks, 1986.

Sabourin, Jean-Guy, and Madeleine Greffard. *Le Théâtre Québécois*. Boréal, 1997.

Saddlemyer, Ann, editor. *Early Stages: Theatre in Ontario 1800–1914*. U of Toronto P, 1990. Ontario Historical Studies.

Sadowski-Smith, Claudia. "Canada-US border Narratives and US Hemispheric Studies." *Comparative American Studies: An International Journal*, vol. 3, no. 1, 2005, pp. 63–77. *Taylor and Francis Online*, doi: 10.1177/1477570005050950.

Salter, Denis. "William Rufus Blake and the Gentlemanly Art of Comic Acting." Knowles, *Proceedings*, pp. 68–99.

Salutin, Rick. "The Meaning of it All." Rubin, *Canadian*, pp. 381–88.

Samuel, Raphael. *Theatres of Memory*. Verso, 1994.

Schechner, Richard. "A New Paradigm for Theatre in the Academy." *TDR*, vol. 36, no. 4, 1992, pp. 7–10.

Schneider, Rebecca. *The Explicit Body in Performance*. Routledge, 1997.

---. *Performing Remains: Art and War in Times of Theatrical Reenactment*. Routledge, 2011.

Schweitzer, Marlis. "Casting Clara Fisher: Phrenology, Protean Farce, and the 'Astonishing' Career of a Child Actress." *Theatre Journal*, vol. 68, no. 2, 2016, pp. 167–90.

---. "Networking the Waves: Ocean Liners, Impresarios, and Broadway's Atlantic Expansion." *Theatre Survey*, vol. 53, no. 2, 2012, pp. 241–67.

---. "An 'Unmanly and Insidious Attack': Child Actress Jean Davenport and the Performance of Masculinity in 1840s Jamaica and Newfoundland." *Theatre Research in Canada*, vol. 35, no. 1, 2014, pp. 49–68.

Scudamore, H.B, R.W. Downie, W.L. McGeary, and H.R. Dillon. *The P.B.I. or Mademoiselle of Bully Grenay*. *Canadian Forum* vol. 11, no. 12, Sept. 1921, pp. 368–74; vol. 11, no. 13, Oct. 1921, pp. 400–05; vol. 11, no. 14, Nov. 1921, pp. 430–36; vol. 11, no. 15, Dec. 1921, pp. 464–69.

---. *The P.B.I., or, Mademoiselle of Bully Grenay*. Mount Saint Vincent University, Canadian Drama Collection, C.D.Coll 11.01.

"Search Programs." *University Study*. *Universities Canada*, www.universitystudy.ca /search-programs/.

Service Records for Simon Jauvoish, regimental no. 910140. Library and Archives Canada, Canadian Expeditionary Force personnel files, RG 150, accession number 1992–93/166, box 4799, file 22.

Service Records for William Stabler Atkinson, regimental no. 420016. Library and Archives Canada, Canadian Expeditionary Force personnel files, RG 150, accession number 1992–93/166, box 293, file 33.

Shea Murphy, Jacqueline. *The People Have Never Stopped Dancing: Native American Modern Dance Histories*. U of Minnesota P, 2007.

Shepherd-Barr, Kirsten. "Modernism and Theatrical Performance." *Modernist Cultures*, vol. 1, no. 1, 2010, pp. 59–68. *Edinburgh University Press*, dx.doi.org/10.3366/E2041102209000057.

Sherriff, R.C. *Journey's End*. Brentano's, New York, 1929.

Shortt, Mary. *From Douglas to The Black Crook: A History of Toronto Theatre, 1809–1874*. U of Toronto, 1977. M.A. dissertation.

Shrive, Norman. "What Happened to Pauline?" *Canadian Literature*, no. 13, 1962, pp. 25–38.

Shypula, Brian. "Banking on Support for Pauline Johnson." *Brant News*, 24 Mar. 2016, brantnews.com/news-story/6404911-banking-on-support-for-pauline-johnson/.

Sidnell, Michael. Foreword. Conolly, pp. ix–x.

Simpson, Audra. *Mohawk Interruptus: Political Life Across the Borders of Settler Colonial States*. Duke UP, 2014.

Simpson, Leanne. *Dancing on Our Turtle's Back: Stories of Nishnaabeg Re-Creation, Resurgence and a New Emergence*. Arbeiter Ring, 2011.

---. *Islands of Decolonial Love: Songs and Stories*. Arbeiter Ring, 2013.

Simpson, Leanne Betasamosake, with Edna Manitowabi. "Theorizing Resurgence from-Within Nishnaabeg Thought." *Centering Anishinaabe Studies: Understanding the World through Stories*, edited by Jill Doerfler, et al., Michigan State UP/U of Winnipeg P, 2013, pp. 279–93.

Smith, Graham Hingangaroa. "Protecting and Respecting Indigenous Knowledge." *Reclaiming Indigenous Voice and Vision*, edited by Marie Battiste. U of British Columbia P, 2000.

Smith, Mary Elizabeth. "Freeman's *Creeps* and *Battering Ram*: Variations on a Theme." *Canadian Drama/L'Art dramatique canadien*, vol. 4, 1978, pp. 25–33.

---. *Too Soon the Curtain Fell: A History of Theatre in Saint John, 1789–1900*. Brunswick, 1981.

Smith, Sidonie, and Julia Watson, editors. *Getting a Life: Everyday Uses of Autobiography*. U Minnesota P, 1996.

---, editors. *Interfaces: Women/Autobiography/Image/ Performance*. U of Michigan P, 2002.

"'So This is Canada' for Walker Soon." *Winnipeg Tribune*, 4 Sept. 1926. *Newspapers.com*, www.newspapers.com/image/39559191/.

Sofer, Andrew. "Spectral Readings." *Theatre Journal*, vol. 64, no. 3, 2012, pp. 323–36.

Soldevila, Philippe, and Christian Essiambre. *Les Trois exils de Christian E.* Dramaturges Éditeurs, 2013.

Souchotte, Sandra. "Firehall's Performance Doesn't Live Up To Herbert's Poetry." *The Varsity* [U Toronto], 1 Dec. 1972.

Sperdakos, Paula. "Canada's Daughters, America's Sweethearts: The Careers of Canadian 'Footlight Favorites' in the United States." *Theatre Research in Canada*, vol. 20, no. 2, 1999, pp. 1–23.

Spiderwoman Theater. *Material Witness*. Formerly *Women in Violence—The Next Generation*, directed by Muriel Miguel, 12–29 May 2016, La MaMa Theater, New York City. Performance.

Spivak, Gayatri Chakravorty. "Translator's Preface." *Of Grammatology*, Jacques Derrida, translated by Spivak, Johns Hopkins UP, 1976, pp. ix–lxxxvii.

"Stage." *Winnipeg Tribune*, 22 Sept. 1926. *Newspapers.com*, www.newspapers.com /image/39560385/.

Statistics Canada. "Drama/Theatre Arts and Stagecraft Enrollments and Graduates." CANSIM Postsecondary Student Information System, 2016.

Stone, Martin (Oscar Ryan). "Voices from Quebec." *Canadian Tribune* [Toronto], 29 Nov. 1972.

Strain, J. Frank "The Financial Problems Facing Canadian Universities: Some Unpleasant Economic Principles." *Liberal Education and the Small University in Canada*, edited by Christine Storm, McGill-Queen's UP, 1996, pp. 155–80.

Strong-Boag, Veronica, and Carole Gerson, editors. *Paddling Her Own Canoe: The Times and Texts of E. Pauline Johnson Tekahionwake.* U of Toronto P, 2000.

Stuart, Ross. "Alberta, Theatre in." Benson and Conolly, *Oxford*, pp. 9–12.

Stuart, Ross, and Ann Stuart. "University Theatre." *Later Stages: Essays in Ontario Theatre from the First World War to the 1970s*, edited by Ann Saddlemyer and Richard Plant, U of Toronto P, 1997, 305–32. Ontario Historical Studies.

Szondi, Peter. *Théorie du Drame Moderne 1880–1950*. 1956. Translated by Patrice Pavis, with Jean and Mayotte Bollack, L'Âge d'Homme, 1983.

Tannahill, Jordan. *Theatre of the Unimpressed*. Coach House, 2015.

Taylor, Diana. *The Archive and the Repertoire: Performing Cultural Memory in the Americas.* Duke UP, 2003.

---. "Remapping Genre Through Performance: From 'American' to 'Hemispheric' Studies." *PMLA*, vol. 122, no. 5, 2007, pp. 1416–30. *U of the Fraser Valley*, jstor.org.proxy.ufv.ca:2048/stable/25501794.

Tennyson, Brian Douglas. *The Canadian Experience of the Great War: A Guide to Memoirs.* Scarecrow Press, 2013.

"Theatre." *Acadian Recorder*, 1 June 1833, p. 3.

Thériault, Joseph Yvon. *Évangéline: Contes d'Amérique*. Québec Amérique, 2013.

Titley, E. Brian. A *Narrow Vision: Duncan Campbell Scott and the Administration of Indian Affairs in Canada.* U of British Columbia P, 1986.

Todd, R.B. "British Columbia, Theatre in." Benson and Conolly, *Oxford*, pp. 60–63.

Toronto City Council. By-Law No. 6, "An Act Concerning Licences," 31 May 1834. The Metropolitan Toronto Archives.

---. By-Law No. 50, "An Act to Regulate Theatrical Performances and other Exhibitions," 3 Aug. 1840. The Metropolitan Toronto Archives.

"Toronto Coloured Young Men's Amateur Theatrical Society." "Venice Preserved, or A Plot Discovered," by Thomas Otway, with "Several Scenes from Shakespeare"; Royal Lyceum Theatre; King Street; *Mirror* [Toronto], 20–23 Feb. 1849. Advertisement.

Toten-Beard, Deanna M. *Sheldon Cheney's Theater Arts Magazine: Promoting a Modern American Theater: 1916–1921.* Scarecrow, 2010.

Tourangeau, Rémi. "Les Jeux Scéniques du Québec et la Théâtralisation de l'Histoire." *L'Annuaire Théâtral: Revue Québécoise d'ÉtudesTthéâtrales*, no. 5–6, 1988–89, pp. 171–82.

Towsen, John H. *Clowns*. Hawthorn, 1976.

Toye, William, and Eugene Benson, editors. *The Oxford Companion to Canadian Literature.* Oxford UP, 1987.

Trencsényi, Katalin. *Dramaturgy in the Making: A User's Guide for Theatre Practitioners.* Bloomsbury Methuen Drama, 2015.

Trudeau, Pierre Elliott. *House of Commons Debates, 28th Parliament, 3rd Session.* Volume 8, 8 Oct. 1971, p. 8545. *Library of Parliament*, parl.canadiana.ca/view/oop.debates_HOC2803_08/811?r=0&s=2.

Truth and Reconciliation Commission of Canada. *Honouring the Truth, Reconciling for the Future: Summary of the Final Report of the Truth and Reconciliation Commission of Canada*. Truth and Reconciliation Commission of Canada, 2015.

"TSF 2017—Kwèykw`áystway." *Full Circle First Nations Performance*, fullcircle.ca/tsf17-kweykwaystway-speaking-with-one-another/.

Tuck, Eve. "Suspending Damage: A Letter To Communities." *Harvard Educational Review*, vol. 79, no. 3, 2009, pp. 409–27.

Tuck, Eve, and W. Yang, editors. *Youth Resistance, Research, and Theories of Change*. Routledge, 2013.

Upchurch, Anna. "Linking Cultural Policy from Great Britain to Canada." *International Journal of Cultural Policy*, vol. 13, no. 3, 2007, pp. 239–54.

Urquhart, Hugh M. *The History of the 16th Battalion (The Canadian Scottish) Canadian Expeditionary Force in the Great War, 1914–1919*. Macmillan, 1932.

Usmiani, Renate. "Antonine Maillet, 2. Recycling an Archetype. The Anti-Evangelines." *Canadian Theatre Review*, vol. 46, 1986, pp. 65–71.

---. *Second Stage: The Alternative Theatre Movement in Canada*. U of British Columbia P, 1983.

Van Steen, Marcus. *Pauline Johnson: Her Life and Work*. Musson Book Company, 1965.

Vance, Jonathan. *Death So Noble: Memory, Meaning and the First World War*. U of British Columbia P, 1997.

---. *A History of Canadian Culture*. Oxford UP, 2009.

---. "The Soldier as Novelist: Literature, History, and the Great War." *Canadian Literature*, vol. 179, 2003, pp. 22–37.

Varty, Anne. *Children and Theatre in Victorian Britain: 'All Work, No Play'*. Palgrave, 2008.

Veinstein, André. *La Mise en Scène Théâtrale et sa Condition Esthétique*. Flammarion, 1955.

Viehmann, Martha L. "Speaking Chinook: Adaptation, Indigeneity, and Pauline Johnson's British Columbia Stories." *Western American Literature*, vol. 47, no. 3, 2012, pp. 258–85. *Project Muse*, doi: 10.1353/wal.2012.0064.

Vizenor, Gerald. *Fugitive Poses: Native American Indian Scenes of Absence and Presence*. U of Nebraska P, 1998.

---. *Manifest Manners: Narratives on PostIndian Survivance*. U of Nebraska P, 1999.

---. "Trickster Discourse." *American Indian Quarterly*, vol. 14, no. 3, 1990, pp. 277–88.

Wagner, Anton, editor. *Contemporary Canadian Theatre: New World Visions*. Simon & Pierre, 1985.

Walker, Barrington, editor. *The History of Immigration and Racism in Canada: Essential Reading*. Canadian Scholars', 2008.

Walkes, W.R. *A Pair of Lunatics: A Dramatic Sketch*. Revised version, Samuel French, [1895?]. *Hathi Trust Digital Library / University of Pennsylvania*, babel.hathitrust.org/cgi/pt?id=nnc1.1002356988;view=1up;seq=5.

War Diary, 16th Canadian Infantry Battalion. War Diaries of the First World War, Library and Archives Canada.

"War Play at Auditorium Great Success." *Winnipeg Tribune*, 14 May 1934. *Newspapers.com*, newspapers.com/image/39311898/.

"War Play, With Timely Touch, To Be Given Two Performances." *Winnipeg Tribune*, 12 May 1934. *Newspapers.com*, www.newspapers.com/image/39311527/.

Warren, Jean-Philippe. "Petite Typologie Philologique du 'Moderne' au Québec (1850–1950). Moderne, Modernisation, Modernisme, Modernité." *Recherches Sociographiques*, vol. 46, no. 3, 2005, pp. 495–525.

Wasserman, Jerry. " 'It's the Do-Gooders Burn My Ass': Modern Canadian Drama and the Crisis of Liberalism." *Modern Drama*, vol. 43, no. 1, 2000, pp. 32–47.

---, editor. *Modern Canadian Plays*. Talonbooks, 1985.

---. "Transnational Cross-dressing, Intercultural Pageantry: Zouave Costume in Performance." *Inter-disciplinary.net*, 2010, www.inter-disciplinary.net/wp-content/uploads/2010/10/jwassermanpaper.pdf.

Watson, Richard A. "Spastics, Like Others, Aren't Pure of Mind." Review of *Creeps*, by David Freeman, Arts Club Theatre, Vancouver. *Vancouver Sun*, 15 Oct. 1973, p. 5.

Werry, Margaret. "Oceanic Imagination, Intercultural Performance, Pacific Historiography." *The Politics of Interweaving Performance Cultures: Beyond Postcolonialism*, edited by Erika Fischer-Lichte, Torsten Jost, and Saskya Iris Jain, Routledge, 2014, pp. 97–118.

Whittaker, Herbert. "*Creeps* Excellent Starter for Tarragon Theatre." Review of *Creeps* by David Freeman, Tarragon Theatre, Toronto, *The Globe and Mail*, 6 Oct. 1971, p. 16.

---. "Little Theatre and Amateur Theatre." Benson and Conolly, *Oxford*, pp. 301–09.

---. "Showbusiness: Ballet Offers New View if Saunders Interested." *The Globe and Mail*, 8 May 1954, p. 12.

---. "*Le Temps Sauvage* short on vigor." *The Globe and Mail*, 24 Nov. 1972.

---. "The Theatre." Rubin, *Canadian*, pp. 216–27.

Whittaker, Robin C. "Entirely Free of Any Amateurishness: Private Training, Public Taste and the Women's Dramatic Club of University College, Toronto (1905–21)." *Nineteenth Century Theatre and Film*, vol. 38, no. 2, 2011, pp. 51–66.

---. "The Trades of T.R.I.C.: There Are No Macrohistories Here." *Theatre Research in Canada/Recherches théâtrales au Canada*, vol. 35, no. 2, 2014, pp. 221–79.

---. *Un/Disciplined Performance: Nonprofessionalized Theatre in Canada's Professional Era.* U of Toronto, 2010. Dissertation.

---. "Walterdale Theatre Associates and the In(ter)vention of the Audience." *Canadian Theatre Review*, vol. 140, 2009, pp. 33–39.

Wilkinson, Joyce A., Anthony Adah, Gordon Peacock, and Laurin Mann. "Theatre Education." *The Canadian Encyclopedia*, 2 July 2006, www.thecanadianencyclopedia.ca/en/article/theatre-education/.

Williams, Beverly A. *Leisure as Contested Terrain in Late Nineteenth Century Halifax.* Saint Mary's U, 1991. M.A. dissertation.

Wilmer, S. E. *Theater, Society and the Nation: Staging American Identities.* Cambridge UP, 2002.

Wilson, Jason. *Soldiers of Song: The Dumbells and Other Canadian Concert Parties of the First World War.* Wilfrid Laurier UP, 2012.

Wilson, Kathleen. "Introduction: Three Theses on Performance and History." *Eighteenth-Century Studies*, vol. 48, no. 4, 2015, pp. 375–90. *Project Muse*, doi: 10.1353/ecs.2015.0028.

Wilson, Martha. "Martha Wilson." *Martha Wilson*, www.marthawilson.com.

Wilton, Carol. " 'Lawless Law': Conservative Political Violence in Upper Canada 1818–41." *Law and History Review*, vol. 1, no. 13, 1995, pp. 111–36.

Winks, Robin W. *The Blacks in Canada: A History*. McGill-Queen's UP, 1971.

Wittmann, Matthew. *Circus and the City: New York, 1793–2010*. Yale UP/Bard Graduate Centre, 2012.

Wrigley's British Columbia. Wrigley Directories, 1920. *British Columbia City Directories, 1860–1955*, Vancouver Public Library, www.vpl.ca/bccd/index.php.

Yeats, William Butler. "Easter 1916." *Academy of American Poets*, www.poets.org/poetsorg/poem/easter-1916.

Zuehlke, Mark *Brave Battalion: The Remarkable Saga of the 16th Battalion (Canadian Scottish) in the First World War.* Harper Collins e-books, 2008.

NOTES ON CONTRIBUTORS

Jill Carter (Anishinaabe/Ashkenazi) is a Toronto-based theatre practitioner and Assistant Professor with the Centre for Drama, Theatre and Performance Studies; the Transitional Year Programme; and Indigenous Studies at the University of Toronto. Her research and praxis base themselves in the mechanics of story creation (devising and dramaturgy), the processes of delivery (performance on the stage and on the page), and the mechanics of Affect.

T. Nikki Cesare Schotzko is Associate Professor at the University of Toronto's Centre for Drama, Theatre and Performance Studies. She has co-edited special issues of *TDR* and *CTR*, and published work in journals including *TDR*, *Performance Research*, *Theatre Journal*, *CTR*, and *TRiC*, and in mainstream online publications including *Artforum* and *Toronto Review of Books*. She is also an occasional dramaturge, having collaborated on experimental music-theatre productions in New York; Toronto; Chicago; and Morelia, Mexico. Her first book, *Learning How to Fall: Art and Culture after September 11*, engages the skewed relationship between twenty-first-century media technologies, perception, and pop culture, and her current research explores *feeling-mothering* and radical acts of care.

Heather Davis-Fisch is Associate Professor of English and Theatre at the University of the Fraser Valley in British Columbia. She is the author of *Loss and Cultural Remains in Performance: The Ghosts of the Franklin Expedition* (Palgrave, 2012) and editor of *Past Lives: Performing Canada's Histories* (Playwrights Canada Press, 2017). Her work has also appeared in the journals *Theatre Research in Canada*, *Canadian Theatre Review*, *Performing Arts Resources*, and *Cultural Studies/Critical Methodologies* and in the books *Theatres of Affect*, *Performance Studies in Canada*, and Bloomsbury's *Cultural History of Theatre* (forthcoming). She is co-editor of *Canadian Theatre Review*'s Views and Reviews section.

Alan Filewod is Professor of Theatre Studies at the University of Guelph. He has published widely on Canadian theatre history, with an emphasis on non-canonical and politically engaged theatre work. His current research focuses on plays written by returned soldiers between 1919 and 1936.

Stephen Johnson works in the Centre for Drama, Theatre and Performance Studies at the University of Toronto, serving as Director for ten years. He has been a member of the Canadian Association for Theatre Research for over thirty years, serving as President from 2012–16. He has taught at the University of Guelph, McMaster University, and the University of Toronto at the St. George and Mississauga campuses. He researches performance and popular culture, and the performance of race, in the nineteenth and early-twentieth centuries. For a full profile see http://sbjohnson.wordpress.com/.

Yves Jubinville is Professor of Theater Studies and current Director of the École supérieure de théâtre of Université du Québec à Montréal. He is a member of the Centre de recherche interuniversitaire sur la littérature et la culture québécoises (CRILCQ). His work focuses, among other topics, on the historiography of theatre in Québec and contemporary theatre practices. He was the editor of the journal *L'Annuaire théâtral* from 2008 to 2014. He also collaborates with the research group "Régimes socio-esthétiques du théâtre au Québec."

Alexandra (Sasha) Kovacs holds a Ph.D. from the Centre for Drama, Theatre and Performance Studies at the University of Toronto. In her 2017–2019 SSHRC-funded post-doctoral fellowship at York University, Kovacs is exploring the restaging of nineteenth-century theatre histories, specifically addressing contemporary representations of E. Pauline Johnson Tekahionwake. She is actively involved in the Toronto arts community, serving as Past Program Director for Scarborough Arts (one of the city's Local Arts Service Organizations). She also is a working actor, dramaturge, and producer, chiefly developing performances with Ars Mechanica, a collective of international and interdisciplinary artists. Kovacs's writing has been published in *Canadian Theatre Review*, *Performance Research*, *Theatre Research in Canada*, and *Digital Studies*. She currently teaches theatre history at Ryerson's School of Performance and serves as secretary and co-treasurer for the Canadian Association of Theatre Research.

Michelle La Flamme (Metis/Creek) is an associate professor in the department of English at the University of the Fraser Valley. She is from Coast Salish territory and graduated with an M.A. from SFU and a Ph.D. from UBC. Her research is on Canadian literature and drama with a special interest in Indigenous performance. Her current work looks at the corporeal complexities and ceremonial aspects involved in the touring exhibition *Walking With Our Sisters* and *The REDress Project*. Her most recent book, *SOMA TEXT*, was published in 2017 by Wilfrid Laurier University Press. Michelle is also a performer and social-justice advocate who believes deeply in the power of theatre to transform communities. In her down time she travels, rides horses, and plays with her grandchildren.

Allana C. Lindgren is Associate Professor and Chair of the Department of Theatre at the University of Victoria. She is the co-editor with Stephen Ross of *The Modernist World*, co-editor of *Renegade Bodies: Canadian Dance in the 1970s* with Kaija Pepper, and Dance Subject Editor for the *Routledge Encyclopedia of Modernism*. In addition, her research has appeared in a variety of journals and collections, including *Contesting Bodies and Nation in Canadian History*, *The Oxford Handbook of Dance and Ethnicity*, *Dance Research Journal*, and *Quarterly Review of Film and Video*.

Glen Nichols is Director of Drama at Mount Allison University, where he teaches studio courses in acting and directing as well as courses in dramatic literature and history. He has published articles on theatre history, theatre translation, and Acadian theatre. In 2003, he published a collection of five contemporary Acadian plays under the collective title, *Angels and Anger: Five Contemporary Acadian Plays in Translation.* Glen Nichols served as president of the Association of Theatre Research in Canada from 2004 to 2008 and, later, editor of *Theatre Research in Canada.*

Nicole Nolette is Assistant Professor at the Department of Languages and Literatures at Acadia University. Her book *Jouer la traduction. Théâtre et hétérolinguisme au Canada francophone* received the Ann Saddlemyer Award from the Canadian Association for Theatre Research. From 2014 to 2016 she was a SSHRC Postdoctoral Fellow affiliated with the Cultural Agents Initiative at Harvard University.

Karyn Recollet is Assistant Professor in the Women and Gender Studies Institute at the University of Toronto. Karyn is an urban Cree, residing in the traditional territories of the Petun, Wendat, Mississauga's of the New Credit, and Dish with One Spoon treaty territory. Karyn's research explores the various intersections of Indigenous artistic activations rooted in the multiple-layered Indigenous territories that are urban spaces. Karyn's focal points are choreographic fugitivity, Indigenous futurities, and decolonial love. Karyn's publications include the articles "Glyphing Decolonial Love" and "Gesturing Indigenous Futurities," and she has co-edited alongside Eve Tuck *Native Feminist Texts* (a special edition of *English Journal*). Karyn is currently working on a manuscript entitled *Urban Glyphs: Fugitivities, Futurities, and Radical Decolonial Love.*

Jessica Riley received her Ph.D. from the School of English and Theatre Studies, University of Guelph. Her work has been published in *Canadian Theatre Review*, *Latina/o Canadian Theatre and Performance* (2013), *OuterSpeares: Shakespeare, Intermedia, and the Limits of Adaptation* (2014), and *The Cambridge Companion to Canadian Literature* (2017). Jessica is also the editor of *A Man of Letters: The Selected Dramaturgical Correspondence of Urjo Kareda* (2017), a project for which she received a Heather McCallum Award from the Canadian Association for Theatre Research.

Dylan Robinson is Canada Research Chair in Indigenous Arts at Queen's University, located on the lands of the Haudensaunee and Anishinaabe people. He is a Stó:lō scholar and sometimes artist, as well as an avid Halq'emeylem language learner. latst á:ylexwstexw te sqwá:ltset. His recent scholarship includes the collection *Arts of Engagement: Taking Aesthetic Action in and Beyond the Truth and Reconciliation Commission of Canada*, co-edited with Keavy Martin.

Marlis Schweitzer is Associate Professor in the Department of Theatre at York University. She is the author of *Transatlantic Broadway: The Infrastructural Politics of Global Performance* and *When Broadway Was the Runway: Theater, Fashion, and American Culture*, and editor (with Joanne Zerdy) of *Performing Objects and Theatrical Things* and (with Laura Levin) *Performance Studies in Canada*. A former editor of *Theatre Research in Canada/Recherches théâtrales au Canada* (2013–2016), Marlis is President of the Canadian Association for Theatre Research / L'association canadienne pour la recherche théâtrale.

Robin C. Whittaker is Associate Professor of Drama at St. Thomas University and Artistic Producer for Theatre St. Thomas (TST). He teaches a variety of practice- and literature-based courses in theatre. His work as a director, playwright, and dramaturg has been seen across Canada, including his most recent play for TST, *No White Picket Fence*, a verbatim piece about women who grew up in the foster care system and are now living well. His publications include *Hot Thespian Action: Ten Premiere Plays from Walterdale Playhouse!* and numerous articles in *Theatre Research in Canada*, *Canadian Theatre Review*, and *Nineteenth-Century Theatre and Film*. He is founding editor of the Fredericton theatre reviews website *STU Reviews*.

INDEX

M

RECYCLED
Paper made from recycled material
FSC® C103567
www.fsc.org

Printed on Rolland Enviro, which contains 100% post-consumer fiber, is ECOLOGO, Processed Chlorine Free, Ancient Forest Friendly and FSC® certified and is manufactured using renewable biogas energy.

PERMANENT 100% BIO GAS® ENERGY PROCESSED CHLORINE FREE Ancient Forest Friendly™